Three Renaissance usury plays

Manchester University Press

The Revels Plays
COMPANION
LIBRARY

E. A. J. HONIGMANN, ROBERT SMALLWOOD and PETER CORBIN
former editors
J. R. MULRYNE, SUSAN BROCK and SUSAN CERASANO general editors

For over forty years *The Revels Plays* have offered the most authoritative editions of Elizabethan and Jacobean plays by authors other than Shakespeare. The *Companion Library* provides a fuller background to the main series by publishing important dramatic and non-dramatic material that will be essential for the serious student of the period.

THE REVELS PLAYS COMPANION LIBRARY

Three Renaissance usury plays

The Three Ladies of London by Robert Wilson
Englishmen for My Money by William Haughton
The Hog Hath Lost His Pearl by Robert Tailor

Edited by
Lloyd Edward Kermode

Manchester University Press
Manchester and New York

distributed exclusively in the USA by Palgrave Macmillan

The right of Lloyd Edward Kermode to be identified as the author of this work has been asserted by him in accordance with the Copyright, Designs and Patents Act 1988.

Published by Manchester University Press
Oxford Road, Manchester M13 9NR, UK
and Room 400, 175 Fifth Avenue, New York, NY 10010, USA
www.manchesteruniversitypress.co.uk

Distributed in the United States exclusively by
Palgrave Macmillan, 175 Fifth Avenue,
New York, NY 10010, USA

Distributed in Canada exclusively by
UBC Press, University of British Columbia, 2029 West Mall,
Vancouver, BC, Canada V6T 1Z2

British Library Cataloguing-in-Publication Data is available

Library of Congress Cataloging-in-Publication Data is available

ISBN 978 0 7190 7263 5 paperback

First published by Manchester University Press in hardback 2009

This paperback edition first published 2014

The publisher has no responsibility for the persistence or accuracy of URLs for any external or third-party internet websites referred to in this book, and does not guarantee that any content on such websites is, or will remain, accurate or appropriate.

Printed by Lightning Source

CONTENTS

GENERAL EDITORS' PREFACE

Since the late 1950s the series known as The Revels Plays has provided for students of the English Renaissance drama carefully edited texts of the major Elizabethan and Jacobean plays. The series includes some of the best-known drama of the period and has continued to expand, both within its original field and, to a lesser extent, beyond it, to include some important plays from the earlier Tudor and from the Restoration periods. The Revels Plays Companion Library is intended to further this expansion and to allow for new developments.

The aim of the Companion Library is to provide students of the Elizabethan and Jacobean drama with a fuller sense of its background and context. The series includes volumes of a variety of kinds. Small collections of plays, by a single author or concerned with a single theme and edited in accordance with the principles of textual modernization of The Revels Plays, offer a wider range of drama than the main series can include. Together with editions of masques, pageants and the non-dramatic work of Elizabethan and Jacobean playwrights, these volumes make it possible, within the overall Revels enterprise, to examine the achievements of the major dramatists from a broader perspective. Other volumes provide a fuller context for the plays of the period by offering new collections of documentary evidence on Elizabethan theatrical conditions and on the performance of plays during that period and later. A third aim of the series is to offer modern critical interpretation, in the form of collections of essays or of monographs, of the dramatic achievement of the English Renaissance.

So wide a range of material necessarily precludes the standard format and uniform general editorial control which is possible in the original series of Revels Plays. To a considerable extent, therefore, treatment and approach are determined by the needs and intentions of individual volume editors. Within this rather ampler area, however, we hope that the Companion Library maintains the standards of scholarship that have for so long characterized The Revels Plays, and that it offers a useful enlargement of the work of the series in preserving, illuminating and celebrating the drama of Elizabethan and Jacobean England.

J. R. MULRYNE
SUSAN BROCK
SUSAN CERASANO

ACKNOWLEDGEMENTS

My thanks are due to the staff at the British Library, Bodleian Library, Huntington Library, Worcester College, Oxford Library, and Guildhall Library, London for making the early texts available to me. Ros Aitken at the Globe Education Centre set apart time and space for me to listen to the tape of the *Englishmen* stage reading, which I discuss in the introduction. I also owe a debt of gratitude to Eileen Klink, Chair of the Department of English at California State University, and to the University's College of Liberal Arts for time release while I was working on this project. I have received valuable and consistent encouragement in this work from Jean Howard, Richard Dutton, Andrew Gurr, and recently Alan Dessen and others. Martine van Elk, David Bevington and Crystal Bartolovich were good enough to read sections of the introduction and texts and offer editorial and critical advice. I am grateful to my editor Susan Cerasano and to Matthew Frost for getting things under way with Manchester University Press. My thanks also go to my copy editor John Banks, who was much more than a copy editor; he improved a number of the glosses and saved me from multiple infelicities. Any problems with the text that remain are of course my own responsibility. I have re-used and reworked sections of earlier work in the introduction to the plays, and this material appeared as 'The Playwright's Prophecy: Robert Wilson's *The Three Ladies of London* and the "Alienation" of the English', *Medieval and Renaissance Drama in England* 11 (1999): 60–87; and 'After Shylock: The Judaiser in England', *Renaissance and Reformation* 20 (1996): 15–26.

LLOYD EDWARD KERMODE

ABBREVIATIONS

The Three Ladies of London

Q1	1584
Q2	1592
Coll 1851	J. Payne Collier, *Five Old Plays, Illustrating the Early Progress of The English Drama* (London: W. Nichol, 1851, for the Roxburghe Club), pp. 157–244.
Haz	W. Carew Hazlitt, *A Select Collection of Old English Plays* (4th ed.), 15 vols (1874–76. Rep. London: Benjamin Blom, 1964), vol. 6, pp. 245–370.
Mithal	Robert Wilson, *An Edition of Robert Wilson's* Three Ladies of London *and* Three Lords and Three Ladies of London, ed. H. S. D. Mithal (PhD Diss. University of Birmingham, 1959. Rep. New York and London: Garland, 1988).

Englishmen for My Money

Q1	1616
Q2	1626
Q3	1631
1830	*The Old English Drama*, 3 vols (London: Thomas White, 1830), vol. 1, pp. 1–72 (4th play, numbering starts again with each play).
Haz	W. Carew Hazlitt, *A Select Collection of Old English Plays* (4th ed.), 15 vols (1874–76. Rep. London: Benjamin Blom, 1964), vol. 10, pp. 469–564.
Mal *Englishmen*	*Englishmen for My Money*, Malone Society Reprints (Oxford: Oxford University Press, 1912).
Baugh	1917 Albert Croll Baugh, 'William Haughton's *Englishmen for My Money*' (PhD Diss. Univesity of Philadelphia, 1917).

The Hog Hath Lost His Pearl

Q	1614 (all copies)
Qc	1614 (corrected state)
Qu	1614 (uncorrected state)
Dod MS	Manuscript editorial notes by Robert Dodsley in Q Bodleian.
Dod	Robert Dodsley, *A Select Collection of Old English Plays* (1st ed.), 12 vols (London, 1744), vol. 3, pp. 177–237.
Reed	Isaac Reed, *A Select Collection of Old English Plays* (2nd ed.), 12 vols (London: J. Nichols, 1780), vol. 6, pp. 375–450.
Scott	Walter Scott (attrib.), *The Ancient British Drama*, 3 vols (London: James Ballantyne, 1810), vol 3, pp. 47–70.
Coll 1825	J. Payne Collier, *A Select Collection of Old English Plays* (3rd ed.), 12 vols (London: S. Prowett, 1825), vol. 6, pp. 327–94.

Haz   W. Carew Hazlitt, *A Select Collection of Old English Plays* (4th
               ed.), 15 vols (1874–76. Rep. London: Benjamin Blom, 1964), vol.
               11, pp. 423–99.
Mal *Hog*   D. F. McKenzie, ed., *The Hogge Hath Lost His Pearle*, Malone
               Society Reprints (Oxford: Oxford University Press, 1972).

OTHER SOURCES AND ACKNOWLEDGEMENTS

Diary   R. A. Foakes and R. T. Rickert, eds, *Henslowe's Diary* (Cambridge:
               Cambridge University Press, 1969).
van Elk   notes written in consultation with Professor Martine van Elk
ES   E. K. Chambers, *The Elizabethan Stage*, 4 vols. (Oxford: Clarendon
               Press, 1923).
Fleay   Frederick Gard Fleay, *A Biographical Chronicle of the English
               Drama 1559–1642*, 2 vols (London: Reeves and Turner, 1891).
McKerrow   *The Works of Thomas Nashe*, ed. Ronald B. McKerrow (1904–10;
               ed. F. P. Wilson, Oxford: Blackwell, 1958).
OED   J. S. Simpson and E. S. C. Weiner, general eds, *The Oxford English
               Dictionary*, 2nd ed. (Oxford: Clarendon, 1989).
Stow   John Stow, *A Survey of London* (1598 and 1602), ed. C. L.
               Kingsford (Oxford: Clarendon Press, 1971).
Tilley   Morris Palmer Tilley, *A Dictionary of the Proverbs in England in
               the Sixteenth and Seventeenth Centuries* (Ann Arbor: University of
               Michigan Press, 1950).

All references to *The Merchant of Venice* and other plays by Shakespeare are from *The
Complete Works of Shakespeare*, 5th ed., ed. David Bevington (New York: Pearson/
Longman, 2004). All references to *The Jew of Malta* are from the Revels edition, ed.
N. W. Bawcutt (Manchester: Manchester University Press, 1978). All quotations from
other sources in the Introduction are in the original spelling, with the exception of the
silent modernization of i/j and u/v.

Frontispiece from John Blaxton, *The English Usurer* (1634). Reproduced by permission of the British Library.

'The Illustration'

The covetous wretch, to what may we compare,
better than swine: both of one nature are,
One grumbles, th'other grunts: both gross and dull,
hungry, still feeding, and yet never full.
Resemblance from their habits may be had
the one in fur, th'other in bristles clad.
Rich men by others sweat augment their pounds:
the Hog's still rooting in the neighbour's grounds.
They neither of them cast an upward eye,
both downward look, and prey on what they spy,
Nor differ they in death, The brawne nought yields
till cut in collers, into cheeks and shields,
Like him the Usurer howsoever fed,
Profits none living, till himself be dead.
Both with the Christmas-box* may well comply
It nothing yields till broke, They till they die.

---

*The 'Christmas-box' or 'Butler's box' was a sealed box for servants to receive 'tips' to be broken open and distributed on an occasion, such as Christmas time. Specifically, the *OED* relates it to money collected by players. In his *The Examination of Usury, in two sermons* (1591), Henry Smith also compares the usurer with a butler's box, 'for as all the Counters at last come to the Butler; so all the money at last cometh to the Usurer' (*The Sermons of Henry Smith* (1675), sig. M4–M4v; pp. 87–8).

INTRODUCTION

Early modern usury: from scriptural discipline to economic necessity

> It is filthy gaines, and a worke of darkenesse, it is a monster in nature: the overthrow of mighty kingdomes, the destruction of flourishing States, the decay of wealthy Cities, the plagues of the world and the misery of the people: it is theft, it is the murthering of our brethren its the curse of God, and the curse of the people. This is usury. By these signes and tokens you may know it: For wheresoever it raigneth all those mischiefs ensue.[1]

> *The name of usurie is not dishonest* of itself, or in the own nature: *the abuse of usurie* or usage *is that which hath made it dishonest*, and of so bad account among men. For *usurie* is properly the use of a thing.[2]

When Francis Bacon wrote that 'few have spoken of *Usury* usefully',[3] he probably intended the play on words. For a *useful* speech on usury might be a gloss to lead us away from sin and closer to God; or, if you are Bacon or any other forward-looking practical man of an expanding economy, your *use* will be in learning how to use usury usefully – what rates make sense, when to borrow money and when to save money, when to trade in goods, when to play the international money market, and when to invest in real estate. The questions of trade, trust, and treachery, property, pelf, and perfidy are used by Robert Wilson in *The Three Ladies of London* (1581–82) to expose usury as a root cause for a city's and its people's misery. William Haughton emphasizes the necessity of using money in pursuit of a clear national identity in *Englishmen for My Money* (1598), and he iterates the dangers of monetary *abuse* to a commonwealth; Wilson had written of the poisonous temptation of 'cankered coin' (17.75), and Haughton gives us a protagonist (unsurprisingly by 1598) 'Not to be fed with words, but won with gold' (1.2.24). Robert Tailor seemingly lets the old problem of usury pale as he foregrounds the behaviour of the young prodigal generation in *The Hog Hath Lost His Pearl* (1613), but the apparent satire on London's morally questionable Mayor keeps questions of usury, avarice, and shady dealings close at hand.

'For the Elizabethans', writes C. T. Wright, 'few moral and economic issues were more significant than the question of usury'.[4] Through the Jacobean period, too, religious and moral authors drew on the Bible and

early churchmen to decry or apologize for usury; economic and political
authors wrote explications and analyses of usury to place it in the early
modern world of trade and international relations; and imaginative
authors used it as a means by which to label characters' 'nature', or as a
trope through which to understand narrow strands or wide swaths of
culture. That usury was at one and the same time a very technical, specific
issue of economic exchange or speculation and a common sign of personal
and public moral degradation made it a tool equally useful for precisely
engineering an argument about trade, investment, aid of the poor, and
government and for working on a moral, economic, and socially hierar-
chical machine that was seen to be failing. On the one hand, lending and
borrowing were essential to finance important excursions into business
and trading ventures; on the other hand, borrowers could borrow beyond
their means and lenders could impose inhumane terms for loans. Indeed,
Jacobean writers were astonished by the quantities of money out at loan,
declaring that 'the mightie sommes imployed by the waye of *Usurye* [. . .]
are thought to be soe hudge, that if all the money of England were layd
on one heape and every *Usurer* should clayme his *parte* there woulde not
be coyne suffycient to pay them'.[5]

Official attempts to curb or eliminate the practice of usury fluctuated
during the Tudor and Stuart years. In 1545, Henry VIII limited the interest rate on usury to 10 per cent. The severe young Edward and his council
banned usury by repealing his father's Act, stating that it had been
misused and misinterpreted by 'dyvers parsons blynded with inordinat
love of themselfes', who allowed usury as an everyday occurrence.
However, prohibition often leads to underground systems and 'black
markets', and Elizabeth, noting that usury as a result of the ban 'hathe
much more excedingly abounded, to the utter undoinge of many Gentlemen Marchauntes Occupiers and other, and to the importable Hurte of
the Common wealth', revived her father's Act in 1571. This Statute was
continued in Elizabethan Acts of 1584–85, 1586–87, 1588–89, 1592–93,
and 1597–98. This is the official context, then, for the (well-grounded)
allegation by Ned Walgrave in *Englishmen for My Money* that Pisaro
'take[s] ten in the hundred more than law. / We can complain: extortion,
simony – / Newgate hath room; there's law enough in England' (4.1.136–
8). Indeed, Ned even comes somewhat short of the mark, for, as Pisaro
himself will admit, 'I take two and twenty in the hundred, / When the
law gives but ten' (5.1.32–3).

There are three main areas of argument involved in the early modern
usury debate. First, the question of the 'unnaturalness' of 'breeding'
barren metal was debated. The problematic Biblical text related to this
issue was of course the parable of the talents, and the moralists had to

address it. On the surface, the parable of the talents apparently praised investment and the return of interest, especially in the service of one's master; but it was a simple shift for the moralists to read the story as a metaphor for practising God-given abilities, to be useful and not idle, not to hide one's light under a bushel, to serve with loyalty, and to understand one's social position and responsibilities. Second, there was the question of whether there were different 'degrees' of usury (depending on who was lending to whom, for what purpose, and at what rate), or whether all usury was equally damnable; this question also raises the issue of differentiating between legitimate *interest* and illegal *usury*, a distinction quite differently drawn by the various writers. And third, the conflict between the moral problems of lending money without charity and the increasing awareness of the necessity of some form of credit to enable trade and economically useful activity needed reconciling – after all, the wealth of the commonwealth was also the health of the commonwealth, and England was up against increasingly sophisticated mercantilist competition from the Continent. Moreover, the question of money in circulation bore on other moral as well as economic issues such as the provision of hospitality, the setting of landowners to work (especially young gentleman with any aspirations to financial, urban success), and the avoidance of idleness and base pursuits.

Probably the best-known dramatic address to the question of 'unnatural' usury is Shylock's joke early in *The Merchant of Venice* (1596). Shylock tells Antonio and Bassanio a parable of the time 'When Jacob grazed his uncle Laban's sheep', and how Jacob won for himself all the parti-coloured lambs, which were born as a response to the rank ewes seeing 'certain' 'peeled' 'wands' before their eyes as they were 'in the doing of the deed' (1.3.69–88). Antonio judges that such a process is in the hands of God, not something that human beings can manipulate against nature's rules. 'Or is your gold and silver ewes and rams?' Antonio asks Shylock, falling unwittingly right into the usurer's trap: 'I cannot tell', triumphs Shylock, 'I make it breed as fast'. Marlowe's Barabas taunts the audience similarly by emphasizing his impossible gains: 'Fie, what a trouble 'tis to count this trash' (1.1.7), he laments, counting his mounds of money before the 'groundlings', and aspiring to 'infinite riches' (1.1.37). Critics like point out that Barabas is portrayed as a merchant, not a usurer. But later in the play, when all his money has been stripped from him by the State and he seems to regain it almost overnight, we are surely meant to understand that there is only one method – usury – by which money can be so rapidly, miraculously, and unnaturally restored. The writers on usury could make much of this breeding of money, bitterly supposing that coins must be gendered, 'for there are some *Edward* peeces, & some *Elizabeth* peeces; and *Phillips, and Maries* may stand for [androgynoi]'.[6] The use of the coining metaphor continues to expose the 'mistake' or sin of illicit breeding or sexual 'looseness' in literary texts: in *Measure for Measure* (1604), the 'sin' of Claudio and Isabella is 'coin[ing] heaven's image / In stamps that are forbid' (2.4.45–6), and in Milton's *Comus*, Comus is attempting to persuade the Lady with 'licker-ish baits' (line 700) when he asserts that 'Beauty is natures coyn, must not be hoorded, / But must be currant, and the good thereof / Consists in mutual and partak'n bliss, / Unsavoury in th' injoyment of it self' (lines 739–42).[7]

The argument over the 'degree' of usury – from regular business money-lending to deliberately 'biting' usury, or '*neshek*' – continued through the Elizabethan, Jacobean, and Caroline periods. Robert Wilson goes some way to addressing a debate over 'honest' money-lending with viable interest and 'biting' usury with impossible terms by contrasting good Gerontus the Jewish usurer in Turkey with evil Usury in London; but, for all the apparent distance between the two characters' moral views of the world, *Three Ladies* suggests that the characters' underlying motive of usury will 'equalize' their effects on the world. Miles Mosse in the next decade still cannot entirely bring himself to make the division between lesser and greater usury. In his *The Arraignment and Conviction of Usurie* (a collection of sermons preached 1592–93 and published 1595), he explains, 'There is a great difference betweene the biting of a flea, and the biting of a dogge, and the biting of a Lyon: yet all are bitings, and the least will draw bloud. So, there is difference betweene him that taketh five, and him that taketh ten, and him that taketh twentie in the hundred: yet all is biting, and the least will consume a man in continuance.'[8] By 1616, the godly person's acceptance of some usury to avoid high abuse is generally embedded in the culture, as illustrated in James Spottiswoode's *The Execution of Neschech and the Confining of his Kinsman Tarbith*: 'the forbidding of all Usury, is the very maintaining of damned Usurie: and therefore that which is lawfull, in my conceit, should bee approved, and the restrictions and stintes clearlie sette down and nominated'.[9]

The inconsistent use of the term 'use' compounded the problem of the question of usury's 'degrees'. There was a move from the earlier use of 'interest' as meaning specifically that portion of return to a lender that represents his or her loss or disadvantage in enacting the loan to the modern meaning of interest as additional moneys charged simply for the benefit of a loan. This latter 'convenience charge', or free money to the lender, with no discernable risk, would have been known as the 'use' to medieval and earlier Tudor writers and thinkers. Further confusion of the term 'use' arises, however, during the sixteenth century because 'use' can refer to the money lent (the *usable* loan) to the borrower, or it can refer to the interest (in the modern sense) paid back to the lender for use of the loan.[10] We have to understand these senses of 'use' in the context of a period in which the idea of the 'loan' or the debt to be paid later was not an oddity or frightening position for a trader: 'All business was conducted on credit', Eric Kerridge reminds us, and 'the ordinary price was the one for sales on credit, with discount allowed in the event of payment on the nail'.[11] 'No loans being given or taken, these credit arrangements normally involved no interest, still less usury.'[12] The assumption was that payment would be made at a later date, and the price was generally fixed for that postponed day. There were several classes of compensation for real loss and potential risk in the system of lending. Interest could be claimed for a delay *past* the agreed-upon date, when the deal became effectively dead (*titulus morae*), but 'the lender had to forbear suing for recovery of his loan, and the interest he received was in return for this forbearance';[13] it is, of course, a central feature of the usurer – good or bad, Gerontus or Shylock – that he should sue in court for his money if he is chasing an overdue legal agreement (rather than having signed away a title or otherwise simply been cozened out of wealth).

In *God and the Moneylenders*, Norman Jones uses the 1571 Parliamentary debate and Statute Against Usury as the pivotal document and historical moment around which to examine the ways in which English law and English morality worked together to define, debate, and allow usury. Kerridge and Jones both respond to, update, and expand R. H. Tawney's influential introduction to his edition of Thomas Wilson's *A Discourse Upon Usury* of 1572.[14] Jones's book is particularly concerned to follow the overt shift from a mid-sixteenth-century debate on usury based on moral and scriptural arguments to the early seventeenth century's acceptance of the necessity of the 'evil' of usury and a consequent debate revolving around the quite different but related questions of economics and personal conscience. In *Trade and Banking in Early Modern England* and *Usury, Interest and the Reformation*, Kerridge painstakingly teases out the moral arguments of the Reformation to extrapolate the differences between 'usury' and 'interest', the former being payment simply for the fact of a loan and the latter justifiable compensation for potential losses taken by the lender.[15] Kerridge explains the complexity of this distinction and its confusion as 'usury' comes inconsistently to be a euphemism for *foenus* or 'biting', harsh lending practices. These distinctions were being made in mid-century: the character Pasquill, in William Harrys's translation of the German *The Market or Fayre of Usurers* (1550) makes just this differentiation in his argument with the character Usury;[16] and in his 1560s sermons entitled *An Exposition upon the Two*

Epistles of the Apostle Saint Paul to the Thessalonians, John Jewel details allowable lending as (1) charge for actual loss incurred after return date, which is interest, not usury, and (2) giving a sum without requirement to ever receive it back, under an agreement to receive an annuity.[17]

The conflict between morality and necessity really lies as a foundation beneath the usury tracts and drama of the late sixteenth and early seventeenth centuries. 'By the last decade of the [sixteenth] century people were beginning to concede that the external definition and regulation of usury were to be left to the magistrates, without reference to theology', writes Jones, adding that Miles Mosse, by the mid-1590s, was 'giving up on God's law as the standard up to which secular law must measure'.[18] We have already seen that Mosse was conflicted, and even such an acceptance was late in coming, for the moralists and preachers were hanging on to a moral message that had been quieted if not silenced for many years by the 1590s. The year 1571 saw the official opening of the Royal Exchange as well as the Statute Against Usury, which, despite its title, effectively *permitted* money-lending at up to 10 per cent. There seems to remain a division well into the seventeenth century between the economically or practically minded economists, commentators, and playwrights, and the preachers who stuck to ethics without embracing the realities of financial liquidity and circulation. Thus Roger Turner, in *The Usurers Plea Answered* (1634), a sermon given at Southampton, Thursday 18 July 1633, even argues that usury should not be allowed from the endowments of widows and orphans – the generally accepted exception to condemnation of usury – for God takes especial care of these people; furthermore, Turner argues, if money is lent out at 8 per cent usury on behalf of these groups, the borrower must exceed this rate to make money: 'And how doe these Widowes know who is opprest or bitten by this Gaine?'; he goes on to argue against 'a supposed necessity of Usury' for trade and traffic. Turner suspects the necessity of trade is in fact because merchants 'cannot live in the pompe they doe, maintaine their wives in those fashions that they doe, drive their Trades to the height which they doe' without it.[19]

In moral writing and popular entertainment, the lure of gold is a lustful temptation to men, and those who openly exercise their desires of excessive consumption and vanity are women. In Dekker's *The Shoemaker's Holiday* (1599), for example, it is Eyre's wife, Margaret, whose taste in fine apparel is emphasized even while Eyre himself exhibits sartorial self-importance – generally read by critics as civic pride. The men of the Rialto who seek Monsieur Money in *A Search for Money* (1609) blame their wives – with a quick theatrical allusion to Will Kempe – for transforming money 'into chaines, jewels, bracelets, tyres, ruffes of the fashion, which still were no longer liv'd then a wonder, nine dayes, then it was stale, and they must have a new'.[20] Turner expands his critique of women's inordinate desire promoting usury by comparing it with other vices: 'A drunkard hath brought his body to such a habit, that unlesse he drinke liberally, even to the turning of his braines, he will be sick againe; is not drunkennesse in that man sinfull, because so necessary? A proud woman hath beene wedded so long to her will, that if shee be crossed in it, shee will grow mad for pride, like *Nabuchadnezzar*, or else dye with fretfulnesse (like a Weezil in a Cage) shall her wilfulnesse be excused, because her devillish stomacke is growne too strong for her wit?'[21] *Englishmen for My Money* ensures that the 'will' of the women directs itself toward beneficial love and marriage, but the joke is of course based on the fear that men cannot control the dangerous desires of women – desires that preachers and dramatists have been connecting directly with trade deficits, usury, and the decline of the English craftsman's standing. Recent studies of *Englishmen* in particular take on these gendered issues, and they are discussed in the introduction to the play, below.

One strong argument in the period for controlling usury and taking care of the economic health of the country was to make money plentiful and decrease interest rates on loans. In the Netherlands, for example, money was generally lent at 6 per cent in the absence of usury constraints. Because interest rates in England were routinely a few percentage points higher than on the Continent, lenders borrowed abroad and did their money lending in England: 'Onely England is the parradise of *Usurers*', notes the anonymous author of the manuscript 'The Usurer Reformed' (fol. 14v), echoing the conversation between Lady Lucre and Usury in *Three Ladies* (2.216–27);[22] the same advantage is clearly available for international merchants to borrow more cheaply than their English counterparts and thus undercut them in the marketplace. In the anonymous *A Tract Against Usurie* (1621), these points are expanded, as the writer supports lower interest rates on loans to increase competition and keep merchants trading goods. The lower interest rates, such as the 6 per cent in Holland, allow trading with less risk of loss by the borrower, greater profit, the ability to trade at lower prices and undercut countries like England, and greater returns of money into the commonwealth.[23]

England's 10 per cent makes borrowing more risky, goods more expensive, and encourages traders to lend at usury, because it is a safer, easier, more lucrative pursuit. High interest rates also cheapen land, which is secure but slower to reap gain. Cheap land leads to lack of investment in improving property and thus neglect of the commonwealth: 'it makes the Lande it selfe of small value, neerer the rate of new-found Lands, than of any other Countrie, where Lawes, governement, and peace, have so long flourished'.[24] This last comment is pertinent, for one of the underlying concerns of the preachers and the secular writers of entertainment is the preservation of a national identity impervious to the terrors of usury and its alien effects on good English behaviour. Such identity for any country lies largely in its efficient use of its own resources and its domestic policy; these are the issues – exporting to England's disadvantage, the decline of hospitality, and so on – that trouble Wilson so deeply, that Haughton makes comic, and that Tailor draws into a study of individual conscience; and these issues of land and honest work underlie Bacon's famous essay 'Of Usury', with which I began this introduction. Merchandising is the most important matter in a healthy economy, writes Bacon: 'as a Farmer cannot husband his Ground so well, if he sit at a great Rent; So the Merchant cannot drive his Trade so well, if he sit at great *Usury*'.[25] The work ethic is strongly in place here, and usury must be allowed at modest levels only to encourage the purchasing of goods and the active intercourse of traffic.

Lower rates and fair lending, from this point of view, then, encourage money circulation and a healthy economy. Money used properly to the benefit of the kingdom has come from the king, the 'heart' of the country's body, and is 'like bloud in the naturall, in the veines of trading, for all and every ones maintenance, and retire to those royall centres againe'.[26] Money circulation sets the poor and middling sort to work and benefits the moneyed to be able to continue employment of their lessers. When rates are allowed to get out of control, however, we are forced to ask 'is not the Usurers money to them like an *Italian* Drugge, pleasant in the taking, and no fault found, untill we see they burst[?]' Moreover, Usury causes debt and prisoners, which are kept 'at the charge of the Countrie, towards which, how little help is had from usurie?'[27] But the opposing argument had its strengths too. Arguing from the point of view of the lender instead of the borrower, the pseudonymous Well-wisher of the Commonwealth points out that abating usury rates encourages lenders instead to put their money into real estate, which (coupled with the population increase of natives and strangers) raises the price of land. Some moneyed men, discouraged by low rates, will attempt and fail at alternative trades in which they have no training; still others will place their money at usury or exchange abroad instead of stimulating the economy at home. The subsequent decline in activity will affect the employment and incomes of native artisans and apprentices.[28]

With the fact being that almost all businessmen and gentlemen were engaged in some form of borrowing and lending, practical minds of the first half of the seventeenth century produced an increasing number of books outlining terms and processes of money-lending. Robert Butler's *The Scale of Interest* is a primer, written in 1632, which differs from the many business-like, unapologetic loan calculation texts like the *Treasurer's Almanacke* (1631, 1636) by basically alleging fraud in English accounting and lending practices to circumvent the usury laws. Wilson's *Three Ladies* provides an early example of harping on the inextricability of usury, fraud, and dissimulation as practices. Butler promises to provide figures that 'doe not onely answer the letter of the Statute, but are also consonant to truth and rules of Art',[29] thus the tract could be presented by borrowers to a lender as a kind of 'blue book' of current, correct, and acceptable valuation of loans. To this end of opening up the whole system of lending to scrutiny, the call for some kind of multi-part banking system arose. The anonymous *Two Knaves for a Penny[,] Or, a Dialogue between Mr Hord the Meal-man and Mr Gripe the Broker* (1647) suggests 'a Lumbardy might be established, and money lent out upon reasonable terms, at the rate of [four] per cent. For the relief of the poor, and supply of young beginners; which being but settled, the poor would not only be relieved of the greatest oppression that can be, but it would greatly advance the honour of the City, and all other men; that shall in the least lend assistance to the promotion of so charitable a work.'[30] But this text appeared half a century and more after the Elizabethan plays in the present collection, and Wilson for one could hardly conceive of such a system. Indeed, it would only be in the 1640s that this text and a good number of others, such as John Benbrigge's *Usura Accommodata, or a Ready Way to Rectifie Usury*, would make the major shift into more complex, practical proposals for managing money based on established and working Continental systems of banking and credit.[31]

The underwriters of loans were not the only ones vilified in the period. Just as reviled, and often more so because more visible to the borrowers, were the scrivener, and especially the broker, whose 'large conscience, is an yll wardrobe for a poor mans goodes'.[32] John Blaxton's extended simile gives us a taste of the opinion of the day:

> Not unaptly may we compare the usurer to the neather milstone, which is slow and sturres not; he sits at home, and spends his time in a devilish Arrithmeticke, in numeration of houres, dayes, and monethes, in Subtraction from other mens estates, and multiplication of his owne, untill he have made division betweene his soule and Heaven, and divided the earth to himselfe, and himselfe to hell. His broker we may compare with the upper milstone (without which the neather milstone may seeme unprofitable) that is quick and stirring, and runs round: the poore (like Corne) who between both these is grinded into powder.[33]

In fact, most brokerage was drawn into the category of a kind of usury of the day, for it was the profession of making money from nothing but sitting in between the two or more parties to a transaction. Related villains were landlords and bawds, both of whom sat back and collected cash. The former is the rent-racking, hard-hearted beast of morality plays such as George Wapull's *The Tide Tarrieth No Man* (1576) and directly linked to Usury in *Three Ladies*, where Usury is Lucre's broker who evicts Conscience from her house and re-lets it to her for four times the rent. A very common complaint of the second half of the sixteenth century was of the rise in rents. Only two years after the character No Good Neighbourhood is ruining Tenant Tormented in Wapull's play and a few years before Wilson wrote *The Three Ladies of London*, John Wharton recounts his dream in which he sees usurers being punished in hell among a company of 'Leasemongers':

> A many of them at this day,
> in Britain soil doth dwell:
> Whom God will fling (for their deserts)
> down to the pit of hell.
> They chop and change, and Leases catch,
> and hoiseth up great rent:
> At general Sessions I do fear,
> for it they will be shent.
> The houses that did lately go,
> but for a mark a year:
> For Nobles seven they do go now,
> how do ye like this gear[?][34]

George Wither adds to this concern and details further types of usury that go by other names but are arguably more damnable. He considers 'usury of Cattle or of Leases' to be 'as monstrous' as direct lending, and the landlord is 'no less a griping Usurer, / Than is the money master: if he breake / the rule of Christian charity, and take / More profit than his Tenant can afford'.[35] The latter – the bawd – is another procurer of unnatural breeding, a fact that Feste in *Twelfth Night* plays with: when Viola gives Feste a tip, he begins, 'Would not a pair of these have bred, sir?' and continues, 'I would play Lord Pandarus of Phrygia, sir, to bring a Cressida to this Troilus' (3.1.49, 51–2), thus drawing on an established connection between money-making and illicit sex. And in his *Lectures on the XV Psalme* (1604), George Downame wrote that usurers 'live in idlenesse: for usurie, as one well sayth, is *quæstuosa segn ties*, gainefull idlenesse; they walk inordinately, seeking gaine by a trade of sinne, even as the common theefe or baud doth: for what is an usurer but as *Bernard* sayth, *fur legatis*, a theefe, which for the hardnesse of mens hearts the lawes do tollerate. The Philosopher matcheth the usurer with the baud: and to the same purpose observe the cohærence, *Deut.* 23. 18. 19.'[36]

Those who 'gripe' to make money of nothing, most often by taking advantage of their social standing as clerks or justices, are also classed as usurers by Wharton and Wither. Thus 'There be of these, that Use for silence take / some others, an Usurious profit make / Of their authorities, and do advance / their wealth by giving others countenance'. And middle-men in deals 'oft, of every hundred, twenty take, / ere payment of our own, to us, they make / They must have bribes, their wives must have Caroches, / or horse, or jewels, after which encroaches / Their servants also'. In the courts of law, 'mean Officers so speedily grow rich. / Although they give large incomes, by this way / their wives so on a sudden grow so gay, / That were but Kitchen-maids few years before / yea many in the blood of Orphans poor / Have dyed their Gowns in scarlet by such courses, / and clothed and fed themselves with Widow's curses'.[37] Along the same lines, Wilson's lawyer in *Three Ladies* 'can make black white, and white black again' (3.138). And finally, a more 'active' mode of bro-kering, and one that pertains particularly to a London that is increasingly concerned with the burgeoning foreign trade into and out of the city, involves particular kinds of agents, or middle-men, known as colourers of strangers' goods. These men would pass off foreign product as their own so as to save the foreign trader the full brunt of extra duties on imported merchandise, in the process taking a cut of the selling price as an agent's fee. Jonathan Gil Harris notes that, for the writer Gerard Malynes, this 'colouring' is another form of usury, feeding as it does into the draining of the domestic economy.[38] We might recall that this is exactly the process in Dekker's *The Shoemaker's Holiday*, and we should take this play more seriously than criticism has done as an economically problematic piece – indeed, for someone like Malynes, it is in part a usury play. The weight of critical history's reading of Eyre as a boisterous, Fal-staffian character has kept the questionable and dangerous nature of his activities as a businessman (and controlling husband and master) largely under wraps.[39]

Usury, trade, foreigners

Two of the three plays included in this collection concern themselves with the presence of foreigners in London, and it is clear that the trope of usury always underlies and drives other concerns in sixteenth- and seventeenth-century plays – from religious reformation to social stability in the morali-ties, from sexual and generational relations to economic expediency in the 'mature' drama. This anthology is also, therefore, in many ways equally a collection of 'city plays' or 'alien plays', since usury provides a foundation for London's wealth and evolving mercantile sense of itself and a means for Anglo-foreign relations and intercourse. 'Strangers' or 'aliens' appear in well-known moral comedies of the 1550s, 1560s, and 1570s, such as *Wealth and Health* and *Like Will to Like*. They continue to be a staple of all historical genres in Elizabethan and Jacobean drama. Foreigners provide avenues for stereotypical xenophobic commentary (both harsh and light-hearted), and even physical attack, as we see played out in Anthony Munday (et al.), *The Play of Sir Thomas More* (c. 1594). Usurers of earlier plays tend to be more clearly foreign, whereas the seventeenth-century drama is more inclined to portray English usurers.

Foreigners in sixteenth-century England were welcomed, employed, given religious privileges, and imitated; they were also mocked, feared, driven out of towns and the country, and killed. Craftspersons and merchants had reason to love and hate foreigners coming to England to live and work. They certainly brought new markets and new skills, but they also seemed to take native positions in the marketplace at the expense of the English. Merchants and businessmen saw the necessity of foreign presence in England, while long-term alien residency in late Elizabethan London was aggravating the significant tensions of overcrowding, inflation, and poverty. For the nobility and royalty, the issue of foreignness was one of nationwide importance. Questions about the security of the State from the reign of Henry VIII to James I were often underlain by concerns with foreign relations.[40] Foreign relations in turn impacted domestic relations: if one rank of persons wanted to benefit from the advantages of the presence of foreigners while those foreigners imposed hardship on another rank of English citizens, there would be internal conflict in the country. This division is manifest in the Dutch Church Libel, a threatening notice against the strangers of London affixed to the wall of the Dutch Church in Broadstreet Ward on 5 May 1593. It complains of the resident aliens:

> With Spanish gold, you all are infected
> And with yt gould our Nobles wink at feats
> Nobles said I? nay men to be rejected,
> Upstarts yt enjoy the noblest seat*es*
> That wound their Countries brest, for lucres sake
> And wrong our gracious Queene & Subjects good
> By letting strangers make our harts to ake
> For which our swords are whet, to shedd their blood
> And for a truth let it be understoode
> Flye, Flye, & never returne.[41]

Census records of the immigrant population in London show quite a range of residents, from primarily economic migrants to legitimate religious refugees. Looking back on the situation from a mid-Jacobean perspective, John Fenton sees usury as an insidious foreign growth among a weak-willed native populace:

> many Christians of reformed Churches being urged to fly for persecution, and to convert their goods into money, yet wanting skill to imploy the same in a strange countrie; tender hearts thought it pitie that Usurie in such a case were not lawfull; and nimble wits began to search, if the matter might not be so handled, and qualified by cautions and limitations, that some such thing as that we call Usurie might be practised. For such is the subtilty of Satan, that if he cannot hinder the growth of good corne, yet tares shall grow up with it. He thought that when men were so busied about the reforming of those grosse abuses of superstition; that then was the onely time to begin a new seed-plot of Usurie, of Sacriledge, of liberty and profanenes in the other extreme. Which vices, howsoever they were little feared or thought upon in those days; yet by this time we may easily perceive to what ripenesse they be growne, which then were but as seedes under the ground.[42]

Indeed, in the year of *The Hog Hath Lost His Pearl*, not only were writers lamenting the fact that usury and avarice had entered the commonwealth under the stalking horse of reformed religion, but they were noting the good name the practice was gaining. In his *Abuses Stript and Whipt* (1613), a diatribe against almost everything and everyone in England, and dedicated to himself as really the only person he can trust to appreciate it, George Wither continues to illustrate the slippage between usurious practice, foreign identity, and class division. His section 'Of Covetousness' notes of the vicious and privileged:

> And yet in these dayes, if that men have ritches,
> Though they be *hangmen, Usurers or witches,*
> *Divels-incarnate*, such as have no shame
> To act the thing that I shall blush to name,
> Doth that disgrace them any whit? Fie no,
> The world it meanes not for to use them so;
> There is no shame for Ritch-men in these times,
> For wealth wil serve to cover any crimes:
> Thats truely noble [. . .]
>   [. . .] *report that he is poore,*
> And there's no way for to disgrace him more[.]

To be a 'devil incarnate' would suggest a common refrain to the readership of the period, in which 'An Englishman Italianate is a devil

incarnate', and Wither goes on to confirm this connection just a couple
of pages later:

> For, say they use extortion, no men more,
> Undoe their *Country*, hurt and wrong the poore,
> Be damn'd Usurers, and keep a house,
> That yeelds not crums enough to feed a mouse:
> Yet they'l not say hee's covetous; oh no,
> *Hee's thrifty, a good wary man, or so.*
> Another though in pride he doe excell,
> Be more ambitious then the *Prince of hell*;
> If his apparell be in part like us,
> *Italian, Spanish, French* and *Barbarian*,
> Although it be of twenty severall fashions,
> All borrowed from as many forraine nations;
> Yet hee's not vaine, nor proude; what is he than?
> *Marry a proper, fine neat Gentleman*[.][43]

This foreign-influenced infecting of proper English social harmony brings
in a focus on selfish ambition that the Jacobean usury drama will draw
out potently in such characters as Middleton's Quomodo (*Michaelmas
Term*) and especially Massinger's vulgar Overreach (*A New Way to Pay
Old Debts*). But this is to leap ahead, for, before these very English usurers
of the seventeenth century are on the stage, Elizabethans are attempting
to work through the hybrid identities of merchants, brokers, and artisans
who display the ability to move and morph between the realms of work
and leisure, city and country, poverty and riches, Englishness and alien
identity.

The money-minded and nationality-concerned Elizabethan morality
plays were already bringing in foreign characters in threatening roles to
remind their audiences of the ever-present real threat of foreign influence
in England. As the century got older, such influence ranged from the
benign to the fatal: at the lighter end of the spectrum, foreign habits such
as smoking (or 'drinking' tobacco, as it was often termed in the period)
were supported and lambasted by turns; foreign fashion was paradoxi-
cally mocked and imitated; there was the worrying phenomenon of foreign
luxury goods entering the markets and being exchanged for staple English
product; low-priced alternatives to English goods – made possible through
new materials, superior technology, and cheaper rates of usury abroad
– hurt English artisans in the markets. At the far extreme of the
foreign threat, the Spanish Armada of 1588 had attempted to invade
England, and rumours of foreign-led insurrection continued to circulate.
The traditional public enemy had shifted in the second half of the sixteenth century from the French to the Spanish, which perhaps lends

Englishmen a less threatening air, with its choice of French, Dutch, and Italian foreigners.[44] Pisaro, however, is Portuguese, and such scandals as the Lopez affair of 1593–94 (to which I return below) and the harbouring of the pretender Don Horatio of Portugal in London would not yet have been forgotten.

The French and Dutch were hardly neutral groups, either. There was a significant body of Protestant foreigners in England in the 1550s when Mary ascended the throne, some of whom fled the country and some of whom went underground, hoping for a return to Protestantism in the near future.[45] Significant influxes of immigrants occurred again in the 1560s (mostly from the Low Countries), and following the 1572 massacre of Huguenots in Paris, an event dramatized by Marlowe. 'Dutch' and 'French' immigrants (many Flemish and French Walloon) made up by far the largest proportion of settled foreigners in England, primarily in London, Norwich, and Colchester, but also in south-coast towns for shorter periods. In the second half of the sixteenth century, one-third of Norwich's population was immigrant, leading to some complaints of overcrowding and redistribution of the alien families. Awareness (and exaggeration) of the large number of aliens allowed local and national scaremongers to use the threat of aliens to drum up support against the foreigners themselves or against the monarch. Kett's rebels, who surrounded Norwich in 1549, used the threat of foreigners as impetus to gain support for their uprising, and the famous Ridolfi plot of 1571, 'a proposed operation against Elizabeth [. . .] had as its primary component a foreign invasion of England coordinated with an internal rebellion'.[46] It does not seem surprising, then, that by the closing decades of the sixteenth century relations between foreigners and the English were strained, and dramatists recognised the artistic and commercial benefits of entering such an arena of conflict.

Nor did it necessarily take threats of alien-based rebellion to rouse the suspicions and anger of the capital's populace. The established presence of foreign traders in London by the 1590s – their numbers artificially emphasized by the clustering of alien communities in a few London parishes – was enough to lay a foundation of fear against which a backlash could be directed to any new foreign 'insurgency'. Political action connected powerfully with drama in the period, and it was just five years prior to the staging of *Englishmen* that the Dutch Church libel threatened:

> Your Machiavellian Marchant spoyles the state,
> Your usery doth leave us all for deade
> Your Artifex, & craftesman works our fate,
> And like the Jewes, you eate us up as bread

[...]
Weele cutt your throtes, in your temples praying
Not paris massacre so much blood did spill.
(ll. 5–8, 39–40)[47]

The Paris Massacre allusion and a marginal manuscript note mentioning
Tamburlaine may suggest that the population of London was finally ready
to take what it saw as its only remaining option, that of violence. These
references, being titles of Marlowe's plays, seem more than coincidental,
the perpetrators knowing quite well the transference they were making
from stage depiction to the scenes on the city streets. The libel may
contain direct references to Wilson's play, too. David Bevington has noted
the important contemporary shift that Wilson makes in adding to the
earlier drama's French and Flemish aliens his Italian 'Machiavellian
Marchant', Mercadorus;[48] and the 'Artifex' of the libel, precisely like the
Artifex of *Three Ladies*, is in the middle of a scheme in which foreign
goods are made poorly but dressed well and sold to the impoverishment
of the honest English worker. The slippage between identifying Protestant
aliens as 'Machiavellian', 'Jewish', and involved in 'usery' demonstrates
the ease with which usurers and other 'anti-Christian' and 'un-English'
practitioners could be linked with Jews,[49] and why bringing foreigners
into the midst of dramatic representation of England's socio-economic
problems was so inflammatory and marketable.

Usurers, Jews, Jewishness
England's medieval Jewry spread itself across the country to survive;
living in small villages and major towns, the French-stock Jews found
assimilation difficult, and the spates of violence and forced local
expulsion, centred in historical records around the 1190 massacres coin-
cident with the coronation of Richard I the previous year, kept the communities marginalized through the following century. In 1275, the
Statutum de Judeismo attempted to ban all Jewish usury. It encouraged
Jews to engage in other merchandising and trades, promised rights to
property, and limited protections from civil action. Between 18 June and
1 November 1290, the Jews of England were expelled; as wards of the
monarch, their goods enriched the Crown coffers and their absence pla-
cated a sector of the king's restless, moneyed class. Historians continue
to argue over the reasons for the expulsion – anti-semitism, jealousy, the
need for cash, political positioning in relation to court favour (or, con-
versely, the court gaining the good graces of nobility). Robin Mundill
points out that Edward I does not seem to have reaped the full financial
rewards of the expulsion of some two thousand propertied Jews, leaving

equivocal the argument of a solely economic impetus. There was probably internal conflict among the English, too; many Jews were third- and fourth-generation residents and thus well settled into their location, and several towns apparently did not join in the request to expel their Jews. The *Statutum de Judeismo* focused on usury, 'which the Jews have madde in Time past, and that divers Sins have followed thereupon', and Edward cited the continuation of usury under colour of another name as his prime reason for carrying out the expulsion.[50]

The usury plays with which we are concerned (and all Marian, Elizabethan, Jacobean, and Caroline works of literature) were thus written and/or performed in a city and country officially devoid of Jews – the medieval house of conversion, the *Domus Conversorum*, still standing and very occasionally occupied. In practice, Jewish contact with England returned in the sixteenth century by means of several political and economic avenues.[51] When the (officially converted) Jews began settling in London in small but significant numbers from about 1540, they were concentrated in Tower Ward and Aldgate, locations that are relevant to *The Three Ladies of London*, and to *Englishmen for My Money* in particular, for they may suggest that Pisaro's address in Crutched Friars is meant as a hint that he is Jewish. During the 1580s and early 1590s the Jewish community of London became more noticed, owing in part to the presence of the Portuguese 'New Christian' doctor, Rodrigo (Ruy) Lopez. He was the Earl of Leicester's physician before becoming attendant on the Queen in 1586;[52] tried for treason in the autumn of 1593, he was hanged at Tyburn on 7 June 1594.[53] There is a consensus among literary historians that the Lopez affair strongly influenced the revival and reception of *The Jew of Malta* in 1594 and the writing of *The Merchant of Venice*. Furthermore, as I have already indicated, the Portuguese connection would probably have resonated with audiences watching *Englishmen*'s Pisaro.

The medieval legacy of the English Jews as usurers could still be used by Elizabethan and Jacobean writers, as could the myths of Jewish blood lust for Christian sacrifice. Some Elizabethan authors took pains to defend the English as the mildest usurers, for the Jews

> tooke after 60.70.80. in the 100. It appeares in *Graftons* Chronicle that about the yeere of our Lord 1264. and in the 47. yeere of the raigne of *Henry* the 3. King of England, five hundreth *Jewes* were slaine by the Citizens of London, because one Jewe would have forced a Christian man to pay more then two pence for the *usurie* of twentie shillings the weeke: as for our *usurie* in money after the rate of 10. in the 100. it comes not to an halfe penny a weeke for twentie shillings: and therefore I take it to be the least *usurie* that is used this day in the land.[54]

That does not mean that it is acceptable practice, however, and the writer goes on to remind his readers that usury is condemned by Exodus 22 (do not exact interest from the poor), Leviticus 25 (take in your poor brother and do not abuse him with interest on loans), Deuteronomy 23 (do not lend upon interest to your brother, but to a foreigner you may lend upon interest), Proverbs 28, and Ezekiel 18 and 22 (the righteous man does not lend at interest; Jerusalem is condemned for doing so). Jacobeans kept with the same thirteenth-century illustrative incident: 'In 46 of. H.3. 700 Jewes wer slayne in London, the rest spoyled & ther synagogue defaced, for that one Jewe, forced a Christian to pay moor then 2d. a weeke for the usury of 20s. wherby it is plaine that brokers & Jewes are of like quality.'[55]

Still others emphasized instead the *similarity* between the English and the Jews or the extent to which the English now *exceeded* the Jews at their own vice. Usury is, writes Philip Caesar in 1569, 'A vice whiche none but infidels will use, and no godlie men can abide. And yet a vice which infidels detest, and Christians, so called, in deede no Christians, delight in. A vice whiche among the Turkes and Indians is not allowed: and so odious among the Jewes, as they use it not, but towardes strangers.'[56] In the first year of James's reign, Thomas Pie is particularly saddened. He has had to title his tract 'Usury's Spright', because it has already been 'arraigned', 'tried', and put to 'death' in previous tracts, yet still, 'Usurie is as rife in this land, and as commonly and cruelly practized, as ever, I thinke, in any age before: as Jewishly, as when the Jews were heere in their prime: as unmercifully, as when the cursed *Caorsini*, the Popes factors, by his holie countenance, were here in their pride'.[57] By John Blaxton's time, the 1630s, then, it was nothing new to declare that 'Ministers may tell the mercilesse usurer that he is infamously guilty of that sinne, of which a converted Jew, an honest Heathen, a tolerable Turke, would be ashamed and remorsefull'.[58] The mid-Jacobean 'The Usurer Reformed' revived an old idea to make these English usurers recognizable, but also to deal with the aggravating problem of those parasitical brokers: 'what inconvenyence woulde there come to the Comon wealth if every professed *usurer* were enioyned to weare a redde hatt, as the Jewes doe in Ittaly: ffor it would come to passe, either that for pure shame he would leave the wicked trade, or that his hatt might save the charge of a Scryvenor or a Broker to dyverte the needy, to a man that hath money to lett'.[59]

James Shapiro notes the sliding scale in early modern representation of English Jewishness, familiar charges of usury slipping into frightening representations of the other 'Jewish' tenacity – for Christian blood: 'At a time when English men and women were increasingly engaged in lending at interest, sometimes demanding excessive rates of return, it was reassuring to learn that they were not as bad as Jews', writes Shapiro. 'Yet Jewish usury (perhaps because there was less and less difference between it and English financial practice) was insufficiently unnerving in and of itself to stimulate the kind of irrational prejudices still produced by the charge of ritual murder. Only when harnessed to the darker threat of taking the knife to Christians, as in *The Merchant of Venice*, did depictions of Jewish usurers prove so deeply unsettling.'[60] Shapiro's is of course a view from within a book centred relentlessly on Shakespeare *as Englishness*; as the reader of any number of usury plays will discover, *The Merchant of Venice*, for all its breadth, cannot alone represent the quintessential touchstone for the English sense of the genre of the usury plays. We have lost *The Jew*, a play probably from the 1570s, that Stephen Gosson, playwright and, later, anti-theatrical writer, tells us analysed 'the greedinesse of worldly chusers, and bloody mindes of Usurers'.[61] This play, in between the moralities and *Three Ladies*, suggests strongly that 'Jewish' usury *was* a real and pervasive domestic threat through the Elizabethan, Jacobean, and Caroline periods, made even more practically manifest by the increasing English awareness of usury's necessary infiltration into a new mercantilist economy and its existence side-by-side with continued thrashing out of national religious identity.

The stereotypical jokes about Jewish hard hearts (e.g. *Mer* 4.1.70–80) or miserliness (e.g. *Jew of Malta* 4.4.62–6) and the conflation of physical and practical features of the usurer and the stage Jew blend the cultural identities of usurers and Jews such that they are inextricable in these plays. Robert Wilson's Gerontus, a Turkish usurer, is a Jew; the character Usury is alleged to have parents who 'were both Jewes, though thou wert borne in London' (*Three Lords* 1441–2; sig. F4);[62] Barabas is a Jew; and, Shylock is a Jew. Marston's Mamon (*Jack Drum's Entertainment* (1600–1)) is an Englishman, yet he exhibits extreme examples of stereotypically 'Jewish' behaviour in the stage and prose fiction tradition; George Chapman's usurer, Leon, in *The Blind Beggar of Alexandria* (1597), is difficult to separate from sixteenth-century images of the Jew; and, while Pisaro is never called a Jew, his country of origin suggests the possibility, and a number of similarities to Barabas and Shylock seem based in stage-Jewishness as well as usuriousness. Chapman's *Blind Beggar* is, like *The Jew of Malta*, a Rose play, and Leon clearly wears a large, false, stage nose. In *A Search for Money* (1609), William Rowley refers to a usurer with 'an old moth-eaten cap buttoned underneath his chinne: his visage (or vizard) like the artificiall Jewe of Maltaes nose'.[63] If Barabas and Leon both wore large, false noses, it seems likely that such a prop would also be brought out of the cupboard for that other Rose theatre usurer, Pisaro

in *Englishmen*; after all, as Ned Walgrave tells us, Pisaro's 'snout' is 'Able
to shadow Paul's, it is so great' (1.2.15–16). The comic tradition continues as Mamon is listed in the quarto's list of characters as 'Mamon, the
usurer with a great nose'; Hog the usurer's daughter is named Rebecca,
a name that glances at Jewishness, but he himself will eat with Lightfoot,
unlike Shylock with the Christians.

   Alan Dessen draws out the continuity between the Jewish characters –
and by implication the issue of gathering money, largely if not entirely
through usury – in Wilson, Marlowe, and Shakespeare, concluding that
'In morality play, tragedy, or comedy, the stage Jew could function as a
dramatic scalpel with which the Elizabethan dramatist could anatomize
the inner reality of a society Christian in name but not necessarily in
deed'.[64] Indeed, the Turkish Judge makes the slippage between name and
deed clear in scene 14 of *Three Ladies*, where he declares in front of the
Jew Gerontus and Christian Mercadorus that 'One may judge and speak
truth, as appears by this: / Jews seek to excel in Christianity, and Christians
in Jewishness' (14.48–9); Marlowe's Maltese Christians exhibit a 'failure
[. . .] to provide a positive alternative to Barabas's Jewishness'; and Shakespeare, in the character of the bitter Gratiano, 'provides us with a "Jewish"
Christian or a Christian Shylock'.[65] As we contemplate the usury play as
distinct from plays with Jews, we can see that this notion of exposing the
ailing Christian common body (or the 'sick economy', as Jonathan Gil
Harris has coined it)[66] comes also from within: English usurers in their
'Jewishness' are the tools with which to analyse their countrymen's and
women's shortcomings and with which to bleed their own poisons as they
make their way toward a reconciliation with Christian life or even a conversion away from the gods Mammon and Avarice.

The literary stereotype and the representation of the usurer
In *The Three Ladies of London*, the character called Usury gives us what
we would expect. He is 'hard-hearted' (2.171), a 'bloodsucker', a 'thief'
(7.4), and a swinish 'Suck-Swill' (7.25). This last porcine image, possibly
connected to the medieval *Judensau* images, was widely alluded to in the
period. John Blaxton's title-page woodcut includes a commentary on
usurers as hogs (see page xi). I noted above that Usury's 'parents were
both Jewes, though thou wert borne in *London*' (*Three Lords* 1442; sig.
F4), and, in parallel to Simony's unsurprising upbringing in religiously
profane Rome (2.228), Usury is connected to usurious Venice (2.216–17),
with its merchants, popishness, and Italian cunning. Usury claims he
comes to England, however, because of its increasing reputation as the
homeland of Lucre, whom he must serve. Usury walks hand in hand with
Simony (SD 2.84.1), but also causes great rejoicing in Dissimulation when

he is present (10.101–3). His most vituperous hate is for Hospitality
(5.23), whom he murders at the beginning of scene 8. As C. T. Wright
notes, 'One chief Elizabethan grievance against the usurer was his ruin of
the hospitable gentry'.[67] The socio-political valency of Usury murdering
Hospitality in Wilson's play, which itself builds on earlier drama's
concerns with London overcrowding and merciless landlords, multiplies
in the texts of the 1590s and early 1600s, which assume an unequivocal
and direct link between usury and the decline of hospitality in England.[68]
The problem of usury's ruin of the class of native gentleman is a central
concern of Thomas Lodge in his *An Alarum Against Usurers*, which was
published in 1584, the same year as *Three Ladies*.

Arthur Bivins Stonex counted seventy-one plays 'containing or seeming
to contain' usurers between 1553 and the closing of the theatres, forty-five
of which have the usurer as a significant character.[69] Others have Jews
and money-men Lombards. Usurers in literature are usually not *only*
usurers; as embedded as the practice of usury had become in society by
the time of the public theatre plays, it is represented as the occupation of
those who are also engaged in legitimate crafts or merchandising trades.
For some stage usurers, their usury is simply a sideline and impacts little
on their character, while for others it becomes the defining aspect of their
character that determines their rise and fall. 'Usury' plays tend to be
comedies, and the usurers are also often cast as stereotypical or at least
recognizably familiar lustful old men, duped fathers, or even prodigal
themselves. As Norman Jones point out, 'The usurer was often typed as
a prodigal, too, for the moralists were certain that the only reason he
would want money was for consumption and idleness. Thus the desire
for wealth demonstrated by usurers was proof of their reprobate status.'[70]
There is clearly an irony here, for the plays generally seem to pit the
prodigal child *against* the usurer in a familiar extension of the age-old
generation conflict of youth and *senex*. But if the usurer himself is taken
as prodigal in this sense, then there is more to be teased out in this relationship: the repressed desire of the usurer (to be young, to have sex, to
use his money even when the idea of doing so makes him fret), the flam-
boyance of the prodigal, the *success* of the prodigal, the self-flagellation
of the stock usurer – all these psychological, economic, emotional, and
social concerns complicate the rather static binary implied by a dual
usurer–prodigal 'paradigm'. Work remains to be done on the development of the usurer in drama and in particular on his shifting role in a
society at once increasingly reliant on his money but increasingly unwilling to have any personal truck with money-lenders.

In non-dramatic tracts, guides to spot a usurer were frequently drawn
up. Ithamore's evocation of the pickled-grasshopper-eating usurer in *The*

Jew of Malta (which defamation Barabas swiftly dismisses) reminds us of
traditional descriptions of the figure, who 'hath a leane cheeke, a meager
body, as if he were fed at the Divels allowance: his eyes are almost sunke
to the backside of his head with admiration of money. His eares are set
to tell the clocke; his whole Carcase a meere Anatomy.'[71] An extended
comic version of the miserly usurer is found in a French text, translated
into English – once again in 1584 – in which we hear of a usurer who
tried to hang himself, and, when he was cut down by a sympathetic soul,
complained about the cost of his ruined rope; so he drowned himself,
because that would cost nothing:

> He was of stature shorte, and therewithal somewhat thinke, of a swarte
> complection, and of a grimme countanaunce, aunswerable to the disposi-
> tions of his minde, for the worke of Nature is a worke of understanding,
> who frameth everie mans body, agreeable to his minde. He was married,
> yet (through the infection of covetousnesse, which had poisoned his heart)
> he would never or sildome accompany his Wife, for feare he should have
> Chyldren, to put him to charge: He was lothe to use many wordes, least
> by that meanes, drinesse should provoke him to drincke, and so he should
> be at coast with himselfe: his bread was at the least twelve dayes olde,
> before he would eate it, because being thorowe stale, it should last him
> the longer: at dinner tyme he would sleepe tyll Supper, thereby to save a
> meale: he would confesse, that he was lothe to rubbe, where eyther he
> ytched, or the fleas bytte him, least by that meanes he should weare his
> shyrte, and so be at coast to buie a newe: all his studie was howe he might
> live, to spend least money: when he blewe his nose, the wall served him
> for a hankerchar, for he used not to buie any: he would sildome or very
> little walke abroade, eyther because he would not spend any thing, or else
> as some saye, for that he would not weare shooe leather: he used for the
> most parte, water for his drinke, he was seene once in *Paris*, to eate his
> breade with the smoake of the roast meate, and to satisfie his thyrst, with
> the vent and ayre of the wine seller. And to conclude, his miserable quali-
> ties were more then eyther have been reported, or if they were set downe,
> would be believed. Let it suffice that these qualities were more filthie, then
> became humanitie, and more beastlie, then agreede with Christianitie.[72]

The closing sentence of this description reminds us that, for both the
theologians and morally minded readers of great literature, the beastliness
and anti-Christianity (often meaning 'Jewishness') of usurers remained
the most prominent problem, and usurers were closely associated with
Satan and hell, for 'Every forfeit he takes, scores up a new debt to *Lucifer*;
and every morgag'd land he seizeth on, inlargeth his dominions in hell'.[73]
'If but any probable suspicion rose of a man to occupie that filthie trade,
he was taken for a devill in the likenes of a man: his house was called the
devils house, all that hee had was counted the devils: and therefore while

he lived of all sortes he was abhorred'.[74] The morality plays had their covetous and avaricious vices who practised oppressive money-lending, hoarding, and leasing some time before the plays included in this volume; Covetousness in W. Wager's *Enough Is as Good as a Feast* (c. 1560) declares that 'Covetous (saith the wise man) is the root of all evil; / Therefore, Covetous is the chiefest that cometh from the devil'.[75] And when Harvey calls Pisaro 'Signior Bottle-nose' (*Englishmen* 3.2.1), he is using the epithet traditionally applied to the devil, as when Sin calls Satan 'You bottle-nosed knave' (line 363) in T. Lupton's play *All for Money* (1572).[76] Brokers and scrivenors were lesser devils in Satan's service, and marginalia in 'The Usurer Reformed' note of these two professions, 'Ther vomit is full of bills, & obligations. Ariosto'; and moreover, 'It is said that Lucifer is tied in chaines that hee can never come abroade: but the spirits of avarice & lying, Mammon and Belial, in the shape of brokers do him service'.[77] Mammon is in the end always a sad character, as we see in Spenser's depiction of his useless temptation of Red Cross Knight, and in Marston's play *Jack Drum's Entertainment* (1600–1) where the usurer Mamon is a particularly nasty Englishmen who ends up viciously whipped in Bedlam.

Thomas Nashe's *Pierce Penilesse* (1592) makes a similarly hellish alignment as his poor scholar goes off in search for the devil who lends money. He goes to the Exchange:

and thrusting my selfe, as the manner is, amongst the confusion of languages, I asked (as before) whether he were there extant or no? But from one to another, *Non novi Daemonem* was all the answer I could get. At length (as Fortune served) I lighted upon an old straddling Usurer, clad in a damaske cassocke edged with Fox fur, a paire of trunke slops, sagging down like a Shoomakers wallet, and a shorte thrid-bare gown on his backe, fac't with moatheaten budge, upon his head he wore a filthy course biggin, and next it a garnish of night-caps, which a sage butten-cap, of the forme of a cow-sheard over spread very orderly: a fat chuffe it was I remember, with a gray beard cut short to the stumps, as though it were grimde, and a huge woorme-eaten nose, like a cluster of grapes hanging downe-wardes. Of him I demaunded if hee could tell me any tidings of the partie I sought for.

[. . .] thus much I heard by a Broker a friend of mine [. . .] that he is at home sicke of the gout [. . .] hee is busie with *Mammon*, and the Prince of the North, how to build up his kingdome[.][78]

The confluence of usurer and devil (and as we have just seen above, by association, Jew) is also foregrounded in William Rowley's well-known prose piece *A Search for Money* (1609). This reference bears rehearsing from the previous section. A party sets out in search of Monsieur Money,

making their enquiries with a tailor, tapster, shoemaker, barber, gallant,
thief; among mountebanks and prostitutes; and then to 'Jewish brokers',
scriveners, milliners, and drapers, before coming to 'the kennel of a most
dogged usurer'.[79] He is a gargoyle-like figure, whose head, peeping through
a door, is worse 'then ever held a spout of lead in his mouth at the corner
of a Church, an old moth-eaten cap buttoned underneath his chinne: his
visage (or vizard) like the artificiall Jewe of Maltaes nose', and that nose,
like Pisaro's, according to Frisco (4.3.106–11), is full of worms: 'the
worms fearing his bodie would have gone along with his soule, came to
take and indeed had taken possession, where they peept out still at certain
loope holes to see who came neere their habitation: upon which nose,
two casements were built, through which his eyes had a little ken of us'.[80]
The usurer angrily announces that, in spite of all his bills and bonds, he
cannot keep Monsieur Money with him, because he is always abroad at
loan. Eventually Money is found to be confined in hell because 'the divill
had so many children fathered on him that he never begat and so many
of his owne, that hee had no other dowry to bestow on them'.[81]

Ugly, a starved appearance, diseased, old, socially isolated – these are
the common features of the usurer. There is the almost ubiquitous (and
paradoxical) attribution of gout – the disease of luxurious living – to
miserly livers, and the equally contradictory attiring of the usurer in
threadbare clothes lined with furs. As C. T. Wright concludes, 'the
convention ceases to have any relation to facts'.[82] Despite acknowledging
these conventions, however, the plays generally satirize them rather than
demonstrate them. Although Pisaro's 'snout' is said to be huge, this is
said as slander, and there is no other evidence that he is ugly; no one in
the play suggests that Gerontus the usurer dresses poorly; and even
Tailor's Hog is more the beleaguered father of prodigality than the des-
picable devil figures of usurer Barabas or medieval mythical bloodthirsty
Jews. By the time of Massinger's *A New Way to Pay Old Debts* (1621),
the belying of the usurer's stereotypical appearance can be foregrounded
as a bit of metatheatre. Furnace, the cook, notes:

> To have a usurer that starves himself
> And wears a cloak of one-and-twenty years
> On a suit of fourteen groats, bought of the hangman,
> To grow rich, and then purchase, is too common;
> But this Sir Giles feeds high, keeps many servants,
> Who must at his command do any outrage.
> Rich in his habit, vast in his expenses,
> Yet he to admiration still increases
> In wealth and lordships.
>
> (2.2.106–14)

Of course, the fact is that, in the drama at least, it is not at all 'too common' to have a usurer represented in this manner, even while the genres of prose and poetry continue to peddle the stereotype.[83]

The drama's representation of the usurer surprises us in another way, and that is the frequent change of heart in the character of the usurer at the end of the play. Not so in prose tracts. In *The Market or Fayre of Usurers* (1550), the involuntary stubbornness of the usurer is emphasized. Seemingly convinced of his own reprobate status, this usurer admits that there 'should be nothyng worse, nor more pernicious more execrable, detestable and synful then an usurer. [. . .] A man might rather have to do with a Turke, and a Panyme then with a great usurer.' In spite of this confession, he soon declares that repentance is hard and doubts he can leave the money-lender's life.[84] Similarly, in *The Ruinate Fall of the Pope Usury* (c. 1580), we read the familiar conviction that 'as it is impossible to alter the creation, the force of Tigers, the strength of Elephants, the flight of Birdes, the gliding of serpents, the savours of herbes, the waight of mettels, yᵉ moistnes of waters[,] and the droughts of of [*sic*] the Earth: so is it as impossible to alter the natures of perverse greedinesse to liberalitie, for as fire cannot be chaunged into water nor water into fire: no more can an olde Usurer with the inordinate covetouse, be turned into a young minde to become liberall'.[85] However, the plays that portray this moral conflict for the most part remain 'comic' with their endings of willing and sadly amused conversion; in spite of the preachers' insistence on the impossibility of the softening of the usurer's hard heart, these plays time and again play out just that fantasy of returning a lost soul to the moral fold of England. In this way, our two most written-about and read 'usury' plays, by Shakespeare and Marlowe, are not representative of the 'usury play' mode that this collection and the majority of the plays of the period demonstrate. Even when the plot gets complicated and the usurers are severely punished (at least in social terms), as is the case in Middleton's *A Trick to Catch the Old One* (Q1 1608), 'The usurers react, not like men who have suffered grave personal misfortunes, but like men who have lost a game'. For all its intrigue, this play is, in Alexander Leggatt's words, 'surprisingly good-tempered'.[86] I would want to suggest that we keep the other senses of 'tempered' in mind as we read these plays, for they impart a surprising ability to 'temper' (to moderate, restrain, curb) received opinion and to 'temper' (mix, alloy, modify, enrich) their evidence and generic source material as they investigate social or moral issues.

Usury, money, and ambition in Jacobean drama
For all the tracts against money, avarice, and usury, only a selection of which are mentioned in this introduction, the merchandising or investing

moneyed man becomes strangely admired as well as reviled in the late
Elizabethan and Jacobean drama. The dynamics of this new theatre of
economic, sexual, and bloody conflict has drawn most of the critical
attention concerned with usury and financial ethics. John McVeagh points
out that Dekker's Simon Eyre's in *The Shoemaker's Holiday* possesses an
equivocal but effective cunning that 'makes him not a narrow but a hearty
human being, not anti-social but more congenial than before', and
Volpone's insistence that his money is got through 'No common way: I
use no trade, no venture' and no 'usure private' means that 'Volpone's is
clean money, got by witty invention'.[87] Thomas Gresham in Thomas
Heywood's 2 *If You Know Not Me You Know Nobody* (1606), moreover, 'is not just a great merchant; he is a great patriot, and his wealth
enables him to express his love of his monarch and his city'.[88] But this
admiration is hardly the whole story. Theodore Leinwand observes that
as late as Middleton's Quomodo in *Michaelmas Term* (1607) we see this
draper 'not in the role of a trader, but as a usurer and swindler [. . .] both
playwright and audience still identify the usurer with the cunning citizen,
at a time when everyone from knights to scriveners was lending at interest'.[89] Gail Kern Paster notes how embedded such a view of the ubiquitous battle of self-interest had become in the drama by the time of Jonson
and Middleton, where 'Patterns of predatory behavior underlie the action
of all these comedies in varying degrees and turn the comic convention
of the "biter bit" into a summary judgement of urban society. The predatory order comes to take on the universal validity of natural law.'[90]
Leinwand further reads against an entirely celebratory reading of 2 *If You
Know Not Me*, which, he argues, in spite of the growing admiration for
the successful moneyed man, 'explores the embarrassment with which its
financiers encumber themselves', and 'Just as Dekker casts suspicion on
the origins of Simon Eyre's wealth, so Heywood momentarily insinuates
a moral lapse on Gresham's part'.[91] Indeed, we need to take seriously the
early London comedies' inroads into broaching the paradox of questionable financial gain and admirable social mobility – both Simon Eyre
and Pisaro are responsible and intelligently self-interested citizens. Eyre
manages to pitch his rise to power, however, as being embedded in the
service of the city, country, and his craft, and this foreshadows Heywood's
presentation of the new man of money.

   The coexistence of and tension between pro-money and anti-ambition
stances in plays of the 1590s and 1600s reveals something of the difficulty
of tracing a simple chronological progression of dramatic opinion. Real
viciousness of the usurer in London comedy is generally cast as coming
later, in the character of Overreach in Massinger's *A New Way to Pay
Old Debts* (1621). He is 'a positive, destructive force [. . .] too monstrous

for laughter'.[92] The shape of Overreach, however, had to some extent been prefigured in Marston's usurer Mamon, mentioned earlier, a vicious poisoner and who ends up similarly mad and sent to Bedlam. Neither is Massinger's way to pay old debts entirely 'new': the tricks of setting up a sham marriage and substituting the usurer's indebted prodigal for the usurer's preferred son-in-law, or of pretending marriage to a wealthy widow or landed gentlewoman, or of faking an altered state in the prodigal that the usurer perceives to his benefit – these have already been staged in *A Trick to Catch the Old One* and *Englishmen for My Money*. More pointed in Massinger's play is the presentation of his ruthlessness as something real, present, and to be contended with; whereas the representation of the revolting Barabas, the Jew of Malta, for instance, might be dismissed as extreme tragi-comedy, Overreach's own assertions to Wellborn that 'worldly men' such as himself trample further on those who are 'Past hopes sunk in their fortunes' (3.3.50–1) and to Lovell that he is 'insensible of remorse or pity' (4.1.130) are the frightening confirmations of the explosion of the moneyed man, the middle-class, ambitious, self-promoter. '[M]y wealth / Shall weigh his titles down' (3.2.103–4), says Overreach of Lovell, and this faith in the 'democratising' power of money overruns belief in blood ties and humanity.

But striking continually against the practical trajectory that followed the fortunes of rising wealth, the preachers persevered with their condemnations of the old usury figures; while usury as such receded into the background – albeit a concrete background – in the drama of this decade, the usurer figure became most important in the role of unjust father. Leinwand argues that '[a]lthough the playwrights may have tacitly assumed that a usurer was capable of any crime, the villainy the audience *saw* had nothing to do with lending at interest'.[93] Of course, usury continued to provide for the villainy: I have noted that Barabas's miraculous return to wealth is suggestively the result of that 'unnatural' instant-breeding of usury; and in spite of himself, Gerontus's usury is the necessary grease for Mercadorus's destructive wheels. When the vice of the usurer returns with acidity in the Jacobean drama, 'It is like a world, as the drama reflects it to us, in which as the spiritual connections have dissolved away between men, every individual is forced to turn aggressor in self-defence'.[94] In *A Trick to Catch the Old One* we have 'a world which has turned into a vast market place, and in which getting and outdoing are the acknowledged business of life'.[95] But through the mêlée we sense the perhaps grudging, very masculine, slightly repulsed but voyeuristic and envious appreciation for the villains' success. 'Surprisingly enough', writes Laura Stevenson, 'the sin they objected to was not greed, but social ambition.'[96] This draws on a trajectory that Louis B. Wright had noticed some fifty years earlier: 'Materialism and prodigality incidental to it are the bogies of the later stage homilies. Greed is the source of all social evils; the usurer comes to be the Great Devil; Ambition is more detestable even than Pride in the earlier plays.'[97] Stevenson goes on, 'The Jacobean usurer, then, has acquired a new vice; he has lost his morality-play role as a figure of greed only to gain a new stereotype of the social climber'.[98] Examples of this later figure are plentiful in well-edited texts of Middleton, Marston, and Massinger; the present collection provides an alternative piece of drama, for the private-theatre *Hog Hath Lost His Pearl* does not represent this movement of plays, but instead shifts into a parodic, pseudo-Romantic mode of drama and away from the urban anti-sentimentalism of city comedy.

THE PLAYS

The Three Ladies of London

The author and the play
When John Payne Collier announced in 1851 that Robert Wilson was 'indisputably a dramatist of great ability' and 'a most distinguished individual, perhaps only second to Tarlton as an actor, and decidedly his superior as an author', he began what has been a slow process of the recuperation of the reputation of this man who was an important player and author,[99] and one whose ethical representation of the state of things in *The Three Ladies of London* was being discussed in his own time. Stephen Gosson critiques *Three Ladies* and notes a (now lost) response play, *London Against the Three Ladies*, in his *Plays Confuted in Five Actions* of 1582, and that gives us a *terminus ad quem* for our play.[100] The play remained worthy of allusion later in the century:

> The world's so bad that virtue's over-awed,
> And forced, poor soul, to become vice's bawd;
> Like the old moral of the comedy,
> Where Conscience favours Lucar's harlotry.[101]

While Wilson's place as a major comic actor has been acknowledged for some time, his worthiness as a writer of comical, satirical political drama was only glanced at before the new historical, materialist, and new economic criticism began to reread him. In 1930, Louis B. Wright asserted that 'Wilson's *Three Ladies of London* is purely an economic document in theatrical form, severely arrai[g]ning the materialism of the day', and the breadth of recent critical approaches to the play certainly attests to its richness as a source of cultural information.[102] It is to be hoped that this edition will encourage further consideration of Wilson's plays' literary and dramatic value, as prompted at the end of H. S. D. Mithal's biographical introduction to the play: 'Among other things, the Cobbler tradition, the characters of Nobody and the noble Jew, the presentation of the Clown as the leading character in the play and always on the side of right, the use of prose and blank verse for the first time in drama in such a way as to make them characteristic of the occasion and the speaker, the pretty jingle of his fourteeners, his Pedlar and Crackstone suggesting Autolycus and Falstaff respectively – these may be cited as some of his positive contributions to literature.'[103] Richard Dutton has called Wilson 'a true professional of the theatre',[104] and Mithal sees Wilson as 'a writer who stands like a sign post, as it were, on the crossroads of the times', pointing back to the morality tradition, forward with an ability to broach complex relational dramaturgy that will develop in the 1590s, and sideways with pertinent contemporary political and social analysis. Mithal's introduction to Wilson is a comprehensive overview of the extant evidence for the actor-playwright's life and work, and the present introduction has used that work as its basis. I have excised Mithal's references to easily refuted documents or argumentation; interested readers can return to Mithal for that material.

On 3 January 1572, the Proclamation for the Execution of the Laws against Unlawful Retainers was issued to enforce earlier statutes.[105] Leicester's Men apparently responded with a letter to their patron requesting continuation of his favour, and the letter is signed by six of the company, the first signature being James Burbage's and the fifth Robert Wilson's. We have no earlier *terminus a quo* for Wilson's association with the company, which had been in existence from at least June 1559, at which time Dudley, Earl of Leicester asked for a licence for his players to perform in Yorkshire.[106] On 10 May 1574, a patent for Leicester's company to play in the city and liberties of London lists Wilson once more as a member.[107] By the next decade, Wilson is named as a playwright as well as a player in a Latin letter of 25 April 1581, in which a play is requested from him. Mithal suggests that the play written in response to this letter was in fact *Three Ladies*, and I return to this issue below. By 1583, then, when the twelve best players were culled from other companies to form the Queen's Men, Wilson was an established, multi-talented star.[108] He is named first in the list of Queen's players licensed to play in the city of London on 26 November of that year; and John Stow's *Annales* of 1615 rather famously misnames Wilson and sets him side-by-side with his better-remembered contemporary, Tarlton: Stow refers to them as 'two rare men, viz. Thomas Wilson, for a quicke, delicate, refined, extemporall wit, and Richard Tarleton, for a wondrous plentifull pleasant extemporall wit, he was the wonder of his time'.[109]

In a relevant note, Stow mentions that Tarlton 'was so beloved that men use his picture for their signs'.[110] In *The Three Lords and Three Ladies of London* (1588–89), in which the imprisoned ladies are released from prison and match with three Lords of London, Simplicity enters as a poor citizen selling ballads and meets Wit, Will, and Wealth. After a brief, comical singing competition, Will notices a ballad that Simplicity has not shown them. It is about Tarlton (343–74; sig. Cv), and Will finally buys the picture for a groat for his master Lord Pleasure (412–13; sig. C2–C2v). The 'picture' is a poetic one that Will 'cannot read', although 'the finenes' of the picture suggests an image of Tarlton himself heading the ballad, and so not quite the same thing as using a picture for a shop sign; but Simplicity was undoubtedly played by Wilson himself, and this is a touching memorial from a famous comedian as the living man suggests the influence of the late friend and in the process laments the ongoing lack of appreciation for the moral efficacy of their trade. Richard Levin notes that Robert Armin's pseudonymous *Quips upon Questions, or A Clown's Conceit upon Occasion Offered* (1600) contains a likely allusion to *The Three Lords and Three Ladies of London* in telling of a collier who goes to the theatre to see Tarlton. Because Tarlton is dead, the collier is laughed at, but when they show a picture of Tarlton on stage the collier leaves satisfied.[111]

In 1588 a subsidy list does not include Wilson's name as one of the household players of the Queen's Men;[112] this is not an exhaustive list, but the fact that other missing names are those of known dead men has led to speculation that the Wilson we have been discussing so far had by this time died.[113] This would require that the burial record for Wilson in 1600, two wills from 1597, mention of Wilson in the present tense by Francis Meres's *Palladis Tamia* in 1598, his likely authorship of other 1590s publications, including *The Cobbler's Prophecy*, and his name as a prolific collaborator in Henslowe's *Diary* between 1598 and 1600 all to be taken as references to another Wilson.

There are problems with asserting a second, younger Wilson and really rather little difficulty with accepting a young comic actor of the 1570s who develops into a high-achieving actor-playwright of the 1580s and mid-1590s and settles into collaborative piece-work in his twilight years. *Three Ladies, Three Lords, The Cobbler's Prophecy*, and *The Pedlar's Prophecy* (if this last is by Wilson) are all steeped in a concern for the moral wealth and health of a nation embroiled in class and gender war, in trade issues and international relations, and in determining national identities. The moral sermon of *Three Ladies* continues in *The Pedlar's Prophecy*, which, despite its later date of 1595, may be an earlier composition. It is certainly more straightforward, and in many ways cruder, than *Three Ladies* as it addresses its particular concern with the problems of travellers and merchants and the influence of aliens in England. It returns a number of times to the ravages of usurious practice in the land – all the while the Pedlar hollowly echoing the claim that this is not a play about England: 'I speake not of this Realme, you take me amisse, / All my talke is of the noble Citie of *Tyre*' (sig. Gv). The prologue makes clear that it is 'the bankerouts and usurers' (sig. A3) the play is here to condemn, for borrowing has become obsessive and is leading to inevitable bankruptcy and prodigality (sig. C2). The ruthless landlords (sig. D2, E) are present as ever, but the hardness of the culprits' hearts (sig. D3, E3v) will serve to bring them down in the end.

We might assess Wilson's age by association, and in that vein Mithal notes that it would be odd to find a very young man 'howsoever precocious collaborating with men like forty-years-old Munday'.[114] Moreover, we might note that another playwright represented in this edition, William Haughton, is specifically referred to in Henslowe's *Diary* as 'yonge horton' in 1597, and we might especially expect some such qualifier if we indeed had a very young Wilson in collaboration with older peers. Thomas Heywood's reference to Wilson as being 'before my time' in his *Apology for Actors* (1612) could be taken as suggesting that Wilson was no longer around by the mid-1590s, when Heywood was working; but Heywood is a man of the mature theatre and seventeenth century, and he probably would have considered Wilson as representing an old guard of moral playwrights. Meres's *Palladis Tamia*, by contrast, seems to confirm the ongoing presence in London of the single Wilson. After referring to Tarlton in the past tense, he writes that, as the Greeks had their extemporal wits, 'so is now our wittie *Wilson*, who, for learning and extemporall witte in this facultie, is without compare or compeere, as to his great and eternall commendations he manifested in his chalenge at the Swan on the Bank side'.[115] This latter event dates Wilson's living presence between 1595, when the Swan was built, and 1598 when *Palladis Tamia* was published.

Mithal's suggestion that Wilson 'abandoned his career as an actor' about 1593 at first seems like a clear reading of the gaps in the records, and it allows us to imagine a smooth career track toward the late collaboration. Attempts to slot Wilson into further moments of dramatic history here and there have been made. The 1920s, for example, saw an extended argument – played out in the main by S. R. Golding and S. O. Addy in the pages of *Notes and Queries* – over the possibility of Wilson's hand in *The Play of Sir Thomas More*.[116] This theory has not found favour and is not discussed in Vittorio Gabrieli and Giorgio Melchiori's authoritative modern edition of the play.[117] Moreover, we might want to consider the shift from playing to writing a less certain one. As Mithal notes, Thomas Lodge refers to Wilson in about 1579 as 'a good scholler', which strongly suggests he was already a writer as well as a player; it also suggests to me that Lodge's line 'I should prefer Wilsons shorte and sweete if I were judge' does indeed refer to a lost work entitled *Short and Sweet*, as E. K. Chambers and others assumed, and which Mithal resists.[118] And to look from the other direction, that 'challenge' at the Swan, for instance, suggests he was still willing to put himself on stage in the late period, and the characters of Raph in *The Cobbler's Prophecy* and the pedlar in *The Pedlar's Prophecy* are in many respects reincarnations of *Three Ladies'* and *Three Lords'* Simplicity, tempting us to think that he had himself in mind when writing the roles.[119]

So we have a man on the cusp of a great acting and significant writing career at the time of *Three Ladies'* composition. The Stationers' Register has no record of the play, but Mithal writes:

> The date of the play's composition can, however, be determined with reasonable accuracy on the basis of the reference to Peter's Pence as 'Not much more then 26. yeares, it was in Queene Maries time' [2.276]. As the Act reviving Peter's Pence was passed in the winter of 1554-5, and as Gosson mentions the play in his *Plays Confuted in fiue Actions*, entered in the Stationers' Register on April 6, 1582, *The Three Ladies* was probably written in 1581. Indeed it is just possible that the play written by Wilson in response to Thomas Baylye's Latin letter of 25 April 1581 was this drama.[120]

The letter Mithal refers to commissioned a play for Shrewsbury's Men. Although the suggestion that *Three Ladies* may have been written in response to this letter is a plausible one, we should remember that Shrewsbury's players apparently constituted a provincial organization, and the events of *Three Ladies*, as Mithal indeed acknowledges, 'are taking place not in the land of Nowhere but in the very heart of the city of London'.[121] The significance of London over the provinces is brought out in *The Three Lords and Three Ladies of London*, where the concluding prayer has Lord Pleasure ask, 'On all the rest that in this Land doo dwell, / Chiefly in *London*, Lord poure downe thy grace' (2333-4; I4); the three lords of Lincoln, who come to London to claim brides already taken by the three lords of London, are sent packing with nothing but emblematic stones to remind them of their defeat (2080-169; H4v-Iv); and Simplicity binding Fraud to a post to burn him suggests the London public theatre stage-post.

Another possible prompt for writing the play was the issuance of a proclamation on 19 May 1581 to control usury. It noted that 'frivolous questions' were being asked to get around the 1571 usury statute 13

Elizabeth I c. 8, which was due to expire. This proclamation or the buzz circulating around the topic seems as likely to have prompted Wilson's writing of *Three Ladies* as the general request in the Shrewsbury commission, for in it the monarch (the greatest lady of London) passes judgement on exactly the issues (usury and trade), the location (city of London), and the consequences (the detrimental effect of usury and foreigners on London's native population) that Wilson's play examines.

Whatever the prompt for the work, Wilson wrote and acted in a play that he probably took with him from Leicester's Men to the Queen's Men, and Scott McMillin and Sally-Beth MacLean have pointed out that the connection between Leicester and his players after 1583 remained strong. The sequel play *Three Lords and Three Ladies of London* is a Queen's Men's play, and the second edition of *Three Ladies* in 1592 might suggest a double-bill performance in the years 1588–92 (it certainly suggests the play's popularity); this situation brings together Wilson, Leicester, the Queen's Men, and their politico-moral allegorical drama as spokes in the same Protestant, patriotic wheel of the 1580s and 1590s. Moreover, there is ample evidence to conclude that Wilson continued to think of himself as a dedicated follower of Leicester, whether as a player, writer, or international messenger. He and Will Kempe visited Leicester and a company of his old patron's players in 1585–86 while Leicester was in the Low Countries, and to do so Wilson would have to be 'lured from his new company', the Queen's Men – a feat that further demonstrates the ongoing Leicester–Wilson connection.[122]

Three Ladies is a text that could be used in various playing situations, as might be demanded by a playwright taking it with him between companies and locations. The play hints at economy in casting and some cutting, which may suggest accommodation for touring. Simplicity enters 'with an Officer to whip him, *or two if you can*' (16.0, my emphasis); and we get the doubling direction '*Let Lady Lucre make ready for [Lady] Love quickly, and come with Diligence*' (SD 17.62.2–3), when Lucre in fact has a good eighteen lines to exit and change into Love, and a couple of scenes earlier Love and Lucre appear on stage together and converse, albeit with Love in a 'vizard behind' and a hood, thus disguising the player. But a company of at least seven is required to play *Three Ladies*, and there are *three* leading female parts, which would extend the traditional earlier troupe of 'three men and a boy' somewhat (although Lady Lucre is referred to as 'a lusty lady' (2.198) and the part could comically be taken by a man rather than a boy). When *Three Ladies* was revived presumably for the Queen's Men, then, it would have suited a company that with a 'virtual certainty' divided into two smaller troupes for most of its existence.[123]

Usury and the play

Three Ladies tells the tale of the downfall and corruption of Lady Love and Lady Conscience at the hands of Lady Lucre and her unsavory team of henchmen – Usury, Dissimulation, Simony, and Fraud. An Italian merchant called Mercadorus trades in London with money he has borrowed on usury from Gerontus, a good-natured Levantine Jew. Valuable studies by Emily Bartels and James Shapiro examine the Marlovian and Shakespearean workings-out of the relationships between the alien Jew or 'other' and a (real or assumed) native population,[124] and Alan Dessen and Daryl Palmer have placed Robert Wilson at the beginning of such dramatic examination.[125] Palmer argued in 1997 that the early modern understanding of 'race' is what is being addressed in *The Three Ladies of London*, and it is the irruption of such a powerful socio-political presence into a belated morality play – a 'Generic disturbance' – that gives the play such arresting power over an audience early in England's economic and merchandising boom.[126] There is no doubt that *Three Ladies* was an important precursor to Marlowe and Shakespeare's 'Jewish' plays, in which we hear echoes of Wilson's scenes: Gerontus's 'two thousand ducats' plus 'another thousand' for 'three months' space' (9.3–4) prefigures Shylock's deal of 'Three thousand ducats for three months' in *Merchant of Venice* (1.3.1–3);[127] Gerontus's comment that 'many of you Christians make no conscience to falsify your faith and break your day' (9.9) suggests not only Shylock's observations on the Christians' hypocrisy but also Christian 'policy' in *The Jew of Malta*; and Judge Nemo's maxim, 'One may judge and speak truth, as appears by this: / Jews seek to excel in Christianity, and Christians in Jewishness' (14.48–9) is this play's 'Which is the merchant here, and which the Jew?' (*Mer* 4.1.172).

The portrait of the Ottoman Jew is surprisingly sympathetic, and it prompts Thomas Cartelli's *caveat* reminding us that *Three Ladies*' 'unorthodox treatment of Christian and Jew should [. . .] be enlightening to those critics who continue to subscribe to a view of Elizabethan attitudes toward cultural difference which is as oversimplified as the one Marlowe and Shakespeare persuade us to reject'.[128] Here, a conservative Wilson depicts someone in the Levant who should be a double-devil (both usurer and Turkish Jew) as an honest man, a merciful dealer, and a faithful religious person who is shocked by the Christian merchant's willingness to convert to Islam to avoid debt.[129] We are given a picture not of a precise, cutting usurer but of a man whose place in society has necessitated his role as money-lender, and in this role he is considerate and lenient to his borrowers. We are not told that Gerontus has become rich through his trade and must assume that it is doing him significant financial harm to be left unrepaid of the three thousand ducats loaned to Mercadorus for over two years. There seems to be no malice or irony, then, when Gerontus says, 'Well, I am glad you be come again to Turkey; now I trust I shall / Receive the interest of you so well as the principal' (9.11–12). He is simply desperate for the conclusion of a long-overdue business contract into which both parties presumably entered freely. Gerontus declares, 'Signiore Mercadore, I know no reason why because you have dealt with me so ill. / Sure you did it not for need, but of set purpose and will' (17–18). But still Gerontus is flexible. Having been made familiar with Mercadorus's mercantile reason for returning to Turkey, he offers to help the Italian locate his goods. Later we hear Mercadorus himself admit that 'My Lady Lucre have sent me here dis letter, / Praying me to cozen de Jew for love a her' (12.21–2), and we lose all hope in the reformability of his dealings when he spits out the insult as Gerontus exits, 'Marry, farewell and be hanged, sitten, scald, drunken Jew!' (12.19).

When Mercadorus worms his way out of paying Gerontus by threatening to 'turn Turk', it is significant that the Jew objects so strongly, because the objection would coincide with that of the English playgoer.[130] So we have a problem: the (Catholic) Christian has tricked the Jew, and that in itself is comedy, and the Christian after all does not in fact change his faith, finally declaring, 'Me be a Turk? No' (14.58). But the Turkish Judge himself comes up with the conclusion quoted above (14.48–9), which of course is meant to apply not only to the case before him but also to the general behaviour of so-called Christians in the play. For all the benignity of Gerontus, however, we note that he resides in the country where the Judge can unapologetically use 'Jewishness' as a benchmark of stereotypically lucre-driven bad behaviour (albeit to express surprise at *this* Jew's 'Christianity'). The cozening of Gerontus is set up to be effected through Mercadorus's turning Turk, but it is instead achieved by him *not* turning Turk, and by him relying, rather, on the fact that men and women with religious conviction and good Conscience (which might mean gullibility) are easy to overcome in this harsh world.

As we watch and hear the foreign usurer, we are drawn to compare him with London's Usury. We have to understand that, in spite of the goodness of the Turkish Jew, it is still his money that permits the corruption of England at the hands of the Italian Mercadorus, and the connection between usurers, for all their apparent difference in character, is never severed. The character Usury received his training in Venice under Lady Lucre's 'grandmother, the old Lady Lucre of Venice' (2.216) and has taken up permanent residency in England, since 'England was such a place for Lucre to bide, / As was not in Europe and the whole world beside' (2.222–3). In Wilson's sequel play, *The Three Lords and Three Ladies of London*, Simony lists the aliens for Usury's benefit: ' 'Tis not

our native countrie, thou knowest, I *Simony* am a Roman, *Dissimulation*
a Mongrel, half an Italian, halfe a Dutchman: *Fraud* so too, halfe French,
and halfe Scottish: and thy parents were both Jewes, though thou wert
borne in *London*' (1439–42; sig. F4). Mithal questions whether Wilson
put that last clause in the mouth of Simony precisely because this is
slander and not the truth. The point is, I think, that Usury, whatever his
parentage, is a second-generation English resident whereas the others
(according to the admittedly doubtful testimony of Simony) are all new
immigrants; he was born in London, served in Venice, and now has
returned. The *Three Ladies*' connection with Venice would already suggest
London Usury's 'Jewishness' before *Three Lords*' confirmation of that
identity.

   This London Usury is multi-talented too. We have seen that contemporary commentators considered rent-racking a type of usury, and Wilson
has Usury act as Lucre's real estate manager – an interesting shift, since
Lucre assigns Fraud that position (2.247). Usury is experienced in both
repossessing houses and a sort of second-degree murder, for Simplicity
complains, 'O, that vile Usury! He lent my father a little money, and for
breaking one day / He took the fee-simple of his house and mill quite
away: / [. . .] / So he killed my father with sorrow, and undoed me quite'
(2.101–2, 105). Neither does Usury only pick on poor Conscience or
modest Hospitality, but he boasts early on that 'sith I am so well settled
in this country, / I will pinch all, rich and poor, that come to me' (2.267–
8). Indeed, it is Wilson's concern throughout the play to insist on the
damage that usury and lucre do to all classes in London and England.
Such damage is aggravated by alien immigration and the increase in rents
due to overcrowding in the capital. When Mercadorus encourages Lucre
to rent rooms 'to stranger dat are content / To dwell in a little room, and
to pay much rent' (5.72–3), she replies by telling him she has

> infinite numbers in London that my want doth supply,
> Beside in Bristol, Northampton, Norwich, Westchester, Canterbury,
> Dover, Sandwich, Rye, Portsmouth, Plymouth, and many more,
> That great rents upon little room do bestow?
> Yes, I warrant you, and truly I may thank the strangers for this,
> That they have made houses so dear, whereby I live in bliss.
>
> (5.79–84)

Lucre's list of provincial towns is, furthermore, an accurate representation
of places to which aliens were encouraged to relocate at various times in
the sixteenth century.

   The interplay of geography and ethnicity, morality and practicality,
gender and power, class and corruption in *Three Ladies* insists that we

consider carefully Wilson's combination of telling us a moral tale and showing us an embattled community. Moreover, Wilson seems particularly interested in insisting that any individual allegorical, representational, moral note in the play is directly related to physical, material, somatic, and often economic effects on Londoners. Whereas it is often assumed that the Elizabethan moralities only employ character 'types' that instruct without significant self-awareness, irony, or complexity, this brief analytical summary of the play makes clear Wilson's awareness of the equivocal and moving border between characters that are moral representations and those that are 'real' figures in the world. The two characters called Nemo provide particularly interesting examples. They each raise the same questions of community transaction, trustworthiness, and effectiveness, and they relate to the elusive figures of 'nobody' in other plays. I do not agree, however, with those who see these figures as two guises of a single character.[131] To do so does not appreciate the extent to which Wilson has shifted from pure moral representation into a mature interrogation of the tension between ideas and bodies.

The first 'Nemo' is the fallen nobleman who invites Simplicity to a dinner of nothing and then fades away:

> But come in to dinner with me, and when you have dined,
> You shall have –   *Presently go out.*
>   (4.180–1)

This lack of hospitality foreshadows the dire event four scenes later, when we hear the character Hospitality cry out for help and see him dragged off stage to be murdered by Usury. This is a serious moment for London that demonstrates a shift into a late, mature version of morality drama; for comparison, consider the fact that *Mankind*'s Mercy could not die; when Tityvillus whispers to Mankind that Mercy is hanged, it cannot be true for Mercy is always available to the repentant man. Hospitality, the social and physical provision of Christian teaching, on the other hand, is a material matter on earth and therefore a 'touchable' character. The importance of Hospitality's death is clearly worked out and confirmed in the play as Conscience finds no friendly reception for such a character as herself wherever she goes. The second 'Nemo' is the judge whom we are apparently supposed to take seriously as arbiter of moral rectitude. Of course, for all the severity of the final judgement in this play (and perhaps because it is almost melodramatic), we are forced to reflect on the noble 'No-man' we met earlier in the play, who liberally offered non-existent hospitality, and we ask ourselves the extent to which this judge or the effects of his judgement exist; could he simply be a figure of conscience and not really of the physical world? We are at least partially answered when Judge Nemo reappears in *The Three Lords and Three Ladies of London*, for there he is clearly being taken seriously as a character with spiritual and even godly presence, and whose actions have had material force, for the ladies have physically suffered from their incarceration. A problem remains, however, in the simple fact that the Judge Nemo is never named on stage; how might the audience know him to be Nemo? Should he wear the clothing of No-man, whatever that may be? Should he wear Nicholas Nemo's clothing, since the earlier character is identified repeatedly as No-man?

Wilson's plays consistently comment on the moral and physical culpability of women, and with that in mind it is notable that critics have not focused more cogently on gender in his work. Usury and Lucre are inseparable as economic and social operations, and the gendering of money makes its 'handling' and multiplying by male usurers inevitably if often indirectly a sexualized practice. The withholding of men's money in the usury plays is nearly always to make them unfit for marriage and therefore licit sexual relations – to be impecunious is to be impotent. Feminine money is attractive, deceptive, and corrupting: Lady Lucre's box of abominations is multicoloured; similarly, Thomas Bell claims that his book *The Speculation of Usurie* (1596) has tried 'to paint out fitly in her lively colours, the deformed and impudent ladie Usurie'.[132] Like the wives that demand luxury of their upwardly mobile husbands (according to Turner, Rowley, and Wither, discussed in the first section of the general introduction to usury), money that should be the foil to show off the jewel of a man to society comes to master him and diminish him. *Three Ladies* is particularly interesting in that it adds the dynamic of female–female corruption. The corruption of the feminine is driven home in the parodic blazon of scene 10, where Lady Lucre gloats over the state of Lady Conscience's beauty as she spots her beautiful face with defiling ink (10.105–14).

The Three Lords and Three Ladies of London 'was almost definitely accompanied by the revision and revival of *Three Ladies* in the same year', says Mithal, 'and this is proved by the change in the number of years since when Peter's Pence was abolished from "26. yeares" ago in the first quarto to "33. yeares" ago in the second'.[133] Taken together the two plays present a long tale of English decline and resurrection. In *Three Lords*, Nemo returns, and the three ladies (who have indeed spent years in prison) remain gaoled until the great lords of London appear with the offer to marry them into redemption. Of the evil quartet, only Usury continues to 'livest but too wel' (613; sig. D) in London, and his friend Dissimulation manages to slip back into town during the market-day at Leadenhall and into Westminster to pick up the latest news. The consis-

tent undermining of the goodness of London by the vices that we saw in
Three Ladies is less pervasive here, and London is praised as not just
better than foreign places but better than the provinces too: Dissimulation
lives happily in rural England, while London proves hostile to him. This
is a clear inversion of the consistent writing against London's corruption,
and, when three lords of Lincoln suddenly appear near the end of the
play to claim the hands of the three ladies in marriage, they are dismissed
easily by the witty lords of London (2080–169; sig. H4v–Iv).

   The final, comic attempt of the vices to win back the ladies' favours
fails dismally, although there is no finality to their suppression either.
Usury is branded with 'A litle x. standing in the midd'st of a great C'
(1954; sig. H3) to denote the maximum percentage (10 per cent) he is
allowed to take on usury by law. Of course, this comedy is tempered: just
as the Judge's name 'Nemo' suggests in *Three Ladies*, as Louis B. Wright
noted, that 'the dramatist satirically showed that no judge had yet dared
sentence Lucre', so the branding as punishment is countered by reading
it as a confirmation of the legitimacy of Usury in London.[134] Another
allusion to the 1571 Act, this brand declares that London *owns* Usury,
or that Usury is London's adopted child; as Usury himself said a decade
earlier in *Three Ladies*, Venetian Lucre had in London 'a daughter, which
her far did excel', and that daughter declares that Usury 'shall live here
as pleasantly, / Ay, and pleasanter too, if it may be' (2.221, 226–7). Usury,
then, 'settles' into London just as the idea of usury did among those
closely related to the necessities of trade. Whether we can read this as
Usury 'no longer pos[ing] a threat within the world of the play' is arguable, but Teresa Nugent seems right to emphasize that a suppression of
the danger of usury in *Three Lords* indicates a shift whereby the new
arch-enemy of a merchandising state is the trade-threatening figure of
Fraud.[135] We might even suggest that Fraud's list of evil deeds in *Three
Ladies* (2.68ff) already sets him on a path that prefigures a dangerous
henchman like Marlowe's Ithamore, and it certainly foreshadows the
prominence of Fraud as an ongoing vice in the London of *Three Lords*,
for he escapes from a bungled execution scene where Simplicity, blind-
folded, cannot burn him to death before Dissimulation whisks him away
to safety (2270–320; I3v–I4).[136]

Englishmen for My Money

The author and the play

'Of his birth place, early life and education nothing is known', writes
Albert Croll Baugh in his 1917 introduction to the play.[137] Who was
William Haughton, writer of possibly as many as ten original or adapted

plays, and co-author of a dozen or so? We know little to nothing of his life and career, and without Philip Henslowe's invaluable *Diary* the bulk of what we do know would be lost. Henslowe calls Haughton 'yonge Horton' in the first *Diary* reference to the playwright, 5 November 1597.[138] Baugh has estimated the playwright's birthdate to be around 1573–77, making him between twenty and twenty-four years of age at the time of this reference. This seems probable: since at this time the other major writers for Henslowe were aged twenty-four or older, we should assume that Haughton was younger (perhaps significantly so) than the others; at the same time, his apparent knowledge of some Dutch, Italian, and French (albeit not entirely proved by the comic language usage in *Englishmen*) would seem to require a significant level of education.[139]

Englishmen for My Money, then, paid for in the *Diary* February to May 1598, seems the product of a writer very new on the scene. Only one of his many co-written plays is extant, *Patient Grissil*, with Thomas Dekker. The *Diary* gives us a picture of a prolific playwright, one who was able to (or perhaps often needed to) work with others to produce plays in which Henslowe had enough faith to advance payment continually 'in earnest' of the book of the play; non-extant plays probably written by Haughton alone, as recorded in the *Diary*, include *The Poor Man's Paradise*,[140] *Ferrex and Porrex*,[141] *The English Fugitives*, *Judas*, and 'Roben hood[es] penerthes'. Not that such payment was always enough to keep Haughton out of trouble, for on 10 March 1599 (i.e. 1600)[142] Henslowe put up 10 s to bail him out of the clink, a prison on London's South Bank, where he was confined, probably for debt.

One record of payment to Haughton is for 5 s on 6 May 1600 'in earnest of' *The Devil and His Dam*; this is probably the play published as *Grim the Collier of Croydon* in *A Choice Ternary of English Plays* (1662). The *Diary* entry is crossed out, and this does cast some doubt on the continued involvement of Haughton in the writing of the play; it is also usual for the *Diary* to record further payments towards the total within the month that the first 'in earnest of' payment appears. However, as William Baillie points out in his 1984 edition of *A Choice Ternary*, Henslowe's entries are erratic.[143] *Englishmen for My Money* appears in the *Diary* by the subtitle 'a womon will have her wille' and *Grim* appears by the subtitle announced in the last line of the play: 'This play of ours, *The Devil and His Dame*' (5.2.126). (Both subtitles were probably intended by the author(s) as the main title and subsequently altered for publication.) The 1662 title page lists the author as one 'I.T.' or more likely 'J.T.', and we have to entertain the strong possibility of revision by a later writer. While I am not as confident as is Baillie of Haughton's sole authorship of *Grim*, there are a number of factors that point toward

Haughton. The Anglo-foreign relations in the play, the treatment of 'types' of women, the half-friendly, half-deadly masculine competition, and the phrasing especially of the comic figures in the sub-plot strongly suggest Haughton's hand at points throughout. In fact, the whole tastes more of the Haughton who wrote *Englishmen* than does *Patient Grissil*, in which we can be sure of Haughton's heavy involvement. Grim's amusingly learned affectations and iteration of 'and so forth' (4.1.41; 5.1.50–1) in his quick declamations cannot help but remind us of *Englishmen*'s Frisco (1.2.106–7; 2.2.11–12; 4.3.101–2); and the liberal sprinkling of anti-alien sentiment throughout the text feels as if it comes from the Haughton soap-box. When Belphagor the devil comes to earth, he calls himself 'an incarnate Devil' (1.3.1), which, as I noted earlier in the introduction, would have suggested Italian tendencies to the English audience. However, we find that he advertises himself as a Spaniard (from the hot, hellish country, depicted as such in a play like *The Tide Tarrieth No Man*), and this foreigner allows the English to continue to harp on the problem of international sexual relations, the same issue that Haughton centrally addresses in *Englishmen for My Money*. Grim's Honorea defends herself against the foreigner's advances early in the play:

> Base Alien, mercinary Fugitive,
> Presumptuous Spaniard, that with shameless pride
> Dar'st ask an *English* Lady for thy Wife.
> I scorn, my Slave should honour thee so much[.]
> (1.4.104–7)

And Morgan gives the penultimate speech of the play to make bookends of this sentiment: 'Henceforth we'l strictlier look to Strangers lives, / How they shall marry any English Wives' (5.3.113–14). The Devil, as Castiliano, is, incidentally, repeatedly referred to as 'The Spanish Doctor' (2.4.3; 5.2.104), perhaps reminding the audience once more of that dangerous Iberian physician, Lopez, and perhaps also suggesting a composition date in the mid to late 1590s.

Between 1599 and 1602, the years immediately following the writing and initial production of *Englishmen*, Henslowe's *Diary* lists Haughton as receiving payments for seventeen co-written plays. Another six plays in the same period bear Haughton's name as sole payee, suggesting he was their only author. However, this latter category is hardly stable. Henslowe frequently has several entries for one play, in one instance naming Haughton as sole payee and in another instance naming him as one among several playwrights. Any or all of those six plays, then, could have involved unrecorded payments to other authors. The conclusion has to be that a solo Haughton play is a rare and difficult thing to be certain about. It has generally been accepted that *Englishmen* and perhaps *Grim* are Haughton's extant solo works; I have already suggested putting a question mark next to *Grim*, and we might even do the same for *Englishmen*. By late 1599, Haughton and Dekker are certainly collaborating on *Patient Grissil*; *Englishmen for My Money* and *The Shoemaker's Holiday*, published just one year apart, share a number of echoes of syntax, phrasing, characters' verbal exchanges, English–foreign encounters, and reference to the city's topography that may suggest that the two playwrights had some contact and influence on each other before the known collaboration – whether or not Dekker was involved directly in *Englishmen*, and whether or not *Englishmen* (or Haughton) informed *The Shoemaker's Holiday* remain open questions.

Usury and the play

Englishmen for My Money is a play steeped in its London location, interacting by turn with the physical shape of the theatre in which it is played and the topography and geography of the larger city in which the theatre plays its cultural role. The play looks forward to the family, mercantile, and sexual content of Jacobean London plays, and it reflects back on the traditions of plays and dialogues concerned with the moral place of money in a realm and the relationships between money, nationality, gender, and age.[144] The pivotal character is a Portuguese merchant and usurer named Pisaro. His oral eloquence and sense of superiority are reminiscent of Marlowe's Jew of Malta, Barabas, and Haughton has certainly learned from the style of Marlowe's protagonists in general; Haughton also puts depth in his character by balancing the necessary characteristics of being a father, a usurer, a foreigner, and, in the end, a realist. Pisaro is resident in London, the widower of an English wife, and is attempting to secure matches in marriage for his three daughters with three foreigners – Delion (French), Alvaro (Italian), and Vandal (Dutch). The women themselves do their best to elope with their true English loves, Walgrave, Harvey, and Heigham, who have a double motive to marry the usurer's daughters: they are in love with them, and they wish to recover their properties, which have been mortgaged to Pisaro. With cunning on the part of Anthony (the daughters' tutor) and incidental comical chicanery by the clown Frisco, the Englishmen triumph over the foreigners, and marry the women.

   Theodore Leinwand dismisses *Englishmen for My Money*, for 'unthinkingly champion[ing] one status group over another' and for the 'jingoism that motivates the tedious plot of what is probably the earliest city comedy'. Leinwand goes on, 'Haughton's uncritical endorsement of the careers of three thriftless English gallants, and his wearisome mockery of their rivals – three wealthy, foreign merchants – suggest that he is un-interested in either the conflict, or the sources of conflict, that pitted one status group against another'.[145] This edition of the play, which clearly reveals the irony and authorial distance throughout the text, and the critical work that has been done on Haughton in recent years, which I survey below, demonstrate the insufficiency of such a view. Alexander Leggatt's important study of 1973 noted that – although we may have lost earlier citizen comedy – 'Haughton seems, at times, to use his local colour with the self-consciousness of an innovator';[146] and, for all the pedantry of his approach, even Arthur Bivins Stonex in 1916 understood that there was something in Haughton's play that represented a major step in comic dramatic development.[147]

Stonex traces a supposed development in the 'prodigal-usurer' play, noting elements that progressively get added to the matrix of money-lending, prodigality, rebellious children, and conversion. He has some trouble maintaining a clear trajectory of increasing complexity, noting that in the relatively early *Englishmen for My Money* 'the rebellious daughter *motif* has reached its full development'. He goes on, slightly disturbed by Haughton's sudden achievement: 'In fact, the situation has been so cleverly complicated that one is compelled to wonder if some simpler form had not intervened, or if some foreign model had not been utilized'.[148] He opines that, if *Hog Hath Lost His Pearl* had preceded *Englishmen*, 'it would have been possible to show an entirely regular evolution of the role of the rebellious daughter in the usurer play from the first uncertain step in *The Jew of Malta* to the delightful complexity of *Englishmen for My Money*'.[149] He then moves on to the development of 'the second main usurer plot' in which the usurer is a bachelor in pursuit of a young heiress;[150] Stonex follows this plot element in early seventeenth-century plays, but he does not mention Haughton's story element of Pisaro's lust for Susanna (actually Walgrave in disguise), which might be taken as either a parody of this 'later' plot line or more likely a bridge between the pantaloon figure and the bachelor usurer. Funnily, this ironic wooing scene in *Englishmen* also prefigures in a proleptic parody another plot element that Stonex places much later: 'incredible as it may seem', writes Stonex of Shirley's *Love Tricks* (1625), 'the young prodigal who carries off [the usurer's] daughter also plays the role of the elusive heiress whom the usurer would wed'.[151]

Details such as that Pisaro lives in Crutched Friars, that he is from Portugal, or that his 'snout, / [is] Able to shadow Paul's, it is so great' (1.2.15–16) suggest he is to be taken as a Jew (as noted in the general introduction, above), although neither his religious status nor any identity as *ethnically* Jewish is made a basis for the actions of his very 'English' daughters or the Englishmen against him. The assertion that he suffers from gout draws on the stereotype of the usurer, but Haughton suppresses further traditional stereotypes of the 'stage usurer', such as poor clothing and sparse eating, and maintains something of a 'noble Jew' about this equivocal but beleaguered father. We see Haughton taking on elements of earlier drama – in particular from Marlowe's *Jew of Malta* – but continually refiguring them. He imitates in order to ironize, and he subverts or invents in order to stamp his own authority as a playwright of note. The opening of the play with Pisaro, *solus*, seems like mock imitation of Marlowe's Machiavel and Barabas; it suggests a damnable character type, but it is adapted gradually throughout the play until Pisaro is finally the accepting father of comedy, not the 'Judas-like' (1.1.28) villain his own words proclaim him to be at the beginning. The alien merchants, although ineffectual, are hardly dangerous invaders either. Against the expectation of a relentlessly xenophobic nationalistic drama, Haughton makes the Englishman Ned Walgrave the vicious one, who turns on Pisaro in a way that is reminiscent of Gratiano's attack on Shylock in the trial scene of *The Merchant of Venice*. Walgrave has to be restrained by his fellow Englishmen when he threatens Pisaro that he will lie with the usurer's daughter Mathea 'before thy face, / Against the Cross in Cheap, here, anywhere!' (4.1.141–2). These are unnecessarily violent words that expose the over-zealousness and unguardedness of English pride and illustrate the desperate state of English men reduced by usury.[152]

The usurer's obsession with gold (over love, and all else) is evidenced in Pisaro's lines in the final scene. Harvey, Marina's suitor, enters feigning fatal illness. Pisaro, thinking of the value of Harvey's lands, which he holds in mortgage, says rhetorically, 'Come, my soul's comfort, thou good news bringer; / I must needs hug thee even for pure affection!' (5.1.67–8). The image of Pisaro hugging Harvey and therefore his gold, his 'soul's comfort', is once again strongly reminiscent of Barabas's exclamations to his daughter when he returns to his old house, converted to a nunnery by the State, to receive hidden gold from the hands of his faithful daughter: 'here lives my soul's sole hope' (2.1.29), says Barabas, ambiguously referring to both his daughter and his gold. When Abigail throws down Barabas's bags of gold to him, Barabas rhapsodizes over his wealth, 'O girl, O girl, O beauty, O my bliss!' (2.1.54); the amusing stage direction *'hugs his bags'* follows immediately.

The 'foreignness' and 'strangeness' of the usurer – usually related to being a Jew – that is emphasized in *Three Ladies*, *The Jew of Malta*, and *The Merchant of Venice* is shifted toward a familiarity and domesticity in the endenizened Pisaro, Marston's English Mamon and Middleton's

Hoard and Lucre (*A Trick to Catch the Old One*). The problem of usury therefore becomes more complicated. Whereas it could be dismissed more easily in the earlier plays as something clearly foreign, other, ungodly, or non-English, it is now thoroughly part of the English (and particularly mercantile London) body economic, social, and politic. A 'moral mercantilism' accepted the practice of usury as a promoter of healthy activity against idleness, but it also saw usury as an ethical and theological problem with the concomitant 'infection' and 'infiltration' of England by ideas and practicalities of trade with foreign countries. Usury facilitated linguistic exchange or corruption, bodily exchange and miscegenation, and an ongoing compromising of early modern faith in the traditions of gender roles, family organization, hospitality, friendship, and reformed religion. With a usury and trading play that incorporates three foreigners speaking various versions of English and 'their own' languages, three half-English daughters, a perfectly English-spoken Portuguese father, and a fake French tutor, it is not surprising that the play's criticism has fallen into two camps, discussing money-mercantile issues or the question of identity as revealed through linguistic tropes and practices.

Haughton possesses a clear ability to step back from his work, and Elizabeth Schafer rightly notes that 'Haughton seems to revel in the contradictions' created by his own characters' hypocritical and chauvinistic use and representation of language.[153] Ned's volubility, the daughters' rhetoric, the concentration on languages and education feed the play's emphasis on the power of the tongue, which proves to be another agent that binds the duality of foreignness (language) and 'Jewishness' (usury and economy-wasting) that I discussed earlier in the introduction on usury. Recent critics have been concerned with gendering our understanding of the language in the play. Emma Smith takes the trope of the 'mother tongue' as a marker of national identity to place Pisaro's daughters as defenders of Englishness in opposition to the usurer's continued attempts to hybridize them with foreigners; referring to her dead mother, Mathea insists, 'I have so much English by the mother / That no base, slavering French shall make me stoop' (4.1.45–6).[154] The ability to read 'French' as referring to nationality, language, and disease is apt and reminds us of the physical infections and corruptions imagined throughout the play as resulting from linguistic alteration – we might here recall Frisco's appeal to the Englishmen: 'do not suffer a litter of languages to spring up amongst us' (1.2.104–5). Smith's reading has the play working to resist the period's assumption of female susceptibility to infiltration and penetration, especially a penetration by 'trade [which] is imagined as intercourse with foreigners and thus as a kind of prostitution'.[155] Usury produces a double bind – it either takes potentially productive men away from honest merchandising into idleness and evil or it promotes an active trade that brings the baubles of idleness and luxury into the country.

The notion of vulnerability of the female sex and the nation is taken up by Diane Cady, who argues that the connection between the interference of foreign language into English and the incontinence and availability of women's bodies to be violated by the foreign is a trope in a long history of texts. *Englishmen for My Money* continues this combination as it 'presents foreigners and women as equivalent threats to "cleane and pure" English'.[156] We can see that *Three Ladies* had already strongly engaged with the draining of the commonwealth through prejudicial and selfish trading practices, and that women become the site for the negotiations based on usury that bring in worthless goods for the destruction of domestic marketplaces. Citing William Harrison's *Description of England* (1577), which refers to the imported baubles, 'cockhorses for children' and 'gewgaws for fools', Alan Stewart writes that 'While Harrison sees these trinkets as fodder for children and fools, Wilson's play [. . .] consistently genders their target market as female'.[157] And Jonathan Gil Harris takes the issue further to argue that there is no essential separation between usury and miscegenation; the trade made off usury leads to idleness and whoring (incontinence) at home, to the destruction of manly business endeavours in the city, and to the continuous infiltration of national borders with infecting foreign elements.[158]

All of this socio-political argumentation gets played out in the theatre. Crystal Bartolovich has recently concentrated on the worldliness of the apparently closed theatrical realm of London comedy; the text and performance, she notes, engage powerfully with the economic and social realities of the larger international market of which that theatre and city are part. The central market Exchange scene in the play, she writes, depicts London as 'interconnected to a much broader world, in which distant events, forces, and decisions have the most pressing local impact'.[159] Bartolovich studies *Englishmen* in tandem with 2 *If You Know Not Me* to find the theatre (and turn-of-the-century London) attempting to establish the relatively new and unwieldy force of the international market as a purportedly stable 'place' called the Exchange.[160] Jean Howard has recently read *Englishmen* as an Exchange play that puts strangers at the centre of its city and 'never perfectly succeeds' in its 'attempts to draw and enforce distinctions between strangers and English Londoners, and to subordinate the former to the latter'.[161] As all critics of this play note, *Englishmen* relentlessly attempts to 'map' London. I would add that, in doing so, it carefully argues that London is there for the English to 'possess' as a kind of nationalistic weapon. Even in his stupidity, Frisco betters the foreigners as they all run around London in the dark night. In contrast to the 'naturally' domestic position of the English in the play, Stewart outlines the liminal social existence of Pisaro as, arguably, a 'denizen' resident of London.[162] His daughters bridge the difference by insisting that they are 'English', an insistence that prompts admiration for their verve but also distaste for their unflinching prejudice. Haughton places an array of English and foreign notions of place and identity in dialogue, and these scenes of international, inter-gender, and inter-generational exchange are underlain by the ongoing patriotic attempt to address and redress the problematic situations in which the bonds of usury place English gentlemen.

The Hog Hath Lost His Pearl

The author and the play
The Hog Hath Lost His Pearl was entered in the Stationers' Register on 24 May 1614 and published in the same year. It is the only play – and almost the only text – we can confidently assign to Robert Tailor. He contributed a commendatory sonnet among many poems that preface John Taylor's *The Nipping or Snipping of Abuses* (1614), and in it he plays with the shared name 'Tailor': 'Most commonly one Taylor will dispraise, / Anothers workmanship, envying always / At him that's better then himselfe reputed, / Though he himselfe be but a botcher bruted', and alludes in the couplet to his subject, the 'water poet': 'But I not minding with thy worth to flatter, / Doe know thy wit too good too toyle by water'.[163] A letter from Sir Henry Wotton to Sir Edmund Bacon is one of two documents that give us our primary information about *Hog*:

> On Sunday last at night, and no longer, some sixteen Apprentices (of what sort you shall guess by the rest of the Story) having secretly learnt a new Play without Book, intituled *The Hog hath lost his Pearl*; took up the *White-Fryers* for their Theater: and having invited thither (as it should seem) rather their Mistresses than their Masters; who were all to enter *per buletini* for a note of distinction from ordinary Comedians. Towards the end of the Play, the Sheriffs (who by chance had heard of it) came in (as they say) and carried some six or seven of them to perform the last Act at *Bridewel*; the rest are fled. Now it is strange to hear how sharp-witted the City is, for they will needs have Sir *John Swinnerton*, the Lord *Mayor*, be meant by the *Hog*, and the late Lord Treasurer by the *Pearl*. And now let me bid you good night, from my Chamber in *King-street* this *Tuesday*, at Eleven of the night.[164]

So a performance at the Whitefriars theatre – on 21 February 1613[165] – is recorded because of its irregularity. We know little more about Whitefriars as a playhouse, other than the outlines of the companies that variously played there.[166] A few months after the *Hog* affair, an attempt to erect a

new playhouse in the Whitefriars (or convert it to a public theatre) was
blocked by the Privy Council. The sensitivity of the location is suggested
by the comment that the audience was invited ('*per buletini*') to set off
the 'distinction' of the occasion from one that might be provided by dis-
reputable 'ordinary Comedians'.[167]

That the play was performed without permission on a Sunday night
in Lent was reason enough for it to have been stopped by the authorities,
and the intriguing accusations of its invective against the Lord Mayor
John Swinnerton and others need to be addressed further. While the name
'Hog' seems to ask for an allegorical reading, it is also a very familiar
representation for the stock grubbing usurer, as the general introduction
and Blaxton woodcut and verse on pp. x–xi show. Moreover, it is hard
to see how anything much can be *meant* by Hog's 'pearl', which is not
an actual lost item in the play; in fact there is no pearl at all – it is only
something falsely promised by the 'spirits' that haunt and cozen Hog in
5.1. Rather, the term represents the combination or conflation of the
usurer's daughter and his wealth (a familiar usury play trope, which we
see in Shylock's Jessica and Barabas's Abigail).[168]

There is one further document that sheds light on this performance.
Katherine Duncan-Jones has noticed that 'a pair of extremely obscene
poems' at the end of a Bodleian MS commonplace book refer to the *Hog*
incident detailed in Wotton's letter to Bacon.[169] The first poem, 'The
Counter-skuffle', attributed to Francis Davison, details a food-and-filth
fight in Wood Street Counter debtors' prison. At one point, the fray quiets
as the sheriff enters with the arrested players from *Hog*:

> Noe false report this newes did breed
> For tw'as the very shriffe indeed
> yet were they more afraid then need as chaunced
> For he had bene as they did saie
> in the white friers at a plaie
> and brought the Actors thence away that daunced
> And onelie came with Linckes and lightes
> to see safe Lodgd these worthy wightes
> of whom some were attir'd like sprightes and divels
> A sort of Prentices they were
> that plaid and askt no leave I heere
> for which the shriff made them beare their evells
> When he had safelie lodg'd them there
> forth of the gates he did repaire
> While all the Combattants for feare stood quakinge

This document disagrees with Wotton's placement of the culprits at
Bridewell, although, as Jones points out, by the time of Wotton's letter

on Tuesday, they may well have been transferred to the latter prison. Duncan-Jones goes on to point out that the attire mentioned for the entering players suggests that they were playing either the woodland scene in 4.3 or the magical cozening scene of 5.1. *Pace* Wotton's 'perform the last act at Bridewell', I am inclined to think that the players had got as far as 5.1, since 'divels' suggest underworld and other-worldly costume rather than woodland satyrs, and while 'sprightes' could fall into either category, Haddit as Bazan in 5.1 is specifically referred to in the text as a 'spirit'/spright (line 49 SD, 136). It is of course an interesting and unresolvable matter that the authorities, 'who by chance had heard of it', should come in so late to an unlicensed performance, since they would not have needed to assess the content to shut it down. Duncan-Jones ends her article with the comment 'But what, precisely, it was about this second-rate play that caused it first to be prepared "secretly", and then, on performance, to offend the city authorities, remains obscure'.[170] If we concentrate on Mayor Swinnerton's activities and reputation and on Londoners' relationships with him – rather than the touchy attitude of the 'City' fathers of 1612–13 as a whole – we seem to get into the area of an answer.

Two matters might be addressed in relation to the question: first, a brief turn to Thomas Dekker's *Troia-Nova Triumphans: London Triumphing* (1612), the pageant for the Mayor performed on 29 October 1612, reveals some anxiety on the part of the author and the city as their new Mayor is inaugurated and given 'the cap of maintenance'.[171] Second, evidence suggests that Swinnerton was a powerful and perhaps ruthless wine merchant and customs farmer, who four years before his inauguration as Mayor had managed the purchase of the impressive Essex property of Norman record, Little Birch Hall. With some reputation as a wealthy, aloof, and 'resourceful' businessman of the new and ambitious London mercantile class, we might easily believe that there is indeed a pun on the names 'Hog' and 'Swine-rton'.

In *Troia-Nova Triumphans*, the character of Arete (Virtue) reports that the twelve chief companies of the city gather with magnanimity to welcome the Mayor:

> All arm'd, to knit their Nerves (in One) with Thine,
> To guard this new Troy: And, (that She may shine
> In Thee, as Thou in Her) no Misers kay
> Has bard the Gold up; Light flies from the Day
> Not of more free gift, than from them their Cost:
> For what's now spar'd, that only they count Lost.
>
> (B3–B3v)

And they expect his professional behaviour in kind:

> Shelter with spred armes, the poor'st Citizen.
> Set Plenty at thy Table, at they Gate
> Bounty, and Hospitality: hee's most Ingrate
> Into whose lap the Publicke-weale having powr'd
> Her Golden shewers, from Her his wealth should hoord.
>
> (B3v)

Justice turns from the general persuasions against miserliness and covetousness to urge very specifically that the familiar bipartite category of usury beneficiaries, widows and orphans, be taken care of:

> Let not Oppression wash his hands ith' Teares
> Of Widowes, or of Orphans: Widowes prayers
> Can pluck down thunder, & poore Orphans cries
> Are Lawrels held in fire; the violence flyes
> Up to Heaven-gates, and there the wrong does tell,
> Whilst Innocence leaves behind it a sweet smell.
>
> (D)

A combination of tendentiousness and force is trying to direct the Mayor on a very specific course *away* from usurious miserliness and toward a communal generosity, and the entertainment claims that this is the way to true fame and honour. There is certainly possible allusion to and parody of the mayoral show in the magical cozening scene (5.1) of *Hog*. A disembodied song is heard in the Mayoral entertainment, which calls on 'Honor, eldest child of Fame' (sig. C3v) for inspiration. Welcoming the new Mayor, the song wills 'Goe on nobly, may thy Name, / Be as old, and good as Fame. / [. . .] / So shall SWINERTON nere dye, / But his virtues upward flye' (sig. B4); the spirit Haddit, as Bazan, similarly wishes for Hog, 'But come, my task: I long to rear / His fame above the hemisphere' (5.1.160–1). The fame in *Hog*, however, is the antithesis of Dekker's honorable fame, for it is manifested through general envy for exactly the 'hoord[ing]' Dekker declaims against, not the love and security expected by a community. Thus the Player in *Hog* asks, 'What, would then Croesus list to fill / Some mortal's coffers up with gold, / Changing the silver it doth hold?' (5.1.96–8), and Haddit as Bazan confirms:

> I'm hither come; and now I see
> To what intent I'm raised by thee:
> It is to make that mortal rich,
> That at his fame men's ears may itch
> When they do hear but of his store.
>
> (5.1.148–52)

Thus we see the attractiveness of F. G. Fleay's identification of Haddit with Dekker, which E. K. Chambers dismisses, and which certainly remains a very general allusion.[172]

The Prologue's insistence that 'our swine / Is not, as diverse critics did define, / Grunting at State affairs, or invecting / Much at our city vices' (Pro. 9–12) might be true, and the text of the play may even bear some alteration from the year before. But it appears quite likely that circumstantial allusions to specific issues and persons were found readily in the play's general invective against city greed and sermon on redemption. As Evelyn May Albright points out, the protestations 'would be understood by the intelligent hearers or readers as a hint to look to city frauds for the special application' – this in spite of what she sees as the play's division between the satire on Swinnerton the Hog and the 'ludicrous intermingling' of the romantic plot, apparently part of a deflective strategy to satirize the current stage fashion and take less perceptive attentions away from the central attack on the Mayor.[173] Swinnerton had held lucrative patents on wines for a dozen years under Elizabeth; 'at some time before 1607', however, rights were reassigned to others by Charles Blount, Earl of Devonshire. When the Earl died shortly afterwards, Swinnerton appealed against the legitimacy of these grants and in 1608 records show him paying rent on French wines.[174] Until January 1613, Swinnerton fought the other farmers of the customs with accusations of fraud in obtaining and holding patents, but in the end was denied his claims.[175] Albright sees a January 1613 counter-complaint alleging fraud by Swinnerton as the impetus for getting *Hog* on to the stage a few weeks later to show the Hog's 'unbounded avarice'.[176] General intra-theatrical back-and-forth can be detected in the years preceding and following the performance of *Hog*. Albright notes that Dekker's *If It Be Not a Good Play, the Devil Is In It* (1612) was probably 'being parodied by borrowing its general method to attack a man whom [Dekker] had praised', and D. F. McKenzie suggests that 'W. Smith's *The Hector of Germany* (1615), acted at the Red Bull and the Curtain by a company of young men of the city, perhaps did something to answer the effects of *The Hogge hath Lost his Pearl*: it was dedicated "To the Right Worshipfull, the Great favourer of the Muses, Syr john Swinnerton Knight, sometimes Lord Mayor of this honourable Cittie of London" '.[177]

Albright's attempts to link specific features of Hog's representation with Swinnerton seem less successful, concentrating as she does on his association with wine: he has a wine cellar, and he claims he would have been able to confuse two or three scriveners if he had had Croesus's help earlier, which Albright reads as being 'a hit at the Mayor's efforts to purchase wine grants'.[178] Maybe so, but these are general ideas – Barabas has a wine cellar, too, and plenty of brokers and scriveners are wished away in usury plays. Even the concentration on Hog's obsession with 'mortgages' might be seen as a more general usurer's curse: Pisaro has the three Englishmen's mortgages, for instance, and Middleton's Quomodo lusts after his 'delicate parcel of land, like a fine gentlewoman i' th' waist' (*Michaelmas Term* 2.3.81–2). Albright then turns to the specificity of the 'pearl'. On the morning of Sunday 14 February 1613, Swinnerton had presented the Princess Elizabeth with 'a Chain of Oriental Pearl' for which 'two thousand pounds were paid'.[179] Albright continues:

> the recency and publicity of this ceremony would make it difficult to miss the application to the Mayor [. . . .] In their attempt to identify the 'pearl', or 'treasure' lost, they could think of nothing fitter than the late Lord Treasurer, who had been lined up against the Mayor in his effort to secure the patents on French and Rhenish wines. Sharper-witted persons familiar with the situation would understand that the treasure lost was neither a pearl nor a Treasurer, but the 'farm' of certain fermented wines which the Mayor overreached himself in grasping for, thus losing the aid of these 'powerful spirits' in amassing further treasure to add to the heaps of his gain from the sweet wines patent.[180]

Either the play was already written by 14 February and this literal pearl connection happy coincidence, or Tailor would have had just a few days to work out how to get 'pearl' into the play before the 21 February performance and to write the crux scene in which gold is promised for silver, and pearl is promised for gold.[181]

Among the numerous metadramatic moments in *Hog* are a number of allusions to Shakespeare; such constant reminding of the dramatic genre gives the piece a playful self-consciousness that keeps an audience out of the realm of entire suspension of disbelief when it is asked to consider the quasi-serious situation of the morally lost Albert. The prologue hopes that this play will be as fortunate as Pericles (Pro. 32), alluding either to the play, if it was particularly successful, or to the fortunate title character who finds his daughter. Like Hamlet, Carracus has a 'beautified' beloved (*Hog* 1.3.13, *Ham* 2.2.110–11). Young Lord Wealthy says that his father 'appears more terrible than wildfire at a play' (2.1.27–8), which, if it refers to the fire that burned down the Globe during a performance of *Henry VIII* on 29 June 1613, would have to have been added after that date and before the 1614 printing. Carracus's mad running away from his estranged friend Albert in the countryside with the ludic comment that he'll run 'faster than you, I believe' (4.2.122) recalls Lear's mad 'an you get it, you shall get it by running' (4.6.202–3) as he flees Cordelia's men; and Haddit's alarmed response 'What exclamation's that?' (5.3.54) to Hog's reference to 'the sad-fated Carthaginian queen!' may echo

Sebastian's retort, 'Widow? A pox o' that! How came that "widow" in? Widow Dido!' to Gonzalo's 'widow Dido' in *The Tempest* (2.1.78–80).

Usury and the play

If in *Three Ladies* usury underpins questions of religious fidelity and economic fraud that threaten 'all estates', and if in *Englishmen* usury lies behind but less overtly *forces* prodigal urban machinations and national pride, then in *Hog* usury seems close to a matter-of-fact pastime, an annoyance that plays second fiddle to the painful strains of betrayal, repentance, and (arguably) redemption. But this play is a bit of a cobbler's job: we sense that we might be missing some overt political material cut from early productions (or maybe just from that premiere at Whitefriars); and the drastic shifts between subtle exchanges, tense or comic passages, and melodrama could be shoddiness, or it could be part of the packaging of wide-ranging satire and socio-religious commentary. We are, after all, confronted in this play with a community of men and women on the verges of social, spiritual, and mental isolation or marginalization, and the constantly shifting ground of the play's genre is in sympathy with the characters' oscillating and unstable sense of their relationships to others, and even to themselves – for as Maria confirms when Carracus complains that Albert 'so forgets himself', ' 'tis nothing else' (3.1.47–8). He has indeed forgotten the Albert that he was and removes himself to the margin to rewrite his story on the forest trees until he can re-enter the main story of the city again. Within such episodic structure, the importance of the usurer as a topic dwelt on largely in the second half of the play is just as much a linchpin for the whole as is the affecting single act in the desert woods, or the one scene of gulling around which the denouement pivots. *Hog* is, moreover, a play in which Tailor seems to take the opportunity to put his characters into situations that require their brief working out of one contemporary social issue or other; as such, the play lectures, but it does so with such a self-consciousness that it retains a kind of charm in its own egotism.

The usurer Hog has a daughter Rebecca, whose suitor is, unsurprisingly, a penniless prodigal. Haddit (who 'had it' but no longer does), aided by his friend Lightfoot, plans to revive his fortunes through an impressive display of apparel that will fool the old usurer into thinking well of him. In the parallel plot, Carracus has been wooing Maria for a long time. Albert takes advantage of Carracus's tardiness at his elopement to take his friend's place in bed with Maria; he immediately regrets his decision and withdraws into the 'desert woods' to do penance. In these plots, the play is concerned to air the problem of filial disobedience and broach the issue of male–male relationships. The former surfaces when Carracus tells himself to consider that 'thou art come / Hither to rob a father of that wealth / That solely lengthens his now drooping years' (1.3.31–3), and that loss of a daughter may cause the old man to go mad; Rebecca too worries that 'to rob my father, though 'a be bad, the world will think ill of me' (3.3.6–7). In fact, Maria's father, Old Lord Wealthy, deals with his daughter's escape admirably and is set up as the forgiving and youth-loving father in stark contrast to old Hog (see 2.2). The latter concern reminds us of the Antonio–Bassanio dynamic in *The Merchant of Venice*, since the Carracus–Albert relationship is an intense one overtly pitted against the heterosexual union of Carracus and Maria. As the three 'lovers' – the two men in love, one man in love with the woman, the other man having just made love to the woman – prepare to escape, Carracus assures both his companions:

> Come, fair Maria, the troubles of this night
> Are as forerunners to ensuing pleasures.
> And, noble friend, although now Carracus
> Seems, in the gaining of this beauteous prize,
> To keep from you so much of his loved treasure,
> Which ought not be mixed, yet his heart
> Shall so far strive in your wished happiness,
> That if the loss and ruin of itself
> Can but avail your good –
> *Albert.*   O friend, no more!
>   (1.4.96–105)

By 3.1, when Albert asks after the health of Carracus and his wife but dare not stay to talk to them personally, Carracus returns to the assumption of this gendered conflict:

> What could so move thee? Was't because I married?
> Didst thou imagine I infringed my faith
> For that a woman did participate
> In equal share with thee? Cannot my friendship
> Be firm to thee because 'tis dear to her?
> Yet no more dear to her than firm to thee.
> Believe me, Albert, thou dost little think
> How much thy absence gives cause of discontent.
>   (3.1.11–18)

There is certainly a sense in which Albert's terrible deed can be read not so much as his lustful desire for Maria or even basic jealousy, but his disappointment with the performance of his male friend, or his wanting to *be* Carracus. Indeed, the bed-trick is so self-destructive as to lead us to question it as a spontaneous activity; we suspect instead that, if the 'loved treasure' of his Carracus is withdrawn, then alone Albert is literally worth nothing, and he decides to destroy the self he knows.

The destruction is in fact temporarily of all three friends, for Albert in the woods is reduced to the state of a hermit, affectively and poignantly, but also incredibly, writing twenty-three-line poems on every tree he finds; Maria tells Carracus she is dead and also retreats to the woods where she welcomes starvation until Albert revives her; and Carracus's madness gives us comedy, some great melodramatic poetry, and the ability – as is the wont of madmen – to see into (and voice) the truth of the city's corruption at the hands of double-feed lawyers and lechers (3.1.132–40). With Carracus joining the other two friends by chance (fate), and all coping with their griefs, Act 4 shifts entirely into the woods of retreat. The language changes in this romance section, and the city seems almost forgotten to the play. Act 5, however, provides the great gulling scene, where Lightfoot, Haddit, and the Player steal all Hog's wealth, and we are back in the familiar Jacobean city comedy world of financial and personal revenge as a vicious yet survivable game.

The identity of Hog as a usurer in this urban battle gets injected early on. Lightfoot gives us a brief summary of the fitting nomenclature of the usurer Hog, 'for as a hog in his lifetime is always devouring, and never commodious in aught till his death, even so is he, whose goods at that time may be put to many good uses' (1.1.66–9). The notion was an old commonplace, and in 1584, the date of the first printing of *Three Ladies*, an English reader could find that 'The lyfe of a Usurer, is lyke the lyfe of a Hogge, or a filthie Swine, during the which there is no profite proceeding to man, nor any commoditie yielded to itselfe, tyll the blood be let out of the body therof, and meate made of the fleshe: so a Usurers lyfe is unprofitable to others, and unpleasant to himselfe, tyll death take him away'.[182] Any emphasis on avarice and usury, however, comes as an essential element late in the play. In 3.1 Carracus in his distraction points to distressed widows as one of the most frightening things he imagines – widows and orphans being those excepted from the stricture of usury law; in 3.3 we find Hog ironically claiming access to heaven by 'doing gentlemen pleasure' (l. 39) with ready money, and the play is peppered with reminders that brokers, lawyers, and scriveners are pestering the city.

But it is in the final act that the mechanism of usury is marked as the vehicle for the play's events. In the process, the fact of usury diverts attention and judgement away from misdeeds such as Albert's, which cannot possibly be blamed on anyone else, least of all Hog. Act 5 opens with Hog's Barabas-like praise of gold, both this speech and Barabas's (*Jew of Malta* 1.1) shifting from gold to diamonds in their progression of awe. Not long after this, Lightfoot promises that there will be 'those passions and those frantic fits' (5.1.193) that usurers should display, and indeed Hog himself, on realizing he has been duped, shouts 'I shall run mad! I shall run mad!' (l. 238). Hog does not in fact go mad, but this play's self-positioning as a satirical digest of the state of the fiduciary, moral, and political city requires at least the acknowledgement that the usurer *should* by rights end his days in maddened despair – a possible but less frequent position in the drama than in prose tracts, as we have seen. Several times we hear that accumulating money is a matter of 'labour'. Act 5 opens with Hog's meditation on beds, 'the breeders of disease and sloth' (ll. 5–6), which no soldier or scholar or, apparently, usurer could have invented. The ironic joke of a usurer claiming he engages in any hard work for his money would not have been lost on the amused audience here, nor later in the same scene where he claims that Bazan and his spirits 'would have saved me much *labour* in the purchasing of wealth' (5.1.199–200, my italics) had they come earlier, nor as they hear Hog cry out, 'I am undone, robbed this black night of all the wealth and treasure which these many years I have hourly *laboured* for!' (5.3.25–7, my italics).

Tailor seems to like the method of presenting a scene's main issue from two angles, the one comic and the other serious – or rather the one implied and lightly brushed past and the other embedded in a character or context that has earned some consideration of the spectator or reader. The two friends Haddit and Lightfoot lament the superficiality of society's judgement of men, concluding with Lightfoot's ironic rhetorical question, 'what's a man unless he wear good clothes?' (1.1.95) and Haddit's punning response, 'Good speed attend my suit' (i.e. my plan; my clothing) (1.1.96). These are Robert Wilson's concerns for fashion and William Haughton's for disguise cast into the new anxious mould of Jacobean mistrust. Thus Haddit's comical lament over lack of honesty in the world, 'words and deeds are now more different than Puritans and players' (1.1.99–100), is the benign bedfellow of Overreach's dangerous rejection of words as 'no substances' (*A New Way to Pay Old Debts* 3.2.154). All this joking suppresses the seriousness of impecuniosity and allows the audience to continue to enjoy the expectation of the prodigal's eventual success. A kind of descendant of Haughton's 'mad' Ned Walgrave, Haddit counters the deeper-thinking, calmer characters of both his and the previous generation. He thus enables us to enjoy the thrill of continued prodigality, while we nominally and finally appreciate and side with the moral lessons and actions that dovetail with the play's denouement. Indeed, Haddit's plans for recovery continue to involve obsession with luxury, and the London comedies generally valorize material gain by young Englishmen, whether the accumulation comes through luck, 'fate', cunning, the help of friends, or work.

When Old Lord Wealthy laments the witlessness of his son with the familiar complaint that wit is hardly set by these days, for 'He's counted wise enough in these vain times / That hath but means enough to wear gay clothes / And be an outside of humanity' (2.2.39–41), we sympathize with his commonplaces because his son is *so* stupid. Right on cue, moreover, Haddit enters 'in his gay apparel' (SD 2.3.0) to prove the old man's point. This latter scene begins with a joke on the tailor's 'good works' and salvation, which leads into Haddit's claim that he was never proud of his clothes and Carracus's faux-shocked reply: 'How, not of your clothes? Why, then you were never proud of anything, for therein chiefly consisteth pride' (2.3.4–5). When Haddit goes on *ad nauseam* about the effects of pride, it is a joke on the serious concerns of conservative voices. In Philip Stubbes's *Anatomy of Abuses* (first published 1583), Philoponus says:

> Pride is threefold: namely, the pride of the hearte, the pride of the mouth, and the pride of apparell, the last whereof (unlesse I be deceived) offendeth God more then the other two. For as the pride of the hearte, and of the mouth, are not opposite to the eye, nor visible to the sight, and therefore cannot intice others to vanitie & sin (not withstanding they be grievous sin in the sight of God) so the pride of apparell which is object to the sight, as an *exemplary* of evill induceth the whole man to wickednes & sinne.[183]

Tailor relentlessly tosses off entrees into issues that Wilson wanted to deal with so much more earnestly; but in the end the accumulation of sordidness in the city has caught up with the times such that all *Hog*'s author need do is allude to decades-old problems, and the network of theatrical, moral, allegorical, and urban associations goes to work.

Until its end, this play continues to preach a moral sermon that is constantly undercut by its self-consciousness as 'play'. Haddit's apology for their 'trick of stealth' (5.3.103) against Hog excuses the crime, 'Since it hath saved a soul was hell's by right' (l. 105), and this echo of *The Jew of Malta*, where Ithamore declares 'To undo a Jew is charity, and not sin' (4.4.80), closes a play that has arguably been working all along on the apparent Protestant Reformed assumption that faith will bring the community together into a belief in grace. Meanwhile the questions of conversion, redemption, and active personal penitence remain open. In *Three Ladies*, Lady Love's disfigurement showed us that lust will always be exposed. Albert's obsessive carving of his guilt on the trees, then, is not a necessary deed of penitence, nor is the aiding of his friends a deliberate deed-based path to his redemption; this is the demonstration of lust's inevitable revelation as Albert and his friends comprehend the faith and grace within themselves that encompasses good deeds.

This sense of election over good works is suggested in the numerous appearances of the word 'fortune(s)', which is used sixteen times in the play – '(un)fortunate' appears another three times. The first appearance being in the Prologue's phrase 'fortunate, like Pericles', the iteration seems to insist on scripted or fated outcomes for the characters. The romance element and the economic thread will find closure not because of the personal and individual actions of the characters, not because of human deeds, remuneration, or recompense, but because of faith and grace – and dramatic genre. Albert's soliloquy on conscience in 2.4, where he introduces his catchphrase, 'Who but a damned one could have done like me' (line 8), a line he repeats with slight variation in the same speech and then again at the end of the act as the line he will obsessively carve on trees and plants in the forest, suggests his assessment of his place within or excluded from the elect. That this is the issue being seriously worked out in 2.4 and beyond seems confirmed by the joke in the preceding scene when Haddit notes, 'By this light, coz, this suit does rarely! The tailor that made it may hap to be saved, an't be but for his good works' (2.3.1–2).

All of this has to be taken in the light of a play that jokes about Puritans and players and works under a veneer of political satire, some of which may have been stripped in the version that comes down to us. In whatever strain we decide to read the religious message of the play, we can trace a continued meditation on the moral place of the characters throughout the fourth and fifth acts. Albert advertises the potential effectiveness of his own contrition to the disguised Maria (4.1.144–7) but shortly thereafter cannot accept his deed of bringing Carracus back to sanity as a work of his own power that could have any effect on forgiveness:

> I rather ought to thank the heaven's creator
> That he vouchsafed me such especial grace
> In doing so small a good, which could I hourly
> Bestow on all, yet could I not assuage
> The swelling rancour of my fore-passed crimes.
>   (4.3.64–8)

Carracus approves of this point of view:

> He's happier far
> That sins, and can repent him of his sin,
> Than the self-justifier, who doth surmise
> By his own works to gain salvation,
> Seeming to reach at heaven and clasp damnation.
>   (4.3.74–8)

Hog renounces the vice of avarice (5.3.87–90), and this is called the 'blessed, conversion' of a 'blessed, converted man' (5.3.91, 97), a man of course almost forced into this position by the false magical trickery of 5.1, and one for whom the question of salvation must remain equivocal. This play's usurer-father straddles a traditional binary: that 'The usurer is not a lost sheep to be recovered, but an enemy to be overcome'.[184] Hog is apparently both. While Albert's penitence is expected and caused by self-punishment, and while the 'conversion' of Hog is an on-stage and off-stage surprise, his recovery to the fold of the (nominally) non-avaricious is a lesson learned: the usurer *might* be reclaimed, in spite of all odds. But, as Virginia Larsen points out in her discussion of Witgood in *A Trick to Catch the Old One*, there is a difference between being 'socially reclaimed' and 'spiritually redeemed' – the one matters to a society that needs its social circles to remain intact to carry out personal and public business;[185] the other matters to the legion of anti-usury authors, moral playwrights, and idealistic dramatic characters that want to live in a reformed, penitent, and equitable London and England that they have to know is lost for ever, or rather never existed.

LATER PERFORMANCE HISTORY OF THE PLAYS

I am not aware of a full production of any of the three usury plays in this collection after their respective Elizabethan and Jacobean performances, but two of the plays have received some attention. On 28 October 2006, two scenes from *The Three Ladies of London* were performed at the 'Shakespeare and the Queen's Men' conference in Toronto, Canada. Under the directorship of Peter Cockett, *Poculi Ludique Societas* stage-read the broom-selling and spotting of Conscience (Scene 10) and the Turkish trial scene between Gerontus and Mercadorus (Scene 14). The first performance revealed the possibility of a strong Lady Conscience who rhetorically battles Lady Lucre but is then suddenly turned by the hypnotizing allure of money; the almost magical quality of Lady Conscience's conversion to Lucre with the line 'And sith everyone doth it, why may not I do it too?' (10.70) was a telling moment of moral devastation. This scene had Usury played as a sort of gothic 'Igor' henchman figure, a choice which brought out his subordinate role but perhaps not his independent and central destructive power. The Turkish trial scene certainly indicated how entertaining the wily Mercadorus would have been on stage, and it is interesting that this play's comedy was apparently too politically sensitive to be included in the Conference's intended repertoire of full productions. Violent threats against the Records of Early

English Drama offices in Toronto led organizers to decide against pursu-
ing the public performance of a play they felt had rather raw demonstra-
tions of racial and religious prejudice; it was at the time the Danish
Muhammad editorial cartoon controversy broke after publication in the
Jyllands-Posten newspaper on 30 September 2005.

On 5 November 1995, *Englishmen for My Money* was given a stage
reading in the Bankside Globe Education Centre's 'Read Not Dead' series,
co-ordinated by Ros King. The Globe maintains a well-recorded, mono,
analogue cassette tape of the reading and a copy of the programme. The
script appears to be the Malone Society Reprint, but the Globe archive
does not possess a marked-up or prompt copy of the text. The programme
notes by Maggy Williams claim that Pisaro is a Jew but that 'neither usury
nor Jewishness are [*sic*] the issue' of the play. Williams also notes the
play's 'full use of the theatre' architecture, its very specific and local
concern with the city and its status as the first merchant play set in
England. Of course, *Three Ladies* might have some slight claim to the
latter honour.

Nicholas Day reads the part of Pisaro powerfully, sometimes fitting
the role of an overbearing father figure, sometimes defeating the opportunity for variety in delivery. Very early in the play, Day reads Pisaro's
mock Dutch line of 'Haunce butterkin slowpin' (1.1.182–3) with an
inexplicably mock-Chinese 'Haunce fing blukkerting fling tong gong', and
this sets a tone of improvisation and playfulness that increasingly shifts
the emphasis away from Haughton's text's comedy to the amusement of
the actors on the occasion of the reading. Laurentia and Mathea, read by
Helen McCrory and Julie-Kate Olivier respectively, have their characters
delineated reasonably – Laurentia the softer, older, thoughtful one; and
Jamie Glover as Heigham and Scott Ransome as Harvey each have a good
sense of their parts, Glover to a greater extent. Hermione Gulliford and
Andrew Joseph, playing the parts of Marina and her lover Ned Walgrave,
seem unprepared for the task; Walgrave's part as a dangerous yet comic
'mad-cap, wild-oats' character is utterly lost with this weak reading.
Those reading the foreigners and the servants Frisco and Anthony carry
the play well for the first three acts, showing an appreciation for the
'foreign' language's tendency to be at once apparently nonsensical and
revealing (Nick Hutchison as Anthony, Simon Bridge as Frisco; Delion,
Alvaro, and Vandal read by Rupert Wickham, Mark Knight, and Graham
Christopher, respectively).

In Acts 4 and 5, unfortunately, the reading breaks down somewhat;
the main readers seem unprepared for their cues and lines, the cuts
confuse them, they misread the text frequently (including multiple long
's' and 'f' confusions), and lose place such that the comedy becomes that

no one knows what is being said; no doubt the occasion was enjoyable, but the archive of the play is diminished because Haughton's comedy at the play's climax and denouement gets depleted. Here it would be very useful to have a prompt copy of the text, with the cuts marked (such as the excision of Balsaro, whose lines are given to Anthony); this might perhaps reveal more about the directorial vision. Despite the shortcomings of the performance, and despite the very real difficulty of *reading* a play that is so much about *performing* the cityscape, this is a valuable resource that demonstrates effectively the potential for this play to be played on the one hand with powerful irony, meaningful comedy, and poignancy and on the other hand taken as simple farce.

NOTE ON THE EDITORIAL HISTORY OF THE PLAYS

In summary: *The Hog Hath Lost His Pearl* was the first of the plays in the present collection to be edited in a modern text, appearing in Robert Dodsley's modern-spelling, non-annotated *A Select Collection of Old English Plays* in 1744. In 1830, *Englishmen for My Money* first appeared in a collection entitled *The Old English Drama*, and in 1851 John Payne Collier's *Five Old Plays* included *The Three Ladies of London*. All three plays were included in Hazlitt's 1874–76 edition of Dodsley's *Select Collection*. The Malone society has published reprints of *Hog* and *Englishmen*, but not of *Three Ladies*; *Three Ladies* and *Englishmen* have received twentieth-century, annotated, old-spelling scholarly editions (both as PhD dissertations, 1959 and 1917, respectively) whereas *Hog* has not. Isaac Reed adds notes to *Hog* in the 1780 second edition of *A Select Collection*; and in 1810, *The Ancient British Drama*, attributed to Walter Scott, reprints *Hog* as what it calls an 'ancient' play (i.e. one not still much on the stage in 1810).

In detail: by 1825 Collier brings out a third edition of Dodsley's plays, and in 1851 publishes his *Five Old Plays*, which included for the first time *The Three Ladies of London*. Collier's *Five Old Plays* is an old-spelling edition that does not quite follow its claim to 'notice the principal variations between the two impressions' of *Three Ladies*:[186] there are a number of silent Q2 readings, some unnecessary editorial emendations to Q1, and a number of bizarre Q1 readings that remain unattended to. Collier's 'old spelling' is not always the old spelling of the Q1 text and a number of lines and passages conflate and alternate rapidly between Q1 and Q2 inexplicably. (In Lucre's speech at 2.243–54, for instance, Collier includes three readings unique to Q1 and four readings unique to Q2.) Hazlitt puts Collier's *Three Ladies* into modern spelling for the fourth edition of Dodsley's *Select Collection* of 1874–76. Hazlitt adds a good number of notes to remark on Q1 and Q2 variations missed by Collier, and his common-sense modernizations are included and/or collated in the present edition. Shortly before the reprint of Hazlitt's Dodsley in 1964, *Three Ladies* was edited by H. S. D. Mithal along with Wilson's companion play, *Three Lords and Three Ladies of London*. This is a painstaking and admirable piece of scholarship that gives us an old-spelling edition of the two plays with significant textual collation and an extensive introduction that the present edition has made substantial use of. This 1959 PhD dissertation edition was reprinted in 1988 by Garland in typescript facsimile; the lineation of the poetry is determined by page width rather than verse lineation; there are a good number of informative and well-researched notes.

Englishmen for My Money first appears in *The Old English Drama* of 1830, a very respectably collated and annotated modern-spelling edition. 'The general conviction that a cheap, and, at the same time, a neat and accurate edition of the best productions of our elder dramatists is much wanted, has led to the present undertaking', writes the unlisted editor, adding, with an unwitting premonition of his successors' concerns in starting a series such as the Revels Companion Library, that Shakespeare is now available cheaply to everyone, 'but the ignorance of persons, even in the higher walks of life, of his predecessors, contemporaries, coadjutors, and immediate successors is still remarkable; and with the exception of the more popular names of Ben Jonson, Beaumont and Fletcher, Ford, or Massinger, there are not a few, generally well informed readers, who are scarcely aware that Shakespeare had precursors, rivals, or followers.'[187]

THE PRESENT TEXTS

There are two quarto editions of *The Three Ladies of London*, Q1 of 1584 and Q2 of 1592. Irene Mann argued simply and convincingly that Q1 was used as the copy text for Q2, as revealed by the matching pagination in both editions and the repetition in Q2 of many of the Q1 punctuation and other errors.[188] There are also, however, a large number of substantial revisions to the text, and we can probably assume that the copy of Q1 used by the Q2 compositor was heavily marked up with manuscript alterations. Our conclusion might be that the Q2 changes represent performance choices made some time between 1584 and 1592 – perhaps during a revival of *Three Ladies* to play in repertory with *Three Lords* (c. 1588–90). Whether the revisions were made by Wilson or by members of the Queen's Men's company, Q2 represents a legitimate later version of the play. Q1 should be used where possible, however, as the copy text for an edition of an early 1580s play, and the revisions (which entail new problems and errors and choices that arguably have nothing to do with poetic or dramatic merit, as well as correction and improvement) should be treated as annotations to spice a performance to taste. Mann also noted that a passage in Stephen Gosson's *Plays Confuted in Five Actions* (1582) seems to indicate a scene or passage that is missing from the extant versions of *The Three Ladies of London*.[189] Gosson writes of:

> the play termed the three Ladies of London, which in the Catastrophe maketh Love and Conscience to be examined how thrie good ladishippes like of playes? Love answeres that she detesteth them because her guttes are tourned outward and all her secret convighaunce [conveyance] is blazed with colours to the peoples eye. Conscience like a kind-hearted gentelwoman doth alow them.
>
> In this pointe the Poet makes so much hast to his jorneys end, that he throwes him selfe headlong downe the hill. For neither Love disliked them, before he had married her to Dissimulation, whose propertie is to say one thing and thinke another: nor Conscience allowed them before he had spotted her with all abhomination, whose nature is to allowe that which is like herself filthie, corrupt, spotted, and defiled.[190]

In response to this apparent omission, Mann writes that 'The greater part of *The Three Ladies of London* seems to have been written with little concern for the exigencies of time'. She says that the opening is long and slow and that the didactic, polemical, and satirical sequences interrupt the forwarding of the plot. She then focuses on the contrast of the arguable brevity of the trial scene at the end of the play, which she says betrays a technique 'so obviously different' to the rest that 'one can scarcely fail to infer that excisions have been made from the original version of the final scenes'.[191] Gosson, however, still thinks the play rushes with 'so much hast' even with the additional passage included. It is not clear how exactly such a passage could be fitted into the trial scene; as the play-text stands there would have to be a rather overt segue in the trial proceedings to turn from the moral-sexual judgement of the ladies to their reaction to playing.

This edition uses as the copy text for *Three Ladies* the British Library copy of Q1, which was collated with Q1 texts in the Bodleian and Huntington and Q2 texts in the British Library and Huntington. As indicated above, I do not find the Q2 changes as ubiquitously convincing as some earlier editors, although there are a good number of clear corrections and improvements in the later edition. I have endeavoured to stick with Q1 readings where possible since they give us an early 1580s text. I have chosen the Q1 rather than Q2 where altered words seem a matter of taste rather than quality, and occasionally even where the revision seems to be an improvement, because I want to present the single text of the early 1580s as far as possible. I am concerned to avoid an artificially conflated or cobbled Q1/Q2 production at any point by piecing together the text word by word from the two editions. When Q2 is necessary, I have on occasion brought in whole phrases or lines of Q2, since this at least represents a whole early modern authorial or compositorial thought. A small example is at 5.56, where Q reads 'Marry, very, sir' in response to Mercadorus's question 'how fare-a my lady ...?' and Q2 corrects to 'Marry, well, sir'. I keep the Q2 reading as an acceptable correction instead of adopting Hazlitt's conflation of the two: 'Marry, very well, sir'. No edition before the present one has divided the play into scenes; Q1 and subsequent editions begin the play with the notice 'The first act' and begin what is in the present edition scene 2 with 'The second act'. No other scene divisions are marked.

The copy text for *Englishmen for My Money* is the Huntington copy of Q1 (1616), with a number of Q2 (1621) corrections and a very few Q3 (1631) insertions. All copies of all editions at the Huntington, British Library, and the Bodleian have been collated. Q1 has a better sense of (comic) foreign pronunciation and seems to be printed from a stage-smart copy, perhaps an authorial revision or an unclearly marked-up prompt copy. I say unclearly because there is apparently some doubling of words or metrical stresses, where one should have been deleted, but both have been left in the printing. There are also a number of erroneous entries, exits, and speech prefixes. Q2 and Q3 (1631) correct (anglicize) dialect and accent, but they sometimes make correct foreign words nonsensical (e.g. Dutch 'neit' becomes 'ne it'). Q3, set from Q2, adds some unique changes, and I have not noted them where they are nonsensical or clear mistakes. There are progressive word changes through the editions that support a theory that Q2 was set from a reading of Q1 and Q3 from either reading or hearing Q2: for example at 4.1.231 Q1 'mated' looks in Q2 like 'mared' (an easy 't'/'r' misreading in Elizabethan hand), which in turn becomes Q3 'marred' (a possible mishearing or more likely conscious 'correction' of Q2 without having access to Q1). Q3 does add one or two clarifying readings, however, which have been incorporated in the present edition and collated. The plethora of oaths uttered in Q1 have been trimmed down in Q2 and Q3, and I have retained them in this edition. Where punctuation or spelling choice provides significantly different readings, I have explained the issue in the footnotes and collated the variant. Since Q1 is printed significantly later than the 1598 date of composition, leaving plenty of time for changes in the text, I have been less concerned here than in the case of *Three Ladies* about the problem of 'authenticity' that may occur by substituting Q2 (or very occasionally Q3) words and apparent corrections. The three quarto readings do not *conflate* independently good texts, as is the case with *Three Ladies* Q1 and Q2, so much as lightly correct and modernize them.

The Hog Hath Lost His Pearl is extant only in one edition, the Quarto of 1614; the Huntington copy provides the copy text for the present edition, which was collated with the two copies in the British Museum and the Bodleian copy; the copies in Worcester College, Oxford, and the Guildhall Library were also consulted. There are significant corrections made through the text, and the corrected and uncorrected states of formes are collated in the Malone reprint edition. There are six occasions on which the Qc and Qu differences in copies consulted for the present edition were substantial and warranted collation.

TEXTUAL ISSUES

In accordance with Revels series practice, I have silently modernized spelling, expanded abbreviations and elisions (e.g. 'enou' and 'enow' to 'enough'; 'mo' and 'moe' to 'more'), amended i/j and u/v, regularized repeated English phrases (such as various versions of the oath 'By'r Lady'), corrected non-substantial misprints (such as doubled or turned letters, extra spaces, noun capitalization, and so on) and regularized exit directions. I have used 'O' throughout the texts, whether for apostrophic address or lament.

Character names

In *Three Ladies*, I have chosen to use the form of the name 'Mercadorus' in this text, unless there is an address, implying a vocative, where I use the alternative 'Mercadore'; he introduces himself as Mercadorus at 3.25. I have listed the Lawyer unnamed but parenthetically added (called Creticus). The lawyer is named Creticus late in the play; I am supposing this is not a second lawyer but the one featured earlier, and I want to leave open the possibility that he is deliberately named Creticus – an obvious allusion to the proverbially lying Cretans – only after he 'goes bad' in the play and agrees to carry out deceptive and hurtful law because pleading for Love and Conscience is doing him no good (3.116–48). The old texts' 'Lucar' is modernized to 'Lucre' except where Mercadorus is pronouncing her name with an Italianate inflection at 3.2 and 3.8. In *Englishmen*, the spelling of Vandal's name – Vandalle in the list of characters' names, 'van Dale' in modern Dutch – foregrounds the allusion to barbarity and uncouthness and thus his assault on the English language.

Foreign language

Whereas the Revels series would usually expect a foreign character to be able to speak his or her own language competently and would therefore modernize and correct such speeches, the case of *Englishmen for My Money* demands a different approach. So much of the foreigners' language is macaronic that in a number of cases it is not entirely clear whether a character is speaking a foreign language word or phrase or attempting to pronounce English; furthermore, and perhaps more important to point out, the foreign characters seem to continue the complex joke of the inferior 'gibble-gabble' that is foreign language, as demonstrated by Frisco's appallingly hilarious attempts at 'Dutch', 'French', and 'Italian'. Part of the essential comedy here is the awareness that English actors are playing at being foreigners; this constant awareness adds another layer of irony to the scenes in which Englishmen and foreigners pretend to be each other, in a linguistic version of cross-dressing.

Leaving uncorrected some of the mispronunciations and apparent linguistic mistakes in the foreign languages without doubt introduces some inconsistency to the text, but it is an inconsistency that is in character with the text itself and with the arguments about Anglo-foreign relations that the play raises. Thus Alvaro the Italian's 'dulce' (2.1.34) is not corrected to 'dolce' nor his 'piculo' (2.1.135) to 'piccolo', because his pronunciation of those words should be painful to those who know and insignificant to those who do not; notes are provided where the spelling or pronunciation changes are so radical that they need clarifying. Another simple example would be a word such as 'Mister', which is printed variously as 'Mester', 'Meestere', and 'Meester', the last being correct Dutch. While I have retained this 'correction' as a nod in the direction of Revels' practice, I should note that, when Vandal is speaking a combination of Dutch and English, he is speaking to someone who will be listening for English (whether an Englishman or a non-Dutch foreigner). 'Mester', then, is probably the Dutchman's pronunciation of the English word 'Mister', and the spelling should arguably remain as in the early text. Furthermore, I have retained orthographic hints at pronunciation, such as Vandal's 'huis'/'house' or 'u'/'you' (2.3.263–5) (which in these examples are also correct Dutch words), or combination spelling 'houis' (3.2.78) or even indications of foreignness that are textual/visual only and not aural (which might give us some insight into Haughton's mindset while writing these characters) – an example would be retaining the 'k' in Vandal's word 'kash' (= cash, for 'catch') (2.1.132).

We should remind ourselves also that, even when a foreigner is supposed to be speaking his own language, he may not only make grammatical errors but may make little sense at all; such a case is Alvaro's exclamation of horror when Harvey rises from his apparent death-bed (5.1.150–1). This obviously difficult moment is indicative of the deliberate, Anglocentric motive of having foreign characters in comedy act foolishly to the extent that their own languages are held up for ridicule. We see this overtly in Vandal's soliloquy at the opening of 3.4. There is no reason to have him speaking anything other than pure Dutch while he is on his own, but of course he comically speaks Dutch phrases among English interjections, and all in the context of English grammar. So, to maintain this sense of deliberate carelessness with foreign characters speaking their own language, I correct where it is essential for comprehensibility or where there is no benefit in mistaken language, but I leave grammatical and occasional spelling infelicities that contribute to audience amusement and/or bemusement. I have, moreover, annotated where there may be legitimate reasons for believing apparent mistakes to be intended readings.

Speech assignment
In addition to the usual speech misassignments or omissions, which are easy enough to correct, there are a few questions about speech assignment in *Three Ladies* and *Englishmen*.

(1) The opening lines of scene 4 of *Three Ladies* appear to pose a problem of attribution. The present edition retains Qq speech prefixes, as follows:

> *Sincerity.* Good Cousin Simplicity, do somewhat for me.
> *Simplicity.* Yes, faith, Cousin Sincerity, I'll do anything for thee.
>   What wouldst thou have me do for thee, canst tell that?
>   Mass, I cannot tell what shouldst do for me, except thou
>   wouldst give me a new hat.
> *Sincerity.* Alas! I am not able to give thee a new.
> *Simplicity.* Why, I marvel then how thou dost do:
>   Dost thou get thy living amongst beggars, from door to door?
>   Indeed, Cousin Sincerity, I had thought thou wast not so poor.
>   (4.1–8)

It is quite possible to have Simplicity speaking lines 2–4, although he has to engage in some comic dramatic monologue. He turns in line 4 to contemplate what Sincerity might give him in return for whatever favour she asks and cannot think of anything significant; he suggests a new hat, which Sincerity cannot afford. Simplicity then reacts in lines 6–8 with surprise and disdain. Collier (followed by Hazlitt) gives line 4 to Sincerity and lines 5–8 to Simplicity. This reading has Simplicity responding to Sincerity's request for a hat with surprise that she should be wanting such a trifle. This emendation suffers from a couple of problems, however.

First, Sincerity comes to Simplicity with a request in line 1 and then inexplicably 'cannot tell' what she wants from him, but at lines 11–13 states quite clearly that she wants letters signed and delivered on her behalf. Second, line 6 seems to reply to line 5, so to have them both spoken by Simplicity seems an unlikely emendation.

(2) The entry direction for *Englishmen for My Money* 1.3 reads 'Enter Pisaro, Delion the Frenchman, Vandal the Dutchman, Alvaro the Italian, and other Merchants, at several doors'. Alvaro does not in fact enter until line 236, 'Gentlemen' speak at line 80, and there is an additional unnamed 'Stranger' who speaks at line 202. I have emended 'Gentlemen' to 'All', since there has been no previous division between gentlemen and others and 'All' facilitates a general response from all those within earshot of Browne. At lines 202 and 205, I have left Q's 'Stranger' and 'Merchant' prefixes, which suggest a larger community of English and foreign merchants represented on stage. Since 'stranger' has been used in the scene to refer to our familiar foreigners, one of them could possibly speak the line. The 'Stranger' and 'Merchant' could also be intended as one character, emphasizing the presence of 'stranger merchants' at the Exchange, and these lines certainly read well as a brief back-and-forth between Moore and one other person. There is also arguable stage business between line 88 where a Post enters and Balsaro's entrance at line 157.

(3) In *Englishmen for My Money* 3.3, there are multiple inconsistencies in the speeches of Delion and Alvaro, which cannot be reconciled by emendation. These two foreigners meet Heigham in 3.2, where they are attempting to get access to Pisaro's daughters at the house in Crutched Friars. Heigham tells Alvaro that he is not in Crutched Friars where he thinks he is, but in fact in Leadenhall and must have lost his way in the dark. The Englishmen then tell Delion separately that he is also mistaken and is not in Crutched Friars but in Fenchurch Street. Frisco, disguised as the Dutchman, is in turn told he is in Tower Street. The two foreigners and Frisco go off to find their way to Crutched Friars. In 3.3 all three meet. Frisco declares his location and asks the foreigners where they think they are; now Alvaro claims to be in Fenchurch Street and Delion in Leadenhall:

> *Delion.* Who parle der? In wat plashe, in wat street be you?
> *Frisco.* Why, sir, I can tell where I am: I am in Tower Street. Where a devil be you?
> *Delion.* Io be here in Lede-hall.
> *Frisco.* In Leadenhall? I trow I shall meet with you anon. [*Aside*] In Leaden-hall? What a simple ass is this Frenchman. Some more of this: where are you, sir?

Alvaro. Moy, I be here in Vanshe Street.

Frisco. [*Aside*] This is excellent in faith, as fit as a fiddle. I in Tower Street, you in Leadenhall, and the third in Fenchurch Street; and yet all three hear one another, and all three speak together. Either we must be all three in Leadenhall, or all three in Tower Street, or all three in Fenchurch Street – or all three fools!

Alvaro. Monsieur gentle-homme, can you well tesh de wey to Croshe-frier?

Frisco. How, to Crutched Friars? Ay, ay sir, passing well, if you will follow me.

Delion. Ay, dat me sal, Monsieur gentle-homme, and give you tanks.

Frisco. [*Aside*] And, Monsieur Pharo, I shall lead you such a jaunt that you shall scarce give me thanks for. – Come, sirs, follow me.

(3.3.16–35)

In line 19, Delion uses the Italian 'Io', which might suggest either a speech misattribution, which would explain his claiming to be in Leadenhall, or, less likely, might suggest a misreading of 'Je' (this word is only used once by Delion in the whole play, and that in a French sentence). Frisco, however, follows with a reply that indicates that it is indeed the Frenchman who has just spoken: 'In Leaden-hall? What a simple ass is this Frenchman'. Frisco then milks the comedy, apparently turning to Alvaro, who replies with the French 'Moy'. Alvaro's 'Monsieur gentle-homme' and 'tesh de wey to Croshe-frier' at lines 29–30 all sounds rather French; Delion repeats the address 'Monsieur gentle-homme', which is followed in the next line by Frisco immediately referring again to Alvaro. Frisco's lines mean that the confusion cannot be repaired through reassigning speeches, and the fact that there are plenty of other examples of the foreigners using each other's languages (for example in the scenes we are discussing, Delion exclaims 'O Dio' at 3.3.56, and Alvaro uses the Dutch 'huis' at 3.2.35) suggests a (deliberate?) carelessness for linguistic attribution. The fact that 3.3 is set in the confusing dark adds to the comedy of irreconcilable foreignness. It might be taken, moreover, as part of the ongoing critique of London as a growing center of Babel, with the 'nations, sects, and factions' (1.3.315) brought in by foreign residents like Pisaro, producing the 'litter of languages' (1.2.105) that Frisco warns against, all concentrated around the growing importance of the Exchange, where there is the proverbial 'confusion of languages', as Nashe puts it.[192]

NOTES

1 Bishop John Jewel, quoted in John Blaxton, *The English Usurer* (1634), sig. C3–C3v.

2 Heinrich Bullinger, quoted in Miles Mosse, *The Arraignment and Conviction of Usurie* (1595) (Collection of sermons preached 1592–93), sig. D2.

3 Sir Francis Bacon, *The Essayes or Counsels, Civill and Morall*, ed. Michael Kiernan (Cambridge, MA: Harvard University Press, 1985), p. 125.

4 Celeste Turner Wright, 'Some Conventions Regarding the Usurer in Elizabethan Literature', *Studies in Philology* 31 (1934): 176–97, p. 176.

5 Anon., 'The Usurer Reformed' (Huntington MS EL2468, temp. James I), fol. 14.

6 Thomas Pie, *Usuries Spright Conjured* (1604), sig. F2.

7 John Milton, *Comus*. In *The Riverside Milton*, ed. Roy Flannagan (Boston: Houghton Mifflin, 1998), pp. 155–6.

8 Miles Mosse, *The Arraignment and Conviction of Usurie* (1595), sig. T4v.

9 James Spottiswoode, *The Execution of Neschech and the confining of his Kinsman Tarbith* (1616), sig. Fv.

10 David Hawkes makes important use of this interesting double meaning of 'use' in his analysis of usury and sexuality in Shakespeare's sonnets. See his chapter 'Sodomy, Usury, and the Narrative of Shakespeare's *Sonnets*' in *Idols of the Marketplace: Idolatry and Commodity Fetishism in English Literature, 1580–1680* (New York: Palgrave 2001), pp. 95–114.

11 Kerridge, *Trade and Banking in Early Modern England* (Manchester: Manchester University Press, 1988), pp. 16, 33.

12 Ibid., p. 34.

13 Ibid., p. 34.

14 Norman Jones, *God and the Moneylenders: Usury and the Law in Early Modern England* (Oxford: Blackwell, 1989); Kerridge, *Trade and Banking*.

15 Eric Kerridge, *Usury, Interest and the Reformation* (Aldershot: Ashgate, 2002).

16 William Harrys, trans., *The Market or Fayre of Usurers* (1550), sig. F8.

17 John Jewel, *An Exposition upon the Two Epistles of the Apostle Saint Paul to the Thessalonians* (two sermons from 1560s) (1583 and 1584), pp. 857–8.

18 Jones, *God and the Moneylenders*, pp. 168, 169.

19 Roger Turner, *The Usurers Plea Answered* (1634) (a sermon given at Southampton, Thursday 18 July 1633), sig. D, Dv; pp. 19, 20.

20 William Rowley, *A Search for Money* (1609), sig. C4.

21 Turner, *The Usurers Plea Answered*, sig. Dv–D2, pp. 20–1.

22 Anon., 'The Usurer Reformed', fol. 14v.

23 See Anon., *A Tract Against Usurie* (1621), sig. A4v.

24 Ibid., sig. A4v.

25 Sir Francis Bacon, *The Essayes or Counsels, Civill and Morall*, p. 125.

26 Anon., *Usurie Araigned and Condemned* (1625), sig. A3v.

27 The three preceding sentences refer to *Usurie Araigned*, sig. A3v–A4, B, and Bv respectively.

28 See *Decay of Trade. A Treatise Against the Abatement of Interest* (1641).

29 Robert Butler, *The Scale of Interest* (1632), sig. A2.

30 Anon., *Two Knaves for a Penny[,] Or, a Dialogue between Mr Hord the Meal-man and Mr Gripe the Broker* (1647), sig. A4v.

31 John Benbrigge, *Usura Accommodata, or a Ready Way to Rectifie Usury* (1646).

32 'The Usurer Reformed', fol. 3v.

33 Blaxton, *The English Usurer*, ch. 5, sig. G4v.

34 John Wharton, *Wharton's Dream. Conteyninge an invective agaynst certaine abhominable Caterpillers as Usurers, Extortioners, Leasmongers and such others* [. . .] (1578), sig. D2.

35 George Wither (1588–1667), untitled poem appended to Blaxton's *English Usurer* (sig. M2–M2v in Huntington 96503; L4–L4v in Huntington 28047) (my modernized spelling; original punctuation).

36 George Downame, *Lectures on the XV Psalme* (1604), p. 258, sig. Sv.

37 Wither, in Blaxton, *The English Usurer.*

38 Jonathan Gil Harris, *Sick Economies: Drama, Mercantilism, and Disease in Shakespeare's England* (Philadephia: University of Pennsylvania Press, 2004), p. 57.

39 The questionable practice of Eyre is acknowledged and discussed in David Scott Kastan, 'Workshop and/as Playhouse: Comedy and Commerce in *The Shoemaker's Holiday*', *Studies in Philology* 84 (1987): 324–37; and Brian Walsh, 'Performing Historicity in Dekker's *The Shoemaker's Holiday*', *Studies in English Literature 1500–1900* 46 (2006): 323–48.

40 For discussions of the issues mentioned in this paragraph see Laura Hunt Yungblut, *Strangers Settled Here Amongst Us: Policies, Perceptions, and the Presence of Aliens in Elizabethan England* (London and New York: Routledge, 1996); Lien Luu, *Immigrants and the Industries of London, 1500–1700* (Aldershot: Ashgate, 2005); Lien Luu and Nigel Goose, eds, *Immigrants in Tudor and Early Stuart England* (Brighton: Sussex Academic Press, 2005).

41 Libel text taken from c. 1600 copy by John Mansell, reprinted in Arthur Freeman, 'Marlowe, Kyd, and the Dutch Church Libel', *English Literary Renaissance* 3 (1973): 44–52, pp. 50–1.

42 Roger Fenton, *A Treatise of Usurie* (1612), sig. V3v–V4.

43 George Wither, *Abuses Stript and Whipt* (1613), sig. G2–G2v, G3v.

44 For further discussion of the national stereotypes see A. J. Hoenselaars, *Images of Englishmen and Foreigners in the Drama of Shakespeare and His Contemporaries* (London: Associated University Presses, 1992); Lloyd Edward Kermode, 'After Shylock: the Judaiser in England', *Renaissance and Reformation* 20 (1996): 15–26.

45 For a comprehensive study of Protestant immigrants in England see Andrew Pettegree, *Foreign Protestant Communities in Sixteenth-Century London* (Oxford: Clarendon Press, 1986).

46 Yungblut, *Strangers*, p. 23.

47 See Freeman, 'Marlowe, Kyd'.

48 David Bevington, *Tudor Drama and Politics* (Cambridge, MA: Harvard University Press, 1968), p. 138.

49 In the *Diary* a play called 'matchavell' or *Machiavelli* plays in repertoire with *The Jew of Malta*, two times out of three back-to-back on successive performance nights (pp. 16–18).

50 Robin R. Mundill, *England's Jewish Solution: Experiment and Expulsion, 1262–1290* (Cambridge: Cambridge University Press, 1998), chs 2, 5, 8; transcription of *Statutum de Judeismo*, 291–3.

51 For the history of the return of Jews to England in the sixteenth century see Lucien Wolf's optimistic but revealing 'Jews in Elizabethan England', *Transactions of the Jewish Historical Society of England (TJHSE)* XI (1924–27): 1–91; Cecil Roth, *A History of the Jews in England* (1941; Oxford: Clarendon Press, 1964, 1978), 3rd ed.; David S. Katz, *The Jews in the History of England 1485–1850* (Oxford:

Clarendon Press, 1995); James Shapiro *Shakespeare and the Jews* (New York: Columbia University Press, 1996).

52 This account draws on Claire Hilton, 'St. Bartholomew's Hospital, London, and its Jewish Connections', *TJHSE* 30 (1987–88): 21–50, pp. 23–5.

53 For an extensive account of the Lopez case see Katz, *The Jews*, ch. 2 (pp. 49–106).

54 Anon., *The Death of Usury, or, The Disgrace of Usurers* (1594), p. 10; sig. B4v.

55 'The Usurer Reformed', fol. 3.

56 Philip Caesar, *A General Discourse Against the Damnable Sect of Usurers* (1569; trans.1578), Dedicatory epistle, sig. *3v–*4.

57 Thomas Pie, *Usuries Spright Conjured* (1604), Dedicatory letter, A2v.

58 Blaxton, *The English Usurer*, sig. F3–F3v, citing Mr [Robert] Bolton [1572–1631].

59 'The Usurer Reformed', fol. 24. Francis Bacon's well-known comparable reference comes in his essay 'Of Usury': 'Many have made Wittie Invectives against *Usurie*. [. . .] That *Usurers* should have Orange-tawney Bonnets, because they doe *Judaize*' (*The Essayes or Counsels, Civill and Morall*, pp. 124–5).

60 Shapiro, *Shakespeare and the Jews*, p. 100.

61 Stephen Gosson, *The School of Abuse* (1579), sig. C6v.

62 References to *Three Lords and Three Ladies of London* are to H. S. D. Mithal's edition. Line number is followed by Q signature (*An Edition of Robert Wilson's 'The Three Ladies of London' and 'Three Lords and Three Ladies of London'*, ed. H. S. D. Mithal (PhD Diss. 1959; New York and London: Garland, 1988, hereafter Mithal).

63 Rowley, *A Search for Money*, sig. C2. Cited and discussed in Christopher Marlowe, *The Jew of Malta*, ed. N. W. Bawcutt (Manchester: Manchester University Press, 1978), p. 2.

64 Alan C. Dessen, 'The Elizabethan Stage Jew and the Christian Example: Gerontus, Barabas, and Shylock', *Modern Language Quarterly* 35 (1974): 231–45, p. 244.

65 Ibid., pp. 238, 243.

66 Harris, *Sick Economies*.

67 C. T. Wright, 'Some Conventions', p. 187.

68 For extensive analyses of hospitality in England see Felicity Heal, *Hospitality in Early Modern England* (Oxford: Clarendon Press, 1990); Daryl Palmer *Hospitable Performances: Dramatic Genre and Cultural Practices in Early Modern England* (West Lafayette, IN: Purdue University Press, 1992).

69 Arthur Bivins Stonex. 'The Usurer in Elizabethan Drama', *PMLA* 31 (1916): 190–210, p. 191, n. 3.

70 Jones, *God and the Moneylenders*, p. 147.

71 Blaxton, *The English Usurer*, F4, citing Mr [Thomas] Adams [fl. 1612–53].

72 *A most rare and wonderfull tragedy of all other in our age most admirable, of the life and death of a miserable [u]surer of Fraunce, [. . .] A worthy warning for all covetous Usurers and miserable Misers, how to eschewe the vile vice of Avarice* (Paris, 1583; London 1584 Thomas Hacket), sig. Ciiv–Ciii.

73 Thomas Adams, *Mysticall Bedlam: or The World of Mad-Men* (1615), in *The Workes of Thomas Adams* (1629), sig. Tt6; p. 503.

74 Philip Caesar, *A General Discourse*, Dedicatory epistle, sig. *3v–*4.

75 W. Wager, *The Longer Thou Livest* and *Enough Is as Good as a Feast*, ed. R. Mark Benbow (Lincoln: University of Nebraska Press, 1967), ll. 433–4.

76 T. Lupton, *All for Money* (1577) in *English Morality Plays and Interludes*, ed. Edgar T. Schell and J. D. Shuchter (New York: Holt, Rinehart and Winston, 1969), 419–73, p. 436, line 363.
77 'The Usurer Reformed', sig. 7, 7v.
78 Thomas Nashe, *Pierce Penilesse, His Supplication to the Divell* (1592), ed. G. B. Harrison (New York: Barnes and Noble, 1966), pp. 13–14.
79 Rowley, *A Search for Money*, sig. C, C2. See also note 57.
80 Ibid., sig. C2v.
81 Ibid., sig. E2v.
82 Wright has an extensive investigation of the traditional, if contradictory, gout of the usurer in 'Some Conventions', p. 190. For a litany of citations to paint a motley picture of the habits and effects of the usurer's activities in early modern literature, especially drama, see also Celeste Turner Wright, 'The Usurer's Sin in English Literature', *Studies in Philology* 35 (1938): 178–94.
83 In the Huntington copy 96503 of Blaxton's *The English Usurer*, a later manuscript hand has transcribed several poems and epigrams on usury and usurers from John Cotgrave's *The English Treasury of Wit and Language* (1655) and *Wit's Interpreter; Or, The New Parnassus* (1655 and 1662).
84 Harrys, trans., *The Market*, sig. L2–L2v, L5v.
85 Anon., *The Ruinate Fall of the Pope Usury, Derived from the Pope Idolatrie, Revealed by a Saxon of Antiquitie* (c. 1580), sig. A7v.
86 Alexander Leggatt, *Citizen Comedy in the Age of Shakespeare* (Toronto: University of Toronto Press, 1973), p. 59. I might have chosen this excellent usury play as the third text in the collection, but it is being edited for the Revels series single play editions.
87 John McVeagh, *Tradefull Merchants: The Portrayal of the Capitalist in Literature* (London: Routledge, 1987), pp. 12, 21.
88 Laura Caroline Stevenson, *Praise and Paradox: Merchants and Craftsmen in Elizabethan Popular Literature* (Cambridge: Cambridge University Press, 1984), p. 30.
89 Theodore B. Leinwand, *The City Staged: Jacobean Comedy, 1603–1613* (Madison: University of Wisconsin Press, 1986), p. 53.
90 Gail Kern Paster, *The Idea of the City in the Age of Shakespeare* (Athens: University of Georgia Press, 1985), p. 152.
91 Theodore B. Leinwand, *Theatre, Finance and Society in Early Modern England* (Cambridge and New York: Cambridge University Press, 1999), p. 25.
92 Leggatt, *Citizen Comedy*, p. 31.
93 Stevenson, *Praise and Paradox*, p. 98.
94 McVeagh, *Tradefull Merchants*, p. 11.
95 Ibid., p. 22.
96 Stevenson, *Praise and Paradox*, p. 104.
97 Louis B. Wright, 'Social Aspects of Some Belated Moralities', *Anglia* 54 (1930): 107–48, p. 111.
98 Stevenson, *Praise and Paradox*, p. 105.
99 Coll 1851, p. 12.
100 Stephen Gosson, *Plays Confuted in Five Actions* (1582), p. 185. Cited in *ES* iv, p. 216.
101 Edward Guilpin, *Skialetheia, or a Shadowe of Truth* (1598). Cited in Coll 1851, pp. 14–15.
102 Wright, 'Social Aspects', p. 128.

103 Mithal, p. xcviii.
104 Mithal, p. ii; Richard Dutton, *Mastering the Revels, The Regulation and Censorship of English Renaissance Drama* (London: Macmillan, 1991), p. 66.
105 *ES* ii, p. 86.
106 *ES* ii, p. 85.
107 *ES* ii, p. 87.
108 Richard Dutton warns against confidently connecting Wilson with Leicester's Men: 'The details of Wilson's career in the 1580s are very confused, and there is no evidence that any of his three extant plays was actually written for' Leicester's company (*Mastering the Revels*, p. 71). However, the naming of Wilson in the 1574 patent for Leicester's company and Wilson's connections with Leicester after the formation of the Queen's Men in 1583 do nothing to suppose a break between the two men in the intervening years.
109 *ES* ii, p. 105.
110 John Stow (cont. by Edmond Howes), *The Annales, or, Generall chronicle of England* (1615), p. 697.
111 Richard Levin, 'Tarlton's Picture on the Elizabethan Stage', *N&Q* 47 (245) (2000): 435–6. On the picture of Tarlton see also John Astington, 'Rereading Illustrations of the English Stage', *Shakespeare Survey* 50 (1997): 151–70, pp. 163–4.
112 *ES* ii, p. 107.
113 T. W. Baldwin argues for the death of Robert Wilson the elder in 1588 ('Nathaniel Field and Robert Wilson', *Modern Language Notes* 41 (1926): 32–4).
114 Mithal, p. xci.
115 Francis Meres, *Palladis Tamia* (1598), sig. Oo5v, p. 285; Oo6, p. 286.
116 See S. O. Addy, 'Robert Wilson and "Sir Thomas More": Wilson's First Play', *Notes and Queries* 154 (May 1928): 335–6. Addy's article is a reply to S. R. Golding's piece in the same volume: S. R. Golding, 'Robert Wilson and "Sir Thomas More" ', *Notes and Queries* 154 (April 1928): 237–9.
117 Anthony Munday, and others, *Sir Thomas More*, eds Vittorio Gabrieli and Giorgio Melchiori, Revels edition (Manchester: Manchester University Press, 1990).
118 Thomas Lodge, 'A Reply to Stephen Gosson's Schoole of Abuse in defense of Poetry, Musick, and Stage Plays', pp. 42–3 (p. 28 in Shakespeare Society ed.), cited in Mithal, p. lxvi.
119 *The Pedlar's Prophecy*, published in 1595, however, feels like an earlier work. On the dating of the play see G. L. Kittredge, 'The Date of *The Pedler's Prophecy*', *Harvard Studies and Notes in Philology* 16 (1934): 97–118.
120 Mithal, pp. xx–xxi. The statute is 1 & 2 Philip and Mary c. 8. The letter is reproduced and transcribed by Mithal, plate IV and p. lxxv.
121 Mithal, p. xxv. John Tucker Murray says that 'The only appearance of an Earl of Shrewsbury's company of players in the sixteenth century was at Abingdon in 1580. These men were under the patronage of George Talbot, who was Earl of Shrewsbury from c. 1560 to 1590. [. . .] Nothing more is heard of an Earl of Shrewsbury's company of players till 1616' (John Tucker Murray, *English Dramatic Companies, 1558–1642*, 2 vols (London: Constable, 1910), 2, pp. 66–7). Wilson may already have had *Three Ladies* or another play under way or completed when the Baylye request was conveyed to him; the letter mentions no fee or contract for date of completion, and it is not at all certain that it was expected that Wilson should write a *new* play, nor one exclusively for Shrewsbury's Men.

122 See R. C. Bald, 'Leicester's Men in the Low Countries', *Review of English Studies* 19 (1943): 395–7; Scott McMillin and Sally-Beth MacLean, *The Queen's Men and Their Plays, 1583–1603* (Cambridge: Cambridge University Press, 1998), 18–24, p. 20.

123 McMillin and MacLean, *The Queen's Men and Their Plays*, p. 44. McMillin and MacLean go on to say that 'The most important point' about the habits of the Queen's Men back in London 'may be that they had no fixed home and no evident interest in attaining one. [. . .] Oscar Brownstein's remark that even in London they were on tour seems perceptive on this point: they were following "the pattern of the provincial tour within the limited geographical scope of London, its liberties, and suburbs"' (p. 46). See Oscar Brownstein, 'A Record of London Inn-Playhouses from c. 1565–1590', *Shakespeare Quarterly* 22 (1971): 17–24, p. 22.

124 See Emily Bartels, 'Marlowe, Shakespeare, and the Revision of Stereotypes', *Research Opportunities in Renaissance Drama* 32 (1993): 13–26; Bartels, 'Malta, the Jew, and the Fictions of Difference: Colonialist Discourse in Marlowe's *The Jew of Malta*', *English Literary Renaissance* 20 (1990): 3–16; and Bartels *Spectacles of Strangeness: Imperialism, Alienation, and Marlowe* (Philadelphia: University of Pennsylvania Press, 1993), ch. 4; Shapiro, *Shakespeare and Jews*, pp. 187–9, ch. 6 and *passim*.

125 Dessen, 'The Elizabethan Stage Jew'; Daryl Palmer, 'Merchants and Miscegenation: *The Three Ladies of London, The Jew of Malta*, and *The Merchant of Venice*', in *Race, Ethnicity, and Power in the Renaissance*, ed. Joyce Green MacDonald (London: Associated University Presses, 1997), 36–66.

126 Palmer, 'Merchants and Miscegenation', p. 46.

127 Usual loan periods were six months or twelve months, so this reprisal of three months as a bond date seems unusual and possibly connected.

128 Thomas Cartelli, 'Shakespeare's *Merchant*, Marlowe's *Jew*: The Problem of Cultural Difference', *Shakespeare Studies* 20 (1987): 255–60, p. 259.

129 Alan Stewart emphasizes the fact that *Three Ladies* was written at a moment when 'despite its best efforts, London could no longer see itself as somehow remote from and untainted by the Mediterranean world' (' "Come from Turkie": Mediterranean Trade in Late Elizabethan London', in *Remapping the Mediterranean World in Early Modern English Writings*, ed. Goran V. Stanivukovic (London: Palgrave Macmillan, 2007), 157–77, p. 173. (My gratitude is due to Professor Stewart for providing me with an advance copy of his typescript.) For studies of the Anglo-Turkish relationship as seen through the prism of drama in the period see Daniel Vitkus, *Turning Turk: English Theater and the Multicultural Mediterranean* (New York: Palgrave Macmillan, 2003); also his introduction to *Three Turk Plays from Early Modern England* (New York: Columbia University Press, 2000), which draws on the book.

130 Morris Palmer Tilley's first record of the proverb to 'turn Turk' is in 1598, in *Much Ado About Nothing* (3.4.52), T609.

131 Mithal, pp. 124–5; William R. Dynes, ' "London, Look On!": The Estates Morality Play and the Moralities of Economy', Conference Paper, Group for Early Modern Cultural Studies. Pittsburgh, PA, 1996, http://english.uindy.edu/dynes/estatesmorality.htm, 23 February 2006.

132 Thomas Bell, *The Speculation of Usurie* (1596), sig. G2v.

133 Mithal, p. xxiv.

134 Wright, 'Social Aspects', p. 129 n.

135 Teresa Nugent, 'Usury and Counterfeiting in Wilson's *The Three Ladies of London* and *The Three Lords and Three Ladies of London,* and in Shakespeare's *Measure for Measure*', in *Money and the Age of Shakespeare,* ed. Linda Woodbridge (New York: Palgrave Macmillan, 2003), 201–17, pp. 203–4, 207–8, 213.

136 For further discussion of the end of *Three Ladies* and this scene in *Three Lords* see Lloyd Edward Kermode, 'The Playwright's Prophecy: Robert Wilson's *The Three Ladies of London* and the "Alienation" of the English', *Medieval and Renaissance Drama in England* 11 (1999): 60–87.

137 Albert Croll Baugh, William Haughton's *Englishmen for My Money* (PhD Diss. University of Pennsylvania, 1917), p. 15.

138 This epithet is always mentioned in discussions of Haughton, sometimes being misrepresented. The 1830 editor writes that 'in Henslowe's Diary he is not unfrequently termed "Young Haughton" ' (p. 4); in fact, the appellation is used only for one instance (two entries, but the second is a duplication of the first).

139 However, there is no record of a William Haughton at the Universities at an appropriate time. Baugh notes that Anthony's reference to Oxford University as 'England's pride' at 1.1.39 suggests some sort of affiliation with that institution, but the nature of such a relationship remains obscure.

140 A second payment for *The Poor Man's Paradise* is listed in the *Diary* (p. 123), where the name 'harey Chettle' is crossed out and 'Thomas Hawton' [*sic*] put in interlinearly.

141 This would seem to be an adaptation of Thomas Sackville and Thomas Norton's 1560s play *Gorboduc.*

142 Henslowe's *Diary* uses the old calendar in which the New Year began on 25 March; hence a date of 10 March is still recorded as belonging to the previous year.

143 William M. Baillie, ed., *A Choice Ternary of English Plays: Gratiae Theatrales* (1662) (Binghamton: MRTS, 1984), p. 174. All references to *Grim* are from this edition.

144 See for example, *Wealth and Health* (1554–58) and the dialogue between Man and Money in Anon., *The Bayte and Snare of Fortune* (STC gives 1556 and 1550 as likely publication dates).

145 Leinwand, *The City Staged,* p. 7.

146 Leggatt, *Citizen Comedy,* p. 7.

147 Stonex, 'The Usurer', pp. 199–200.

148 Ibid., pp. 199–200.

149 Ibid., p. 201.

150 Ibid., p. 203.

151 Ibid., p. 209.

152 In personal correspondence Crystal Bartolovich usefully suggested that, in contrast to my representation here, Haughton perhaps did not disapprove of the feisty role he gave Walgrave.

153 Elizabeth Schafer, 'William Haughton's *Englishmen for My Money*: A Critical Note', *RES* n.s. 41 (1990): 536–8, p. 537.

154 Emma Smith sees such assertive power as an inherited and gendered national trait: 'In his play, Haughton has killed off the mother but not her tongue: Pisaro's wife had given her language, and with it her national status, to her daughters' (' "So much English by the Mother": Gender, Foreigners, and the Mother Tongue in William Haughton's *Englishmen for My Money*', *Medieval and Renaissance Drama in England* 13 (2001): 165–81, p. 176).

155 Ibid., p. 169.

156 Diane Cady, 'Linguistic Dis-ease: Foreign Language as Sexual Disease in Early Modern England', in *Sins of the Flesh: Responding to Sexual Disease in Early Modern Europe*, ed. Kevin Siena (Toronto: Centre for Reformation and Renaissance Studies, 2005), 159–86, p. 178.

157 Stewart, 'Come from Turkie', p. 161.

158 Harris, *Sick Economies*, p. 76.

159 Crystal Bartolovich, 'London's the Thing: Alienation, the Market, and *Englishmen for My Money*', *Huntington Library Quarterly* 71 (2008): 137–56, p. 147. (My gratitude is due Professor Bartolovich for providing me with a copy of her typescript.)

160 Ibid., MS, *passim*.

161 Jean Howard, *Theater of a City: The Places of London Comedy, 1598–1642* (Philadelphia: University of Pennsylvania Press, 2007).

162 Alan Stewart, ' "Euery soyle to mee is naturall": Figuring Denization in William Haughton's *English-men for My Money*', *Renaissance Drama* 35 (2006): 55–81.

163 John Taylor's *The Nipping or Snipping of Abuses* (1614), sig. A3v. Some settings for Sandys' *Sacred Hymns* of 1615 have been attributed to one Robert Tailour, and Kathman suggests tentatively that this may be our author; he was 'in the right place at the right time', for we find him playing the lute at the week of celebrations of the marriage of Princess Elizabeth leading up to the date of the *Hog* controversy. (David Kathman, 'London Politics and the Authorship of Two Jacobean Plays', Conference paper, Shakespeare Association of America, 2005. My gratitude is due to Dr Kathman for providing me with a copy of his paper.)

164 Henry Wotton, *Reliquiae Wottonianae*, ed. Isaac Walton (1685), sig. Ee3v–Ee4, pp. 402–3. The late Lord Treasurer was William Cecil, Earl of Salisbury.

165 Fleay and the *DNB* entry for Robert Tailor put this performance on Sunday 14 February 1613, combining evidence from the Wotton letter (dated simply 'Tuesday'), which notes that it was performed 'On Sunday last at night', with Haddit's remark in the play that 'Shrove Tuesday is at hand' (1.1.123). However, Haddit's line continues, 'I have some acquaintance with bricklayers and plasterers', letting us know that this is a device to remind us of the tradition of apprentices' holiday and social inversion on Shrove Tuesday rather than a date placement for a specific performance. The prologue in the quarto of 1614 (a year after the events of the curtailed performance) clearly shows that the published play is a revised and reflective document, and dates in the text do not have to refer to any performance time. E. K. Chambers corrects the performance date to Sunday 21 February 1613, based on the fact that the letter 'refers to the departure of the King, which was 22 Feb. 1613, as on the previous day' (*ES* iii, p. 496) ('The King departed yesterday from hence towards you' (*Reliquiae Wottonianae*, sig. Ee3v, p. 402)).

166 Whitefriars is mentioned in Richard Rawlidge's diatribe against the moral corruption of London, where he notes that Queen Elizabeth's privy council 'obteined leave from her Majesty to thrust those players out of the Citty, and to pull downe the Dicing houses: which accordingly was affected, and the Play-houses in Gracious street, Bishops-gate-streete, nigh Paules, that on Ludgate hill, the White-Friars were put downe, and other lewd houses quite supprest within the Liberties, by the care of those religious Senators' (*A Monster Late Found Out and Discovered* (1628), sig. A3).

167 *Acts of the Privy Council of England* (1613–14), p. 166. Cited in *ES* ii, p. 517.

168 Evelyn May Albright notes and rejects the unlikely assertion that the Hog and Pearl referred respectively to the King and his daughter Elizabeth, who had just been 'lost' to her father through her marriage to the Elector Palatine on 14 February, a week before the performance ('A Stage Cartoon of the Mayor of London in 1613', in *The Manly Anniversary Studies in Language and Literature* (Chicago: University of Chicago Press, 1923), 113–26, p. 114).

169 Katherine Duncan-Jones. 'Prentices and Prodigals: A New Allusion to *The Hogge hath Lost His Pearl*', *Notes and Queries* 44 (242) (1997): 88–90.

170 Ibid., p. 90.

171 Albright writes that Dekker's entertainment invites burlesque because of its 'ineffective combination of romantic and supernatural plot elements with the everyday realistic; sudden and somewhat unconvincing repentance of evil characters; a tendency to use miraculously easy resolutions; extreme lyricism, melodious plaints, and an occasional jarring effect in moving from smooth to rocky blank verse, or from verse to prose' (Albright, 'A Stage Cartoon', p. 119).

172 D. F. McKenzie writes that 'if Dekker is alluded to at all, it is more generally' (Mal *Hog*, p. ix); see Fleay, *A Biographical Chronicle of the English Drama, 1559–1642*, 2 vols (London: Reeves and Turner, 1891), ii, pp. 256–7.

173 Albright, 'A Stage Cartoon', p. 119.

174 Ibid., p. 115.

175 Ibid., pp. 115–17.

176 Ibid., p. 118.

177 Ibid., p. 121; Mal *Hog*, p. ix. Kathman notes echoes between the plays' title pages that talk of 'London Prentices' and 'a Company of Young-men' as the players, and the fact that both plays make 'a point of disavowing any topical interpretations' (Kathman, 'London Politics').

178 Ibid., p. 123.

179 Ibid., p. 125.

180 Ibid., p. 125.

181 Kathman ('London Politics') notes, moreover, that 'Cecil had died on 24 May 1612, nine months before the play's performance, and so would not seem to be a natural subject for topical satire'.

182 *A most rare and wonderfull tragedy*, sig. Cvi.

183 Philip Stubbes, *Anatomy of Abuses* (1595 edition), ed. Margaret Jane Kidnie (Tempe: Arizona Center for Medieval and Renaissance Studies, 2002), pp. 64–5.

184 Leggatt, *Citizen Comedy*, p. 26.

185 Virginia Lee Larsen, 'Thomas Middleton as Social Critic: a Study of Three Plays' (PhD Diss. UC Santa Cruz, 1995), pp. 150, 152.

186 Coll 1825, p. 237.

187 1830, p. 1.

188 Irene Mann, 'The Copy for the 1592 Quarto of *The Three Ladies of London*', *Philological Quarterly* 23 (1944): 86–9, p. 89.

189 Irene Mann, 'A Lost Version of *The Three Ladies of London*', PMLA 59 (1944): 586–9.

190 See Stephen Gosson, *Plays Confuted in Five Actions* (1582), sig. Dv–D2–D2v.

191 Mann, 'A Lost Version', p. 587.

192 Nashe, *Pierce Penilesse*, p. 13.

THE THREE LADIES OF LONDON

THE ACTORS' NAMES

[FAME.
LADY LOVE.
LADY CONSCIENCE.
LADY LUCRE.
DISSIMULATION, ⎫
FRAUD,   ⎬ *Lady Lucre's Employees.*   5
SIMONY,   ⎪
USURY,   ⎭
COGGING, *Dissimulation's man.*
SIMPLICITY, *a miller.*   10
MERCADORUS, *an Italian merchant.*
ARTIFEX, *an artisan.*
LAWYER *(called Creticus).*
SINCERITY.
HOSPITALITY.   15
SIR NICHOLAS NEMO.
PETER PLEASEMAN, *a parson.*
GERONTUS, *a Jewish usurer in Turkey*
TOM BEGGAR.
WILY WILL.   20
JUDGE OF TURKEY.
Serviceable DILIGENCE, *a constable.*
BEADLE.
JUDGE NEMO.
CLERK *in Nemo's court.*   25
Crier *in Nemo's court.*
Beadle's men.]

[FAME . . . Beadle's men.]] *this ed.; not in Q, Q2.*

---

9. *COGGING*] i.e. Cheating, Deceiving.
11. *MERCADORUS*] See the note on character names in the introduction, p. 65.
13. *LAWYER*] See the note on character names in the introduction, p. 65.
16. *SIR NICHOLAS NEMO*] i.e. Sir Nicholas Nobody (see the discussion of this character in the introduction).
18. *GERONTUS*] this name seems related to the protagonist of the English 'Ballad of Gernutus'; also important is the fact that the name probably indicates an old man, from the Greek *gerōn.*

PROLOGUE

To sit on honour's seat, it is a lofty reach,
To seek for praise by making brags, oft times doth get a breach.
We list not ride the rolling racks that dims the crystal skies,
We mean to set no glimmering glance before your courteous eyes.
We search not Pluto's pensive pit, nor taste of Limbo lake,   5
We do not show of warlike fight, as sword and shield to shake.
We speak not of the powers divine, ne yet of furious sprites,
We do not seek high hills to climb, nor talk of love's delights.
We do not here present to you the thresher with his flail,
Ne do we here present to you the milkmaid with her pail.   10
We show not you of country toil, as hedger with his bill,
We do not bring the husbandman to lop and top with skill.
We play not here the gardener's part, to plant, to set and sow,
You marvel then what stuff we have to furnish out our show.
Your patience yet we crave a while, till we have trimmed our
    stall,   15
Then young and old, come and behold our wares, and buy them
    all.
Then if our wares shall seem to you well woven, good and fine,
We hope we shall your custom have, again, another time.

FINIS.

---

13. play] *Q*; p ay *Q*2.   14. stuff] *Q*; wares *Q*2.

---

2. *get a breach*] cause a conflict.
3. *list*] desire.
rolling racks] drifting clouds.
4. *glimmering*] 'Here *glimmering* is used in the sense of *glittering*. The phrase thus means "a bright view of Heaven" ' (Mithal, p. 112).
5. *Pluto's pensive pit*] Hades, the underworld.
Limbo lake] abode of the just who died before Christ's coming (used also as general emphasis for the underworld).
9. *flail*] instrument for threshing corn (wheat).
11. *hedger*] gardener who keeps hedges.
bill] pruning tool with a concave blade.
15. *trimmed*] filled out, stocked, decorated.

THE THREE LADIES OF LONDON

[Sc. 1]

Enter FAME, *sounding before* [LADY] LOVE *and* [LADY] CONSCIENCE.

Lady Love. Lady Conscience, what shall we say to our estates? To
    whom shall we complain?
    Or how shall we abridge such fates as heapeth up our pain?
    'Tis Lucre now that rules the rout: 'tis she is all in all,
    'Tis she that holds her head so stout, in fine 'tis she that works
      our fall.
    O Conscience, I fear, I fear a day,   5
    That we by her and Usury shall quite be cast away!
Lady Conscience. Indeed, I fear the worst, for every man doth sue,
    And comes from countries strange and far, of her to have a
      view,
    Although they ought to seek true Love and Conscience clear,
    But Love and Conscience few do like that lean on Lucre's chair.   10
    Men ought be ruled by us, we ought in them bear sway,
    So should each neighbour live by other in good estate alway.
Lady Love. For Lucre men come from Italy, Barbary, Turkey,
    From Jewry: nay, the pagan himself
    Endangers his body to gape for her pelf.   15
    They forsake mother, prince, country, religion, kiff and kin,
    Nay, men care not what they forsake, so Lady Lucre they win,
    That we poor ladies may sigh to see our states thus turned and
      tossed,

Scene 1] *this ed.;* The first Acte. *Q, Coll;* The first Act. *Q2;* THE FIRST ACT. *Haz.*
8. a view] *Q;* view *Q2.*   18. tossed] *this ed.;* tost *Q, Q2.*

0.1. sounding] blowing her trumpet.
  1. *say to our estates*] do about the condition we are in.
  3. *rout*] (1) group, gang (2) civil disturbance.
  4. *stout*] stubbornly, defiantly.
  in fine] to conclude.
  14. *Jewry*] 'The land of the Jews, Judea; sometimes extended to the whole of Pales-
tine' (*OED* 'Jewry' 1).
  15. *to gape . . . pelf*] to greedily look for her money, riches.
  16. *kiff and kin*] i.e. kith and kin, friends and family.

And worse and worse is like to be, where Lucre rules the roost.
Lady Conscience. You say the truth, yet God, I trust, will not admit
    it so,   20
    That Love and Conscience by Lucre's lust shall catch an
    overthrow.
Fame. Good ladies, rest content, and you no doubt shall see
    Them plagued with painful punishment for such their cruelty.
    And if true Love and Conscience live from Lucre's lust
    lascivious,
    Then Fame a triple crown will give, which lasteth aye victorious.   25
Lady Conscience. God grant that Conscience keep within the bounds
    of right,
    And that vile Lucre do not daunt her heart with deadly spite.
Lady Love. And grant, O God, that Love be found in city, town,
    and country,
    Which causeth wealth and peace abound, and pleaseth God
    Almighty.
Fame. But ladies, is't your pleasure to walk abroad a while,   30
    And recreate yourselves with measure, your sorrows to beguile?
Lady Conscience. Pass on, good Fame, your steps do frame, on you
    we will attend,
    And pray to God that holds the rod, our states for to defend.
                                  Exeunt.

---

19. roost] *Haz;* rost *Q, Q2.*   21. That] *Q;* that *Q2.*   23. plagued] *Q;* plagud *Q2.*
27. daunt] *Q, Q2;* haunt *Haz.*

19. *rules the roost*] Hazlitt's emendation of Qq 'rost' gives us a familiar phrase;
some commentators prefer emending to 'roast'. Cf. *Sir Thomas More* 2.1.2–3.
   24. *live from*] avoid.
   25. *triple crown*] 'a splendid three-ti[e]red crown; the phrase is generally used for
the papal crown, but it has general significance as well' (Mithal, p. 112).
   27. *daunt*] subdue, vanquish.
   30. *abroad*] outside.
   31. *measure*] song or dance (here probably dance, since Lady Conscience talks of
Fame's 'steps' at line 32); 'your steps do frame' could also simply mean 'walk ahead'.
   32. *Pass on . . . attend*] Go ahead, show us the dance steps, and we will follow (also
suggesting 'show us how to behave and we will obey').

[Sc. 2]

Enter DISSIMULATION, *having on a farmer's long coat*
and a cap, and his poll and beard painted motley.

Dissimulation. Nay, no less than a farmer, a right honest man,
But my tongue cannot stay me to tell what I am:
Nay, who is it that knows me not by my parti-coloured head?
They may well think, that see me, my honesty is fled.
Tush, a fig for honesty! Tut, let that go,   5
Sith men, women, and children my name and doings do know.
My name is Dissimulation, and no base mind I bear,
For my outward effects my inward zeal do declare,
For men do dissemble with their wives, and their wives with
    them again,
So that in the hearts of them I always remain.   10
The child dissembles with his father, the sister with her brother,
The maiden with her mistress, and the young man with his lover.
There is Dissimulation between neighbour and neighbour,
Friend and friend, one with another,
Between the servant and his master, between brother and
    brother.   15
Then why make you it strange that ever you knew me,
Seeing so often I range throughout every degree?
But I forget my business. I'll towards London as fast as I can,
To get entertainment of one of the three ladies, like an honest
    man.

Scene 2] *this ed.;* The second Acte *Q, Coll; not in Q2;* THE SECOND ACT
Haz. 0.1 SD *poll*] *Q2;* powle *Q.* 2. to] *Q2;* to to *Q.* 13–14. There . . . another,]
so Q; single line in Q2. 17. throughout] *Q2;* thorowout *Q.* 18. business] *Q;*
basenes *Q2.* 19. ladies] *Haz;* Ladies *Q, Q2.*

0.2. *poll*] head.
0.2. *motley*] multi-coloured, patchwork.
2. *stay*] prevent.
3. *parti-coloured*] multi-coloured. See Sidney Thomas, 'A Note on Shakespeare's
Motley', *Shakespeare Quarterly* 10 (1959): 255, who cites this scene's opening stage
direction and lines to rebut Leslie Hotson's 'confident assertion that "motley" and
"parti-coloured" had completely different meanings in Shakespeare's time' (Hotson,
Shakespeare's Motley (New York: Oxford University Press, 1952)).
5. *a fig*] vulgar expression of dismissal, often accompanied by the action of thrusting
the thumb between first and second fingers of the same hand.
let that go] never mind about that.
8. *outward effects*] outer appearances, visible features.
17. *degree*] (1) social status, class (2) type of person.
19. *To get entertainment*] To gain employment.

Enter SIMPLICITY *like a miller, all mealy,*
with a wand in his hand.

Simplicity. They say that there is preferment in London to have.   20
 Mass, an there be, I'll be passing and brave.
 Why, I'll be no more a miller, because the maidens call me
  Dusty-poll,
 One thumps me on the neck, and another strikes me on the noll,
 And you see I am a handsome fellow – mark the comporknance
  of my stature.
 Faith, I'll go seek peradventures, and be a serving creature.   25
Dissimulation. Whither away, good fellow? I pray thee, declare.
Simplicity. Marry, I'll 'clare thee: to London; would thou didst go
 there.
Dissimulation. What if I did? Would it be the better for thee?
Simplicity. Ay, marry should it, for I love honest company.
Dissimulation. Agreed, there is a bargain, but what shall I call thee?   30
Simplicity. 'Cause thou art an honest man, I'll tell thee: my name is
 Simplicity.
Dissimulation. A name agreeing to thy nature – but stay, here comes
 more company.

Enter FRAUD *with a sword and a buckler, like a ruffian.*

Fraud. Huff once aloft, and if I may hit in the right vein,
 Where I may beguile easily without any great pain.

---

20. SP *Simplicity*] Q2; *not in* Q.   that] Q; *not in* Q2.   22. Dusty-poll,] *Haz*; dusty
pole, Q, Q2.   24. comporknance] Q2; comporknaunce Q.   25. peradventures,] Q
2; paradventures, Q.   28. the] Q; *not in* Q2.   32.1. SD *a buckler,*] Q *(a Buckler)*;
buckler Q2; *Buckler Coll*; buckler, *Haz*.

 19.1. a miller] proverbially a simple rustic, clown, probably played by Robert
Wilson himself.
 19.2. wand] stick (perhaps to strike the horse turning the grindstone at the mill).
 21. *Mass*] i.e. By the Mass (a mild oath).
 an] if.
 passing and brave] i.e. passing brave, exceedingly grand.
 22. *Dusty-poll*] Flour-head.
 23. *noll*] head (variously top of the head and back of the head or neck).
 24. *comporknance*] Simplicity's mistake for 'comportment', i.e. deportment,
bearing.
 25. *peradventures*] uncertainty, chance, accident; Simplicity's mistaken rhetorical
version of 'adventures' (French: *Par aventure*).
 26. *Whither away*] Where are you going.
 27. *'clare*] tell (declare to).
 32. *stay*] wait.
 32.1. buckler] small shield.
 ruffian] hoodlum, perhaps with 'ruffianly' long hair.
 33–6. *Huff . . . lash?*] i.e. 'Get myself in a good position, and if things go well, such

I will flaunt it and brave it after the lusty swash,   35
I'll deceive thousands; what care I who lie in the lash?
Dissimulation. What, Fraud? Well met. Whither travellest thou this
          way?
Fraud. To London, to get entertainment there, if I may,
     Of the three ladies: Lucre, Love, and Conscience.
     I care not whom I serve – the devil – so I may get pence.   40
Simplicity. O Fraud, I know thee for a deceitful knave,
     And art thou gotten so bonacion and brave?
     I knew thee when thou dwelledst at a place called Gravesend,
     And the guests knew thee too, because thou wast not their
          friend,
     For when thou shouldst bring reckoning to the guests,   45
     Thou would, but twice so much, and swear it cost thy dame no
          less.
     So thou didst deceive them and thy dame too,
     And because they spied thy knavery, away thou didst go.

---

40. I care not whom I serve – the devil – ... pence.] *this ed.;* I care not whom I serve
(the Devil) ... pence. *Q;* What care I to serve the Devill, ... pence? *Q2.* 42.
bonacion] *this ed.;* baniacion *Q;* boniacion *Q2;* bonfacion *Coll, Haz.* 43. dwelledst] *Q;*
dwelt *Q2.* 45. shouldst ... the guests,] *Q;* wouldst ... thy gesse, *Q2;* guestes
Coll. 46. Thou would, but twice so much,] *Q;* Thou wouldst say twice so much, *Q2;*
Thou would put twice so much *Haz.*

---

that I can easily cheat others without it costing me much effort (or without getting hurt
myself), I will strut and show off in the manner of the feisty swashbuckler; I'll deceive
thousands, what do I care if my actions leave them in the lurch?' This latter phrase is
idiomatic in the period, and 'to run in, or upon the lash' means to be in debt (*OED*
'lash' 4).

42. *bonacion*] a word of uncertain meaning, probably corrupt. Collier's claim that
his emendation 'bonfacion', meaning showy or bombastic in dress, appears in the 1592
edition is incorrect. He was using the Garrick collection copy now in the British
Museum, which has 'boniacion'. 'Bonfacion' is perpetuated by Hazlitt and the *OED*
cites this Victorian neologism as a sixteenth-century word; the reappearance of the
word at 7.7 seems to make it an adverb for how one might 'flatter'. For brief discussion
of debatable words in Wilson plays and the *OED* see Terence P. Logan, 'Robert Wilson
and the *OED*', *N&Q* 15 (1968): 248, who does not correctly attribute this word's
alteration to 'bonfacion' back to Collier.

43. *Gravesend*] Mithal notes that the Swiss traveller Thomas Platter, whose *Travels
in England* was published in 1599, writes that the town of Gravesend had a lot of inns,
thus making Fraud's claim to be a waiter in an inn apt (Mithal, p. 114).

45–6. *For when ... less*] For when you were supposed to bring the guests their bill,
you did, but you charged them double, and swore that you were only covering the
landlady's expenses; Hazlitt's emendation to 'Thou would put twice so much' may well
be correct, the 'b' and 'p' misplaced in compositing.

48. *spied thy knavery*] saw your trickery.

Then thou didst go into Hertfordshire, to a place called Ware,
And because horses stood at hay for a penny a night there,   50
So that thou couldst get nothing that kind of way,
Thou didst grease the horses' teeth, that they should not eat hay,
Then thou wouldst tell the rider his horse no hay would eat.
Then the man would say, 'Give him some other kind of meat'.
'Sir, shall I give him oats, vetches, peas, barley, or bread?'   55
But whate'er thou gavest him, thou stolest three-quarters when
    he was in bed.
And now thou art so proud with thy filching and cozening art,
But I think one day thou wilt not be proud of the rope and the
    cart.
Take a wise fellow's counsel, Fraud: leave thy cozening and
    filching.
Fraud. Thou whoreson rascal swad, avaunt! I'll bang thee for thy
    brawling.   60
How darest thou defame a gentleman that hath so large a living!
Simplicity. A goodly gentleman ostler! I think none of all you will
    believe him.
Fraud. What a clinchpoop drudge is this – I can forbear him no more!
          Let FRAUD *make as though he would strike him,*
          but let DISSIMULATION *step between them.*

---

53. Then ... wouldst] *Q; And wouldst Q2.*   54. Then] *Q; So Q2.*   55. vetches,]
Haz; Fitches, *Q;* fitches, *Q2.*   56. gavest ... stolest] *Q;* gavst ... stolst *Q2.*   58. not]
Q; not in Q2.   62. none ... him.] *Q;* none of you al beleeve him. *Q2.*

---

49. *Ware*] 'This village in the county of Hertfordshire was known for sports involving the maintenance and upkeep of horses. Fraud might, therefore, well have been an
ostler in Ware' (Mithal, p. 114).

50-1. *And because ... way*] And because horses were kept so cheaply there (only
one penny per day), so that you could not make enough money by doing that job
honestly.

54. *meat*] food.

55. *vetches*] cheap beans.

57. *filching and cozening*] stealing and cheating.

58. *the rope ... cart*] the hanging rope and the cart that takes you to the gallows
(or 'carts' you, drives you around for public shaming); cf. *A Knack to Know a Knave*
(1594), 'And in a cart be towed up Holburne hill' (G4).

60. *whoreson*] son of a whore (general abusive epithet).

swad, avaunt!] rustic (clown), be gone!

bang] strike, beat.

brawling] quarrelling noise.

61. *hath so large a living*] is so wealthily maintained.

63. *clinchpoop drudge*] 'a term of contempt for one considered wanting in gentle-
manly breeding' (*OED*); tight-arsed slave.

Dissimulation. My good friend, Fraud, refrain, and care not
    therefore.
    'Tis Simplicity, that patch; he knoweth not good from bad,   65
    And to stand in contention with him, I would think you were
    mad.
    But tell me, Fraud, tell me, hast thou been an ostler in thy days?
Fraud. Tut, I have proved an hundred such ways,
    For when I could not thrive by all other trades,
    I became a squire to wait upon jades.   70
    But then was then, and now is now, but let that pass,
    I am as thou seest me; what care I the devil what I was?
Dissimulation. You say you go to London; in faith, have with you
    then.
Simplicity. Nay, come and go with me, good honest man,
    For if thou go with him, he will teach thee all his knavery.   75
    There is none will go with him that hath any honesty –
    A bots on thy motley beard! I know thee. Thou art
    Dissimulation,
    And hast thou got an honest man's coat to 'semble this fashion?
    I'll tell thee what, thou wilt even 'semble and cog with thine own
    father,
    A couple of false knaves together: a thief and a broker.   80
    Thou makes townsfolks believe that thou art an honest man: in
    the country,
    Thou doest nothing but cog, lie, and foist with Hypocrisy.
    You shall be hanged together, and go alone together for me,
    For if I should go, the folks would say we were knaves all three.

           Enter SIMONY *and* USURY, *hand in hand.*

---

68. Tut] *Q*; Faith *Q*2.   71. but] *Q*; so *Q*2.   81. makes] *Q*; makst *Q*2.   82.
Hypocrisy] *Haz*; hypocrisie *Q*, *Q*2.   83. alone] *Q*, *Q*2; along *Haz.*

---

   64. *care not therefore*] don't worry about that.
   65. *patch*] clown.
   68. *I have . . . ways*] providing a list of past crimes as a type of résumé is a traditional stage villain's activity.
   70. *a squire . . . jades*] i.e. a pimp for whores.
   71. *let that pass*] never mind about that.
   73. *have with you*] off you go.
   77. *bots*] i.e. pox, plague.
   78. *'semble this fashion*] (1) dissemble in this way (2) abuse this apparel.
   79. *cog*] cheat.
   82. *foist*] cheat, practise roguery; steal off, vanish.
   Hypocrisy] 'Doctor Hypocrisy' is mentioned at 11.28 & 30, although he does not
appear in the play.
   83. *alone together for me*] on your own (i.e. without me) as far as I'm concerned.
   84. *knaves*] dishonourable men.

Simony. Friend Usury, I think we are well near at our journey's end,　　85
　　But knowest thou whom I have espied?
Usury.　　　　　　　　　　　　　　No.
Simony.　　　　　　　　　　　　　　　　　Fraud, our great friend.
Usury. And I see another that is now come into my remembrance.
Simony. Who is that?
Usury.　　　　　　　　Marry, Master Davy Dissimulation, a good
　　helper, and our old acquaintance.
Simplicity. Now all the cards in the stack are dealt about,
　　The four knaves in a cluster comes ruffling out.　　　　　90
Simony. What, Fraud and Dissimulation! Happily found out.
　　I marvel what piece a work you two go about.
Fraud. Faith, sir, we met by chance, and towards London are bent.
Usury. And to London we hie, it is our chiefest intent,
　　To see if we can get entertainment of the ladies or no.　　　95
Dissimulation. And for the selfsame matter even thither we go.
Simony. Then we are luckily well met, and seeing we wish all for one
　　thing,
　　I would we our wills and wishing might win.
Simplicity. Yes, they will be sure to win the devil and all,
　　Or else they'll make a man to spew out his gall.　　　　　100
　　O, that vile Usury! He lent my father a little money, and for
　　breaking one day
　　He took the fee-simple of his house and mill quite away:
　　And yet he borrowed not half a quarter so much as it cost;
　　But I think if he had had but a shilling, it had been lost.
　　So he killed my father with sorrow, and undoed me quite.　　105

---

89. stack] *Q*; stocke *Q2*; stock *Coll, Haz.*　　92. a] *Q*; of *Q2*.　　104. if he had had] *Q*;
if it had been *Q2*.　　105. undoed] *Q*; *undid Q2.*

---

90. *ruffling*] swaggering, bearing themselves arrogantly or proudly (*OED* 'ruffle' v².
2).

92. *a*] of.

93. *bent*] headed.

94. *hie*] go.

98. *wills and wishing*] desires.

100. *spew out . . . gall*] puke up his stomach.

101. *breaking one day*] being one day overdue in repayment of the loan.

102. *fee-simple*] absolute possession (including inheritance rights).

103. *he borrowed . . . cost*] he borrowed less than $12\frac{1}{2}$ per cent of those properties'
value.

104. *if he . . . lost*] probably 'if my father had been so poor as only to have a shilling,
Usury would have taken it from him'; possibly 'if my father had borrowed only a shilling, Usury would have taken the fee-simple of the house and mill'.

105. *undoed me quite*] ruined me utterly (by taking away my source of
inheritance).

An you deal with him, sirs, you shall find him a knave full of spite,
And Simony – ay *per se* ay, Simony too: he is a knave for the
    nonce.
He loves to have twenty livings at once,
And if he let an honest man as I am to have one,
He'll let it so dear that he shall be undone,   110
And he seeks to get parsons' livings into his hand,
And puts in some odd dunce that to his payment will stand:
So, if the parsonage be worth forty or fifty pound a year,
He will give one twenty nobles to mumble service once a month
    there.
Simony and Usury both. What rascal is he that speaketh by us such
    villainy?   115
Dissimulation. Sirs, he was at us erewhile too; it is no matter, it is a
    simple soul called Simplicity.

Enter [LADY] LOVE *and* [LADY] CONSCIENCE.

But here come two of the ladies; therefore make ready.
Fraud. But which of us all shall first break the matter?
Dissimulation. Marry, let Simony do it, for he finely can flatter.

---

107. Simony – ay *per se* ay, Simony too:] *this ed.*; Symony I P[er]se I, Symony too Q;
Simon I per se I, Symonie too, Q2; Simony, I per se I Simony, too, Coll; Simony –
A-per-se-A-Simony – too, *Haz.* 115. speaketh] Q; speakes Q2. 117. ladies]
Haz; Ladyes Q; Ladies Q2.

---

107. *ay* per se *ay*] Simplicity seems to be exclaiming or announcing his recognition
of and approbation for Simony. The phrase is a mistake for the more usual 'O per se
O' cryer's announcement, as, for example, in Thomas Dekker's *English Villanies Eight
Severall Times Prest to Death by the Printers* [...] *Discovered by Lanthorne and
Candle-light, and the Helpe of a New Cryer, Called O-Per-Se-O* (1648). Simplicity's
version suggests a reading of 'oh yes, him(self) (i.e. that one), yes', with emphasis on
the repeated character name, Simony; Mithal thinks that the emphasis is on the word
'ay' ('yes') rather than on the character (Mithal, p. 115).
for the nonce] for the purpose.
108–10. *He loves...undone*] Simony practises several professions (or perhaps
earns twenty livings' worth of money from selling church preferments and benefices),
and he permits others only to have their living at such great cost (from extortionate
fees) that they are soon financially ruined.
111–14. *And he...there*] Simony gets control of parishes, places someone in the
role of the parson who will do the job for Simony's small salary; if Simony gets £40
or £50 per year through the parish's tithes and payments to the church, he only gives
twenty nobles (£6 13s 4d) away to have his man do minimum work to keep the job
of parson.
114. *nobles*] gold coins worth 6s 8d (one-third of a pound).
115. *speaketh by us*] accuses us of.
116. *he was...erewhile*] he was railing against us a short while ago.
118. *first break the matter?*] begin, broach the topic?

Usury. Nay, sirs, because none of us shall have pre-eminence above
    other,   120
We will sing in fellowship together, like brother and brother.
Simony. Of troth, agreed, my masters, let it be so.
Simplicity. Nay, an they sing, I'll sing too.

    The Song.
    [*All Men.*] Good ladies, take pity and grant our desire.
    Conscience's Reply. Speak boldly and tell me what is't you
        require.   125
    Their Reply. Your service, good ladies, is that we do crave.
    Her Reply. We like not, nor list not such servants to have.
    Their Reply. If you entertain us, we trusty will be,
        But if you refrain us, then most unhappy.
        We will come, we will run, we will bend at your beck,   130
        We will ply, we will hie, for fear of your check.
    Her Reply. You do feign, you do flatter, you do lie, you do
        prate,
        You will steal, you will rob, you will kill in your hate.
        I deny you, I defy you, then cease of your talking,
        I refrain you, I disdain you, therefore get you walking.   135

Lady Conscience. What, Fraud, Dissimulation, Usury, and Simony,
    How dare you for shame presume so boldly,
    As once to show yourselves before Love and Conscience,
    Not yielding your lewd lives first to repentance?
    Think you not that God will plague you for your wicked
        practices,   140
    If you intend not to amend your vile lives so amiss?
    Think you not God knows your thoughts, words, and works,
    And what secret mischiefs in the hearts of you lurks?
    Then how dare you to offend his heavenly majesty
    With your dissembling deceit, your flattery and your usury?   145

---

124. SP [*All men.*]] *this ed.; not in* Q, Q2.   130. your] *Q;* our Q2.   134. of] *Q;* off
Q2.   140. you for] *Q; not in* Q2.   141. vile lives so amiss] *Q;* lives so far amisse
Q2.   143. the hearts of you] *Q;* your hearts there Q2.   144. to] *Q; not in* Q2.

---

   122. *Of troth*] In faith, truly.
   124–35.] The song of request and denial is 'a sort of ditty common in the plays of
the period. There are similar songs in *Wit and Science*, 11.935 ff., *Nice Wanton*, A4v,
(Iniquitie and Dalila singe), and *The Marriage of Wit and Wisdom*, II.vi. ed. J. S.
Farmer, (1908), (Wisdom and Wit sing.)' (Mithal, p. 115).
   129. *refrain*] refuse, check.
   130. *beck*] indication, command.
   131. *check*] reprimand.
   132. *prate*] chatter.

Fraud. Tut, sirs, seeing Lady Conscience is so scrupulous,
  Let us not speak to her, for I see it is frivolous.
  But what say you, Lady Love, will you grant us favour?
Lady Love. I'll no such servants, so ill of behaviour,
  Servants more fitter for Lucre than Love,   150
  And happy are they which refrain for to prove
  Shameless, pitiless, graceless, and quite past honesty,
  Then who of good conscience but will hate your company?
Usury. Here is scrupulous Conscience and nice Love indeed.
  Tush! If they will not, other will, I know we shall speed.   155
Simplicity. But, lady, I stand still behind, for I am none of their
  company.
Lady Conscience. Why, what art thou? O, I know, thou art
  Simplicity.
Simplicity. I'faith, I am Simplicity, and would fain serve ye.
Lady Conscience. No, I may have no fools to dwell with me.
Simplicity. Why, then Lady Love will you have me then?   160
Lady Love. Ay, Simplicity, thou shalt be my man.
Simplicity. But shall I be your goodman?
Lady Love. Ay, my good man, indeed.
Simplicity. Ay, but I would be your goodman, and swap up a
  wedding with good speed.
Lady Love. No, Love may not marry in any case with Simplicity,   165
  But if thou wilt serve me, I'll receive thee willingly,
  And if thou wilt not, what remedy?
Simplicity. Yes, I will serve ye, but will ye go into dinner, for I am
  hungry?
Lady Love. Come, Lady Conscience, pleaseth you to walk home
  from this company?

---

146. scrupulous] Q2; scrippolous Q; scripolous *Haz.* 147. Let us] Q; I will
Q2. 154. scrupulous] Q2; scripolous Q. 155. other] Q; others Q2. 161. Ay] Q
(I); Yes Q2. 163. Ay] Q *(I);* Yea Q2. 164. good] Q; not Q2. 166. thee] Q; it
Q2. 168. I will] Q; ile Q2. will ye] Q; will you Q2. 169. pleaseth you to] Q;
wil you Q2.

---

146. *scrupulous*] finicky, suspicious in matters of right and wrong.
151. *refrain for to prove*] stop themselves from becoming.
154. *nice*] foolish, fastidious, unwilling, shy.
155. *Tush!*] 'An exclamation of impatient contempt or disparagement' (OED).
speed] succeed.
156. *none*] not one.
162–4. *goodman … good man … goodman*] Simplicity is asking Love to marry
him, and she interprets his first use of 'goodman' as servant (good man) rather than
his intended meaning of 'husband'.
164. *swap up*] quickly carry out.

Lady Conscience. With right goodwill, for their sights pleaseth not
   me.   170
                Exeunt LADY LOVE *and* [LADY] CONSCIENCE.
[Simplicity.] Fraud is the clubbish knave, and Usury the hard-hearted
   knave,
   And Simony the diamond dainty knave,
   And Dissimulation the spiteful knave of spade.
   Come there any more knaves, come there any more?
   I see four knaves stand in a row.   175
            Let FRAUD *run at him, and let* SIMPLICITY *run in,*
                       and come out again straight.
Fraud. Away, drudge! Begone quickly.
Simplicity. I wous, do thrust out my eyes with a lady.   *Exit.*
Usury. Did you ever see gentlemen so 'rated at before?
   But it skills not; I hope one day to turn them both out of door.
Simony. We were arrantly flouted, railed at, and scoffed in our kind.   180
   That same Conscience is a vile terror to man's mind.
   Yet, faith, I care not, for I have borne many more than these
   When I was conversant with the clergy beyond the seas.
   And he that will live in this world must not care what such say,
   For they are blossoms blown down, not to be found after May.   185
Fraud. Faith, care that care will, for I care not a point.

---

170. pleaseth] *Q; likes Q2.* 171. SP [*Simplicity.*]] *Haz;* Fraud *Q, Q2.* 172.
diamond] *Q2;* dyamon *Q.* 177. wous] *Q;* wis *Q2.* lady] *Haz;* Lady *Q, Q2;.*
179. of] *Q;* at *Q2.*

171–2. *clubbish . . . hard-hearted . . . dainty*] rude, rough . . . unsympathetic . . .
fastidious.
171–3. *Fraud is . . . spade*] i.e. all four are knaves of the same pack, related in their
evil.
175.1. *run in . . . straight*] exit and return immediately.
177. *wous*] Apparently Simplicity's mistake for 'wis' (know); Q2 prints 'wis'.
do . . . lady] Mithal has this as Simplicity's mistake for 'throw out my eyes for',
meaning 'to look out for' (*OED* 'eye' n¹. 5. a). Usury's (mock) offended reply in the
next line, however, seems to suit another meaning better: Simplicity is offering Usury
money or is asking Usury to pay for him to get service with a Lady, for 'to put out
one's eyes with gifts' = to bribe (*OED* 'eye' n¹ 3.b). There is also the possibility that 'I
wous, do' is a misreading of 'Ay, would you', thus again asking Usury for help to Lady
Lucre; however, this option does not seem so clearly to prompt Usury's reply about
being ''rated at'.
178. *'rated at*] berated, railed at.
179. *skills not*] doesn't matter.
180. *arrantly flouted . . . kind*] utterly disrespected, insulted, and mocked for our
characters, professions.
186. *a point*] a bit.

I have shifted hitherto, and whilst I live I will jeopard a joint;
And at my death I will leave my inheritor behind,
That shall be of the right stamp to follow my mind.
Therefore let them prate till their hearts ache, and spit out their
    evil.   190
She cannot quail me if she came in likeness of the great devil.
Dissimulation. Mass, Fraud, thou hast a doughty heart to make a
    hangman off,
For thou hast good skill to help men from the coff.
But we were arrantly flouted, yet I thought she had not known
   me,
But I perceive, though Dissimulation do disguise him, Conscience
    can see.   195
What though Conscience perceive it? All the world cannot
    beside.
Tush! There be a thousand places where we ourselves may
    provide.
But look, sirs; here cometh a lusty lady towards us in haste;
But speak to her, if you will, that we may be all placed.

Enter LADY LUCRE.

Usury. I pray thee do, for thou art the likeliest to speed.   200
Dissimulation. Why then I'll to it with a stomach in hope of good
    speed.
Fair lady, all the gods of good fellowship kiss ye – I would say
    bless ye.

---

187. I have . . . joint] Q2; I have shift it hitherto, and whilst I live I will ieobard a
ioynt Q.   192. off] Q; of Q2.   201. to it] Q2(toit); tout Q.   202. – I . . . ye.] *this
ed.;* (I would say blisse ye, Q; (I would say blesse ye) Q2.

---

  187. *jeopard a joint*] put a joint (esp. finger) in jeopardy, thus 'take a risk'.
  189. *right stamp*] appropriate figure (i.e. like me).
  191. *quail*] discourage, scare.
  192. *doughty*] valiant, formidable.
  to make . . . off] This Q1 reading suggests that Fraud is clever enough to avoid or
get rid of the hangman; the next line says that he helps others from the 'coff', which
might be a version of 'cuff', or handcuff, or it might be a version of 'corf', a basket,
which word can also mean 'cage' (*OED* corf 1.b.4), suggesting that Fraud helps people
get out of gaol. The Q2 reading 'to make a hangman of' suggests that Fraud will
improve a hangman's lot (which is more difficult to reconcile with the context), or that
he is 'doughty' enough to be a hangman himself.
  195. *him*] himself.
  196. *All the . . . beside*] No one else can.
  197. *we ourselves . . . provide*] we will be able to make a living.
  199. *placed*] given employment.
  201. *to it with a stomach*] get started, get on with it with gusto.

Lady Lucre. Thou art very pleasant, and full of thy rope-ripe – I
    would say rhetoric.
Dissimulation. Lady, you took me at the worst: I beseech you,
    therefore,
    To pardon my boldness, offending no more.   205
Lady Lucre. We do; the matter is not great, but what wouldest thou
    have?
    How shall I call thee, and what is't thou dost crave?
Dissimulation. I am called Dissimulation, and my earnest request
    Is to crave entertainment for me and the rest,
    Whose names are Fraud, Usury, and Simony,   210
    Great carers for your health, wealth, and prosperity.
Lady Lucre. Fraud, Dissimulation, Usury, and Simony,
    Now truly I thank you for proffering your service to me;
    You are all heartily welcome, and I will appoint straight way
    Where each one in his office in great honour shall stay.   215
    But Usury, didst thou never know my grandmother, the old Lady
    Lucre of Venice?
Usury. Yes, madam, I was servant unto her and lived there in bliss.
Lady Lucre. But why camest thou into England, seeing Venice is a
    city
    Where Usury by Lucre may live in great glory?
Usury. I have often heard your good grandmother tell   220
    That she had in England a daughter, which her far did excel,
    And that England was such a place for Lucre to bide,
    As was not in Europe and the whole world beside.
    Then, lusting greatly to see you and the country, she being dead,
    I made haste to come over to serve you in her stead.   225

---

203. – I . . . rhetoric.] *this ed.;* (I would say Retorick) *Q;* I would say rhetorick *Q2;*
– I . . . rethoric. *Haz.* 206. wouldest] *Q;* wouldst *Q2.* 224. and the country, she]
Q2; the countrey, and she *Q.*

---

   203. *rope-ripe*] Lucre's ironic pun, playing on Dissimulation's previous rhetorical
correction and on rope-ripe's double meaning of (1) rhetorical extravagance, and (2)
readiness ('ripeness') for the hangman's rope.
   204. *you took . . . worst*] Mithal compares *Henry V*'s 'Thou hast me, if thou hast
me, at the worst' (5.2.215–16) as meaning 'caught me at a disadvantage'; this is an
arguable reading, for Henry is overtly saying that Catherine has him at his physical
worst, because, as he says, 'old age . . . can do no more spoil upon my face' (214–15).
Dissimulation may indeed be acknowledging Lady Lucre's superiority in the rhetorical
exchange, but there is also the sense that he is protesting with something like 'you
mistook what I said and (deliberately?) interpreted it badly'; at line 205 he acknowledges his insulting blunder.
   214. *straight way*] immediately.
   222. *bide*] reside.
   225. *stead*] place.

Lady Lucre. Gramercy, Usury, and I doubt not but that you shall
          live here as pleasantly,
     Ay, and pleasanter too, if it may be. But, Simony, from whence
          came ye, tell me?
Simony. My birth, nursery, and bringing-up hitherto hath been in
          Rome, that ancient religious city.
     On a time, the monks and friars made a banquet, whereunto
          they invited me,
     With certain other some English merchants, which belike were of
          their familiarity.   230
     So, talking of many matters, amongst others one began to debate
     Of the abundant substance still brought to that state.
     Some said the increase of their substance and wealth
     Came from other princes, and was brought thither by stealth.
     But the friars and monks, with all the ancient company,   235
     Said that it first came, and is now upholden by me, Simony,
     Which the English merchants gave ear to; then they flattered a
          little too much,
     As Englishmen can do for advantage, when increase it doth touch;
     And being a-shipboard, merry and overcome with drink on a day,
     The wind served, they hoist sail, and so brought me away,   240
     And landing here, I heard in what great estimation you were,
     Made bold to your honour to make my repair.
Lady Lucre. Well, Simony, I thank thee, but as for Fraud and
          Dissimulation,

---

226. and . . . shall] *Q;* doubt not but to *Q2.*   227. Ay] *Q (I); not in Q2.*   229.
whereunto] *Q;* whereto *Q2.*   230. some] *Q; not in Q2.*   234. was] *Q2; not in Q.*
thither] *Haz;* thether *Q, Q2.*   237. English merchants] *Q;* Englishmen *Q2.*   238.
Englishmen] *Q (English mē);* English merchants *Q2.*

---

     226. *Gramercy*] Thanks (French: *Grant* [*grand*] *merci* = great thanks).
     229. *On a time*] Once.
     230. *some*] few.
belike were . . . familiarity] no doubt knew them (or, were known by them).
     232. *substance*] goods, wealth.
     237-8. *English merchants . . . Englishmen*] These terms are in this order in Q1 (and
inverted in Q2); the Q1 order moves from the specific type of Englishmen encountered
to a general comment on the nature of Englishmen, national comments like this lying
at the core of the play.
     237. *gave ear*] listened.
     238. *for advantage, when increase it doth touch*] to benefit themselves, when the
subject is making money.
     240. *served*] blew in a favourable direction.
     241. *in what great estimation*] how well respected.
     242. *make my repair*] present myself.

I know their long continuance, and after what fashion.
Therefore, Dissimulation, you shall be my steward,   245
An office that every man's case by you must be preferred.
And you, Fraud, shall be my rent-gatherer, my letter of leases,
    and my purchaser of land,
So that many old bribes will come to thy hand.
And, Usury, because I know you be trusty, you shall be my
    secretary,
To deal amongst merchants, to bargain and exchange money.   250
And Simony, because you are a sly fellow, and have your tongue
    liberal,
I will place you over such matters as are ecclesiastical,
And though I appoint sundry offices where now you are in,
Yet jointly I mean to use you together ofttimes in one thing.
All. Lady, we rest at your command in aught we can or may.   255
Lady Lucre. Then, Master Davy, to my palace haste thee away,
    And will Crafty Conveyance, my butler, to make ready
    The best fare in my house to welcome thee and thy company.
    But stay, Dissimulation, I myself will go with thee.
    Gentlemen, I'll go before, but pray, in any case,   260
    So soon as ye please resort to my place.
                    Exeunt DISSIM[ULATION] *and* [LADY] LUCRE.
Simony. I warrant you, lady, we will not long absent be.
Usury. Fellow Simony, this fell out pat, so well as heart could wish.
    We are cunning anglers: we have caught the fattest fish.
    I perceive it is true that her grandmother told,   265
    Here is good to be done by use of silver and gold.
    And sith I am so well settled in this country,
    I will pinch all, rich and poor, that come to me.
Simony. And sirrah, when I was at Rome, and dwelt in the Friary,
    They would talk how England yearly sent over a great mass of
        money,   270
    And that this little island was more worth to the Pope

---

252. I] *Q; we Q2.* 253. I] *Q; we Q2.* you] *Q; ye Q2.* 254. I] *Q; we Q2.* 258.
my] *Q; the Q2.* 259. I] *Q; not in Q2.* 260. pray] *Q; see Q2.* 262. I warrant
you] *Q; Doubt not faire Q2.* 265. I perceive] *Q; Certainly Q2.* 267. sith I am] *Q;
seeing we are Q2.* 268. I . . . me] *Q; Rich and poore shall be pincht whosoever come
to me Q2.* 269. And . . . dwelt] *Q; Sirra, being at Rome, and dwelling Q2.*

---

256. *Master Davy*] i.e. Dissimulation (see 2.88).
257. *will*] order.
258. *fare*] hospitality, food.
263. *fell out pat*] worked out suitably.
267. *sith*] since.
268. *pinch*] squeeze, hurt (financially).

Than three bigger realms which had a great deal more scope,
For here were smoke-pence, Peter-pence, and Powle-pence to be
  paid,
Besides much other money that to the Pope's use was made.
Why, it is but lately since the Pope received this fine,   275
Not much more than twenty-six years – it was in Queen Mary's
  time.
But I think England had never known what this gear had meant,
If Friar Austin from the Pope had not hither been sent,
For the Pope, hearing it to be a little island, sent him with a
  great army over,
And winning the victory, he landed about Rye, Sandwich, or
  Dover: 280
Then he erected laws, having the people in subjection,
So for the most part, England hath paid tribute so long.
I, hearing of the great store and wealth in the country,
Could not choose but persuade myself the people loved Simony.
Usury. But stay your talk till some other time; we forget my lady. 285
Simony. Of troth you say true, for she bade us make haste,
But my talk, methought, savoured well, and had a good taste.
                                                  Exeunt ambo.

272. which] Q; that Q2.   276. twenty-six years –] Haz; 26. yeares, Q; 33. yeares
since, Q2.   277. I think] Q; not in Q2.   278. If . . . had not] Q; Had . . . not Q2.
282. So] Q; and Q2.

---

273. *smoke-pence*] William Petty, *A Treatise of Taxes and Contributions* (1662) 'Of
all the accumulative excises, that of hearth-money or smoak-money seems the best' (p.
86) (*OED* 'smoke' n. 11).
  Peter-pence] 'An annual tax or tribute of a penny from each householder having land
of a certain value, paid before the Reformation to the papal see at Rome; also, a similar
tribute paid by several northern lands'; apparently instigated in the late seventh century,
it was discontinued by a statute of 1534 (*OED* 'Peter-penny, Peter's penny' 1).
  Powle-pence] i.e. poll (head)-pence, a poll tax; I retain the Q1 reading, which high-
lights the pun on the names Peter and 'Paul'.
  276. *twenty-six years*] Q2 updates this period to '33. yeares since'.
  277. *gear*] stuff, goings on.
  278. *Friar Austin*] 'Augustine, the prior of the monastery of St. Andrew on the
Caelian hill at Rome, chosen by Pope Gregory the Great as the leader of a mission
which arrived in England in 597 A.D. to convert the country from heathenism to
Christianity'; Mithal also notes that the 'reference to an army is interesting and apparently unique. Since the reference itself seems to be quite serious, one wonders if possibly
it might reflect some piece of folk legend, possibly inspired by anti-Catholic animus'
(Mithal, p. 118).
  280. *Rye, Sandwich, or Dover*] ports on the south coast of England.
  282. *tribute*] tax imposed by one state on another as the fee-payer's admission of
submission and/or payment for maintenance of peace.
  286. *bade*] willed.
  287.1. Exeunt ambo] Leave together.

[Sc. 3]

Enter MERCADORUS *like an Italian Merchant.*

Mercadorus. I judge in my mind-a dat me be not vare far
From da place where dwells my Lady Lucar.
But here come an shentlyman-a, so he do.

Enter DISSIMULATION.

Shentleman, I pray you heartily, let me speak you.
Pray you, do you not know a shentleman dat Master Davy do
call?   5
Dissimulation. Yes, marry, do I; I am he, and what would you
withal?
Mercadorus. Good-a my friend, Master Davy, help me, I pray you
heartily,
For-a some-a acquaintance-a with Madonna Lucar, your lady.
Dissimulation. Sir, upon condition, I will, therefore I would you
should know,
That on me and my fellows you must largely bestow,   10
Whose names are Fraud, Usury, and Simony, men of great credit
and calling,
And to get my lady's goodwill and theirs it is no small thing.
But tell me, can you be content to win Lucre by Dissimulation?

0.1 MERCADORUS] *this ed.;* Mercadore *Q, Q2;* Mercatore *Haz.*   1. I] *Q;* Me *Q2.*
2. da] *Q;* de *Q2.*   3. here] *Q2;* he *Q.*   4. Shentleman ... let] *Q;* Pray ye heartely
signior leta *Q2.*   5. Pray ... call?] *Q;* Pray ye do ye know un shentleman dat meshier
Davie doo call? *Q2.*   6. Yes ... he] *Q;* Yes sir, my selfe am he *Q2;.*   7. Master ... heartily] *Q;* meshier Davie, helpa me pray ye heartely *Q2;* Gooda my friend,
Maister Davy, helpe me, pray you hartely *Coll.*   8. For-a some-a] *this ed.;* for a
sum ma *Q;* for have sum *Q2.*   lady] *Haz;* Lady *Q, Q2.*   9. SP *Dissimulation]*
Coll; not in *Q; catchword provided in Q2 on preceding page, but speech prefix
omitted.*

---

1. *vare*] i.e. very.
3. *shentlyman-a*] i.e. gentleman.
8. *Madonna*] Italian form of address: My Lady, Madam (first OED citation is to
this play's second occurrence, at 3.25).
9. SP *Dissimulation*] Collier supplies this missing prefix. Mithal notes that this
'speech-heading is missing from both the 1584 and 1592 editions' (Mithal, p. 118) and
follows with a lengthy justification for the assignation of 'Dissim.'; Q2 in fact does
provide the catchword 'Dissim.' on B2 but fails to print it at the top of B2v as a speech
prefix.
10. *largely bestow*] bribe, pay off generously.
13. *Dissimulation*] capitalized because Dissimulation is of course referring to himself
as broker of Mercadorus's advancement.

Mercadorus. Ah, good-a my friend, do ax-a me no shush-a question,
    For he dat will live in the world must be of the world sure,   15
    And de world will love his own, so long as the world endure.
Dissimulation. I commend your wit, sir – but here comes my lady.

            Enter [LADY] LUCRE.

Mercadorus. Come hither, here's two, tree crowns for de speak me.
Dissimulation. Well, sir, I thank you. I will go speak for you.
Lady Lucre. Master Davy Dissimulation, what new acquaintance
    have ye gotten there?   20
Dissimulation. Such a one, madam, that unto your state hath great
    care;
    And surely in my mind the gentleman is worthy
    To be well thought on for his liberality, bounty, and great care
    to seek ye.
Lady Lucre. Gentleman, you are heartily welcome. How are you
    called, I pray you tell us?
Mercadorus. Madonna, me be a mershant, and be called Signiore
    Mercadorus,   25
Lady Lucre. But, I pray you, tell me what countryman?
Mercadorus. Me be, Madonna, an Italian.
Lady Lucre. Yet let me trouble ye: I beseech ye, whence came ye?
Mercadorus. For *salva vostra buona grazia*, me come from Turkey.
Lady Lucre. Gramercy, but Signiore Mercadore, dare you not to
    undertake   30
    Secretly to convey good commodities out of this country for my
    sake?
Mercadorus. Madonna, me do for love of you tink no pain too mush,
    And to do anyting for you me will not grush.
    Me will-a forsake-a my fader, moder, king, country, and more
    dan dat;
    Me will lie and forswear meself for a quarter so much as my hat.   35
    What is dat for love of Lucre me dare, or will not do?
    Me care not for all the world, the great devil, nay, make my
    God angry for you.

---

14. do] *Q; not in* Q2. 15. the] *Q;* de Q2. 18. hither] *Q;* hider Q2. two,
tree] *this ed.;* to tree *Q;* too tree Q2. 24. heartily] Q2; hartly *Q.* 29. *salva vostra
buona grazia*] *Haz;* sarva voutra boungrace Q, Q2. 30. to] *Q; not in* Q2. 32. SP
Mercadorus.] Q2; Lucar. *Q.* 34. dan] *Q;* den Q2. 35. meself] *Haz;* me selfe *Q;*
my selfe Q2.

---

29. salva vostra buona grazia] saving (Italian: *salvare*) your good grace.
33. *grush*] i.e. grudge.

Lady Lucre. You say well, Mercadorus, yet Lucre by this is not
    thoroughly won,
    But give ear, and I will show what by thee must be done:
    Thou must carry over wheat, peas, barley, oats, and vetches, and
      all kind of grain,   40
    Which is well sold beyond sea, and bring such merchants great
      gain.
    Then thou must carry beside leather, tallow, beef, bacon, bell-
      metal and everything,
    And for these good commodities trifles to England thou must
      bring,
    As bugles to make baubles, coloured bones, glass, beads to make
      bracelets withal,
    For every day gentlewomen of England do ask for such trifles
      from stall to stall.   45
    And you must bring more, as amber, jet, coral, crystal, and every
      such bauble,
    That is slight, pretty and pleasant, they care not to have it
      profitable.
    And if they demand wherefore your wares and merchandise
      agree,
    You must say jet will take up a straw, amber will make one fat,
    Coral will look pale when you be sick, and crystal will staunch
      blood.   50

---

38. SP *Lady Lucre.*] *Q*2; SP *misaligned to precede line 40 in Q.* thoroughly] *Q*;
throwly *Q*2. 40. vetches] *Haz;* fitches *Q, Q*2. 43. to] *Q;* into *Q*2. 44. baubles]
this ed.; bables *Q, Q*2. 46. bauble] *this ed.;* bable *Q, Q*2; babble *Haz.*

    42. *bell-metal*] 'The substance of which bells are made; an alloy of copper and tin,
the tin being in larger proportion than in ordinary bronze' (*OED*). The *OED* quotes
the Act of 1541 ordering that 'No person . . . should . . . convey anie brasse . . . laten,
bell metall, gun metal . . . into . . . partes beyonde the sea'.
    44. *bugles to make baubles*] A bugle was 'a tube-shaped glass bead, usually black,
used to ornament wearing apparel' (*OED* 'bugle' n^3. 1); a bauble is a toy of little price,
often used to refer to a child's toy.
    47. *they . . . profitable*] the women are not looking for things that are useful or have
cultural value.
    48. *And if . . . agree*] And if they ask you to explain what good your products may
do.
    49. *jet will . . . straw*] Thomas Browne adds a number of other 'Electrick bodies' to
the Ancients' knowledge of jet and amber, which will attract straw when rubbed. See
Thomas Browne's Pseudodoxia Epidemica [1668–69], 2 vols, ed. Robin Robbins
(Oxford: Clarendon Press, 1981), i, ch. 4, p. 116.
    amber . . . fat] probably referring to ambergris, wax-like fatty substance from whale
intestine, used in cookery and perfumery; the resin of amber was known in the period
and, interestingly, is particularly electrified by rubbing.
    50. *coral . . . pale . . . sick*] Browne only cites the questionable use of coral for

So with lying, flattering, and glozing you must utter your ware,
And you shall win me to your will, if you can deceitfully swear.
Mercadorus. Tink ye not dat me have carried over corn, ledar, beef
    and bacon too all tis while,
And brought hedar many baubles dese countrymen to beguile?
Yes, shall me tell you, Madonna? Me and my countrymans have
    sent over   55
Bell-metal for make ordnance, yea, and ordnance itself beside,
Dat my country and oder countries be so well furnished as dis
    country, and has never been spied.
Lady Lucre. Now I perceive you love me, and if you continue in this
    still,
You shall not only be with me, but command me when and
    where you will.
Mercadorus. Lady, for to do all dis, and more for you, me be
    content,   60
But I tink some skall knave will put a bill in da Parliament,
For dat such-a tings shall not be brought here.
Lady Lucre. Tush, Mercadore! I warrant thee, thou needest not to
    fear.
What an one do? There is some other will flatter and say
They do no hurt to the country, and with a sleight fetch that bill
    away.   65
And if they do not so, that by Act of Parliament it be passed,
I know you merchants have many a sleight and subtle cast,
So that you will by stealth bring over great store,

---

54. baubles] *this ed.;* bables *Q, Q*2; babbles *Haz.*   55–6. Yes ... beside] *so Q*2;
single line in Q.   57. oder] *Q;* other *Q*2.

---

securing men's teeth, loosening children's teeth, and for warding off 'fascination' or
spells (Robbins, ed., pp. 435–6).
    crystal will staunch blood] Browne writes, 'Crystall is cold and dry, ... Mathiolus,
Agricola, and many commended it in dysenteries and fluxes; all for the increase of
milke ... Which occult and specificall operations, are not expectable from Ice; for being
but water congealed, it can never make good such qualities' (Robbins, ed., p. 82).
    51. *glozing*] Qq have 'glosing', which Mithal takes to mean 'glossing' or 'giving a
superficial lustre', but the line gives various verbs for deception, thus 'glozing' – talking
smoothly, deceitfully – seems the obvious interpretation.
    utter] sell.
    53. *ledar*] leather.
    61. *skall*] i.e. 'scald', scurvy.
    65. *and with a sleight ... away*] and with trickery, cunning get that bill
withdrawn.
    67. *cast*] a multivalent word: (1) way of doing things, inclination (2) stroke, touch
(3) device, trick (4) skill, art.

And say it was in the realm a long time before.
For being so many of these trifles here as there are at this day,   70
You may increase them at pleasure, when you send over sea.
And do but give the searcher an odd bribe in his hand,
I warrant you, he will let you 'scape roundly with such things in
     and out the land.
But, Signiore Mercadore, I pray you walk in with me,
And as I find you kind to me, so will I favour ye.   75
Mercadorus. Me tank my good lady. But, Master Dissimulation, here
     is for your fellows, Fraud, Usury, and Simony, and say me
     give it dem.   *Exeunt* [LADY] LUCRE *and* MERCADORUS.
Dissimulation. Ay, marry, sir, these bribes have welcome been.
Good faith, I perceive Dissimulation, Fraud, Usury, and Simony
     shall live,
In spite of Love and Conscience, though their hearts it doth
     grieve.
Mass, masters, he that cannot lie, cog, dissemble, and flatter
     nowadays   80
Is not worthy to live in the world, nor in the court to have
     praise.

Enter ARTIFEX, *an Artificer.*

Artifex. I beseech you, good Master Dissimulation, befriend a poor
     man
To serve Lady Lucre, and sure, sir, I'll consider it hereafter, if I
     can.
Dissimulation. What, consider me? Dost thou think that I am a
     bribe-taker?
Faith, it lies not in me to further thy matter.   85
Artifex. Good Master Dissimulation, help me. I am almost quite
     undone,

---

70. are] *Q; is Q2.*   76. Me tank] *Q, Q2; Me tanke you Coll; Me tank you Haz.*
77. welcome] *Q2; not in Q;* [welcome] *Coll.*   78. Usury . . . live] *Q; Symonie and*
Usurie shall live *Q2.*   83. it] *Q; not in Q2.*

72. *searcher*] customs house officer; also applied to 'An official appointed by a guild
or company to resist the violation of its customs and laws, and to prevent the production of work below a certain standard of excellence' (*OED* 'searcher' 2), which reminds
us of Lucre's call for deceptive work and foreshadows events later in this scene when
the artisan Artifex shows his willingness to do shoddy, deceptive work to make a living
under the command of Fraud.
73. *roundly*] completely, thoroughly.
75. *kind*] helpful, good (with probable pun on kind as meaning of the same character; cf. Hamlet's 'a little more than kin and less than kind' (1.2.65)).
84. *consider*] remember, return the favour.
86. *undone*] ruined.

But yet my living hitherto with good Conscience I have won,
But my true working, my early rising, and my late going to bed
Is scant able to find myself, wife and children dry bread,
For there be such a sort of strangers in this country,   90
That work fine to please the eye, though it be deceitfully,
And that which is slight, and seems to the eye well,
Shall sooner than a piece of good work be proffered to sell,
And our Englishmen be grown so foolish and nice,
That they will not give a penny above the ordinary price.   95
Dissimulation. Faith, I cannot help thee, 'tis my fellow Fraud must
     pleasure thee.
Here comes my fellow Fraud, speak to him, and I'll do what I
     can.

Enter FRAUD.

Artifex. I beseech you, be good unto me, right honest gentleman.
Fraud. Why and whereto? What wouldest thou have me do?
Artifex. That my poor estate you will so much prefer,   100
     As to get me to be a workman to Lady Lucre;
     And sir, I doubt not but to please you so well for your pain,
     That you shall think very well of me, if I in her service remain.
Dissimulation. Good fellow Fraud, do so much, for I see he is very
     willing to live,
     And some piece of work to thee for thy pains he will give.   105
Fraud. Well, upon that condition I will, but I care not so much for
     his gifts,
     As that he will by my name declare how he came by his great
        thrifts,
     And that he will set out in every kind of thing
     That Fraud is a good husband, and great profit doth bring.
     Therefore, the next piece of work that thou dost make,   110
     Let me see how deceitful thou wilt do it for my sake.

87. good] *Q; not in Q2.* 99. wouldest] *Q;* wouldst *Q2.* 100. poor] *Q; not in Q2.* 110. dost] *Q;* doest *Q2.*

89. *scant*] hardly.
90. *strangers*] foreigners.
93. *proffered*] offered.
94. *nice*] simple, silly.
95. *That they ... price*] They will not pay a fair amount (i.e. more than the cheap, 'ordinary' foreigners' prices) for good English work.
100. *That my ... prefer*] That you raise my meagre situation through your recommendation.
102. *please you ... pain*] pay you back, return the favour for your effort.
109. *husband*] manager, caretaker.

Artifex. Yes sir, I will, sir, of that be you sure,
    I'll honour your name, while life doth endure.
Dissimulation. Fellow Fraud, here comes a citizen, as I deem.
Fraud. Nay, rather a lawyer, or some pettifogger he doth seem.   115

                    Enter a LAWYER [called Creticus].

Lawyer. Gentlemen, my earnest suit is to desire ye,
    That unto your lady's service you would help me,
    For I am an attorney of the law, and pleader at the bar,
    And have a great desire to plead for Lady Lucre.
    I have been earnest, sirs, as is needful in such a case,   120
    For fear another come before me, and obtain my place.
    I have pleaded for Love and Conscience till I was weary,
    I had many clients, and many matters that made my purse light,
        and my heart heavy.
    Therefore let them plead for Conscience that list for me;
    I'll plead no more for such as brings nothing but beggary.   125
Dissimulation. Sir, upon this condition, that you will keep men in
        the law
    Ten or twelve years for matters that are not worth a straw,
    And that you will make an ill matter seem good and firmable
        indeed,
    Faith, I am content for my part you shall speed.
Fraud. Nay, fellow, thou knowest that Simony and Usury hath an ill
        matter in law at this time;   130
    Now, if thou canst handle the matter so subtle and fine,
    As to plead that ill matter good and firmable at the bar,
    Then thou shalt show thyself worthy to win Lady Lucre.
    Therefore tell me if you can and will do it or no.
    If you do it, be sure to get my lady's goodwill, ere you go.   135
Dissimulation. By my honesty, well remembered, I had quite forgot;
    'Tis about that a fortnight ago fell out the matter I wot.
Lawyer. Tush, sir, I can make black white, and white black again,

---

115. pettifogger] *Haz;* petty fogger *Q, Q2.*   116. Gentlemen] *Q;* Gentleman *Q2.*
120. sirs] *this ed.;* Sir *Qq.*   125. brings] *Q;* bring *Q2.*   127. that are] *Q; not in*
Q2.   134. can and will] *Q, Q2;* can or will *Haz.*   137. that] *Coll, Haz;* that, *Q,*
Q2.

---

   115. *pettifogger*] mean, rascally practising lawyer.
   124. *that list for me*] who care to do for me I care; who want to instead of me
   128. *firmable*] This is the only instance of this word recorded in the *OED,* which
interprets it as '?worthy to be ratified'; 'firm' as a verb can mean 'ratify', but perhaps
the sense of 'settling' (*OED* 'firm' v. 5. a) or winning the suit is most appropriate.
   136. *wot*] know.

Tut, he that will be a lawyer must have a thousand ways to feign,
And many times we lawyers do one befriend another,   140
And let good matters slip. Tut, we agree like brother and
    brother.
Why, sir, what shall let us to wrest and turn the law as we list,
Seeing we have them printed in the palms of our fist?
Therefore doubt you not, but make bold report,
That I can and will plead their ill cause in good kind of sort.   145
Fraud. Of troth, how likest thou this fellow, Dissimulation?
Dissimulation. Marry, I like him well, he is a cunning clerk, and one
    of our profession.
But come, sir, go with us, and we will prefer you.
Artifex. Good Master Fraud, remember me.
Fraud. Leave thy prating. I will, I tell thee.   150
Artifex. Good Master Dissimulation, think on me.
Dissimulation. Thou art too importunate and greedy.
Fraud. Come after dinner, or some other time when we are at leisure.
            Exeunt DISSIM[ULATION], FRAUD, *and* LAWYER.
Artifex. Come after dinner, or some other time – I think so indeed,
For full little do they think of a poor man's need.   155
These fellows will do nothing for pity and love,
And thrice happy are they that hath no need them to prove.
God, he knows the world is grown to such a stay,
That men must use Fraud and Dissimulation too, or beg by the
    way.
Therefore I'll do as the most doth, the fewest shall laugh me to
    scorn,   160
And be a fellow amongst good fellows to hold by St Luke's
    horn.   *Exit.*

---

139. be] Q2; qe *(turned 'b')* Q.   145. can] Q2; came, Q.   153. SD *Exeunt . . .* LAWYER] *this ed.;* Dsssim [*sic*] Fraud. and Lawyer exeunt. Q; Dissim. Fraud
and Lawyer exeunt. Q2; Dissimulation, Fraud, and Lawyer exeunt. *Haz.*   154. I think
so] Q; *not in* Q2.

---

141. *let good matters slip*] turn a blind eye to things.
142. *let us to wrest and turn*] hinder us in twisting and turning.
145. *can and will*] This is a familiar phrase from Q2, and it responds to Fraud's use
of the same phrase at line 134; Q1 has 'came and will'.
147. *profession*] i.e. he 'professes' dissimulation and fraud; cf. note to 16.15 and
the use of 'profession' to suggest deceit throughout Marlowe's *The Jew of Malta.*
150. *prating*] babbling.
152. *importunate*] troublesome, persistent.
157. *them to prove*] to put Dissimulation and Fraud to the test.
158. *stay*] condition, state of impasse, immovable difficulty.
161. *by St Luke's horn*] a mild oath, swearing blasphemously by the horn of power
and salvation found in Luke 1:69.

[Sc. 4]

Enter SIMPLICITY *and* SINCERITY.

Sincerity. Good Cousin Simplicity, do somewhat for me.

Simplicity. Yes, faith, Cousin Sincerity, I'll do anything for thee.
> What wouldst thou have me do for thee, canst tell that?
> Mass, I cannot tell what shouldst do for me, except thou
>   wouldst give me a new hat.

Sincerity. Alas! I am not able to give thee a new.   5

Simplicity. Why, I marvel then how thou dost do:
> Dost thou get thy living amongst beggars, from door to door?
> Indeed, Cousin Sincerity, I had thought thou wast not so poor.

Sincerity. Nay, Cousin Simplicity, I got my living hardly, but yet I
>   hope just,
> And with good conscience too, although I am restrained from
>   my lust.   10
> But this is it, Cousin Simplicity, I would request you to do for
>   me,
> Which is, to get Lady Love's and Lady Conscience's hand to a
>   letter,
> That by their means I may get some benefice, to make me live
>   the better.

Simplicity. Yes, I'll do so much for thee, cousin, but hast thou any
>   here?

Sincerity. Ay, behold, they are ready drawn, if assigned they were.   15

Let SIMPLICITY *make as though he read it,*
and look quite over; meanwhile let [LADY] CONSCIENCE *enter.*

Simplicity. Let me see, cousin, for I can read.
> Mass, 'tis bravely done, didst thou it indeed?

---

1. somewhat] *Q*; something *Q*2.   3. What . . . that?] *Q*2; What wouldst for me do
for thee canst tell that? *Q*; What wouldst for me to do for thee? canst tell that? *Haz.*
6. I marvel then] *Q*; then I marvell *Q*2.   6–7. dost] doest *Q, Q*2.   11. is it] *Q*; it
is *Q*2.   to] *Q; not in Q*2.

1–8.] For the apparent difficulty of the speech prefixes here see the introduction.

4. *for me*] i.e. in return for whatever favour I grant.

9. *hardly*] with difficulty.

10. *restrained from my lust*] denied my wish, desire.

12. *hand*] signature.

13. *benefice*] good deed, favour.

15. *drawn . . . assigned*] drawn up, written . . . signed.

15. SD–17] The joke would seem to be that Simplicity cannot in fact read, and the
direction and lines that follow suggest comic stage business where Simplicity transpar-
ently attempts to cover up his ignorance.

17. *bravely*] excellently.

Mistress Conscience, I have a matter to bequest you to.
Lady Conscience. What is't? I doubt not but 'tis some wise thing, if
    it be for you.
Simplicity. Marry, my cousin Sincerity wad besire to 'scribe these
    papers here,   20
    That he may get some preferment, but I know not where.
Lady Conscience. Be these your letters? What would you have me
    do, and how shall I call ye?
Sincerity. Lady, my name is Sincerity.
Lady Conscience. And from whence came ye?
Sincerity. I came from Oxford, but in Cambridge I studied late;   25
    Having nothing, thought good, if I could, to make better my
    state.
    But if I had, instead of divinity, the law, astronomy, astrology,
    Physiognomy, palmistry, arithmetic, logic, music, physic, or any
    such thing,
    I had not doubted, then, but to have had some better living.
    But divines that preach the word of God sincerely and truly   30
    Are in these days little or nothing at all set by.
    God grant the good preachers be not taken away for our
    unthankfulness.
    There was never more preaching and less following, the people
    live so amiss.
    But what is he that may not on the Sabbath day attend to hear
    God's word?
    But we will rather run to bowls, sit at the alehouse, than one
    hour afford,   35
    Telling a tale of Robin Hood, sitting at cards, playing at kettles,
    or some other vain thing,
    That I fear God's vengeance on our heads it will bring.
    God grant amendment. But Lady Conscience, I pray,
    In my behalf unto Lucre do what ye may.

---

20. wad besire] *Q, Q2; wad desire Coll, Haz.*   24. came] *Q2; come Q.*   25. studied
late] *Q2; not in Q.*   31. at all] *Q; not in Q2.*   36. kettles] *this ed.; kettels Q, Q2;*
skittles *Haz.*   37. our heads] *Q; your head Q2.*

---

18. *bequest*] Simplicity's mistake for 'request'.
19. *I doubt . . . thing*] I'm sure it's some wise request (said ironically).
20. *wad besire*] Simplicity's mistake for 'would require'.
28. *physic*] medicine.
31. *set by*] regarded, respected.
35. *bowls*] bowling, perhaps referring to alley-bowling with skittles.
36. *Robin Hood*] Nottingham folk hero of the Middle Ages and Renaissance.
kettles] skittles (*OED* earliest citation is 1649).

Simplicity. Mass, my cousin can say his book well. I had not thought
    it.   40
    He's worthy to have a benefice, an it will hit.
Lady Conscience. God be blessed, Sincerity, for the good comfort I
    have of thee.
    I would it lay in us to pleasure such, believe me.
    We will do what we can, but *ultra posse non est esse*, you know,
    It is Lucre that hath brought us poor souls so low.   45
    For we have sold our house, we are brought so poor,
    And fear by her shortly to be shut out of door.
    Yet to subscribe our name we will with all our heart;
    Perchance for our sakes something she will impart.
    Come hither, Simplicity, let me write on thy back.   50
Simplicity. Here is the right picture of that fellow that sits in the
    corner.

        Enter HOSPITALITY *while she is a-writing.*

Hospitality. Lady, methinks you are busy.
Lady Conscience. I have done, sir. I was setting my hand to a letter
    to Lucre for our friend Sincerity,
    But I would Lady Love were here too.
Hospitality. She is at home with me, but, if you please, so much in
    her behalf I will do.   55
Lady Conscience. I pray you heartily, and it shall suffice the turn
    well enough.
    Good Simplicity, once more thy body do bow.
Simplicity. I think I shall serve to be a washing-block for you.

---

49. sakes] *Q;* sake *Q2.*   55. if you please . . . I will do] *Q;* if it please you . . . ile doo
Q2; if it please, . . . I will do *Haz;* if it please, . . . I will doo *Coll.*   56. you] *Q2; not
in Q.*   enough] *this ed.;* inow *Q, Q2;* enou' *Haz.*   58. I shall serve] *Q;* youle make
me serve *Q2.*

    40. *say his book*] (1) preach (2) be a scholar.
    41. *an it will hit*] if the plan succeeds.
    43. *lay in us to pleasure such*] were in our power to help people such as you.
    44. ultra posse non est esse] Latin: we cannot do more than is in our power.
    50. *write on thy back*] i.e. use your back as a writing table.
    51. *that fellow*] perhaps referring insultingly and clownishly to an audience member;
Mithal thinks Simplicity is simply referring to himself (p. 122).
    53. *setting my hand to*] signing.
    54. *would*] wish.
    57. *bow*] bend, to be a writing table again.
    58. *washing-block*] 'a wooden block or board on which clothes are beaten while
being washed' (*OED* 'washing' III.9.a).

I would do it for you, but I am afraid yonder boy will mock me.
Hospitality. No, I warrant thee.   60
Lady Conscience. Here, take thy letters, Sincerity, and I wish them
    prosperous to thee.
Sincerity. I yield you most hearty thanks, my good lady.
Hospitality. Lady Conscience, pleaseth it you to walk home to dinner
    with me?
Lady Conscience. I give you thanks, my good friend Hospitality;
    But I pray you, sir, have you invited to dinner any stranger?   65
Hospitality. No, sure; none but Lady Love, and three or four honest
    neighbours.
Simplicity. Mass, my lady is gotten to dinner already;
    I believe she rose at ten o'clock, she is so hungry –
    What, an I should come to dinner: hast thou any good cheer?
Hospitality. I have bread and beer, one joint of meat, and welcome,
    thy best fare.   70
Simplicity. Why, art thou called Hospitality, and hast no better cheer
    than that?
    I'll tell thee, if thou hast no more meat for so many, they'll ne'er
    be fat.
    What, if my cousin – nay, I myself alone – to dinner should
    come?
    Where should my lady and the rest dine, for I could eat up every
    crumb?
    Thou art an old miser; dost thou keep no better fare in thy
    house?   75
    Hast no great bag pudding, nor hog's face that is called souse?
Hospitality. My friend, hospitality doth not consist in great fare and
    banqueting,

---

59. but I am] *Q;* but am Q2. 60. I] *Q;* ile Q2. 61. I wish them prosperous] *Q;*
prosperous be they Q2. 63. to dinner] *Q;* and dine Q2. 64. I give you] *Q; not in*
Q2. 65. I pray you] *Q;* tell me Q2; I pray, sir *Coll, Haz.* 69. hast thou] *Q;* is there
Q2. 70. I have] *Q;* Theres Q2. 72. I'll tell thee, if] *Q;* Faith and Q2. 73. I] *Q;*
not in Q2. 74. could] *Q;* would Q2.

---

59. *yonder boy*] Cf. line 51, perhaps referring to another audience member; however,
Hospitality's reply suggests the line is directed at him, and Mithal notes that 'Hospital-
ity is an old man and the statement of Simplicity is intended to be a clown's joke'
(Mithal, p. 122).

67–8. *dinner...ten o'clock*] Simplicity supposes that Lady Conscience craves
dinner, a meal eaten at midday, because she rose from bed only at ten o'clock, and
therefore, presumably, missed breakfast and has not yet eaten.

70. *fare*] food (with regard to its quality).

76. *bag pudding*] pudding (stomach, entrails, minced meat, seasoning, oatmeal)
boiled in a bag.

souse] pickled parts of a pig, especially feet and ears.

But in doing good unto the poor, and to yield them some
    refreshing.
Therefore, if thou and Sincerity will come and take part,
Such as I have I'll give you with a free and willing heart.   80
          Exeunt HOSPITALITY *and* [LADY] CONSCIENCE.
Simplicity. He speaks well, cousin; let's go to dinner with him.
    The old man shall not think but we will pleasure him.
    Faith, he might have richer fellows than we to take his part,
    But he shall never have better eating fellows, if he would swelt
        his heart.
    Here be them that will eat with the proudest of them.   85
    I am sure my mother said I could eat so much as five men.
    Nay, I have a gift for eating, I tell ye,
    For our maids would never believe I put all the meat in my belly.
    But I have spied a knave, my Lady Lucre's cogging man.
    Give me your letters, cousin; I'll prefer ye, if I can.   90

          Enter DISSIMULATION.

Sincerity. Dissimulation! Out upon him! He shall be no spokeman
    for me.
Simplicity. Why then you are a fool, Cousin Sincerity.
    Give me 'em, I tell ye, I know he'll do it for me.
Sincerity. Seeing thou wilt have it, here receive it, but yet it grieves
    my heart
    That this dissembling wretch should speak on my part.   95
Simplicity. Hear ye, sir. I would bequest to 'liver this letter
    To your good wholesome mistress, Lady Lucre.
Dissimulation. Where hadst thou it, tell me?
Simplicity. Marry, of my Cousin Sincerity.
Dissimulation. Why, I have nothing to do in it; 'tis not to me thou
    shouldst come.   100
    I have not to do with Sincerity's matters; 'tis my fellow Simony's
    room.

---

80. I have] *Q; there is Q2.* 83. than we] *Q; not in Q2.* 86. I am sure] *Q; For
Q2.* so] *Q; as Q2.* 87. Nay . . . ye] *Q;* Nay I am sure the gift of eating is given to
me *Q2.* 89. I have spied] *Q;* yonder comes *Q2.* 90. ye] *Q;* you *Q2.* 93. Give . . .
ye] *Q;* Give me am then, for *Q2.* 94. yet] *Q; not in Q2.* 96. bequest] *Q;* request
Q2; request [you] *Haz.* 100. shouldst] *Q;* should *Q2.*

---

84. *swelt . . . heart*] 'to exert oneself to the uttermost' (*OED* 'swelt' II.7).
89. *cogging*] cheating (and the name of Dissimulation's servant).
91. *spokeman*] spokesman, representative.
96. *bequest*] Simplicity's mistake for 'request'.
'liver] i.e. deliver.
100. *in*] with.

Sincerity. Thou art akin to the lawyer: thou wilt do nothing without
    a fee;
But thou, Fraud, Usury, nor yet Simony, shall have nothing of me.
An thou wilt do it, do it; an thou wilt not, choose,
Both thee and their dealing I hate and refuse.   105
Dissimulation. Why, and I am not bound to thee so far as knave go,
And therefore, in despite of thee and thy cousin, there thy letters
    be.
What, thinkest thou by captious words to make me do it?
Let them deliver your letters that hath a stomach to it.
Simplicity. Faith, cousin, he's such a testern and proud, 'sembling
    knave,   110
That he'll do nothing, 'less some bribery he have.
There's a great many such promoting knaves, that gets their
    living
With nothing else but facing, lying, swearing, and flattering.
Why, he has a face like a black dog, and blusheth like the back-
    side of a chimney.
'Twas not for nothing thy godfathers a cogging name gave thee.   115

            Enter LADY LUCRE.

But here comes his mistress, Lady Lucre.
Now, cousin, I'll 'liver your letter.
Mistress Lady Lucre, here's a letter for ye.
Lady Lucre. Hast thou a letter for me?
Simplicity. Ay, by St Mary –   120
How say you, cousin? She reads your letter:
An you can flatter, perhaps you shall speed better.
Sincerity. Thou speakest the truth, Simplicity, for flatterers nowadays
Live gentlemen-like, and with prating get praise.

---

103. have nothing of] *Q2;* do nothing for *Q.*   108. thinkest] *Q;* thinkst
Q2.
110. proud, 'sembling] *Q;* semblation *Q2.*   120. Ay] *Q (I);* Yes *Q2.*   123. speakest]
Q; speakst *Q2.*

---

108. *captious*] fault-finding, carping.
109. *a stomach to it*] a taste for it.
110. *testern*] perhaps *testy, irritable,* but *OED* suggests it is a form of 'tester', which
does not entirely fit here, although a tester could refer to a debased coin (teston) of
Henry VIII; also one who tests or proves a situation (*OED* 'tester'[4] a.), hence perhaps
a difficult person.
    'sembling] i.e. dissembling.
111. *'less*] i.e. unless.
112. *gets*] makes.
114. *a face ... chimney*] a version of the proverbial phrase 'to blush like a black
dog', i.e. to have no shame and not be able to blush; cf. Tilley D507.

Lady Lucre. Sir, I have read the tenure of your letter, wherein I find   125
  That at the request of Love and Conscience I should show
   myself kind
  In bestowing some spiritual living on ye, parsonage, or benefice.
  It seems it stands greatly in need, as appears by this,
  And, trust me, I would do for you, but it lies not in me,
  For I have referred all such matters to my servant Simony.   130
  You must speak to him, and if you can get his goodwill,
  Then be sure of mine, their minds to fulfil.
Sincerity. Lady, I shall never get his goodwill, because I want ability,
  For he will do nothing, except I bring money.
  And if you grant it not, then 'tis past all doubt,   135
  I shall be never the better, but go quite without.
Dissimulation. Madam, I can tell you what you may give,
  Not hurting yourself, whereby he may live,
  And without my fellow Simony's consent,
  If to follow my mind you are any whit bent.   140
Lady Lucre. Pray thee, what is it? For thou knowest, while for their
  house I am in bargaining,
  An it be never so little, I must seem to do something.
Dissimulation. Why, have not you the parsonage of St Nihil to
  bestow?
  If you give him that, Simony shall never know.
Lady Lucre. Indeed, thou sayest true. Draw near, Sincerity.   145
  Lo, for their sakes I will bestow frankly on thee.
  I'll give thee the parsonage of St Nihil to pleasure them withal,
  And such another to it, if thou watch till it fall.

---

127. In bestowing] *Q*; And bestow *Q*2.   128. It seems it stands] *Q*; For you stand
*Q*2.   129. I] *Q*; *not in Q*2.   130. For . . . matters] *Q*; For all such matters are
referred *Q*2.   133. because I want] *Q*; for want of *Q*2.   134. I] *Q*; one *Q*2.   135. 'tis]
Q; it is *Q*2.   137. I can] *Q*; ile *Q*2.   141. in] *Q*; *not in Q*2.   145. Indeed, thou
sayest true] *Q*; Thou saiest true indeed *Q*2.   147. I'll . . . Nihil] *Q*; The parsonage of
saint Nihil ile give thee *Q*2.

125. *tenure*] tenor, main theme.
133. *want*] lack.
134. *except*] unless.
140. *any whit bent*] at all inclined.
143. *St Nihil*] i.e. Saint Nothing (as Sincerity points out at line 159)
146. *frankly*] freely, liberally.
148. watch . . . fall] not entirely clear: perhaps 'wait until it becomes vacant, comes
to pass' (as in 'falls to you'), which of course 'St Nihil' never will; or (again ironically)
'watch until it collapse'.

Simplicity. My lady axes you when you will take possession of your
    house, and lend the rest of the money.
Lady Lucre. What, are they so hasty? Belike they spent it merrily.   150
Simplicity. Faith, no; for they would eat it, if they could get it, when
    they are a-hungry.
    (*Speaking to Sincerity*) But you may be happy, for you have sped
    well today;
    You may thank God and good company that you came this way.
    The parsonage of St Michael's; by'r Lady, if you have nothing
    else,
    You shall be sure of a living, beside a good ring of bells.   155
    Cousin, I'll tell thee what thou shalt do: sell the bells, and make
    money.
Sincerity. Thou mayest well be Simplicity, for thou showest thy folly.
    I have a parsonage, but of what? Of St Nihil, and Nihil is
    nothing,
    Then, where is the church, or any bells for to ring?
    Thou understandest her not; she was set for to flout.   160
    I thought, coming in their names, I should go without.
    'Tis easy to see that Lucre loves not Love and Conscience,
    But God, I trust, will one day yield her just recompense.
Simplicity. Cousin, you said that something to me you would give,
    When you had gotten preferment of Lucre to live,   165
    And I trust you will remember your poor cousin Simplicity –
    You know to Lady Conscience and e'rybody I did speak for you.
Sincerity. Good Simplicity, hold thy peace; my state is yet nought.
    I will help thee, sure, if ever I get aught.

---

152. *(Speaking to* SINCERITY*)*] *at end of line in* Q, Q2.   154. St Michael's] S. Michels
Q, Q2.   158. but of what?] Q2; but what Q.   163. trust] Q2; ttust Q.

---

  149. *My lady . . . money*] Lady Lucre will take the house that Love and Conscience
live in as collateral for a loan that Lady Conscience receives between scenes 4 and 5.
    axes] Simplicity's mistake or rusticism for 'ask'.
  150. *merrily*] carelessly, prodigally.
  154. *St Michael's*] Qq have 'S. Michels'. In an interesting note, Mithal writes that
Simplicity is 'deliberately misconstruing' 'Nihil' (nothing) for 'mickle' (much) and
turning that word into the Saint's name, Michael, to encourage Sincerity to pay him
for his pains (Mithal, pp. 123–4); the pun is convincing, but whether Simplicity is doing
this deliberately or ignorantly remains open to question.
    by'r Lady] i.e. an oath, swearing 'By Our Lady'.
  155. *ring of bells*] a set, a peal of bells.
  156. *sell the bells*] i.e. for the value of the metal; bell-metal could be used to make
armaments (Mercadorus tells Lady Lucre he has shipped out of England 'Bell-metal for
make ordnance' (3.56)).
  160. *set for to flout*] predetermined to mock.
  168. *yet*] still, at this point.

But here comes Sir Nicholas Nemo; to him I will go,   170
And see if for their sakes he will anything bestow.

Enter SIR NICHOLAS NEMO.

Nicholas Nemo. You come from Love and Conscience, as seemeth
 me here,
 My special good friends, whom I account of most dear;
 And you are called Sincerity, your state shows the same.
 You are welcome to me for their sakes, and for your own name,   175
 And for their sakes you shall see what I will do for you,
 Without Dissimulation, Fraud, Usury, or Simony;
 For they will do nothing without some kind of gain,
 Such cankered corruption in their hearts doth remain.
 But come in to dinner with me, and when you have dined,   180
 You shall have –   *Presently go out.*
Sincerity. You shall have – but what? A living that is blown down
 with the wind.
Simplicity. Now, cousin, dismember your friends, seeing two livings
 you have:
 One that this man promised, and another that Lady Lucre gave.
 Mass, you'll be a jolly man, an you had three or four more;   185
 Let's beg apace, cousin, and we shall get great store.
 Do thou get some more letters, and I'll get them 'scribed of
  Mistress Love and Conscience,
 And we'll go beg livings together; we'll beg no small pence.
 How sayest thou, Cousin Sincerity? Wut do so mich?
 If we can speak fair and 'semble, we shall be plaguey rich.   190
Sincerity. Good Simplicity, content thee: I am never the better for
 this,
 I must of force leave off, for I see how vain it is.
 It boots not Sincerity to sue for relief;

---

187. 'scribed] *this ed.;* scribed Q, Q2.   189. Sincerity] *Q; not in* Q2.   192. I must
of force] *Q;* But of force must Q2; But must of force *Coll, Haz.*   193. It boots not
Sincerity to sue] *Q;* Nor bootes it Sinceritie to looke Q2.

---

 170. *Sir Nicholas Nemo*] See the discussion of this character in the introduction.
Mithal considers this 'Nemo' and Judge Nemo the same character in two roles; I take
them to be two characters related in kind but not in personal identity.
 179. *cankered*] diseased, ulcerated.
 183. *dismember*] Simplicity's mistake for 'remember'.
 186. *apace*] with speed.
 187. *'scribed of*] i.e. ascribed by (signed, not written).
 189. *Wut do so mich?*] Would you do so much?
 190. *plaguy*] extremely (cf. expressions like 'stinking rich' and 'filthy rich').
 193. *boots*] benefits, does any good for.
 sue] petition.

So few regard, that to me is a grief.
This was Nicholas Nemo, and No-Man hath no place;   195
Then how can I speed well in this heavy case?
If no man bid me to dinner, when shall I dine?
Or how shall I find him? Where, when, and at what time?
Wherefore the relief I have had, and shall have, is small;
But to speak truth, the relief is nothing at all.   200
But come, Simplicity, let us go see what may be had.
Sincerity in these days was, sure, born to be sad.
Simplicity. Come, let's go to dinner, cousin, for the gentleman, I
    think, hath almost dined.
But, an I get victuals enough, I warrant you, I will not be behind.
Sincerity. What if thou canst not get it, then how wilt thou eat?   205
Simplicity. Marry, on this fashion, with both hands at once; ye shall
    see when I get meat.
Sincerity. Why, his name was Nemo, and Nemo hath no being.
Simplicity. I believe, cousin, you be not hungry, that you stand
    prating.
Faith, I'll go do him a pleasure, because he hath need;
Why, an he will needs have meat eat, 'a shall see how I'll feed.   210
I believe he will not bid me come again to him;
Mass, an he do, 'a shall find a fellow that has his eating.
                                        Exeunt ambo.

[Sc. 5]

                    Enter USURY *and* [LADY] CONSCIENCE.

Usury. Lady Conscience, is there anybody within your house, can
    you tell?
Lady Conscience. There is nobody at all, be ye sure, I know certainly
    well.
Usury. You know, when one comes to take possession of any piece
    of land,

195. No-Man] *Haz;* no man *Q, Q2.*   196. heavy] *Q;* kind of *Q2.*   199. I have had,
and shall have] *Q;* had and to be had *Q2.*   204. an I] *Q (and I);* if I *Q2;* and I do
Haz.   victuals] *Haz;* vittals *Q;* vittels *Q2.*   I warrant ... I will] *Q;* ile warrant ... ile
Q2; I'll warrant ... I will *Haz.*   210. he will] *Q;* hele *Q2.*

206. *Marry, on this fashion*] By Mary (a mild oath), in this manner.
210. *eat*] (pronounced 'et') eaten.
'*a*] he.

3–4. *when one ... stand*] Mithal cites Holdsworth, *A History of English Law,*
which states the medieval law that 'There can be no livery of seisin unless the land is
left vacant', and notes 'we find in certain places a ceremony of abjuration of the land
performed by the person who is conveying it' (7 vols (Boston: Little, Brown, 1923), iii,
p. 222).

There must not be one within, for against the order of law it
     doth stand.
Therefore I thought good to ask you, but I pray you think not
     amiss,   5
For both you, and almost all others knows, that an old custom it
     is.
Lady Conscience. You say truth. Take possession when you please;
     good leave I render ye.
Doubt you not, there is neither man, woman, nor child that will
     or shall hinder ye.
Usury. Why, then, I will be bold to enter.   *Exit.*
Lady Conscience. Who is more bold than Usury to venter?   10
He maketh the matter dangerous where is no need at all,
But he thinks it not perilous to seek every man's fall.
Both he and Lucre hath so pinched us, we know not what to do.
Were it not for Hospitality, we knew not whither to go.
Great is the misery that we poor ladies abide,   15
And much more is the cruelty of Lucre and Usury beside.
O Conscience, thou art not accounted of; O Love, thou art little
     set by,
For almost every one true love and pure conscience doth deny:
So hath Lucre crept into the bosom of man, woman, and child,
That every one doth practise his dear friend to beguile.   20
But God grant Hospitality be not by them over-pressed,
In whom all our stay and chiefest comfort doth rest;
But Usury hates Hospitality, and cannot him abide,
Because he for the poor and comfortless doth provide,
Here he comes, that hath undone many an honest man,   25
And daily seeks to destroy, deface, and bring to ruin, if he can.
Now, sir, have you taken possession, as your dear lady willed
     you?

Enter USURY.

---

6. others] *Q;* other *Q*2.   7. I render] *Q;* have *Q*2.   8. ye] *Q;* you *Q*2.   9. be bold
to] *Q;* boldly *Q*2.   27. taken] *Q;* tooke *Q*2.

6. *others knows*] The singular verb with plural subject was common early modern
usage.
   10. *venter?*] i.e. venture; but *OED* also notes early seventeenth-century uses of the
word associated with selling, and 'One who utters or gives vent to a statement, doctrine,
etc., esp. of an erroneous, malicious or objectionable nature' ('venter' 1).
   17. *accounted of*] valued, respected.
   20. *practise his . . . beguile*] make it their business to cheat their friend.
   21. *over-pressed*] oppressed.
   22. *stay*] support, strength.

Usury. I have done it, and I think you have received your money,
    But this to you: my lady willed me to bid you provide some
      other house out of hand,
    For she would not by her will have Love and Conscience to
      dwell in her land.   30
    Therefore I would wish you to provide ye,
    So ye should save charges, for a less house may serve ye.
Lady Conscience. I pray you heartily, let us stay there, and we will
    be content
    To give you ten pound a year, which is the old rent.
Usury. Ten pound a year! That were a stale jest,   35
    If I should take the old rent to follow your request;
    Nay, after forty pound a year you shall have it for a quarter,
    And you may think, too, I greatly befriend ye in this matter.
    But no longer than for a quarter to you I'll set it,
    For perhaps my lady shall sell it, or else to some other will let it.   40
Lady Conscience. Well, sith we are driven to this hard and bitter drift,
    We accept it, and are contented to make bare and hard shift.
Usury. Then get you gone, and see at a day your rent be ready.
Lady Conscience. We must have patience perforce, seeing there is no
    remedy.   *Exit* [LADY] CONSCIENCE.
Usury. What a fool was I! It repents me I have let it so reasonable.   45
    I might so well have had after three score as such a trifle,
    For, seeing they were distressed, they would have given largely.
    I was a right sot, but I'll be overseen no more, believe me.

---

28. it] *Q; not in* Q2.   30. in] *Q;* on Q2.   31. I would wish you] *Q;* tis best Q2.
32. ye should] *Q;* shall you Q2.   serve ye] Q2; serve *Q.*   38. I . . . ye] *Q;* you are
befriended Q2.   40. For . . . else] *Q;* For my lady perhaps will sell it, or Q2.   45. It . . .
it] *Q (*it . . . it*);* to let it Q2.

28–40.] Lady Conscience receives a loan from Lucre/Usury, but she is immediately
forced to use it on her new rent, which Usury has quadrupled.
    29. *my lady . . . hand*] my Lady ordered me to tell you to make provision for
(arrange, furnish) another house immediately.
    35. *stale jest*] bad joke.
    37. *after*] at the rate of.
    39. *set*] agree to, contract, place in possession (*OED* 'set' 21. a, 22, 23, 27, etc.).
    41. *sith . . . drift*] since we are forced into this difficult and hurtful circumstance.
    42. *make . . . shift*] do with difficulty what we have to with the little that we have.
    43. *at a day*] Mithal interprets this to mean 'at the end of a quarter' (Mithal, p.
126); it could also mean an unspecified 'at a certain day of payment', but Usury's
assumed cruelty would seem more likely to lead to the interpretation 'at a day's length',
or 'within a day from now'.
    44. *perforce*] by constraint, without choice.
    46. *so well . . . three score*] as easily have got sixty pounds.
    48. *sot*] fool.
    overseen] mistaken, imprudent.

Enter MERCADORUS.

Mercadorus. Ah, my good-a friend-a Master Usury. Be my trot', you
    be very well-met.
    Me be much beholding unto you for your good will; me be in
    your debt.   50
    But-a me take-a your part so much against a scald old churl
    called Hospitality,
    Did speak against you, and says you bring good honest men to
    beggary.
Usury. I thank you, sir. Did he speak such evil of me, as you now say?
    I doubt not but to reward him for his treachery one day.
Mercadorus. But, I pray, tell-a me how fare-a my lady all dis while?   55
Usury. Marry, well, sir; and here she comes, if myself I do not
    beguile.

Enter [LADY] LUCRE.

Lady Lucre. What, Signiore Mercadore. I have not seen you many a
    day;
    I marvel what is the cause you kept so long away?
Mercadorus. Shall me say to you, Madama, dat me have had much
    business for you in hand,
    For send away good commodities out of dis little country
    England.   60
    Me have now sent over brass, copper, pewter, and many oder
    ting,
    And for dat me shall ha' for gentlewomans fine trifles, that great
    profit will bring.
Lady Lucre. I perceive you have been mindful of me, for which I
    thank ye.
    But, Usury, tell me, how have you sped in that you went about?
Usury. Indifferently, lady: you need not to doubt,   65
    I have taken possession, and because they were destitute,
    I have let it for a quarter. My tale to conclude:

---

51. old] *Q; not in Q2.*   53. thank you] *Q2;* thank *Q;* thanke, [you] *Coll.*   56. Marry,
well, sir] *Q2;* Marie verie Sir *Q;* Marie, verie, sir *Coll;* Marry, very well, sir *Haz.*
57. you many] *Q;* you this many *Q2.*   59. much] *Q;* such *Q2.*

---

   49. *Be my trot'*] i.e. By my troth.
   51. *scald*] scurvy, scabby.
   54. *reward*] repay, revenge.
   56. *Marry, well, sir*] Hazlitt's conflation of Q1's 'Marie verie Sir' with this Q2
reading to give 'Marry, very well, sir' is a good emendation, but Q2 makes sense as it
stands and provides an original phrase from an early text that frequently corrects
Q1.

Marry, I have a little raised the rent, but it is but after forty
    pound by the year;
But if it were to let now, I would let it more dear.
Lady Lucre. Indeed, 'tis but a trifle; it makes no matter: 70
    I force it not greatly, being but for a quarter.
Mercadorus. Madonna, me tell ye vat you shall do: let dem to
    stranger dat are content
    To dwell in a little room, and to pay much rent,
    For you know da Frenchmans and Flemings in dis country be
        many,
    So dat they make shift to dwell ten houses in one very gladly,   75
    And be content-a for pay fifty or threescore pound a year
    For dat which da Englishmans say twenty mark is too dear.
Lady Lucre. Why, Signiore Mercadore, think you not that I
    Have infinite numbers in London that my want doth supply,
    Beside in Bristol, Northampton, Norwich, Westchester,
       Canterbury,   80
    Dover, Sandwich, Rye, Portsmouth, Plymouth, and many more,
    That great rents upon little room do bestow?
    Yes, I warrant you, and truly I may thank the strangers for this,
    That they have made houses so dear, whereby I live in bliss.
    But Signiore Mercadore, dare you to travel undertake,   85
    And go amongst the Moors, Turks, and pagans for my sake?
Mercadorus. Madonna, me dare-a go to de Turks, Moors, pagans,
    and more too.
    What do me care, an me go to da great devil for you?
    Command-a me, Madam, and you shall see plain,

---

70. 'tis] *Q;* it is *Q2.*   72. me tell ye] *Q;* me a you *Q2.*   73. and to pay] *Q;* and pay
Q2.   75. dwell] *Q;* be *Q2.*   80. Bristol] *this ed.;* Bristow *Q, Q2.*   81. Portsmouth]
this ed.; Porchmouth *Q, Q2, Coll, Haz.* more] *this ed.;* moe *Q;* mo *Q2.*   87. dare-a]
*Q (*dare a*);* dare *Q2.*   89. Madam] *Q;* Madona *Q2;* madam *Haz.*

---

71. *I force it not*] I don't press the point, I don't worry about it.

75. *houses*] households, families.

77. *mark*] an exchange value, weighed in gold or silver, worth about two-thirds of
a pound in Elizabethan England: see *Englishmen*, 1.1.142 note.

80–1. *Bristol . . . Plymouth*] Bristol: important harbour city on the River Severn in
south-west England, in Gloucestershire county (now Avon); Northampton: midlands
town; Norwich: second largest city in England in Elizabethan England, with a large
immigrant population; Canterbury: south-eastern town (in Kent), seat of one of the
Archbishoprics of England; Dover, Sandwich, Rye, Portsmouth, Plymouth: strategic
port towns on the south and south-east coast of England. 'Westchester' is not a modern
town name. It appears in a play title in Henslowe's *Diary* (*Wise Man of West Chester;*
also *Wise Man of Chester*). The actor Edward Alleyn tells his wife in a 1593(?) letter
to write to him at 'shrowsbery or to west chester or to york'.

Dat-a for your sake me refuse-a no pain.   90
Lady Lucre. Then, Signiore Mercadore, I am forthwith to send ye
From hence, to search for some new toys in Barbary or Turkey;
Such trifles as you think will please wantons best,
For you know in this country 'tis their chiefest request.
Mercadorus. Indeed, de gentlewomans here buy so much vain toys,   95
Dat me strangers laugh-a to tink wherein dey have their joys.
Fait', Madonna, me will search all da strange countries me can
tell,
But me will have such tings dat please dese gentlewomans vell.
Lady Lucre. Why, then, let us provide things ready to haste you away.
Mercadorus. A *vostro commandamento*, Madonna, me obey.   100
                                                            Exeunt.

[Sc. 6]

Enter SIMONY *and* PETER PLEASEMAN, *like a parson.*

Simony. Now proceed with your tale, and I'll hear thee.
Peter Pleaseman. And so, sir, as I was about to tell you,
This same Presco and this same Cracko be both my parishioners
now,
And, sir, they fell out marvellously together about you.
The same Cracko took your part, and said that the clergy   5
Was upholden by you, and maintained very worshipfully.
So, sir, Presco he would not grant that in no case,
But said that you did corrupt the clergy, and dishonour that holy
place.

---

92. or] *Q;* or in *Q2;* and in *Coll, Haz.*   96. me] *Q, Q2;* we *Coll.*   98. such] *Q;* sush
Q2.   100. *vostro commandamento*] *Haz;* voutro commaundemento *Q;* voutro commaundemento *Q2.*

0.1. SD *parson*] *Q (Parson);* Priest *Q2.*   1. your] *Q;* thy *Q2.*   4. together] *Q; not
in Q2.*   6. upholden . . . maintained] *Q;* maintained . . . upholden *Q2.*   7. no] *Q;*
any *Q2.*

---

92. *Barbary*] North Africa.

96. *me*] Q2 confirms this Q1 reading. Collier emends to 'we', which makes more
immediate sense; however, Mercadorus's imperfect English could well use 'me' for 'my'
or to indicate the sense of 'strangers like me'.

100. A vostro commandamento] Italian: At your command.

0.1. *parson*] the alteration to 'Priest' in Q2 may indicate a deliberate change in a
post-Armada, anti-Catholic environment.

3. *Presco and . . . Cracko*] perhaps indicating prescient and crack-brained characters, since the former rejects Simony and the latter praises him.

7. *no*] double negatives are common in early modern texts.

Now, sir, I was weary to hear them at such great strife,
For I love to please men, so long as I have life.   10
Therefore I beseech your mastership to speak to Lady Lucre,
That I may be her chaplain, or else to serve her.
Simony. What is your name?
Peter Pleaseman. Sir Peter.
Simony. What more?   15
Peter Pleaseman. Forsooth, Pleaseman.
Simony. Then your name is Sir Peter Pleaseman.
Peter Pleaseman. Ay, forsooth.
Simony. And please woman too, now and then.
Peter Pleaseman. You know that *homo* is indifferent.   20
Simony. Now, surely, a good scholar in my judgement.
    I pray, at what university were ye?
Peter Pleaseman. Of no university, truly.
    Marry, I have gone to school in a college, where I have studied
        two or three places of divinity,
    And all for Lady Lucre's sake, sir, you may steadfastly believe
        me.   25
Simony. Nay, I believe ye. But of what religion are you, can ye tell?
Peter Pleaseman. Marry, sir, of all religions: I know not myself very
        well.
Simony. You are a Protestant now, and I think to that you will
        grant.
Peter Pleaseman. Indeed, I have been a Catholic; marry, now for the
        most part, a Protestant.
    But, an if my service may please her – hark in your ear, sir –   30
    I warrant you my religion shall not offend her.
Simony. You say well, but if I help you to such great preferment,
    Would you be willing that for my pain
    I shall have yearly half the gain?

---

18. Ay] *Q (I);* Yea *Q2.*   22. at] *Q;* you of *Q2.*   28. you will grant] *Q;* now wil
grant *Q2.*   33. that] *Q; not in Q2.*   33–4. Would . . . gain] *so lineated in Q2; single
line in Q.*   34. half] *Q2;* hale *Q.*

---

15. *Sir*] Not in the modern sense of Knighthood but a title used of ordinary priests,
sometimes (and in this case) specifically in opposition to the address 'Master' (i.e. university graduate): Sir Peter says he is 'Of no university, truly'.

20. *homo is indifferent*] i.e. the Latin word 'homo' is not gendered, so the suggestion
that the name means, homosexually, 'Peter please *man*' – thus the joke 'woman too' – is
denied.

24. *I have . . . divinity*] (1) I have got myself two or three academic qualification in
divinity studies (2) I have found myself two or three jobs (placements) as a divine.

27. *I . . . well*] (1) I, myself, am not sure of my religion (2) I am not sure of my own
identity, it is so variable.

For it is reason, you know, that if I help you to a living,   35
That you should unto me be somewhat beholding.
Peter Pleaseman. Ay, sir, and reason good, I'll be as your mastership
    please.
I care not what you do, so I may live at ease.
Simony. Then this man is answered. Sir Peter Pleaseman, come in
    with me,
And I'll prefer ye straightway to my lady.   40
Peter Pleaseman. O sir, I thank ye.   *Exeunt.*

[Sc. 7]

       Enter SIMPLICITY, *with a basket on his arm.*

Simplicity. You think I am going to market to buy roast meat, do ye
    not?
I thought so, but you are deceived, for I wot what I wot.
I am neither going to the butcher's to buy veal, mutton, or beef,
But I am going to a bloodsucker; and who is it? Faith, Usury,
    that thief.
Why, sirs, 'twas no marcle he undoed my father, that was called
    Plain Dealing,   5
When he has undone my lady and Conscience too with his
    usuring.
I'll tell ye, sirs, trust him not, for he'll flatter bonacion and sore,
Till he has gotten the baker's vantage, then he'll turn you out of
    door.

---

37. Ay] *Q (I);* Yea *Q2.*   39. in] *Q; not in Q2.*   40. ye] *Q; you Q2.*

2. I thought . . . wot.] *Q;* But see how you are deceived, for well I wot, *Q2.*   3. veal,
mutton, or beef] *Q;* mutton, veale nor beefe *Q2.*   4. I] *Q; not in Q2.*   5. marcle] *Q,*
Q2 (marckle).   undoed] *Q, Q2 (undood);* undid *Haz.*   7. I'll . . . not] *Q;* Trust him
not sirs *Q2.*   bonacion] *Q, Q2;* bonfacion *Haz.*

---

    40. *prefer*] recommend.
    1. *You*] Simplicity is addressing the audience, or a member of it.
    2. *wot*] know.
    5. *marcle*] miracle.
    7. *bonacion*] See note to 2.42.
    sore] greatly, severely (cited only as an adjective in *OED*).
    8. *gotten the baker's vantage*] i.e. got the better of you, swindled you (and got your
money); bakers were notorious for their alleged tendency to make loaves on the light
side of legally required weights.

Enter DISSIMULATION.

Dissimulation. Simplicity, now of my honesty, very heartily well met.
Simplicity. What, Semblation, swear not, for thou swearest by that
    thou couldst not get.   10
    Thou have honesty now? Thy honesty is quite gone.
    Marry, thou hadst honesty at eleven o'clock, but it went from
      you ere noon.
    Why, how canst thou have honesty, when it dare not come nigh
      thee?
    I warrant, Semblation, he that has less honesty than thou may
      defy thee.
    Thou hast honesty, Sir Reverence! Come out, dog, where art
      thou?   15
    Even as much honesty as had my mother's great hoggish sow.
    No, faith, thou must put out my eye with honesty, an thou hadst
      it here:
    Hast not left it at the alehouse, in gage for a pot of strong beer?
Dissimulation. Pray thee, leave prating, Simplicity, and tell me what
    thou hast there.
Simplicity. Why, 'tis nothing for thee; thou dost not deal with such
    kind of ware.   20
    Sirrah, there is no beceit in a bag pudding, is there? Nor in a
      plain pudding-pie?
    But there is beceit, and knavery too, in thy fellow that is called
      Usury.
    Sirrah, I'll tell thee; I will not tell thee – and yet I'll tell thee,
      now I 'member me, too.

9. my] *Q;* mine *Q2.*   10. not get] *Q;* never get *Q2.*   12. Marry . . . noon] *Q2 (*xi.
of clocke*);* Mary thou hadst honestie at xi. of the clock, and went from thee at noone
Q; Mary thou hadst honestie at xi. of the clock, and went from you at noone *Coll.*
16. much] *Q2;* must *Q.*   had] *Q;* hath *Q2.*   17. my] *Q;* mine *Q2.*   21. beceit] *Q,*
Q2; deceit *Coll, Haz.*   -pie] *Q2;* -thy *Q.*   22. But . . . Usury] *so Q; line missing in*
Q2.   23. will not] *Q2;* wonnot *Q;* won not *Coll, Haz.*

   10. *Semblation*] Simplicity's (deliberate or mistaken) blunder for 'Dissimulation'.
that] i.e. honesty.
   15. *Come out . . . thou?*] Simplicity seems to be imagining a dog called 'honesty' or
even 'Sir Reverence' hiding away from Dissimulation because 'it dare not come nigh
thee' (13); in general the phrase seems to mean 'reveal the truth' or 'come clean'.
   17. *thou must . . . eye*] See note to 2.177.
   18. *gage*] surety.
   21-2. *beceit*] (1) Simplicity's blunder for 'deceit' (2) compositor's error in replacing
'd' with 'b' (thus Collier et al. emend).
   21. *bag pudding*] See note to 4.76.

Canst tell, or wouldst know whither with this parlament I go?
Faith, even to Suck-Swill, thy fellow, Usury, I am sent,   25
With my Lady Love's gown, and Lady Conscience's too, for a
    quarter's rent.
Dissimulation. Alas, poor Lady Love, art thou driven so low?
Some little pittance on thee I'll bestow.
Hold, Simplicity: carry her three or four ducats from me,
And commend me to her even very heartily.   30
Simplicity. Duck eggs? Yes, I'll carry 'em, an 'twere as many as this
    would hold.
Dissimulation. Tush, thou knowest not what I mean: take this, 'tis
    gold.
Simplicity. Mass, 'tis gold indeed: why, wilt thou send away thy
    gold? Hast no more need?
I think thou art grown plaguy rich with thy dissembling trade.
But I'll carry my lady the gold, for this will make her well apaid.   35
Dissimulation. And, sirrah, carry Lady Love's gown back again, for
    my fellow Usury
Shall not have her gown, I am sure so much he will befriend me.
Simplicity. But what shall Conscience's gown do? Shall I carry that
    back again too?
Dissimulation. Nay, let Conscience's gown and skin to Usury go.
If nobody cared for Conscience more than I,   40
They would hang her up like bacon in a chimney to dry.
Simplicity. Faith, I told thee thou caredst not for Conscience nor
    honesty;
I think, indeed, it will never be the death of thee.
But I'll go conspatch my arrant so soon as I can, I tell ye,

---

31. 'em] *Haz;* am *Q;* them *Q*2.   33. Hast no] *Q* *(*hast no*);* hast thou no *Q*2.
38. that] *Q;* it *Q*2.   44. I tell ye] *Q;* tell ye *Q*2.

---

24. *parlament*] Simplicity's mistake for 'parament', a decorated robe or robe of state
(*OED*). As Mithal notes, this usage is ironic, because Lady Love's and Lady Conscience's gowns, which he is taking to pawn to Usury, are hardly elaborate garments.
    25. *Suck-Swill*] suitably hoggish name for a usurer, proverbially like a pig in that
he is useless or even destructive until dead.
    29. *Hold*] Wait.
    ducats] gold coins of Italy.
    31. *Duck eggs?*] Simplicity mishears 'ducats'.
    an 'twere] if it were.
    this] probably referring to his belly (he would 'carry' the eggs by eating them).
    33. *Mass*] i.e. By the Mass (a mild oath).
    35. *apaid*] (1) satisfied, contented, pleased (2) repaid, requited, rewarded.
    39. *gown and skin*] this suggests an inextricable connection between the morality
character's substance and their representation by clothing.
    44. *conspatch my arrant*] Simplicity's bungle for 'dispatch my errand'.

For now I ha' gold, I would fain have some good meat in my
  belly.   45
                                                                      Exit.
Dissimulation. Nay, I'll hie me after, that I may send back Lady
    Love's gown,
  For I would not have Love bought quite out of town.
  Marry, for Conscience, tut, I care not two straws,
  Why I should take care for her, I know no kind of cause.
                                                                      Exit.

[Sc. 8]

Enter HOSPITALITY.

Hospitality. O, what shall I say? Usury hath undone me, and now he
    hates me to the death,
  And seeks by all means possible for to bereave me of breath.
  I cannot rest in any place, but he hunts and follows me
    everywhere,
  That I know no place to abide, I live so much in fear.
  But out, alas! Here comes he that will shorten my days.   5

Enter USURY.

Usury. O, have I caught your old grey beard? You be the man whom
    the people so praise.
  You are a frank gentleman, and full of liberality.
  Why, who had all the praise in London or England, but Master
    Hospitality?
  But I'll master you now, I'll hold you a groat.
Hospitality. What, will you kill me?
Usury.   No, I'll do nothing but cut thy throat.   10
Hospitality. O help, help, help, for God's sake!

Enter [LADY] CONSCIENCE, *running apace.*

Lady Conscience. What lamentable cry was that I heard one make?
Hospitality. O Lady Conscience, now or never help me!
Lady Conscience. Why, what wilt thou do with him, Usury?
Usury. What will I do with him? Marry, cut his throat, and then no
    more.   15

---

  5. *out*] 'An exclamation expressing lamentation, abhorrence, or indignant reproach'
(*OED* 'out *int.*' 2).
  9. *hold*] bet, wager.

Lady Conscience. O, dost thou not consider, that thou shalt dearly
    answer for Hospitality, that good member? Refrain it
    therefore.
Usury. Refrain me no refraining, nor answer me no answering,
    The matter is answered well enough in this thing.
Lady Conscience. For God's sake, spare him! For country's sake,
    spare him; for pity's sake, spare him;
    For love's sake, spare him; for Conscience's sake, forbear him!   20
Usury. Let country, pity, love, conscience, and all go in respect of
    myself,
    He shall die. Come, ye feeble wretch, I'll dress ye like an elf!
Lady Conscience. But yet, Usury, consider the lamentable cry of the
    poor:
    For lack of Hospitality, fatherless children are turned out of door.
    Consider again the complaint of the sick, blind, and lame,   25
    That will cry unto the Lord for vengeance on thy head in his
    name.
    Is the fear of God so far from thee that thou hast no feeling at all?
    O, repent, Usury! Leave Hospitality, and for mercy at the Lord's
    hand call.
Usury. Leave prating, Conscience: thou canst not mollify my heart.
    He shall, in spite of thee and all other, feel his deadly smart.   30
    Yet I'll not commit the murder openly,
    But hale the villain into a corner, and so kill him secretly.
    Come, ye miserable drudge, and receive thy death.

---

16. dost] *Haz;* doest *Q, Q2, Coll.*   consider] *Q; remember Q2.*   O . . . therefore] *so
in Q; two lines may be intended in Q2 (for / Hospitality), to rhyme* 'for' *and* 'therefore';
two lines in Haz: 'answer / For'.   19–20. For . . . him] *so lineated in Coll, Haz; single
line in Q, Q2.*   26. unto] *Q2; unro Q.*   30. thee] *Q; theee Q2.*

---

16. *O . . . therefore.*] Hazlitt divides these lines into two heptameter lines, but the
play concentrates on couplets, and the metre is not regular enough here to justify
emendation.
    16. *answer*] i.e. answer for it in heaven.
    19–20. *For . . . him!*] This lineation by Collier maintains the couplet rhyming
scheme.
    21. *in respect of myself*] as subordinate to me, in service to me.
    22. *I'll dress ye like an elf*] 'give you a thrashing as I would a rogue or a demon'
(Mithal, p. 128); alternatively, the elf is the frightening being delivering the beating.
The *OED* cites Henry Smith's *The Works of Henry Smith*, ed. Thomas Fuller, 2 vols
(Edinburgh: James Nichol, 1867), ii, p. 483 'The wrathful fosters and defies / Frenzies,
furies (wayward elves): / What need ye call for whip or scourge?' These lines appear
in the verse prayer, 'Micro-Cosmo-Graphia: The Little World's Description or, The
Map of Man', put together from Smith's 'Latin sapphics' by Joshua Sylvester.
    29. *mollify*] soften.
    32. *hale*] drag, pull forcibly.

Hospitality. Help, good lady, help! He will stop my breath.
Lady Conscience. Alas! I would help thee, but I have not the power.   35
Hospitality. Farewell, Lady Conscience: you shall have Hospitality in
    London nor England no more.   *Hale him in.*
Lady Conscience. O help, help, help, some good body!

    Enter DISSIMULATION *and* SIMPLICITY *hastily.*

Dissimulation. Who is that that calls for help so hastily?
Lady Conscience. Out, alas! Thy fellow Usury hath killed Hospitality.
Simplicity. Now, God's blessing on his heart: why, 'twas time that he
    was dead.   40
    He was an old churl, with never a good tooth in his head.
    And he ne'er kept no good cheer that I could see;
    For if one had not come at dinner time, he should have gone
        away hungry.
    I could never get my belly full of meat;
    He had nothing but beef, bread, and cheese for me to eat.   45
    Now I would have had some pies, or bag puddings with great
        lumps of fat,
    But, I warrant ye, he did keep my mouth well enough from that.
    Faith, an he be dead, he is dead. Let him go to the devil, an he
        will;
    Or if he will not go thither, let him even lie there still.
    I'll ne'er make wamentation for an old churl,   50
    For he has been a great while, and now 'tis time that he were
        out of the world.

    Enter LADY LUCRE [with SIMONY].

Lady Lucre. What, Conscience, thou lookest like a poor pigeon,
    pulled of late.
Lady Conscience. What, Lucre, thou lookest like a whore, full of
    deadly hate.

---

36. SD *Hale him in.*] Q, Q2, *placed after line 33.* 38. that that] Q; that
Q2. hastily] Q, Q2; lustily *Haz.* 40. that he was] Q; he were Q2. 47. I warrant
ye] Q; *not in* Q2. 50. wamentation] Q; a lamentation Q2. churl] *Haz;* churlde Q,
Q2. 51. been] Q *(beene);* livde Q2. 52. lookest] Q; lookst Q2. 53. lookest] Q;
lookst Q2.

---

41. *churl*] rustic, boor.
42. *cheer*] hospitality, victuals.
47. *I warrant ye*] I assure you.
50. *wamentation*] Simplicity's mistake for 'lamentation'.
51.1. Enter ... SIMONY.]] Simony requires an entrance not given in the early texts;
he should enter here with Lucre because he has told Peter Pleaseman in scene 6 that
he will go to his lady to plead for Pleaseman.
52. *pulled*] plucked, naked.

Lady Lucre. Alas! Conscience, I am sorry for thee, but I cannot weep.
Lady Conscience. Alas! Lucre, I am sorry for thee that thou canst no
  honesty keep: 55
  But such as thou art, such are thy attenders on thee,
  As appears by thy servant Usury that hath killed that good
    member, Hospitality.
Simplicity. Faith, Hospitality is killed, and hath made his will,
  And hath given Dissimulation three trees upon a high hill.
Lady Lucre. Come hither, Dissimulation, and hie you hence so fast
  as you may,   60
  And help thy fellow Usury to convey himself out of the way.
  Further, will the justices, if they chance to see him, not to know
    him,
  Or know him, not by any means to hinder him.
  And they shall command thrice so much at my hand.
  Go, trudge, run! Out, away! How, dost thou stand?   65
Dissimulation. Nay, good lady, send my fellow Simony,
  For I have an earnest suit to ye.
Lady Lucre. Then, Simony, go do what I have willed.
Simony. I run, Madam; your mind shall be fulfilled.   *Exit.*
Lady Conscience. Well, well, Lucre, *Audeo et taceo*: I see and say
  nothing,   70
  But I fear the plague of God on thy head it will bring.
Dissimulation. Good lady, grant that Love be your waiting-maid,
  For I think, being brought so low, she will be well apaid.
Lady Lucre. Speakest thou in good earnest, or dost thou but
  dissemble?
  I know not how to have thee, thou art so variable.   75

---

54. I cannot] *Q;* cannot *Q2.* 59. a] *Q2;* an *Q.*

59. *three trees . . . hill*] 'meaning, of course, the gallows, supposed to be erected in a conspicuous place' (Coll., p. 240); there is also a nod toward the three 'trees' or crosses of Golgotha and the death of Christ, the champion of Hospitality.

60. *hie you hence*] get going.

62. *will*] order, persuade. Also 11.35.

know] recognize.

64. *command . . . hand*] I will do them three times the favour in return.

65. *trudge*] this could be a variant of 'drudge'; however, 'trudge' as a verb is common in the sixteenth century, and *OED* cites this word as a noun meaning 'one who trudges' from 1748, and we could here have a much earlier use of this term.

70. Audeo et taceo] Latin tag, translated in the same line.

73. *apaid*] See note to 7.35.

75. *have*] take, understand.

Dissimulation. Lady, though my name be Dissimulation, yet I speak
   bona fide now.
   If it please you my petitions to allow.

Enter SIMONY.

Lady Lucre. Stand by, I'll answer thee anon. What news, Simony,
   Bringest thou of thy fellow Usury?
Simony. Marry, madam, good news, for Usury lies close   80
   Hid in a rich man's house, that will not let him loose
   Until they see the matter brought to a good end,
   For Usury in this country hath many a good friend,
   And late I saw Hospitality carried to burying.
Lady Lucre. I pray thee, tell me who were they that followed him?   85
Simony. There were many of the clergy, and many of the nobility,
   And many right worshipful rich citizens,
   Substantial, gracious, and very wealthy farmers;
   But to see how the poor followed him, it was a wonder;
   Never yet at any burial I have seen such a number.   90
Lady Lucre. But what say the people of the murder?
Simony. Many are sorry and say 'tis great pity that he was slain,
   But who be they? The poor beggarly people that so complain.
   As for the other, they say 'twas a cruel, bloody fact,
   But I perceive none will hinder the murderer for this cruel act.   95
Lady Lucre. 'Tis well. I am glad of it. Now, Dissimulation, if you
   can get Love's goodwill,
   I am contented with all my heart to grant thereuntil.
Dissimulation. I thank you, good lady, and I doubt not but she
   With a little entreaty will thereto agree.
Simplicity. Now I have it in my breeches, for I can tell   100
   That I and my lady with Mistress Lucre shall dwell.
   But if I be her serving fellow, and dwell there,
   I must learn to cog, lie, foist, and swear,
   And sure I shall never learn; marry, an 'twere to lie abed all day,

---

88. gracious] *Q, Q*2; graziers *Coll.*   90. I have] *Q*; was *Q*2.   96. can] *Q*; canst
*Q*2.   97. thereuntil] *Haz*; there untill *Q, Q*2.   98. I...lady] *Q (Ladie);* Thankes to
you ladie *Q*2.   100. for I] *Q*; and very well *Q*2.   104. sure] *Q*; surely *Q*2.

---

  76. *bona fide*] 'with good faith', truthfully.
  77. *my petitions*] i.e. request to employ Lady Love.
  78. *anon*] directly, immediately.
  88. *gracious*] Collier's emendation to 'graziers' ('One who grazes or feeds cattle for
the market' *OED*) is worth consideration; as the line stands in Qq, however, 'substantial' and 'gracious' are acceptable adjectives for the farmers or landowners at Hospitality's funeral.
  100. *I have ... breeches*] 'have sure and private knowledge of it' (Mithal, p. 128).
  103. *foist*] cheat.

I know to that kind of living I can give a good say,   105
Or if 'twere to eat one's meat, then I knew what I had to do.
How say ye, sirrah, can I not? I'll be drudge by you.
Lady Lucre. Now to you, little mouse: did I not tell you before
That I should, ere 'twere long, turn you both out of door?
How say you, pretty soul, is't come to pass, yea or no?   110
I think I have pulled your peacock's plumes somewhat low,
And yet you be so stout, as though you felt no grief;
But I know, ere it be long, you will come puling to me for relief.
Lady Conscience. Well, Lucre, well, you know pride will have a fall.
What advantageth it thee to win the world, and lose thy soul
    withal?   115
Yet better it is to live with little, and keep a conscience clear,
Which is to God a sacrifice, and accounted of most dear.
Lady Lucre. Nay, Conscience, an you be bookish, I mean to leave ye,
And the cold ground to comfort your feet I bequeath ye.
Methink you, being so deeply learned, may do well to keep a
    school: 120

---

105. I know . . . say] *Q;* To that kind of lying I should give a good say *Q2;* I know to that kind of living I should give a good 'ssay *Haz.*   106. I had] *Q;* for *Q2.*   107. ye] *Q;* you *Q2.*   drudge] *Q, Q2;* judg'd *Haz.*   111. I think] *Q;* Me thinkes *Q2.*   113. I know] *Q; not in Q2.*   115. advantageth] *Q* (avauntageth*);* availeth *Q2;* avantageth *Haz.*   118. I mean to] *Q;* ile *Q2.*   119. I] *Q;* ile *Q2.*

---

105. *I know . . . say*] (say = 'assay', 'testing the quality or fitness of a person or thing' *OED* 'say' n². 1), thus I know I can do well at (practise, put to the test) that kind of lifestyle; Q1's 'living' is replaced in Q2 with 'lying', which provides a nice pun on the 'lie abed' of the preceding line.

107. *How say ye, sirrah*] It would be dangerous for Simplicity to address anyone on stage at this point with 'sirrah', a mode of address for a social inferior, thus he may be addressing an audience member; on the other hand, he can be careless in just this manner, as when he calls Dissimulation 'knave' just sixteen lines later at 8.124.

I'll be drudge by you] Addressed to Lucre, drudge as a verb means 'to perform mean or servile tasks', hence 'drudged' as a participle, 'set to laborious or servile tasks' (*OED* 'drudge' v. 1, 3).

108. *mouse*] a term of affection, here ironic or patronizing.

112. *stout*] proud.

113. *puling*] whining, crying (like a baby).

118. *bookish*] addicted to book learning; here, patronizing, moral, and impractical.

119. *cold ground . . . bequeath ye*] cf. Ulpian Fulwell, *Like Will to Like* (1568), where Nichol Newfangle promises Tom Tosspot and Rafe Roister some land; when they lose all they have at gambling and prodigality, Nichol reveals that their reward of land is the country to go through at will, begging (D4v–E1v).

120. *keep a school*] (1) 'to be the master or mistress of a school' (*OED* 'school' 1.d) (2) Conscience should keep 'a-school' herself in the ways of the world, because, as the following line warns, even the most learned can fall.

Why, I have seen so cunning a clerk in time to prove a fool.

Exeunt [LADY] LUCRE and SIMONY.

Simplicity. Sirrah, if thou shouldst marry my lady, thou wouldst keep
  her brave,
  For I think now thou art a plaguy rich knave.
Dissimulation. Rich I am, but as for knave, keep to thyself.
  Come, give me my lady's gown, thou ass-headed elf!   125
Simplicity. Why, I'll go with thee, for I must dwell with my lady.
Dissimulation. Pack hence, away! Jack Drum's entertainment! She will
  none of thee.   *Exit.*
Simplicity. This is as my cousin and I went to Master Nemo's house:
  There was nobody to bid a dog drink, or to change a man a louse.
  But Lady Conscience – nay, who there? – scratch that name away! 130
  Is she be a lady that is turned out of all her beray?
  Do not be called no more lady, an if you be wise,
  For everybody will mock you, and say you be not worth two
    butterflies.
Lady Conscience. What remedy, Simplicity? I cannot do withal.
  But what shall we go do, or whereto shall we fall?   135
Simplicity. Why, to our victuals: I know nothing else we have to do,
  And mark if I cannot eat twenty times as much as you.
Lady Conscience. If I go lie in an inn, I shall be sore grieved to see

---

123. I think now] *Q;* me thinkes *Q2.* 131. Is she] *Q;* can she be *Q2.* 132. nobody]
Haz; no bodie *Q;* no man *Q2.* 133. – nay, who there? –] *Haz;* (nay whoe there) *Q;*
(nay who there) *Q2;* (nay, whoe there) *Coll.* beray] *Q;* array *Q2.* 136. I
know … have] *Q;* what else have we *Q2.* 137. as] *Q;* so *Q2.* 138. I shall … gri
eved] *Q;* it will greeve me *Q2.*

---

  122. *brave*] splendid.
  124. *keep to thyself*] speak for yourself (with punning suggestion of 'keep that to
yourself', 'be secret').
  127. *Pack*] Get out, get going.
  Jack Drum's entertainment] sometimes 'Tom Drum's entertainment', a phrase
meaning to get rid of someone, kick them out of doors. It is the title of a play by John
Marston (1600–1), in which the usurer Mamon is expelled from London to a whipping
in Bedlam.
  She will … thee] She wants nothing to do with you.
  128. *as*] just like, the same as.
  129. *nobody to … louse*] i.e. nobody to do the most basic task or even attend to a
man as if he were worth no more than a louse (*OED* 'louse' 1.b.: something worthless
or contemptible).
  130. *nay, who there?*] i.e. hold on a minute!.
  131. *beray?*] Simplicity's scatological ('beray' = befoul) mistake for 'array'.
  132. *Do … Lady*] No longer call yourself 'Lady' (when you are in such a low state
of affairs and lacking appropriate apparel).
  134. *cannot do withal*] 'cannot help it' (*OED* A.2.b.).

The deceit of the ostler, the polling of the tapster, as in most
    houses of lodging they be.
If in a brewer's house, at the over-plenty of water, and
    scarceness of malt I should grieve,   140
Whereby to enrich themselves, all other with unsavoury thin
    drink they deceive.
If in a tanner's house, with his great deceit in tanning,
If in a weaver's house, with his great cozening in weaving,
If in a baker's house, with light bread, and very evil working,
If in a chandler's, with deceitful weights, false measures, selling
    for a halfpenny that is scant worth a farthing,   145
And if in an alehouse, with the great resort of poor unthrifts,
    that with swearing at the cards consume their lives,
Having greater delight to spend a shilling that way, than a groat
    at home to sustain their needy children and wives;
For which I judge it best for me to get some solitary place,
Where I may with patience this my heavy cross embrace,
And learn to sell broom, whereby to get my living,   150
Using that as a quiet mean to keep myself from begging.
Wherefore, Simplicity, if thou wilt do the like,
Settle thyself to it, and with true labour thy living do seek. *Exit.*
Simplicity. No, faith, Mistress Conscience, I'll not, for, an I should
    sell broom,
The maids would cozen me too competually with their old
    shoon.   155
And, too, I cannot work, and you would hang me out of the
    way,
For when I was a miller, Will did grind the meal while I did
    play.

---

150. sell] *Q2;* seek *Q.*   155. too] *Q2;* to *Q.*

139. *polling*] practising extortion (*OED* 'poll' III.5.b).

144. *light bread*] bread that has not used the required quantity of ingredients (cf. note to 'baker's vantage' at 7.8).

147. *shilling ... groat*] a coin worth six pence ... a coin worth four pence (no longer minted in Elizabethan England).

150. *sell broom*] be a street vendor of the simplest sort, selling brooms.

155. *The maids ... shoon*] another of Simplicity's odd syntactical moments. Mithal notes 'competually' as 'a portmanteau word made up of "continually" and "perpetually" ' (Mithal, p. 130). The whole line appears to mean something like 'Women would mock me terribly by throwing old shoes at me'. Q1's 'too competually' might mean something like 'to a great extent'; a broomseller might also engage in the second-hand clothing trade and thus he would have old shoes thrown at him for collection; shoes might also be thrown ironically at poor Simplicity, since to throw a shoe after someone was a gesture to wish them good luck – Frisco alludes to the practice in *Englishmen for My Money* 3.2.103–4.

Therefore I'll have as easy an occupation as I had when my
father was alive.
Faith, I'll go even a-begging: why, 'tis a good trade; a man shall
be sure to thrive,
For I am sure my prayers will get bread and cheese, and my
singing will get me drink.   160
Then shall not I do better than Mistress Conscience? Tell me as
you think.
Therefore god Pan in the kitchen, and god Pot in the buttery,
Come and resist me, that I may sing with the more meliosity.
But, sirs, mark my cauled countenance when I begin –
But yonder is a fellow that gapes to bite me, or else to eat that
which I sing.   165
Why, thou art a fool; canst not thou keep thy mouth strait
together,
And when it comes, snap at it, as my father's dog would do at a
liver?
But thou art so greedy,
That thou thinkest to eat it before it come nigh thee.

SIMPLICITY *sings*.
    Simplicity sings it, and 'sperience doth prove,   170
No biding in London for Conscience and Love.
The country hath no peer,
    where Conscience comes not once a year;

---

163. resist] Q, Q2.   170. it] Q; *not in* Q2.   172. peer] *Haz*; peare Q, Q2.

---

160. *prayers . . . singing*] (1) prayers to God for help (2) prayers on behalf of
another, paying patron . . . street entertainment, ballad singing.
   162. *Therefore god . . . buttery*] Pan is a Greek rural deity with the front (top) half
of a man and the rear (bottom) half of a goat; Simplicity plays on this name with the
invented god of butteries, Pot.
   163. *resist*] Simplicity's mistake for 'assist'.
   meliosity] Simplicity's mistake for 'mellifluousness' (sweetness, honey-like).
   164. *cauled*] (1) The word 'caul' often refers close-fitting cap, and it can refer to a
sheepfold, hence here perhaps meaning tight, fitting, prepared (some kind of grimace?)
(2) Perhaps more simply and more likely is the meaning 'cabbage-head' since 'caul' can
mean cabbage (*OED* 'caul' n.[2]) – and Simplicity goes on to joke that an audience
member is looking at him hungrily.
   165. *yonder . . . me*] i.e. an audience member with his mouth open; this might be a
joke (see note to line 166) about the word 'caul', or it may simply suggest either the
stupidity or the fatigue of the audience member, or both.
   166. *strait*] tight.
   170–8. *Simplicity . . . Love.*] Qq print lines 170–1 and 177–8 in black letter, and
lines 172–6 in roman font.
   172. *The country hath no peer*] 'On 4th September 1565 William Pickering had a
license to print, among other ballads, one called "The Countrye hath no pere", which

And Love so welcome to every town,
  as wind that blows the houses down.   175
Sing down adown, down, down, down.
  Simplicity sings it, and 'sperience doth prove,
No dwelling in London, no biding in London, for Conscience
  and Love.
Now, sirrah, hast eaten up my song? An ye have, ye shall eat no
  more today,
For everybody may see your belly is grown bigger with eating up
  our play.   180
He has filled his belly, but I am never a whit the better,
Therefore I'll go seek some victuals, and 'member, for eating up
  my song you shall be my debtor.   [*Exit.*]

[Sc. 9]

  Enter MERCADORUS, *the Merchant, and* GERONTUS, *a Jew.*

Gerontus. But, Signiore Mercadorus, tell me, did ye serve me well or
  no,
That having gotten my money would seem the country to forgo?
You know I lent you two thousand ducats for three months'
  space,
And, ere the time came, you got another thousand by flattery
  and your smooth face.
So when the time came that I should have received my money, 5
You were not to be found, but was fled out of the country.
Surely, if we that be Jews should deal so one with another,
We should not be trusted again of our own brother,
But many of you Christians make no conscience to falsify your
  faith and break your day.

---

179. SP] *not in this ed.;* Simpli. *Q;* Simp. *Q*2; Simplicitie. *Coll;* Simplicity
Haz. 182. [Exit.]] *Haz; not in Q, Q*2.

3. months'] *Haz;* monthes *Q, Q*2. 4. your] *Q;* thy *Q*2.

---

may have been this very song, and of which, we may presume, Simplicity only sings
one stanza. We cannot suppose that the broadside entered by Pickering consisted of no
more' (Coll. 1851, p. 241).
 179. *sirrah*] referring again to the audience member.
 181. *never a whit*] not at all, none at all (*OED* 'wit' 1.b).
 182. *'member*] i.e. remember.

 2. *forgo*] leave (to evade the debt).
 4. *ere*] before.
 9. *break your day*] forfeit the loan bond by not paying back on the stipulated
day.

I should have been paid at three months' end, and now it is two
  year you have been away.   10
Well, I am glad you be come again to Turkey; now I trust I
  shall
Receive the interest of you so well as the principal.
Mercadorus. Ah, good-a Master Geronto! Pra' heartly, bear-a me a
  little while,
And me shall pay ye all without any deceit or guile.
Me have-a much business for buy pretty knacks to send to
  England.   15
Good-a sir, bear-a me four or five days, me'll despatch your
  money out of hand.
Gerontus. Signiore Mercadore, I know no reason why because you
  have dealt with me so ill.
Sure you did it not for need, but of set purpose and will;
And, I tell ye, to bear with ye four or five days goes sore against
  my mind,
Lest you should steal away and forget to leave my money
  behind.   20
Mercadorus. Pra' heartly, do tink-a no such ting, my good friend-a
  me.
Be me trot' and fait', me'll pay you all, every penny.
Gerontus. Well, I'll take your faith and troth once more; I'll trust to
  your honesty,
In hope that for my long tarrying you will deal well with me.

---

10. three months'] *Q2 (three monthes)*; the monthes *Q.*   11–12. Well . . . principal]
so this ed.; single line in Q, Q2.   13. Pra'] *Q (pra)*; pray *Q2.*   15. have-a] *Q (have
a)*; have *Q2.*   16. Good-a] *Q (Good a)*; Good *Q2.*   four or five] *Q*; foure five *Q2*;
for five *Haz.*   hand] *Q2; not in Q*; [hand] *Coll.*   19. I tell ye] *Q; not in Q2.*   21. Pra']
Q, Q2; Pray *Haz.*   tink-a] *Q (tink a)*; tink *Q2.*   23. Well] *Q; not in Q2.*   I'll
trust] *Q (ile)*; & trust *Q2.*

---

10. *three months' end*] this is Q2's reading; Q1's 'the month's end' could work if
the present month were the third month in question, but the action is clearly taking
place much later than the loan's due date. In scene 14, we find out that the loan has
remained unpaid for two years now; Shylock's loan term of 3000 ducats for three
months provides an obvious echo (*Merchant of Venice* 1.3.1–9). See also note to
14.3–6.
  13. *bear-a me*] bear with me.
  16. *out of hand*] at once, immediately (*OED* 'hand' I.33.a); cf. 5.29.
  18. *for need*] out of necessity.
  22. *Be . . . fait'*] By my troth and faith.

    Tell me what ware you would buy for England, such necessaries
       as they lack.   25
Mercadorus. O, no – lack some pretty fine toy, or some fantastic
       new knack,
    For da gentlewomans in England buy much tings for fantasy.
    You pleasure-a me, sir, what me mean-a dereby?
Gerontus. I understand you, sir, but keep touch with me, and I'll
       bring you to great store,
    Such as I perceive you came to this country for,   30
    As musk, amber, sweet powders, fine odours, pleasant perfumes,
       and many such toys,
    Wherein I perceive consisteth that country gentlewomen's joys.
    Besides I have diamonds, rubies, emeralds, sapphires,
       smaradines, opals, onacles, jacinths, agates, turquoise, and
       almost of all kind of precious stones,
    And many more fit things to suck away money from such green-
       headed wantons.
Mercadorus. Fait'-a, my good friend, me tank you most heartly
       alway.   35
    Me shall-a content your debt within dis two or tree day.
Gerontus. Well, look you do keep your promise, and another time
       you shall command me.
Come, go we home, where our commodities you may at pleasure see.
                                   [Exeunt.]

---

25. Tell . . . lack] *Q;* Tell me what good ware for England you do lacke. *Q2.* 27.
much] *Q;* mush *Q2.* 30. perceive] ; know *Q2.* 32. gentlewomen's] *Coll, Haz;*
gentlewomans *Q;* Gentlewomans *Q2.* 33. emeralds, sapphires . . . jacinths . . .
turquoise] *this ed.;* Emerodes, Safiors . . . Jasinkes . . . Turkasir *Q;* Emerodes, Saphires
. . . Jacynthes . . . Turkasir *Q2;* emerands, sapphires . . . jacinths . . . turquoise *Haz.*
34. more] *this ed.;* moe *Q;* not in *Q2;* mo *Haz.* away] *Q;* not in *Q2.* 35. Fait'-a,
my] *this ed.;* Fatta my *Q;* Fatta me *Q2;* Faith-a My *Haz.* 37. look you do keep] *Q;*
see you hold *Q2.* 38. SD [Exeunt.]] *Haz;* not in *Q, Q2.*

---

   25. *Tell . . . lack.*] Gerontus asks Mercadorus to describe the necessary goods that
England requires; the line could be pointed as an interrogative so that Gerontus asks
Mercadorus whether it is 'necessaries' that he is importing, and he answers in the
negative.
   28. *pleasure-a me*] help me, provide for me.
   33. *smaradines*] of smaragdite, emerald-green stone.
   onacles] onyx stone, 'A variety of quartz allied to agate, consisting of plane layers
of different colours: much used for cameos' (*OED* 'onyx' 1) (cameos = relief
carvings).
   jacinths] in early usage, a precious blue stone, probably sapphire.
   34. *green-headed*] (1) naive (2) envious, covetous (green is the colour of jealousy).

[Sc. 10]

Enter [LADY] CONSCIENCE, *with brooms at her back,*
singing as followeth:

New brooms, green brooms, will you buy any?
Come maidens, come quickly, let me take a penny.

My brooms are not steeped,
    but very well bound,
My brooms be not crooked,   5
    but smooth cut and round.
I wish it should please you
    to buy of my broom,
Then would it well ease me
    if market were done.   10

Have you any old boots,
    or any old shoon,
Pouch-rings or buskins
    to cope for new broom?
If so you have, maidens,   15

---

12. shoon] Q *(shoone)*; shooes Q2.

1–20. *New brooms . . . penny*] Qq print lines 1–2 and 19–20 in black letter, and
lines 3–18 in roman font. 'According to "Extracts from the Stationer's Registers", I.88.
William Griffith was licensed in 1563–4 to print a ballad entitled "Buy, Broomes,
buye". This may be the song here sung by Conscience. A song to the tune is inserted
in the tract of "Robin Goodfellow", 1628, 4to. but no doubt first published many years
earlier' (Coll. 1851, p. 242). Mithal notes that a ballad, 'Conscience Crye to all estates
in sellinge of broom', was licensed 25 July 1592, and that the Weaver's song in Thomas
Deloney's *Jack of Newbury* (1596) has the line 'While Conscience went not selling
broom' and another line referring to Lucre, 'Then men to Lucar did not yield'. Conscience is also a broom-man in Kent Street in 1592, in Greene's *A Quip for an Upstart
Courtier*, and 'From all this it appears that presumably the concept of Conscience as a
broom seller derives directly from *The Three Ladies* and is a testimony of its popularity'
(Mithal, p. 133).

3. *steeped*] (1) soaked (presumably to make supple) (2) tilted, sloped (therefore not
straight); Conscience either claims that *although* her brooms are not steeped (soaked)
they are well bound and straight, or she claims that are brooms are not steeped (i.e.
not bent) and are therefore well-bound and straight.

11–14. *Have . . . broom*] these items seem to have become proverbial barter for
brooms; Mithal notes Mackay's *Songs of the London Prentices*, which quotes 'Broomes
for old shoes, pouchrings, bootes and buskings' (Mithal, p. 134).

13. *Pouch-rings*] a ring (or clip) for closing a pouch or a purse (*OED* cites this
line).

buskins] a high boot.

14. *cope*] exchange, barter.

I pray you bring hither,
That you and I friendly
        may bargain together.

New brooms, green brooms, will you buy any?
Come maidens, come quickly, let me take a penny.   20

                [LADY] CONSCIENCE *speaketh.*

Thus am I driven to make a virtue of necessity,
And, seeing God almighty will have it so, I embrace it
    thankfully,
Desiring God to mollify and lessen Usury's hard heart,
That the poor people feel not the like penury and smart.
But usury is made tolerable amongst Christians as a necessary
    thing,   25
So that, going beyond the limits of our law, they extort, and
    many to misery bring.
But if we should follow God's law, we should not receive above
    that we lend,
For if we lend for reward, how can we say we are our
    neighbour's friend?
O, how blessed shall that man be that lends without abuse,
But thrice accursèd shall he be that greatly covets use.   30
For he that covet over-much, unsatiate is his mind,
So that to perjury and cruelty he wholly is inclined:
Wherewith they sore oppress the poor by diverse sundry ways,
Which makes them cry unto the Lord to shorten cutthroats' days.
Paul calleth them thieves that doth not give the needy of their
    store,   35
And thrice accursed are they that take one penny from the poor.
But while I stand reasoning thus, I forget my market clean,

---

16. hither] Q2; hether Q.   23. lessen] *Haz;* lesten Q, Q2; soften *Coll.*   28. neighb
our's] *this   ed.;* neighbors   Q, Q2; neighbours' *Haz.* 31. covet] Q;   covets
Q2.   unsatiate] Q *(unsaciate);* insaciate Q2; insatiate *Haz.*

---

23. *lessen*] Collier suggests that Qq's 'lesten' is a misreading or misprint for 'soften',
but 'l' is not easily misread for 's' in secretary or italic hands. The line also already
gives us 'mollify' to complement 'lessen'.

30. *use*] usury.

33. *diverse sundry*] many different.

35. *Paul calleth . . . store*] 'There is no reference in Paul's canon to his calling such
people thieves as do not share their wealth with the community' (Mithal, p. 135).

36. *And thrice . . . poor*] Paul discusses duty to the poor in 2 Corinthians 9; he does
not call the covetous usurer 'thrice accursed', but this is a general rhetorical mode of
emphasis, as in 'thrice happy are they' at 3.157.

37. *clean*] utterly.

And sith God hath ordained this way, I am to use the mean.

Sing again.

Have ye any old shoes,
Or have ye any boots?   40
Have ye any buskins,
Or will ye buy any broom?

Who bargains or chops with Conscience?
What, will no customer come?

Enter USURY.

Usury. Who is it that cries brooms? What, Conscience, selling
      brooms about the street?   45
Lady Conscience. What, Usury, it is great pity thou art unhanged
      yet.
Usury. Believe me, Conscience, it grieves me thou art brought so
      low.
Lady Conscience. Believe me, Usury, it grieves me thou wast not
      hanged long ago,
      For if thou hadst been hanged before thou slewest Hospitality,
      Thou hadst not made me and thousands more to feel like
      poverty.   50

Enter [LADY] LUCRE.

Lady Lucre. Methought I heard one cry brooms along the door.
Usury. Ay, marry, madam; it was Conscience, who seems to be
      offended at me very sore.
Lady Lucre. Alas, Conscience, art thou become a poor broom-wife?
Lady Conscience. Alas, Lucre, wilt thou continue a harlot all days of
      thy life?
Lady Lucre. Alas, I think it is a grief to thee that thou art so poor.   55
Lady Conscience. Alas, Lucre, I think it is no pain to thee, that thou
      still playest the whore.
Lady Lucre. Well, well, Conscience, that sharp tongue of thine hath
      not been thy furtherance:

39–42. Have . . . broom] *so this ed.; one line in Q, Q2.* 43–4. Who . . . come] *so
this ed.; one line in Q, Q2.* 43. bargains or chops] *Q2; bargen or chop Q.* 50. like
poverty] *Q; the like poverty Q2.* 55. I think] *Q; me thinks Q2.* 56. I think] *Q;
me thinkes Q2.*

38. *And . . . mean*] And since God has determined this mode of life for me, I must
follow the course (make use of this means to do his bidding).
53. *broom-wife*] woman who sells brooms.

If thou hadst kept thy tongue, thou hadst kept thy friend, and
    not have had such hindrance.
But wottest thou who shall be married tomorrow? Love with my
    Dissimulation.
For I think to bid the guests – they are by this time well nigh
    gone,   60
And having occasion to use brooms, I care not if I buy them all.
Lady Conscience. Then give me a shilling, and with a goodwill have
    them you shall.
Lady Lucre. Usury, carry in these brooms, and give them to the
    maid,
For I know of such store she will be well apaid.
                               Exit USURY *with the brooms.*
Hold, Conscience; though thy brooms be not worth a quarter so
    much,   65
Yet to give thee a piece of gold I do it not grudge,
And if thou wouldst follow my mind, thou shouldst not live in
    such sort,
But pass thy days with pleasure store of every kind of sport.
Lady Conscience. I think you lead the world in a string, for
    everybody follows you,
And sith every one doth it, why may not I do it too?   70
For that I see your free heart and great liberality,
I marvel not that all people are so willing to follow ye.
Lady Lucre. Then, sweet soul, mark what I would have thee do for
    me:
That is, to deck up thy poor cottage handsomely;

---

59. But ... Dissimulation] *so this ed.; two lines in Q, Q2 (to* morrow? / Love*).*
60. guests] *Haz;* gesse *Q, Q2.*   61. use] *Q;* buy *Q2.*   66. grudge] *this ed.;* grutch
Q, Q2.

---

58. *kept ... kept*] silenced ... maintained.
   59. *wottest*] know.
   60. *guests*] The Qq 'gesse' can be made sense of if it is emended to 'guess', but
Hazlitt's emendation seems confirmed by the guest list in scene 11, and by 2.45 (Q1
'guests'; Q2 'gesse') and 11.31 (Q1 'gestes'; Q2 'gesse').
   they ... gone] This statement is not entirely clear; 'they' may refer to Love and Dissimulation 'gone' to prepare for their wedding, thus requiring guests to be summoned
quickly.
   well nigh] almost.
   66. *grudge*] begrudge.
   69. *lead ... string*] 'to have [the world] under control, to be able to do what one
likes with [the world]' (*OED* 'string' n. I.1.f).
   74. *deck up*] decorate.

And for that purpose I have five thousand crowns in store,   75
And when it is spent, thou shalt have twice as much more.
But only see thy rooms be neat when I shall thither resort
With familiar friends, to play and pass the time in sport;
For the deputy, constable, and spiteful neighbours do spy, pry,
     and eye about my house,
That I dare not be once merry within, but still mute like a
     mouse.   80
Lady Conscience. My good Lady Lucre, I will fulfil your mind in
     every kind of thing,
So that you shall be welcome at all hours, whomsoever you do
     bring.
And all the dogs in the town shall not bark at your doings, I
     trow,
For your full pretence and intent I do throughly know,
Even so well as if you had opened the very secrets of your heart,   85
For which I doubt not but to rest in your favour by my desert.
But here comes your man, Usury.

                    Enter USURY.

Lady Lucre. I'll send him home for the money.
Usury, step in and bring me the box of all abomination that
     stands in the window;
It is little and round, painted with diverse colours, and is pretty
     to the show.   90
Usury. Madam, is there any superscription thereon?
Lady Lucre. Have I not told you the name? For shame, get you
     gone!   [*Exit* USURY.]
Well, my wench, I doubt not but our pleasures shall excel,
Seeing thou hast got a corner fit, where few neighbours dwell,
And they be of the poorest sort, which fits our turn so right,   95
Because they dare not speak against our sports and sweet
     delight;

76. as] *Q; so Q2.*   78. play and] *Q; not in Q2;* play, and *Coll, Haz.*   79. deputy] *Q2*
(Deputie); Debutie *Q, Coll.*   82. whomsoever] *Q;* whosoever *Q2.*   92. gone!] *this*
ed.; gone. *Q, Q2, Haz;* gone. – *Coll.*   SD [*Exit* USURY.]] *Haz; not in Q, Q2.*

75. *crowns*] coins worth 5 shillings each (one-quarter of a pound), thus Lucre is
investing the large sum of £1250 in setting up her 'house of resort' and offers £2500
more if necessary.
     78. *sport*] games, merriment (often with sexual suggestion).
     83. *dogs . . . bark*] cf. *Richard III* 1.1.23, where the dogs reveal Richard's evil and
strangeness by barking at him.
     trow] trust, believe.

And if they should, alas, their words would naught at all be
    weighed,
And for to speak before my face they will be all afraid.

Enter USURY, *with a painted box of ink in his hand.*

Usury. Madam, I deem this same be it, so far as I can guess.
Lady Lucre. Thou sayest the truth, 'tis it indeed, the outside shows
    no less.   100
    But Usury, I think Dissimulation hath not seen you since your
        coming home,
    Therefore go see him; he will rejoice when you to him are
        shown.
    It is a busy time with him; help to further him, if you can.
Usury. He may command me to attend at board to be his man.
                                                              Exit.
                    Here let [LADY] LUCRE *open the box,*
                        and dip her finger in it, and spot [LADY]
                    CONSCIENCE['s] *face, saying as followeth.*
Lady Lucre. Hold here, my sweet, and then over to see if any
    want.   105
    The more I do behold this face, the more my mind doth
        vaunt.
    This face is of favour, these cheeks are reddy and white.
    These lips are cherry-red, and full of deep delight.
    Quick-rolling eyes, her temples high, and forehead white as
        snow,
    Her eyebrows seemly set in frame, with dimpled chin below.   110
    O, how beauty hath adorned thee with every seemly hue,
    In limbs, in looks, with all the rest, proportion keeping due.
    Sure, I have not seen a finer soul in every kind of part,
    I cannot choose but kiss thee with my lips that love thee with
        my heart.

---

97. should, alas, their words] *this ed.*; should (alas their wordes) Q; should (alas) their
wordes Q2; should, alas! their words *Haz.*   99. this] Q2; the Q.   102. you to
him] Q; to him you Q2.   105. then Q2; them Q.   if any] Q; what doth Q2.

104. *attend at board*] serve at table.
    105. *to see if any want*] (1) to see if there are any places on your face I've missed
with the ink (2) to check all the money is there (which Conscience confirms at line
115); Lucre seems to spot Conscience while talking to her so that Conscience does not
notice
    106. *vaunt*] boast, appear with pride.
    107. *of favour*] beautiful.
    reddy and white] red and white in balance gives the proverbial complexion of female
beauty.

Lady Conscience. I have told the crowns, and here are just so many
    as you to me did say.   115
Lady Lucre. Then, when thou wilt, thou mayst depart, and
    homewards take thy way;
    And I pray thee, make haste in decking of thy room,
    That I may find thy lodging fine, when with my friend I come.
Lady Conscience. I'll make speed, and where I have with brooms
    ofttimes been roaming,
    I mean henceforth not to be seen, but sit to watch your coming.   120
                                                     Exit.
Lady Lucre. O, how joyful may I be that such success do find!
    No marvel, for poverty and desire of Lucre do force them follow
    my mind.
    Now may I rejoice in full contentation,
    That shall marry Love with Dissimulation,
    And have spotted Conscience with all abomination –   125
    But I forget myself, for I must to the wedding,
    Both vauntingly and flauntingly, although I had no bidding.
                                                     Exit.

[Sc. 11]

    Enter DISSIMULATION *and* COGGING *his man, and* SIMONY.

Cogging. Sir, although you be my master, I would not have you to
    upbraid my name,
    But I would have you use the right skill and title of the same,
    For my name is neither Scogging, nor Scragging, but ancient
    Cogging.
    Sir, my ancestors were five of the four worthies, and yourself are
    of my near kin.
Dissimulation. Indeed thou sayst true, for Cogging is a kinsman to
    Dissimulation.   5

---

3. Cogging] *Q;* Coggin *Q2.*   4. Sir . . . kin] *so this ed.; two lines in Q, Q2 (worthies,*
/ And).

---

    115. *told*] counted.
    123. *contentation*] content, satisfaction.
    127. *flauntingly*] overtly, ostentatiously.

    1. *upbraid*] speak reproachfully of.
    3. *Scogging*] 'Not spelt with a capital in the old copies, but apparently an allusion
to the old court-fool Scoggin, or Scogging, of whose jests a volume is extant' (Coll.
1851, p. 242).
    4. *my ancestors . . . worthies*] there were in fact nine worthies, historical figures
from history representing great deeds and heroism: Hector, Alexander the Great, and
Julius Caesar; Joshua, David, and Judas Maccabaeus; King Arthur, Charlemagne,
Godfrey of Bouillon.

But tell me, have you taken the names of the guests?

Cogging. Yea, sir.

Dissimulation. Let me hear after what fashion.

The names of the guests told by COGGING.

Cogging. There is, first and foremost, Master Forgery and Master
    Flattery, Master Perjury and Master Injury,   10
    Master Cruelty and Master Pickery, Master Bribery and Master
      Treachery,
    Master Wink-at-wrong and Master Headstrong, Mistress
      Privy-theft and Master Deep-deceit, Master Abomination and
      Mistress Fornication his wife, Ferdinando False-weight and
      Frisset False-measure his wife –

Dissimulation. Stay! Fornication and Frisset False-measure: they are
    often familiar with my Lady Lucre, and one of them she
    accounts her friend.
    Therefore they shall sit with the bride in the middest, and the
    men at each end.
    Let me see: there are sixteen, even as many as well near is able   15
    To dine in the summer parlour at the playing table,
    Beside my fellow Fraud, and you, fellow Simony;
    But I shall have a great miss of my fellow Usury.

Simony. Take no care for that; he came home yesterday even, no
    longer:
    His pardon was quickly begged, and that by a courtier.   20
    And, sirrah, since he came home he had like to have slain Good
      Neighbourhood and Liberality,
    Had not True Friendship stepped between them very suddenly.
    But, sirrah, he hit True Friendship such a blow on the ear,
    That he keeps out of all men's sight, I think for shame or for
      fear.

---

12. Master ... wife –] *so* Q2; *line division at* 'Privy-theft / And' *in* Q. Mistress
Fornication] Q2 *(mistris)*; maister fornication Q.   21. home] Q; *not in* Q2.   24. I
think] Q; *not in* Q2.

---

   6. *taken*] noted down.

   8. *after what fashion*] in what order, i.e. 'who are they?'.

 11. *Pickery*] petty theft.

 12. *Privy-theft*] secret thievery.

 13. *Stay!*] Wait!

 17. *Beside*] In addition to, as well as.

 18. *I shall have ... Usury*] i.e. I wish Usury were due to be there.

 21. *had like to have*] had very likely have.

Dissimulation. Now, of my troth, it is a pretty jest: hath he made
    True Friendship hide his head?   25
        Sure, if it be so, Good Neighbourhood and Liberality for fear are
        fled.
Simony. But, fellow Dissimulation, tell me, what priest shall marry ye?
Dissimulation. Marry, that shall an old friend of mine, Master
    Doctor Hypocrisy.
Simony. Why will you not have Sir Peter Pleaseman to supply that
    want?
Dissimulation. Indeed, Sir Peter is a good priest, but Doctor
    Hypocrisy is most ancient.   30
    But Cousin Cogging, I pray you go to invite the guests,
    And tell them that they need not disturb their quietness.
    Desire them to come at dinner time, and it shall suffice,
    Because I know they will be loath so early to rise.
    But at any hand will Doctor Hypocrisy   35
    That he meet us at the church very early,
    For I would not have all the world to wonder at our match.
    It is an old proverb: 'Tis good having a hatch before the door,
        but I'll have a door before the hatch.
Cogging. Sir, I will about it as fast as I can hie;
    I'll first to that scald, bald knave, Doctor Hypocrisy.   *Exit.* 40
Simony. But fellow Dissimulation, how darest thou marry with Love,
    bearing no love at all?
    For thou dost nothing but dissemble, then thy love must needs
    be small.
    Thou canst not love but from the teeth forward.
    Sure the wife that marries thee shall highly be preferred.
Dissimulation. Tush, tush, you are a merry man; I warrant you I
    know what I do,   45

---

31. guests] *Q* (*gestes*); gesse *Q2*. 34. loath] *this ed.*; loth *Q, Q2*. 45. warrant
you] *Q*; warrant *Q2*.

---

29. *Why will*] 'Why' could be punctuated with a comma for a different emphasis.
38. *'Tis good . . . hatch.*] perhaps to keep out 'all the world' who would get in
through the open hatch.
39. *hie*] hasten.
40. *scald, bald knave*] scabby, bald villain (suggesting Hypocrisy is a Catholic friar
and/or suffering from venereal disease, which includes loss of hair as a symptom).
43. *but from . . . forward*] i.e. Dissimulation (as a hypocrite) can only say love but
cannot feel it any deeper than the mouth that says 'love'.
44. *preferred*] raised in social standing (apparently ironic).
45. *merry*] joking.
warrant] assure.

And can yield a good reason for it, I may say unto you.
What an if the world should change, and run all on her side?
Then might I by her means still in good credit abide.
Thou knowest Love is ancient and lives peaceably without any
    strife,
Then sure the people will think well of me, because she is my
    wife.   50
Simony. Trust me, thou art as crafty to have an eye to the main
    chance
As the tailor, that out of seven yards stole one and a half of
    durance.
He served at that time the devil in the likeness of St Katherine;
Such tailors will thrive, that out of a doublet and a pair of hose
    can steal their wife an apron.
The doublet sleeves three fingers were too short;   55
The Venetians came nothing near the knee.
Dissimulation. Then for to make them long enough, I pray thee what
    did he?
Simony. Two pieces set a handful broad to lengthen them withal,
Yet for all that below the knee by no means they could fall.
He, seeing that, desired the party to buy as much to make
    another pair;   60
The party did, yet, for all that he stole a quarter there.
Dissimulation. Now, sure, I can him thank, he could his occupation.
My fellow Fraud would laugh to hear one dressed of such a
    fashion.
But, fellow Simony, I thank you heartily for comparing the tailor
    to me,

---

55. sleeves] *Q;* sleeve *Q2.*   58. a] *this ed.;* an *Q, Q2.*

---

51. *an eye . . . main chance*] look to the likeliest course of action for most success. 'Main chance' is a term from the dice game of Hazard.

52. *durance*] i.e. 'durant', a stout woollen cloth also known as 'everlasting' (*OED* 'durant' B).

53. *He served . . . Katherine*] either the tailor was devil-serving under the guise of an impeccably good Saint, or the devil whom he was serving as a client was clothed *by* the tailor to look saintly.

55. *doublet sleeves*] loose, puffed, or slit sleeves of a close fitting upper-body garment.

    three fingers] three fingers' breadth ($3 \times {}^3/_4$ inch).

56. *Venetians*] a fashion of hose or breeches.

58. *pieces*] i.e. of cloth.

    a handful broad] the width of a hand.

59. *fall*] reach.

60. *party to buy as much*] customer to buy that quantity of cloth all over again.

62. *could*] knew.

As who should say his knavery and my policy did not agree.   65
Simony. Not so, but I was the willinger to tell thee, because I know
        it to be a true tale,
    And to see how artificers do extol Fraud, by whom they bear
        their sale.
    But come, let us walk, and talk no more of this,
    Your policy was very good, and so, no doubt, was his.   *Exeunt.*

[Sc. 12]

> *Enter* MERCADORUS *reading a letter to himself, and let* GERONTUS
>   *the Jew follow him, and speak as followeth.*

Gerontus. Signiore Mercadore, why do you not pay me? Think you I
        will be mocked in this sort?
    This is three times you have flouted me, it seems you make
        thereat a sport.
    Truly pay me my money, and that even now presently,
    Or by mighty Mahomet I swear I will forthwith arrest ye.
Mercadorus. Ha, pray-a bare wit me tree or four days; me have
        much business in hand.   5
    Me be troubled with letters, you see here, dat comes from
        England.
Gerontus. Tush, this is not my matter; I have nothing therewith to do.
    Pay me my money, or I'll make you, before to your lodging you
        go.
    I have officers stand watching for you, so that you cannot pass
        by,
    Therefore you were best to pay me, or else in prison you shall
        lie.   10
Mercadorus. Arrest me, dou scald knave? Marry, do, an if thou dare,
    Me will not pay de one penny; arrest me, do, me do not care.

---

65. not] *Q; not in Q2.*

5. much] *Q;* mush *Q2.*   6. with] *Q;* wit *Q2.*   11. an if thou] *Q (and);* if dou *Q2.*

---

65. *did not agree*] Collier notes that 'The negative is omitted in edit 1592, and
perhaps rightly' (Coll. 1851, p. 243) but both Q1's reading, adopted here, and Q2's
omission of 'not' can make sense. Q1 requires that 'As who should say' means 'For
who would dare say (the tailor and I did not agree)' and Simony follows up with 'Not
so' (i.e. indeed there is no one that could say so); Q2 requires that the phrase means
'As if you were someone saying (the tailor and I agreed)'.

3. *even now presently*] straight away, this instant.
11. *dou*] i.e. thou.
an if] if.

Me will be a Turk, me came heder for dat cause,
Darefore me care not for de so mush as two straws.
Gerontus. This is but your words, because you would defeat me;   15
   I cannot think you will forsake your faith so lightly.
   But seeing you drive me to doubt, I'll try your honesty;
   Therefore be sure of this, I'll go about it presently.   *Exit.*
Mercadorus. Marry, farewell and be hanged, sitten, scald, drunken
     Jew!
   I warrant ye, me shall be able very vell to pay you.   20
   My Lady Lucre have sent me here dis letter,
   Praying me to cozen de Jew for love a her.
   Darefore me'll go to get-a some Turk's apparel,
   Dat me may cosen da Jew, and end dis quarrel.   *Exit.*

[Sc. 13]

      Enter three beggars, that is to say, TOM BEGGAR,
        WILY WILL, *and* SIMPLICITY, *singing.*

The Song.

To the wedding, to the wedding, to the wedding go we,
To the wedding a-begging, a-begging all three.

Tom Beggar shall brave it, and Wily Will too,
Simplicity shall knave it, wherever we go;
With lustly bravado, take care that care will,   5
To catch it and snatch it, we have the brave skill.

Our fingers are lime-twigs, and barbers we be,
To catch sheets from hedges most pleasant to see;
Then to the alewife roundly we set them to sale,
And spend the money merrily upon her good ale.   10

13. heder] *Q;* hedar *Q2.*

5. lustly] *Q;* lustily *Q2;* lustely *Coll.*

---

  13. *heder*] hither.
  17. *try*] test.
  19. *sitten*] probably '(be)shitten'.
  scald] scurvy, scabby.

  1–12. *To the wedding . . . all three*] Qq print lines 1–2 and 11–12 in black letter, and lines 3–10 in roman font.
  7. *lime-twigs*] i.e. sticky (lime was a sticky substance used to spread on tree branches to catch birds).
  barbers] i.e. because barbers 'cut' or steal in their trade.
  8. *To . . . hedges*] to steal sheets from hedges, on which they have been placed to dry after washing.
  9. *roundly*] promptly.

To the wedding, to the wedding, to the wedding go we,
To the wedding a-begging, a-begging all three.

FINIS.

Tom Beggar. Now truly, my masters, of all occupations under the
    sun, begging is the best,
For when a man is weary, then he may lay him down to rest.
Tell me, is it not a lord's life in summer to louse one under a
    hedge,   15
And then, leaving that game, may go clip and coll his Madge?
Or else may walk to take the wholesome air abroad for his
    delight,
Where he may tumble on the grass, have sweet smells, and see
    many a pretty sight?
Why, an emperor for all his wealth can have but his pleasure,
And surely I would not lose my charter of liberty for all the
    king's treasure.   20
Wily Will. Shall I tell thee, Tom Beggar? By the faith of a gentleman,
    this ancient freedom I would not forgo,
If I might have whole mines of money at my will to bestow.
Then a man's mind should be troubled to keep that he had,
And you know it were not for me, it would make my valiant
    mind mad.
For now we neither pay Church money, subsidies, fifteens, scot
    nor lot;   25
All the parings we pay is to pay the good ale-pot.
Simplicity. But fellow beggars, you cozen me, and take away all the
    best meat,
And leave me nothing but brown bread or fin of fish to eat.
When you be at the alehouse, you drink up the strong ale, and
    give me small beer,
You tell me 'tis better than the strong to make me sing clear.   30

12.1. FINIS.] *Q; not in* Q2.

15. *louse*] to remove lice from oneself; here the term may also be a corruption of
'lounge'.
16. *clip and coll*] hug, embrace.
Madge] generic name for a country lass.
20–1. *liberty . . . freedom*] playing on the honour of being given the 'liberty' or
'freedom' to practise a legitimate trade in a city as a master.
25. *Church-money . . . scot nor lot*] various required contributions and taxes.
26. *parings*] small amounts; lit. 'shavings', suggesting clipping or filing coins to get
gold.
29. *small beer*] weak, low-quality beer.

Indeed, you know, with my singing I get twice so much as ye,
But, an you serve me so, you shall sing yourselves, and beg alone
    for me.
Tom Beggar. We stand prating here; come, let us go to the gate.
Mass, I am greatly afraid we are come somewhat too late.
Good gentle Master Porter, your reward do bestow   35
On a poor lame man, that hath but a pair of legs to go.
Wily Will. For the honour of God, good Master Porter, give
    somewhat to the blind,
That the way to the alehouse in his sleep cannot find.
Tom Beggar. For the good Lord's sake, take compassion on the poor.

    Enter FRAUD, *with a basket of meat on his arm.*

Fraud. How now, sirs! You are vengeance hasty: can ye not tarry,   40
But stand bawling so at my lady's door?
Here, take it amongst you – yet 'twere a good alms-deed to give
    you nothing,
Because you were so hasty, and kept such a calling.
Tom Beggar. I beseech ye, not so, sir, for we were very hungry:
That made us so earnest, but we are sorry we troubled ye.   45
Simplicity. [*Aside*] Look how greedy they be, like dogs that fall
    a-snatching.
You shall see that I shall have the greatest alms, because I said
    nothing.
Fraud knows me, therefore he'll be my friend, I am sure of that.
They have nothing but lean beef; ye shall see, I shall have a piece
    that is fat. –
Master Fraud, you have forgot me; pray ye, let me have my
    share.   50
Fraud. Faith, all is gone, thou comest too late; thou seest all is given
    there.
By the faith of a gentleman, I have it not; I would I were able to
    give thee more.
Simplicity. O sir, I saw your arms hang out at a stable-door.

---

31. so] *Q; as Q2.*   37. For . . . Master] *Q (Mas);* For Gods sake good mas *Q2.*
42. alms-deed] *Q (almes deede);* almesse deed *Q2.*   44. were] *Q;* are *Q2.*   49. that
is] *Q;* thats *Q2.*   51. comest] *Q;* comst *Q2;* com'st *Haz.*

32. *for me*] as far as I am concerned.
40. *vengeance*] extremely, intensely (*OED* 'vengeance' 5).
tarry] wait.
51. *Faith*] i.e. In faith, truly.
53. *arms*] i.e. coat of arms; Collier sees 'a pun, probably, upon *almes* and *arms*'
(Coll. 1851, p. 243).

Fraud. Indeed, my arms are at the painter's; belike, he hung them
    out to dry.
    I pray thee, tell me what they were, if thou canst them descry.   55
Simplicity. Marry, there was never a scutcheon, but there was two
    trees rampant,
    And then over them lay a sour tree passant,
    With a man like you in a green field pendent,
    Having a hempen halter about his neck, with a knot under the
    left ear, because you are a younger brother.
    Then, sir, there stands on each side, holding up the crease,   60
    A worthy ostler's hand in a dish of grease.
    Besides all this, on the helmet stands the hangman's hand,
    Ready to turn the ladder whereon your picture did stand.
    Then under the helmet hung tables like chains, and for what
    they are I cannot devise,
    Except it be to make you hang fast, that the crows might pick
    out your eyes.   65
Fraud. [*Aside*] What a swad is this? I had been better to have sent
    him to the back door,
    To have gotten some alms amongst the rest of the poor. –

---

57. passant] *Haz*; parsant *Q, Q2*. 59. hempen] *Coll, Haz*; hempten *Q, Q2*. 60.
side] *Q*; hand *Q2*. crease] *Q, Q2*; cres' *Haz*. 64. tables] *Q, Q2*; cables
Haz. 66. SD [*Aside*.]] *this ed.; not in Q, Q2*.

---

  54. *belike*] probably, it is likely that.
  55. *descry*] discern, describe.
  56. *scutcheon*] i.e. escutcheon, small shield shape as a background for coat of
arms.
  rampant] with forefeet raised in proud, aggressive stance.
  57. *sour tree passant*] an ironic reference to a gallows (a bitter 'tree'); in heraldry,
'passant' refers to an animal walking left to right, looking right and raising the right
front paw as it walks.
  58. *pendent*] hanging.
  59. *hempen*] made of hemp.
  60. *crease*] i.e. crest: A figure or device (originally borne by a knight on his helmet)
placed on a wreath, coronet, or chapeau, and borne above the shield and helmet in a
coat of arms (*OED* 'crest' n. 3.a).
  63. *turn the ladder*] i.e. to drop the condemned man so that he hangs.
  your picture] your likeness.
  64. *tables*] tables or 'tablets' could refer to weights to pull on the ropes and 'make
you hang fast', as Simplicity puts it (and a number of weights threaded together would
resemble a 'chain'); Hazlitt's emendation to 'cables' is possible, since a small 't' could
look like a 'c' in secretary hand manuscript, and the meaning – that the hempen ropes
are as stout as cable and therefore efficient for hanging a man – is apt.
  66. *swad*] rustic, clown.

Thou prat'st thou canst not tell what, or else art not well in thy
    wit;
I am sure my arms are not blaz'd so far abroad as yet.
Simplicity. O yes, sir, your arms were known a great while ago,   70
    For your elder brother, Deceit, did give those arms too.
Marry, the difference is all, which is the knot under the left ear;
    The painter says, when he is hanged, you may put out the knot
    without fear.
I am sure they were your arms, for there was written in Roman
    letters round about the hempen collar:
Given by the worthy valiant Captain Master Fraud, the ostler.   75
Now, God be wi' ye, sir; I'll get me even close to the back door.
Farewell, Tom Beggar and Wily Will; I'll beg with you no more.
Exit.

Tom Beggar. O farewell, Simplicity: we are very loath to lose thy
    company.
Fraud. Now he is gone, give ear to me. You seem to be sound men
    in every joint and limb,
And can ye live in this sort, to go up and down the country
    a-begging?   80
O base minds! I trow, I had rather hack it out by the
    highway-side,
Than such misery and penury still to abide.
Sirs, if you will be ruled by me, and do what I shall say,
I'll bring ye where we shall have a notable fine prey.
It is so, sirs, that a merchant, one Mercadorus, is coming from
    Turkey,   85
And it is my lady's pleasure that he robbed should be.
She hath sworn that we shall be all sharers alike,
And upon that willed me some such companions as you be to
    seek.
Tom Beggar. O worthy Captain Fraud, you have won my noble
    heart;
You shall see how manfully I can play my part.   90

---

73. hanged] *Q2* (hangd); hang *Q*; hung *Haz.*   76. wi'] *Haz*; wie *Q*; with *Q2.*

69. *blaz'd*] (1) 'To inscribe or portray conspicuously, as on a heraldic shield; to
adorn or inscribe *with* heraldic devices, words, etc.' (2) 'To celebrate, extol, 'blaze
abroad'; to render illustrious' (*OED*).
    73. *when he ... fear*] i.e. you may remove the marker of your status as younger
brother, because your elder brother, Deceit, will be dead.
    79. *give ear*] listen.
    81. *trow*] trust, believe.
    hack it out] put up with it, brave it out.

And here's Wily Will, as good a fellow as your heart can wish,
To go a-fishing with a crank through a window, or to set lime-
    twigs to catch a pan, pot, or dish.
Wily Will. He says true, for I tell you I am one that will not give
    back,
    Not for a double shot out of a black-jack.
    O sir, you bring us a-bed when ye talk of this gear,   95
    Come, shall we go, worthy Captain? I long, till we be there.
Fraud. Ay, let us about it, to provide our weapons ready,
    And when the time serves, I myself will conduct ye.
Tom Beggar. O, valiantly spoken. Come, Wily Will, two pots of ale
    we'll bestow
    On our captain courageously for a parting blow.   *Exeunt.* 100

[Sc. 14]

Enter the JUDGE OF TURKEY,
with GERONTUS *and* MERCADORUS.

Judge of Turkey. Sir Gerontus, because you are the plaintiff, you first
    your mind shall say:
    Declare the cause you did arrest this merchant yesterday.
Gerontus. Then, learned judge, attend. This Mercadorus, whom you
    see in place,
    Did borrow two thousand ducats of me but for a five weeks'
    space.
    Then, sir, before the day came, by his flattery he obtained one
    thousand more,   5
    And promised me at two months' end I should receive my store.
    But before the time expired, he was closely fled away,
    So that I never heard of him at least this two years' day;
    Till at the last I met with him, and my money did demand,

9. my money did] *Q*; did the money did *Q*2.

---

92. *To go ... dish*] i.e. stealing for household or shop goods by reaching with a catching device through windows; for lime-twigs see note to 13.7.
94. *double ... black-jack*] two swigs out of a large, leather beer jug.
95. *you bring ... gear*] you give us comfort when you talk of these doings.

3–6. *This Mercadorus ... store*] Collier writes 'This representation of the transaction, it will be noted, does not tally with the statement of it by Gerontus [earlier]. Perhaps for 'five', just above, we ought to read *few*' (Coll. 1851, p. 243). The detail is also inconsistent in how much was lent at each stage; the outcome, however, is still a loan of three thousand ducats over (a little more than) three months (see also note to 9.10).
7. *closely*] cunningly, secretly.
8. *this two years' day*] two years since.

Who sware to me at five days' end he would pay me out of
    hand.   10
The five days came, and three days more, then one day he
    requested;
I, perceiving that he flouted me, have got him thus arrested.
And now he comes in Turkish weeds to defeat me of my money,
But, I trow, he will not forsake his faith, I deem he hath more
    honesty.
Judge of Turkey. Sir Gerontus, you know if any man forsake his
    faith, king, country, and become a Mahomet,   15
All debts are paid: 'tis the law of our realm, and you may not
    gainsay it.
Gerontus. Most true, reverend judge, we may not, nor I will not
    against our laws grudge.
Judge of Turkey. Signiore Mercadorus, is this true that Gerontus
    doth tell?
Mercadorus. My lord judge, de matter and de circumstance be true,
    me know well;
But me will be a Turk, and for dat cause me came here.   20
Judge of Turkey. Then, it is but folly to make many words. Signiore
    Mercadorus, draw near:
Lay your hand upon this book, and say after me.
Mercadorus. With a goodwill, my lord judge; me be all ready.
Gerontus. Not for any devotion, but for Lucre's sake of my money.
Judge of Turkey. Say: I, Mercadorus, do utterly renounce before all the   25
    world my duty to my Prince, my honour to my parents, and my
    goodwill to my country.
Mercadorus. Furthermore, I protest and swear to be true to this country
    during life, and thereupon I forsake my Christian faith –
Gerontus. Stay there, most puissant judge! Signiore Mercadorus,
    consider what you do.   30
Pay me the principal; as for the interest, I forgive it you,
And yet the interest is allowed amongst you Christians, as well
    as in Turkey;
Therefore, respect your faith, and do not seem to deceive me.

---

17. reverend judge] *Haz;* (reverent Judge) *Q;* (reverend judge) *Q2.*   21. but folly] *this
ed.;* but a follie *Q;* but a folly *Q2.*   22. upon] *Q;* on *Q2.*   33. seem] *Q, Q2;* seek
Haz.

---

10. *sware*] swore.
out of hand] immediately (see 9.16 and n.).
13. *defeat me of*] cheat me out of.
14. *I deem*] I judge, I am of the opinion.
16. *gainsay*] deny, contradict.

Mercadorus. No point da interest, no point da principal.
Gerontus. Then pay me the one half, if you will not pay me all.   35
Mercadorus. No point da half, no point denier: me will be a Turk, I
    say.
    Me be weary of my Christ's religion, and for dat me come away.
Gerontus. Well, seeing it is so, I would be loath to hear the people
    say, it was 'long of me
    Thou forsakest thy faith, wherefore I forgive thee frank and free,
    Protesting before the judge and all the world never to demand
    penny nor halfpenny.   40
Mercadorus. O, Sir Gerontus, me take-a your proffer, and tank you
    most heartily.
Judge of Turkey. But, Signiore Mercadorus, I trow ye will be a Turk
    for all this.
Mercadorus. Signiore, no: not for all da good in da world me
    forsake-a my Christ.
Judge of Turkey. Why, then, it is as Sir Gerontus said: you did more
    for the greediness of the money
    Than for any zeal or goodwill you bear to Turkey.   45
Mercadorus. O sir, you make a great offence:
    You must not judge-a my conscience.
Judge of Turkey. One may judge and speak truth, as appears by this:
    Jews seek to excel in Christianity, and Christians in Jewishness.
                                     Exit.
Mercadorus. Vell, vell; but me tank you, Sir Gerontus, with all my
    very heart.   50
Gerontus. Much good may it do you, sir; I repent it not for my part.
    But yet I would not have this 'bolden you to serve another so:
    Seek to pay, and keep day with men, so a good name on you
    will go.   *Exit.*
Mercadorus. You say vel, sir; it does me good dat me have cozened
    de Jew.
    Faith, I would my Lady Lucre de whole matter now knew.   55

---

36. denier] *Haz;* denere *Q, Q2.*   37. Me] *Q;* me *Q2.*   38. loath] *this ed.;* loth *Q,*
Q2.   50. with] *Q;* wit *Q2.*

---

   34. *No point . . . no point*] Not a bit . . . not a bit (not the tiniest part, scruple)
(OED A.III.6.a and b).
   36. *denier*] French coin; from sixteenth century, a small copper coin, hence proverbially used for 'a small sum'.
   38. *'long*] along of, owing to.
   39. *wherefore*] therefore, which is the reason why.
   41. *proffer*] offer.
   52. *'bolden*] embolden.

What is dat me will not do for her sweet sake?
But now me will provide my journey toward England to take.
Me be a Turk? No. It will make my Lady Lucre to smile
When she knows how me did da scald Jew beguile.   *Exit.*

[Sc. 15]

Enter [LADY] LUCRE, *and* [LADY] LOVE *with a vizard behind.*

Lady Lucre. Mistress Love, I marvel not a little what coy conceit is
     crept into your head,
     That you seem so sad and sorrowful since the time you first did
          wed.
     Tell me, sweet wench, what thou ailest, and if I can ease thy
          grief,
     I will be pressed to pleasure thee in yielding of relief.
     Sure, thou makest me for to think something has chanced amiss;   5
     I pray thee, tell me what thou ailest, and what the matter is.
Lady Love. My grief, alas, I shame to show, because my bad intent
     Hath brought on me a just reward, and eke a strange event!
     Shall I be counted Love? Nay, rather lascivious Lust,
     Because unto Dissimulation I did repose such trust.   10
     But now I moan too late, and blush my hap to tell,
     My head in monstrous sort, alas, doth more and more still swell!
Lady Lucre. Is your head then swollen, good Mistress Love? I pray
     you let me see.
     Of troth it is! Behold a face that seems to smile on me.
     It is fair and well-favoured, with a countenance smooth and
          good;   15
     Wonder is the worst, to see two faces in a hood.
     Come, let's go, we'll find some sports to spurn away such toys.
Lady Love. Were it not for Lucre, sure Love had lost her joys.
                                                      Exeunt.

56. What] *Q*; Vat *Q2*.

5. something] *Haz, Q* (some thing*)*; somewhat *Q2*.

---

59. *scald*] See notes to 3.61, 5.51, 11.40, 12.19.

0.1. vizard behind] i.e. a mask on the back of the head (giving her two faces).
3. *what thou ailest*] what you suffer from, what ails you.
8. *eke*] also.
9. *counted*] accounted, credited with the name of.
11. *hap*] fortune, chance.
16. *Wonder is the worst*] The strangest part of this is.

[Sc. 16]

> *Enter* Serviceable DILIGENCE, *the Constable, and* SIMPLICITY,
> *with an Officer to whip him, or two if you can.*

Simplicity. Why, but must I be whipped, Master Constable, indeed?
    You may save your labour, for I have no need.
Diligence. I must needs see thee punished, there is no remedy.
    Except thou wilt confess, and tell me
    Where thy fellows are become that did the robbery.   5
Simplicity. Indeed, Master Constable, I do not know of their stealing,
    For I did not see them since we went together a-begging.
    Therefore pray ye, sir, be miserable to me, and let me go,
    For I labour to get my living with begging, you know.
Diligence. Thou wast seen in their company a little before the deed
    was done;   10
    Therefore it is most likely thou knowest where they are become.
Simplicity. Why, Master Constable, if a sheep go among wolves all
    day,
    Shall the sheep be blamed if they steal anything away?
Diligence. Ay, marry, shall he, for it is a great presumption
    That, keeping them company, he is of like profession.   15
    But despatch, sirs; strip him and whip him –
    Stand not to reason the question.
Simplicity. Indeed, 'twas Fraud, so it was, it was not I,
    And here he comes himself, ask him if I lie.

> *Enter* FRAUD.

Diligence. What sayest thou, villain? I would advise thee hold thy
    tongue: 20
    I know him to be a wealthy man and a burgess of the town. –
    [*To Fraud.*] Sir, an it please your mastership, here's one slanders
    you with felony.
    He saith you were the chief doer of a robbery.
Fraud. What says the rascal? But you know,
    It standeth not with my credit to brawl.   25
    But good Master Constable, for his slanderous report

---

14. Ay] *Q (1)*; Yea *Q2.*

---

    5. *the robbery*] i.e. the robbery of Mercadorus that Fraud reveals at 13.86, as
ordered by Lady Lucre, and cited by the Judge at 17.18.
    8. *miserable*] Simplicity's mistake for 'commiserable'.
    15. *profession*] the word carries the sense of ill-doing; cf. note to 3.147.
    17. *reason the question*] discuss, debate the issue.
    21. *burgess*] this title could refer simply to a citizen or freeman of a city; here it
probably suggests a magistrate or member of the town council.
    25. *standeth not with my credit*] does not accord with my social standing.

Pay him double, and in a greater matter command me you shall.

Exit.

Simplicity. Master Constable, must the countenance carry out the
     knave?
Why, then, if one will face folks out, some fine reparlment he
     must have.

                    BEADLE *put off his clothes.*

Beadle. Come, Sir Jack Sauce, make quick despatch at once,   30
     You shall see how finely we will fetch the skin from your bones.
Simplicity. Nay, but tell me whether you be both right-handed or no?
Beadle. What is that to thee? Why wouldst thou so fain know?
Simplicity. Marry, if you should be both right-handed, the one would
     hinder the other,
     Then it would not be done finely, according to order,   35
     For if I be not whipped with credit, it is not worth a pin.
     Therefore, I pray, Master Constable, let me be whipped upon my
     skin.
Diligence. Whereon dost thou think they would whip thee, I pray
     thee declare,
     That thou puttest us in mind, and takest such great care?
Simplicity. I was afraid you would have worn out my clothes with
     whipping,   40
     Then afterward I should go naked a-begging.
Beadle. Have no doubt of that; we will favour thy clothes.
     Thou shalt judge that thyself by feeling the blows.
     Lead him once or twice about, whipping him, and so ex[eun]t.

---

27. a greater] *Q*; as great a *Q2*.   29. reparlment] *Q, Q2*; repariment *Coll,
Haz.*   32. whether you be] *Q*; be you both *Q2*.   34. be both] *Q*; both be *Q2*.   36.
For ... credit] *Q*; For if you whip me not with credite *Q2*.   37. I pray] *Q*; I pray you
Q2.   upon my] *Q*; on the *Q2*.   39. such] *Q*; so *Q2*.   43.1. SD ex[eun]t.] *this ed.*;
Exit. *Q*; exit. *Q2, Coll, Haz.*

---

27. *Pay him double*] punish him particularly harshly.

29. *reparlment*] Not in *OED*; Collier's emendation to 'repariment' is cited in the
OED, but credited to Hazlitt as the only instant of a word meaning '?repairment';
Simplicity could mean 'apparel'.

29.1. *put off his clothes*] take off his (Simplicity's) clothes. The dialogue that follows
suggests that Simplicity is still wearing his clothes, and the direction may be better
placed several lines later.

30. *Jack Sauce*] Impudent fellow; cf. *Englishmen for My Money* 4.1.34 and
4.1.147.

33. *fain*] like to.

39. *puttest us in mind*] remind us (of our duty).

42. *doubt of*] fear for.

43.1. *Lead him ... ex[eun]t.*] It seems simplest here to have all characters exit by
one door and re-enter by another door, Diligence taking up the rear.

[Sc. 17]

> *Enter* JUDGE NEMO, *the* CLERK *of the 'size, the Crier,*
> *and* Serviceable DILIGENCE; *the* JUDGE *and* CLERK *being set,*
> *the Crier shall sound three times.*

Judge Nemo. Serviceable Diligence, bring hither such prisoners as are
    in your custody.
Diligence. My diligence shall be applied very willingly.
    Pleaseth it you, there are but three prisoners, so far as I know,
    Which are Lucre and Conscience, with a deformed creature
      much like Bifrons, the base daughter of Juno.
Judge Nemo. No! Where is that wretch Dissimulation?   5
Diligence. He hath transformed himself after a strange fashion.
Judge Nemo. Fraud: where is he become?
Diligence. He was seen in the streets, walking in a citizen's gown.
Judge Nemo. What is become of Usury?
Diligence. He was seen at the Exchange very lately.   10
Judge Nemo. Tell me, when have you heard of Simony?
Diligence. He was seen this day walking in Paul's, having conference
    and very great familiarity with some of the clergy.
Judge Nemo. Fetch Lucre and Conscience to the bar.
Diligence. Behold, worthy judge, here ready they are.

> *Enter* [LADY] LUCRE *and* [LADY] CONSCIENCE.

Judge Nemo. Stand forth. Diligence, divide them asunder.   15
Clerk. Lucre, thou art indicted by the name of Lucre,
    To have committed adultery with Mercadorus the merchant and
      Creticus the lawyer.
    Thou art also indicted for the robbery of Mercadorus.
    Lastly, and chiefly, for the consenting to the murder of
      Hospitality.
    What sayest thou, art thou guilty or not in these causes?   20
Lady Lucre. Not guilty. Where are mine accusers? They may shame
    to show their faces.
    I warrant you, none comes, nor dare, to discredit my name.

0.3. three times] *Q; thrise Q2.*   11. have] *Q; not in Q2.*   18. Mercadorus] *this ed.;*
Mercadore *Q; mercadore Q2; Mercatore Haz.*   22. dare,] *Coll, Haz; dare Q, Q2.*

    0.1. 'size] assize, court.
    0.3. sound] call out.
    4. *Bifrons, the . . . Juno*] Bifrons is a monster from demonology, and Lady Love has
been given a monstrous two faces (*bi-frons*); the name derives from the figure of Janus,
and the Janus–Juno confusion presumably makes Dilligence call Bifrons Juno's daughter – Juno's *son* was Mars.
    12. *Paul's*] St Paul's cathedral.

     In despite of the teeth of them that dare I speak in disdain.
Judge Nemo. Impudent! Canst thou deny deeds so manifestly known?
Lady Lucre. In denial stands trial. I shame not; let them be shown.   25
     It grinds my gall they should slander me on this sort:
     They are some old, cankered, currish, corrupt carls that gave me
          this report.
     My soul craves revenge on such my secret foes,
     And revengement I will have, if body and soul I lose.
Judge Nemo. Thy hateful heart declares thy wicked life,   30
     In the abundance of thy abomination all evils are rife.
     But what sayest thou, Conscience, to thy accusation,
     That art accused to have been bawd unto Lucre, and spotted
          with all abomination?
Lady Conscience. What should I say; nay, what would I say in this
          our naughty living?
Lady Lucre. Good Conscience, if thou love me, say nothing.   35
Clerk. Diligence, suffer her not to stand prating.
                                        Let him put her aside.
Judge Nemo. What letter is that in thy bosom, Conscience?
          Diligence, reach it hither.   *Make as though ye read it.*
     Conscience, speak on; let me hear what thou canst say,
     For I know in singleness thou wilt a truth bewray.
Lady Conscience. My good lord, I have no way to excuse myself,   40
     She hath corrupted me by flattery and her accursed pelf.
     What need further trial, sith I, Conscience, am a thousand witnesses?
     I cannot choose but condemn us all in living amiss.
     Such terror doth affright me, that living, I wish to die;
     I am afraid there is no spark left for me of God's mercy.   45
Judge Nemo. Conscience, where hadst thou this letter?
Lady Conscience. It was put into my bosom by Lucre,
     Willing me to keep secret our lascivious living.

28. secret] *Haz;* sacred *Q, Q2.*   37. SD ye] *Q, Q2;* he *Haz.*

---

   23. *In despite . . . teeth*] In defiance.
   26. *It grinds my gall*] It rubs me the wrong way; it afflicts me with bitterness (the secretion of the liver, bile).
   27. *cankered, currish, corrupt . . . report*] They are some infected, beastly (dog-like), base rustics who spoke of me in this manner.
   28. *secret foes*] mysterious, anonymous enemies.
   29. *if*] even if.
   37. ye] Hazlitt emends this Q1 reading to 'he'; either word is possible and a manuscript secretary 'h' with its dropped tail could read like a 'y'.
   39. *singleness*] alone, speaking for yourself.
   bewray] reveal, expose (Conscience, being Conscience, cannot help but tell the truth and will reveal deception).
   41. *pelf*] money.
   42. *sith I*] since I.

I cannot but condemn us all in this thing.

Judge Nemo. [*To Lady Lucre.*] How now, malapert! Stand you still
    in defence or no?   50
    This letter declares thy guilty Conscience. How sayest thou: is it
    not so?
    Tell me, why standest thou in a maze? Speak quickly.
    Hadst thou thy tongue so liberal, and now stand to study?

Lady Lucre. O, Conscience, thou hast killed me! By thee I am
    overthrown.

Judge Nemo. It is happy that by Conscience thy abomination is
    known,   55
    Wherefore I pronounce judgement against thee on this wise:
    Thou shalt pass to the place of darkness, where thou shalt hear
        fearful cries,
    Weeping, wailing, gnashing of teeth, and torment without end,
    Burning in the lake of fire and brimstone because thou canst not
        amend;
    Wherefore, Diligence, convey her hence, throw her down to the
        lowest hell,   60
    Where the infernal sprites and damned ghosts do dwell,
    And bring forth Love.

Ex[*eun*]*t* [LADY] LUCRE *and* DILIGENCE.
Let [*Lady*] *Lucre make ready for* [*Lady*] *Love quickly,*
and come with Diligence.

    Declare the cause, Conscience, at large how thou comest so
        spotted,
    Whereby many by thee hath been greatly infected,
    For under the colour of Conscience thou deceivedst many,   65
    Causing them to defile the temple of God, which is man's body.
    A clean conscience is a sacrifice, God's own resting place;
    Why wast thou then corrupted so, and spotted on thy face?

Lady Conscience. When Hospitality had his throat cut by Usury,
    He oppressed me with cruelty and brought me to beggary,   70
    Turning me out of house and home, and in the end
    My gown to pay my rent to him I did send.
    So driven to that extremity, I have fallen to that you see,
    Yet after judgement I hope of God's mercy.

Judge Nemo. O, Conscience, shall cankered coin corrupt thy heart?   75
    Or shall want in this world cause thee to feel everlasting smart?

62.1. SD *Ex*[*eun*]*t*] *this ed.;* Exit *Q, Q2, Coll, Haz.* 63. comest] *Q;* commest *Q2.*
75. coin] *Haz;* quoyn *Q;* quoin *Q2.*

---

50. *malapert!*] Impudence! Saucy person!
52. *in a maze*] amazed.
53. *stand to study*] stand speechless.
56. *on this wise*] in this fashion, as follows.
75. *cankered coin*] infected money.

O, Conscience, what a small time thou hast on earth to live;
Why dost thou not, then, to God all honour give,
Considering the time is everlasting that thou shalt live in bliss,
If by thy life thou rise from death to judgement, mercy, and
    forgiveness?   80

Enter [LADY] LOVE *with* DILIGENCE.

Stand aside, Conscience. Bring Love to the bar.
What sayest thou to thy deformity? Who was the cause?
Lady Love. Lady Lucre.
Judge Nemo. Did Lucre choke thee so, that thou gavest thyself over
    unto Lust?
And did prodigal expenses cause thee in Dissimulation to trust?   85
Thou wast pure, Love, and art thou become a monster,
Bolstering thyself upon the lasciviousness of Lucre?
Love, answer for thyself, speak in thy defence.
Lady Love. I cannot choose but yield, confounded by Conscience.
Judge Nemo. Then judgement I pronounce on thee: because thou
    followed Lucre,   90
Whereby thou hast sold thy soul, to feel like torment with her,
Which torments comprehended are in the worm of Conscience,
Who raging still shall ne'er have end, a plague for thine offence.
Care shall be thy comfort, and sorrow shall thy life sustain;
Thou shalt be dying, yet never dead, but pining still in endless
    pain.   95
Diligence, convey her to Lucre. Let that be her reward,
Because unto her cankered coin she gave her whole regard.
But as for Conscience, carry her to prison,
There to remain until the day of the general session.
Thus we make an end,   100
Knowing that the best of us all may amend,
Which God grant, to his goodwill and pleasure,
That we be not corrupted with the unsatiate desire of vanishing
    earthly treasure;
For covetousness is the cause of wresting man's conscience;
Therefore restrain thy lust, and thou shalt shun the offence.   105
                          [*Exeunt.*]

FINIS.

84. unto] *Q*; to *Q*2. 86. pure, Love,] *this ed.*; pure (Love) *Q*; pure Love, *Q*2.
97. coin] *Q* (coine); coyne *Q*2. 105.1. SD [*Exeunt.*]] *this ed.; not in Q, Q2, Coll, Haz.*

---

   86. *pure, Love,*] This punctuation, which follows Q1's equivalent parentheses
around 'Love', addresses love as a realistic entity who is being criticized for losing her
purity; Q2's alteration to 'pure Love,' suggests the ongoing view of 'pure Love' as a
moral concept that has been tainted.
   103. *unsatiate*] insatiable, cannot be satisfied.

Title page from the first edition (Q 1616) of *Englishmen for My Money*.
Reproduced by permission of the British Library.

ENGLISHMEN FOR MY MONEY

THE ACTORS' NAMES

PISARO, *a Portingale [merchant and usurer].*

LAURENTIA
MARINA } *Pisaro's daughters.*
MATHEA

ANTHONY, *a schoolmaster to them.* 5

HARVEY [*suitor to Marina*].

(FERDINAND) HEIGHAM [*suitor to Laurentia.*]

(NED) WALGRAVE [*suitor to Mathea.*]

DELION, *a Frenchman.*
ALVARO, *an Italian.* } [*Rival*] *suitors.* 10
VANDAL, *a Dutchman.*

FRISCO, *a clown, Pisaro's man.*

MOORE [*a merchant*].

TOWERSON, *a merchant.*

BALSARO [*a Spanish merchant*]. 15

BROWNE, *a clothier.*

POST.

BELLMAN.

[MERCHANT.]

[STRANGER.] 20

[Servant, other Merchants and Strangers.]

(FERDINAND) HEIGHAM] *this ed.; Ferdinand,* or *Heigham Qq.* (NED)
WALGRAVE] *this ed.; Ned,* or *Walgrave Qq.*

---

1. *Portingale*] Portuguese.

11. *VANDAL*] See the note on character names in the introduction.

12. *FRISCO*] 'A brisk movement in dancing' (*OED*, 'Frisco' 1), suggesting friskiness.

18. *BELLMAN*] a town crier; one employed to make public announcements, ringing his bell for attention.

ACT I

Enter PISARO.

Pisaro. How smug this grey-eyed morning seems to be:
    A pleasant sight; but yet more pleasure have I
    To think upon this moistening south-west wind
    That drives my laden ships from fertile Spain.
    But come what will, no wind can come amiss,   5
    For two and thirty winds that rules the seas,
    And blows about this airy region,
    Thirty-two ships have I to equal them,
    Whose wealthy fraughts do make Pisaro rich.
    Thus every soil to me is natural.   10
    Indeed, by birth I am a Portingale,
    Who, driven by western winds on English shore,
    Here liking of the soil, I marrièd,
    And have three daughters. But impartial Death
    Long since deprived me of her dearest life,   15
    Since whose decease, in London I have dwelt,
    And by the sweet loved trade of usury,
    Letting for interest, and on mortgages,
    Do I wax rich, though many gentlemen
    By my extortion comes to misery: 20
    Amongst the rest, three English gentlemen
    Have pawned to me their livings and their lands,
    Each several hoping – though their hopes are vain –
    By marriage of my daughters to possess
    Their patrimonies and their lands again.   25
    But gold is sweet, and they deceive themselves,

---

11. Portingale] *Q*; Portugale *Q2, Q3*; Portingal *1830.*   23. – though . . . vain –] *this ed.*; , though their hopes are vaine, *Qq*.

---

1. *smug*] smooth, fair; often used of persons (as at 4.3.21); cf. Thomas Dekker, *Wonderful Year*: 'the skie got a most cleare complexion, lookte smug and smoothe, and had not so much as a wart sticking on her face' (sig. B).
9. *fraughts*] cargoes.
10. *natural*] native, a homeland.
11. *a Portingale*] a Portugal, Portuguese.
19. *wax*] grow.
23. *Each several*] each one.

For though I gild my temples with a smile,
It is but Judas-like, to work their ends.
But soft, what noise of footing do I hear?

Enter LAURENTIA, MARINA, MATHEA, *and* ANTHONY.

Laurentia. Now master, what intend you to read to us?   30
Anthony. Pisaro your father would have me read moral philosophy.
Marina. What's that?
Anthony. First tell me how you like it.
Mathea. First tell us what it is.
Pisaro. [*Aside*] They be my daughters and their schoolmaster;   35
  Pisaro, not a word, but list their talk.   [*He withdraws.*]
Anthony. Gentlewomen, to paint philosophy
  Is to present youth with so sour a dish
  As their abhorring stomachs nil digests.
  When first my mother Oxford (England's pride)   40
  Fostered me pupil-like, with her rich store,
  My study was to read philosophy.
  But since, my headstrong youth's unbridled will,
  Scorning the leaden fetters of restraint,
  Hath pruned my feathers to a higher pitch.   45
  Gentlewomen, moral philosophy is a kind of art,
  The most contrary to your tender sexes.
  It teacheth to be grave, and on that brow,
  Where beauty in her rarest glory shines,
  Plants the sad semblance of decayèd age.   50
  Those weeds that with their riches should adorn,
  And grace fair nature's curious workmanship,
  Must be converted to a black-faced veil,
  Grief's livery, and sorrow's semblance.
  Your food must be your hearts' abundant sighs,   55

---

39. nil] *Q, Q2 (*nill*);* ill *Q3.*   41. pupil-like] *Q3;* puple-like *Q, Q2.*   55. abundant] *Q3;* aboundant *Q;* aboudant *Q2.*

---

27. *gild*] literally, plate in gold; hence, adorn.
28. *Judas-like*] Judas, the disciple who betrayed Jesus. Pisaro's hypocrisy is aligned with the Jewish opposition to Christianity.
31. *moral philosophy*] philosophical studies into human nature, and therefore moral behaviour.
39. *nil*] nothing.
40. *Oxford*] i.e. Oxford University.
45. *pruned*] preened.
pitch] gloss, colour; also, in falconry, the highest point of a falcon's flight before diving toward its prey.
51. *weeds*] clothes; here, body's own adornment (facial expression, etc.).
54. *livery*] uniform apparel provided by a master for servants.

    Steeped in the brinish liquor of your tears,
    Daylight as dark night, dark night spent in prayer;
    Thoughts your companions, and repentant minds
    The recreation of your tired spirits.
    Gentlewomen, if you can like this modesty,   60
    Then will I read to you philosophy.
Laurentia. Not I!
Marina. Fie upon it!
Mathea. Hang up philosophy! I'll none of it!
Pisaro. [*Aside*] A tutor said I? A tutor for the devil!   65
Anthony. No, gentlewomen, Anthony hath learned
    To read a lecture of more pleasing worth.
    Marina, read these lines – young Harvey sent them.
                                    [*Gives her a letter.*]
    There every line repugns philosophy;
    Then love him, for he hates the thing thou hates.   70
    Laurentia, this is thine from Ferdinand.   [*Gives her a purse.*]
    Think every golden circle that thou seest
    The rich unvalued circle of his worth.
    Mathea, with these gloves thy Ned salutes thee,   [*Gives gloves.*]
    As often as these hide these from the sun,   75
    And, wanton, steals a kiss from thy fair hand,
    Presents his serviceable true heart's zeal,
    Which waits upon the censure of thy doom.
    What, though their lands be mortgaged to your father,

---

79. father,] *Haz;* Father; *Qq.*

56. *brinish*] salty.

60. *modesty*] 'moderation, dullness (?)' (Baugh).

63. *Fie*] expression of disgust or annoyance.

64. *Hang up*] forget (it), leave it alone; cf. *Romeo and Juliet*, where Romeo declares to Friar Laurence, 'Yet "banished"? Hang up philosophy!' (3.3.57).

68. *these lines*] the stage direction follows earlier editors in interpreting this action as Anthony giving Marina a letter; the emphasis on 'lines' might also suggest that Harvey has written Marina a love poem (perhaps a sonnet) against philosophy (van Elk).

71. *this*] i.e. a purse of gold coins ('golden circle').

73. *unvalued*] (1) not yet 'tested', as gold (or silver) metal in a coin (2) not highly considered, lacking value.

75. *these . . . these*] i.e. gloves . . . i.e. hands.

76. *wanton*] unrestrained, unabashed.

77. *serviceable*] (1) ready to do service (2) able, sufficient to do service (perhaps sexually).

79. *father,*] Qq stop the line with a semicolon, which may suggest an interrogative in early modern pointing.

Yet may your dowries redeem that debt.   80
Think they are gentlemen, and think they love;
And be that thought their true loves' advocate.
Say you should wed for wealth (for to that scope
Your father's greedy disposition tends),
The world would say that you were had for wealth,   85
And so fair beauty's honour quite distinct.
A mass of wealth being poured upon another
Little augments the show, although the sum,
But being lightly scattered by itself,
It doubles what it seemed, although but one.   90
Even so yourselves: for wedded to the rich,
His style was as it was, a rich man still.
But wedding these, to wed true love, is duty;
You make them rich in wealth, but more in beauty.
I need not plead. That smile shows heart's consent;   95
That kiss showed love, that on that gift was lent;
And last thine eyes, that tears of true joy sends
As comfortable tidings for my friends.
Marina. Have done, have done. What needst thou more procure,
When long ere this I stooped to that fair lure?   100
Thy ever loving Harvey I delight it;
Marina ever loving shall requite it.
Teach us philosophy? I'll be no nun.
Age scorns delight; I love it being young.
There's not a word of this, not a word's part,   105

---

80. debt] *Q;* dept *Q2, Q3.*   83–4. (for . . . tends),] *this ed.;* ; for . . . tendes, *Qq.*
86. distinct] *Qq;* extinct *Haz.*   95. plead. That smile] *this ed.;* plead that smile, that
smile *Qq;* plead, that smile *1830;* plead: that smile *Haz.*   99. procure] *Q;* procures
Q2, Q3.   102. requite it] *Q2, Q3;* requite it young *Q.*   104. being young.] *Q2, Q3;*
being: *Q.*

---

80. *dowries*] gifts the wife('s family) brings to the husband at the wedding.
86. *distinct*] 'extinct' would seem more appropriate here; the sense could be argued
that beauty's honour would be distinguished or separated off as something shamed.
87–90. *A mass . . . one*] One hardly notices the difference when a great amount of
wealth is added to a pre-existing mass, but if one takes that augmented amount and
spreads it around, it appears to be twice as much as one thought, even though it's the
same amount as that great pile.
95–8. *That smile . . . friends.*] The women are addressed in the following order:
Marina, Laurentia, Mathea.
100. *ere*] before, previous to.
stooped] in falconry, the action of a falcon descending from its height in response
to the lure.
lure] in falconry, feathered decoy to lure the falcon to return after flight.
101. *delight*] delight in.

But shall be stamped, sealed, printed on my heart.
On this I'll read, on this my senses ply,
All arts being vain, but this philosophy.
Laurentia. Why was I made a maid, but for a man?
And why Laurentia, but for Ferdinand?   110
The chastest soul these angels could entice;
Much more himself, an angel of more price.
Were't thy self present, as my heart could wish,
Such usage thou shouldst have, as I give this.
Anthony. Then you would kiss him?
Laurentia.   If I did, how then?   115
Anthony. Nay, I say nothing to it, but 'amen'.
Pisaro. [*Aside*] The clerk must have his fees; I'll pay you them.
Mathea. Good God, how abject is this single life!
I'll not abide it. Father, friends, nor kin
Shall once dissuade me from affecting him.   120
A man's a man, and Ned is more than one;
I'faith I'll have thee Ned, or I'll have none.
Do what they can, chafe, chide, or storm their fill,
Mathea is resolved to have her will.
Pisaro. [*Coming forward.*] I can no longer hold my patience.   125
Impudent villain, and lascivious girls!
I have o'er-heard your vile conversions:
You scorn philosophy, you'll be no nun,

---

120. him] *Q2, Q3; not in Q.* 125. SD *coming forward*] *1830.* 126. villain] *Q2,*
Q3; villanie *Q.*

---

106. *stamped, sealed, printed*] the permanence of Marina's declaration is implied
by using technological terms from coin-making, letter sealing with wax, and printing.
107. *ply*] work.
111–12. *these angels . . . an angel*] an 'angel' was a gold coin worth ten shillings.
Laurentia puns on the divine meaning of the word (and perhaps the halo imagery of
'golden circle'). Such punning occurs frequently in the period; a prime example would
be in *Measure for Measure* (1.1.27–49, 2.4.16, 3.1.492); see also *The Merchant of*
Venice 2.7.55–9.
114. *usage*] punning on the 'use' of money in practising usury, and sexual 'usage'
as she is kissing and handling the coin.
117. *The clerk . . . them*] Pisaro promises to 'pay' Anthony (with revenge) for his
labour.
118. *abject*] miserable, wretched.
120. *affecting*] loving, being attracted to.
127. *conversions*] Baugh asks if it means 'conversations,' but the sense seems to be
the daughters' conversion to a pseudo-religious devotion to their Englishmen (hence
the kissing of the coins, and Anthony's 'amen' to it).
128–32. *You scorn . . . forsooth*] these lines could be pointed with question marks,
but the phrasing also suggests ironic rhetorical statements leading to a final question.

You must needs kiss the purse, because he sent it,
And you, forsooth, you flurjill, minion!   130
A brat scant folded in the dozens at most,
You'll have your will, forsooth! What will you have?
Mathea. But twelve year old? Nay, father, that's not so;
Our sexton told me I was three years more.
Pisaro. I say but twelve; you're best tell me I lie.   135
What, sirrah, Anthony!
Anthony. Here, sir.
Pisaro. Come here, sir – and you light huswives get you in.
Stare not upon me; move me not to ire –
                  Exeunt sisters [and ANTHONY *following].*
Nay, sirrah, stay you here, I'll talk with you.   140
Did I retain thee, villain, in my house,
Give thee a stipend twenty marks by year,
And hast thou thus infected my three girls,
Urging the love of those I most abhorred?
Unthrifts, beggars – what is worse,   145
And all because they are your countrymen!
Anthony. Why, sir, I taught them not
To keep a merchant's book, or cast account:

---

130. flurjill] *this ed.;* flurgill *Qq.*   142. Give] *Q2, Q3;* Gave *Q.*   145–6. Unthrifts . . .
countrymen!] *this ed.;* Unthrifts, Beggers; what is worse, / And all because they are
your Country-men? *Qq;* Unthrifts [and] beggars – what is worse – / And . . . countrymen. *Haz.*   147–9. Why, . . . 'account'] *so lineated in 1830; set in prose in Qq.*
148–9. account . . . 'account'] *this ed.;* accompt . . . [A]ccount[e] *Qq;* account . . .
account *Haz.*

130. *flurjill*] sexually 'light' woman; cf. *Romeo and Juliet,* where the Nurse defends
her sexual morality, 'Scurvy knave! I am none of his flirt-jills' (2.4.136–7).
  minion] darling, favourite; here used contemptuously.
  131. *a . . . dozens*] 'i.e., as we would say now, "scarcely in her teens" ' (1830).
  134. *sexton*] church caretaker.
  135. *you're . . . lie*] you'd do well to tell me I lie (ironic; i.e. just you try it, and see
what happens).
  136. *sirrah*] brief term of address to inferiors.
  138. *huswives*] hussies, loose women.
  139. *ire*] anger.
  142. *marks*] variable quantity of wealth; a mark usually represented a weight in
gold or silver (about 8 oz.); coins representing such weight in silver, often equated to
about two-thirds of a pound sterling in Elizabethan England.
  145. *what is worse,*] I follow the Q punctuation closely here, which suggests that
these words mean 'moreover' or 'and in addition'; an alternative, and attractive, reading
would be to place a question mark or exclamation mark after the words, expressing
Pisaro's disgust at the Englishmen's status as unthrifts and beggars.
  148. *cast account*] calculate the accounts, balance the books.

Yet to a word much like that word 'account'.
Pisaro. A knave past grace is past recovery.   150
Why, sirrah, Frisco! Villain, loggerhead,
Where art thou?

Enter FRISCO, *the clown.*

Frisco. Here's a calling indeed! A man were better to live a lord's life
and do nothing, than a serving creature and never be idle. O
Master, what a mess of brewess stands now upon the point of   155
spoiling by your hastiness. Why, they were able to have got a good
stomach with child even with the sight of them; and for a vapour
– O precious vapour! – let but a wench come near them with a
painted face, and you should see the paint drop and curdle on her
cheeks, like a piece of dry Essex cheese toasted at the fire.   160
Pisaro. Well, sirrah, leave this thought, and mind my words:
Give diligence, enquire about
For one that is expert in languages,
A good musician, and a Frenchman born,
And bring him hither to instruct my daughters –   165
I'll ne'er trust more a smooth-faced Englishman.

---

149. *'account'*] Anthony jokes that he is teaching the daughters something very
similar to 'account': (1) how to settle the accounts of their lovers, now mortgaged to
their father, and (2) how to use 'a cunt'. Pisaro's 'countrymen' in line 146 may prompt
Anthony's reply. A similar joke appears in Chapman's Rose theatre play, *The Blind
Beggar of Alexandria*, where Elimine declares that she cannot name the title of a
Spanish 'count,' because 'it comes so neare a thing that I knowe' (5.19, sig. D2), instead
resorting to the phrase, 'a what you cal't' (5.15) (*The Plays of George Chapman*, ed.
Lloyd E. Berry (Urbana: University of Illinois Press, 1970), gen. ed. Allan Holaday).
Eric Partridge notes the pronunciation of 'coun', the first syllable in 'country,' as being
the same as the word Princess Catherine protests to in *Henry V* 3.4.47–53 (*Shakespeare's Bawdy*, 3rd edn (London: Routledge, 1990)).

150. *A knave . . . recovery*] suggesting a reformed theological outlook in which
recovery, or entry into heaven, cannot be purchased by good works or indulgences, but
is available only through predestined grace.

knave] untrustworthy, cheating person (used to refer to the jack in a pack of cards
and related to the 'jack' used in a number of combinations in this play: 1.3.256,
2.3.179, 4.1.34, 4.1.147).

151. *loggerhead*] stupid, thick-headed person, 'blockhead'.

155. *mess of brewess*] serving, quantity of beef and vegetable stew or broth, often
thickened with bread or meal.

157. *stomach with . . . them*] proverbial; cf. Tilley C317 'To be with child to hear
(see) something', i.e. to be eager for, anticipate

158–9. *a painted face*] a face with (a lot of) make-up.

159–60. *drop and curdle . . . fire*] the make-up will blister and bubble like toasted
cheese.

162. *enquire about*] ask around.

Frisco. What, must I bring one that can speak languages? [*Aside*] What
    an old ass is my master. [*To him again.*] Why, he may speak *flaunte*
    taunte as well as French, for I understand him.
Pisaro. If he speak French, thus he will say: 'Awee, awee'. What, canst 170
    thou remember it?
Frisco. O, I have it now, for I remember my great grandfather's grand-
    mother's sister's cousin told me that pigs and Frenchmen speak
    one language, 'awee awee'. I am dog at this. But what must he
    speak else? 175
Pisaro. Dutch.
Frisco. Let's hear it.
Pisaro. Haunce butterkin slowpin.
Frisco. O, this is nothing, for I can speak perfect Dutch when I list.
Pisaro. Can you? I pray, let's hear some. 180
Frisco. Nay, I must have my mouth full of meat first, and then you
    shall hear me grumble it forth full mouth, as *Haunce butterkin*
    slowpin frokin; no, I am a simple Dutchman. Well, I'll about it.
Pisaro. Stay, sirrah, you are too hasty, for he must speak one language
    more. 185
Frisco. More languages? I trust he shall have tongues enough for one
    mouth. But what is the third?
Pisaro. Italian.
Frisco. Why that is the easiest of all, for I can tell whether he have any
    Italian in him even by looking on him. 190

178. *slowpin*] *Qq*; flowpin *1830*.

167–9.] The aside could be applied to all of these lines, but Pisaro seems to respond in his next speech to hearing Frisco's statement that 'I cannot understand him'.

168–9. flaunte taunte] exaggerated bombast (flaunting himself); OED has a single entry for 'Flaunt-tant' from 1661.

170. Awee, awee] i.e. oui, oui (yes, yes).

173–4. pigs and Frenchman . . . language] i.e. they both squeal, 'awee'.

174. dog] 'experienced or adept in' (Baugh); Tilley cites this line as a version of the proverb 'To be old dog at it' (D506). A. J. Hoenselaars's opposing reading that Frisco is saying 'I am a dog at this', i.e. very *bad*, would be equally funny, but it requires forcing a slight misreading of the line by adding the indefinite article.

178. Haunce butterkin slowpin] Flemish and Dutch characters were often called Hance or Haunce (i.e. Hans) in sixteenth-century drama (e.g., *Wealth and Health, Like Will to Like*); the Dutch proverbially had a penchant for butter (-kin being a diminutive ending), and were slandered with related accusations of greasiness and obesity.

181. my . . . meat] mocking the sound to English ears of Dutch pronunciation.

183. frokin] this word seems to relate to the diminutive form of 'woman': in modern Dutch, *vrouwke*. To Frisco, it is probably simply another convenient nonsense word.
no] Hazlitt emends to O.
simple] mere (absolute), pure (OED 'simple', adj. III).

184. too hasty] i.e. comically in accordance with the meaning of his name (see notes to dramatis personae).

Pisaro. Can you so, as how?

Frisco. Marry by these three points: a wanton eye, pride in his apparel,
and the devil in his countenance. Well, God keep me from the devil
in seeking this Frenchman. But do you hear me, Master: what shall
my fellow Anthony do? It seems he shall serve for nothing but to   195
put Latin into my young mistresses.

Pisaro. Hence ass! Hence loggerhead! Be gone, I say!   *Exit* FRISCO.
And now to you that reads philosophy:
Pack from my house; I do discharge thy service.
And come not near my doors; for if thou dost,   200
I'll make thee a public example to the world.

Anthony. [*Aside*] Well, crafty fox, you that work by wit,
It may be I may live to fit you yet.   *Exit.*

Pisaro. Ah, sirrah, this trick was spied in time,
For if but two such lectures more they'd heard,   205
For ever had their honest names been marred.
I'll in and 'rate them – yet that's not best:
The girls are wilful, and severity
May make them careless, mad, or desperate.
What shall I do? O, I have found it now!   210

197.1. SD *Exit* FRISCO] *placed after line 196 in Qq; placed after line 186 in Haz.*
210. O, I . . . now] *this ed.;* Oh! I . . . now *Qq;* O, I . . . now *Haz.*

192–3. *a wanton eye . . . countenance*] Italians were traditionally represented in
English drama as lusty; pride in apparel was often applied to Spaniards, but each
country exchanged similar slanderous representation of each other. The connection of
the Italians with the devil was common in Elizabethan and Jacobean English literature.
John Deacon, for instance, discussing the foreign fashions in England in the early
seventeenth century, writes of 'the *Italian* proverbe which pourtrayeth forth an
English-man, thus: *Englese Italienato, e un diabolo incarnato: An English man
Italienate, is a very divell incarnate*' (*Tobacco Tortured* (1616; Facs. Amsterdam: Da
Capo Press, 1968), sig. Cv (p. 10)). See also Robert Greene, *A Notable Discovery of
Cozenage* (1591), in *Cony-Catchers and Bawdy Baskets* (London: Penguin, 1972), ed.
Gamini Salgado, p. 158, for a reference to the same ubiquitous proverb.

202. *crafty fox*] the fox is proverbially crafty; fox's fur is often associated with
usurer's apparel (see Celeste Turner Wright, 'Some Conventions Regarding the Usurer
in Elizabethan Literature', *Studies in Philology* 31 (1934): 176–97).

203. *fit*] suit, belong; Anthony uses the term in the sense (1) he will adapt himself
so that Pisaro will think he 'fits' into his household once more, and (2) he will get
revenge on Pisaro (a related sixteenth-century term would be the challenge, 'I am for
you').

204. *spied*] caught, seen.

207. *'rate*] berate, scold

210. *O . . . now!*] Baugh rightly points out that 'now' 'would indicate that the foreigners were simply a device to prevent a match with the three English lovers. But Pisaro
has already sent for a tutor to teach them the strangers' languages', thus the improvi-
sational quality of Pisaro's line is false.

There are three wealthy merchants in the town,
All strangers, and my very special friends.
The one of them is an Italian,
A Frenchman and a Dutchman be the other.
These three entirely do affect my daughters,   215
And therefore mean I they shall have the tongues,
That they may answer in their several languages.
But what helps that? They must not stay so long,
For whiles they are a-learning languages,
My English youths both wed and bed them too,   220
Which, to prevent, I'll seek the strangers out.
Let's look: 'tis past eleven, Exchange time full.
There shall I meet them, and confer with them.
This work craves haste: my daughters must be wed,
For one month's stay saith farewell maidenhead.   *Exit.*   225

[1.2]

Enter HARVEY, HEIGHAM, *and* WALGRAVE.

Heigham. Come gentlemen, w'are almost at the house.
I promise you, this walk o'er Tower Hill,
Of all the places London can afford,
Hath sweetest air, and fitting our desires.

---

217. languages] *this ed.;* Language: *Qq;* language *1830.*   225. saith] *1830;* sayth *Q;* then Q2, Q3.

---

212. *strangers*] i.e. foreigners; the word 'foreigner' in the sixteenth century was usually used to refer to a person from outside the speaker's town or locality, often another Englishman without freedom or citizenship of the city in question.

216. *mean I*] I intend.

216–17. *they shall . . . languages*] i.e. the daughters shall learn Italian, French, and Dutch so that they will be able to converse with the foreign suitors.

218. *stay*] wait, delay.

222. *Exchange*] The Royal Exchange, founded by Sir Thomas Gresham and called 'the burse' (see 1.3.11, 195); founded in 1565 on the north side of Threadneedle Street, south of Cornhill (see Appendix), and renamed 'The Royal Exchange' by Elizabeth I in January 1571.

Exchange time full] trading is in full swing (the Exchange hours were 11 am–12 noon and 5 pm–6 pm).

224. *craves*] demands.

225. *For one . . . maidenhead*] a delay of one month will certainly see the daughters lose their virginity.

2. *Tower Hill*] the city district north-west of the Tower of London (see Appendix). The sweet air may be a joke, since they are near the notorious prison.

Harvey. Good reason so, it leads to Crutchèd Friars   5
    Where old Pisaro and his daughters dwell.
    Look to your feet: the broad way leads to hell.
    They say hell stands below, down in the deep;
    I'll down that hill, where such good wenches keep.
    But, sirrah, Ned, what says Mathea to thee?   10
    Will't fadge? Will't fadge? What, will it be a match?
Walgrave. A match, say you? A mischief 'twill as soon.
    'Sblood, I can scarce begin to speak to her,
    But I am interrupted by her father:
    'Ha, what say you?' and then put o'er his snout,   15
    Able to shadow Paul's, it is so great.
    Well, 'tis no matter, sirs, this is his house.
    Knock for the churl; bid him bring out his daughter.
    Ay, 'sblood, I will, though I be hanged for it!
Heigham. Hoyda, hoyda! Nothing with you but up and ride!   20
    You'll be within ere you can reach the door,
    And have the wench before you compass her.
    You are too hasty. Pisaro is a man

---

11. fadge . . . fadge] *Qq*; fudge . . . fudge *1830*.   13. 'Sblood] *this ed.*; Sbould *Q*; For *Q2, Q3*.   19. Ay, 'sblood] *Haz*; Ile, sbloud *Q*; Ile, that *Q2, Q3*.   23. man] *this ed.*; man, *Qq*.

---

5. *Crutchèd Friars*] the location of a small crypto-Jewish community in sixteenth-century London (see Appendix).

7. *the . . . hell*] proverbial; the road to holiness, by contrast, is narrow; the joke here is that the Englishmen are heading down the (Tower) hill to 'hell' (Crutched Friars), where the 'devil' (4.1.118), Pisaro, lives. Cf. *Merchant of Venice* 2.3.2–3: Jessica to Launcelot, 'Our house is hell, and thou, a merry devil, / Didst rob it of some taste of tediousness'.

11. *fadge*] come together, suit the purpose.

13. *'Sblood*] an oath, abbreviation of 'Christ's blood'.

15–16. *his snout . . . great*] Renaissance stage usurers traditionally had large, false noses, connecting them with (often grotesque) representations of Jewish physiognomy. In Marston's *Jack Drum's Entertainment* (1600–1), the list of characters includes 'Mamon, a usurer with a great nose'.

16. *shadow Paul's*] cast a shadow over St Paul's cathedral.

18. *churl*] here, niggardly, miserly person (often boorish, rustic person).

19. *Ay*] This is Hazlitt's emendation. Q's 'I'll' suggests an intended threat, which he swallows despite his anger, but 'Ay' reads well before 'I will' (knock on the door), since he is impatient for anyone else to do it. Heigham then has to calm him down.

20. *Hoyda*] obsolete from 'hey-day', 'an exclamation denoting frolicsomeness, gaiety, surprise, wonder, etc.' (*OED*).

22. *compass*] encompass (i.e. put your arms around).

23. *man*] Q's comma after 'man' emphasizes the meaning that all men in general are to be won with gold rather than words; this edition's removal of the comma assumes the line-ending comma was not intended to change the meaning and has Heigham saying that Pisaro *specifically* is such a man.

Not to be fed with words, but won with gold.
But who comes here?

Enter ANTHONY.

Walgrave.   Whom? Anthony our friend?   25
Say man, how fares our loves? How doth Mathea?
Can she love Ned? How doth she like my suit?
Will old Pisaro take me for his son?
For, I thank God, he kindly takes our lands,
Swearing, 'Good gentlemen, you shall not want   30
Whilst old Pisaro and his credit holds'.
He will be damned, the rogue, before he do't!
Harvey. Prithee, talk milder. Let but thee alone,
And thou in one bare hour will ask him more
Than he'll remember in a hundred years. –   35
Come from him Anthony, and say what news?
Anthony. The news for me is bad, and this it is:
Pisaro hath discharged me of his service.
Heigham. Discharged thee of his service? For what cause?
Anthony. Nothing, but that his daughters learn philosophy.   40
Harvey. Maids should read that. It teacheth modesty.
Anthony. Ay, but I left out mediocrity,
And with effectual reasons urged your loves.
Walgrave. The fault was small. We three will to thy master
And beg thy pardon.
Anthony.   O, that cannot be.   45
He hates you far worser than he hates me,
For all the love he shows is for your lands,
Which he hopes sure will fall into his hands.
Yet, gentlemen, this comfort take of me:
His daughters to your loves affected be.   50
Their father is abroad, they three at home.

---

41. read that. It] *this ed.*; reade, that it *Q, Q2*; reade that, it *Q3*; read that; it *1830*.

---

30. *want*] lack.
33. *Prithee*] Pray you, Beseech you.
Let but thee alone] leave you to your own devices; allow you to go on.
34. *one bare hour*] solely one hour.
36. *him*] i.e. Walgrave.
42. *mediocrity*] (1) moderation (2) modesty (3) 'a quasi-technical term with reference to the Aristotelian theory of "the mean" (*NED*)' (Baugh).
43. *effectual*] potent, having effect.
51. *abroad*] out of doors.

Go cheerly in, and seize that is your own,
And for my self, but grace what I intend,
I'll overreach the churl, and help my friend.
Heigham. Build on our helps, and but devise the means.   55
Anthony. Pisaro did command Frisco his man –
A simple sot, kept only but for mirth –
To enquire about in London for a man
That were a Frenchman and musician,
To be, as I suppose, his daughters' tutor.   60
Him if you meet, as like enough you shall,
He will enquire of you of his affairs.
Then make him answer, you three came from Paul's,
And in the middle walk one you espied
Fit for his purpose. Then describe this cloak,   65
This beard and hat, for in this borrowed shape
Must I beguile and overreach the fool.
The maids must be acquainted with this drift –
The door doth ope. I dare not stay reply,
Lest being descried. Gentlemen, adieu,   70
And help him now that oft hath helpèd you.   *Exit.*

Enter FRISCO, *the Clown.*

Walgrave. How now, sirrah? Whither are you going?
Frisco. Whither am I going? How shall I tell you when I do not know
    my self, nor understand my self?

---

52. seize] *Haz;* cease *Q, Q2;* ceaze *Q3.*   70. Lest] *Q3;* Least *Q, Q2.*

52. *seize*] with the suggestion of taking property, but also sexual endeavour, as in
'to rape' (cf. Latin: *rapere* = to seize).

57. *sot*] fool (sometimes drunkard).
mirth] comic entertainment.

61. *Him*] i.e. Frisco.

62. *He . . . affairs*] 'He will tell you about his business', perhaps with the suggestion
that he will ask them ('enquire of you') for help in his task.

63. *Paul's*] i.e. St Paul's Cathedral, Westminster (west of the City of London) (see
Appendix).

64. *the middle walk*] central aisle of St Paul's Cathedral. St Paul's was used as a
meeting place to transact business, including the sale of books. In his edition of Stow's
Survey, C. L. Kingsford notes the words of James Pilkington, bishop of Durham:
'The south alley [is used] for Popery and usury, the north for simony, and the horse
fair in the midst for all kinds of bargains, meetings, brawlings, murders, conspiracies'
(Stow ii, p. 316).

65 6. *this cloak . . . shape*] 'borrowed shape' (i.e. imitation) suggests that Anthony
is carrying a cloak, false beard, and hat, rather than referring to the ones he already
wears. Anthony will play the part of such a tutor as Frisco seeks.

67. *beguile*] cheat.

68. *drift*] plan.

Heigham. What dost thou mean by that?   75
Frisco. Marry, sir, I am seeking a needle in a bottle of hay, a monster
    in the likeness of a man. One that instead of good morrow, asketh
    what porridge you have to dinner, *parley vous signiour*? One that
    never washes his fingers, but licks them clean with kisses, a clipper
    of the King's English, and to conclude, an eternal enemy to all good   80
    language.
Harvey. What's this? What's this?
Frisco. Do not you smell me? Well, I perceive that wit doth not always
    dwell in a satin doublet. Why, 'tis a Frenchman, *bassimon cue*,
    how do you?   85
Harvey. I thank you, sir, but tell me what wouldest thou do with a
    Frenchman?
Frisco. Nay, faith, I would do nothing with him, unless I set him to
    teach parrots to speak. Marry, the old ass my master would have
    him to teach his daughters, though I trust the whole world sees   90
    that there be such in his house that can serve his daughters' turn
    as well as the proudest Frenchman. But if you be good lads, tell
    me where I may find such a man.
Heigham. We will. Go hie thee straight to Paul's.
    There shalt thou find one fitting thy desire.   95
    Thou soon mayst know him, for his beard is black,
    Such is his raiment. If thou runnst apace
    Thou canst not miss him, Frisco.

---

78. *parley*] Q (*Parley*); *Parlee* Q2, Q3.   93. man.] *this ed.*; man? *Qq.*   97. Such . . .
raiment] *Qq*; And such his raiment *Haz.*

---

   76. *a needle . . . hay*] proverbial: 'a needle in a haystack' (i.e. very difficult to find,
and not worth the search if successful).

   79–80. *a clipper . . . English*] to 'clip' coins was to get gold by cutting around the
edges. To 'clip' English would be to cut off parts of words through poor pronunciation,
leaving it debased.

   80. *King's*] an obvious alteration in the 1616 Q from 'Queen's' in the original 1598
version.

   83. *smell*] understand, divine.

   83–4. *wit doth . . . doublet*] the rich (satin-wearers) are not always the cleverest; a
doublet is a tight-fitting upper-body garment.

   84. bassimon cue] Frisco's blunder for *comment allez-vous*, which he then trans-
lates, 'how do you?' What he is actually saying is *Baissez mon cul* (Kiss my arse).

   91. *serve his daughter's turn*] (1) do the job (2) fulfil their desires.

   97. *Such is his raiment*] So are his clothes (i.e. black: he is wearing scholarly
robes).

   apace] fast, at a good pace.

Frisco. Lord, Lord, how shall poor Frisco reward your rich tidings,
gentlemen? I am yours till Shrove Tuesday, for then change I my   100
copy, and look like nothing but red-herring cobs and stock-fish.
Yet I'll do somewhat for you in the mean time. My master is
abroad and my young mistresses at home. If you can do any good
on them before the Frenchman come, why so! Ah, gentlemen, do
not suffer a litter of languages to spring up amongst us. I must to   105
the walk in Paul's, you to the vestry. Gentlemen, as to my self, and
so forth.   *Exit.*
Harvey. Fools tell the truth, men say, and so may he.
Wenches, we come now, love our conduct be.
Ned, knock at the door – but soft, forbear.   110

Enter LAURENTIA, MARINA, *and* MATHEA
[*at the door; Heigham and Laurentia talk apart.*]

---

100. *Shrove Tuesday*] the day before Ash Wednesday (first day of Lent); generally
a time for merriment and celebration, since it leads to Lent's forty working days of
fasting and penitence.

100–1. *change I my copy*] 'to change one's style, tone, behaviour, or course of
action, to assume another character' (*OED* 'copy' 11).

101. *red-herring cobs and stock-fish*] smoked herring heads and dried codfish; a
cod's head = fool, blockhead; hard-dried stock-fish, smoking red heads, and stiff fish
in the context of a holiday would seem to be bawdy (cf. a more generally comical use
of the term in Nashe's *The Unfortunate Traveller*, where Jack Wilton titles himself,
'Lord high regent of rashers of the coles and red herring cobs,' McKerrow ii, p. 209).

102. *I'll do somewhat*] I'll do something, I'll do you a favour.

103–4. *do any good on them*] get somewhere with them (with probable play of
doing good on top of them, sexually).

105. *litter*] multiple birth of offspring, used of animals.

106. *vestry*] anteroom for dressing of priests and choir in church; here, perhaps
referring both to the hoped-for result of marriage in a church, and more immediately
to getting into the women's chambers.

106–7. *Gentlemen, . . . and so forth.*] Baugh sees this as a probable cue for the
clown's improvisation, and cites as comparable instances 1.3.147 'and so forth' and
3.3.21–2 'some more of this.' This is probable, but Frisco also seems like the kind of
frisky, flippant character who would openly display his impatience with completing
verbose etiquette, and would curtail the decorum of closing his speeches eloquently.
The Post's 'A little money, and so forth' is arguable, but Frisco's 'some more of this'
seems to be a quite different case. See note to 3.3.21–2.

109. *now, love*] This is Qq's punctuation; placing the pause before 'now' gives a
pleasing caesura. The 1830 editor places a semi-colon before 'now'.

love our conduct be] 'love guides us', or 'love, be our guide'; Q capitalizes 'Love',
suggesting the common early modern personification of love (Cupid).

110.2. Here, and for the passage following, Heigham and Laurentia probably talk
apart, since at lines 134–5, she tells her sisters that he has told her of Anthony's
plan.

The cloud breaks up, and our three suns appear.
To this I fly. Shine bright my life's sole stay,
And make grief's night a glorious summer's day.
Marina. Gentlemen, how welcome you are here
Guess by our looks, for other means by fear   115
Prevented is. Our father's quick return
Forbids the welcome else we would have done.
Walgrave. Mathea, how these faithful thoughts obey –
Mathea. No more, sweet love. I know what thou wouldst say.
You say you love me; so I wish you still.   120
Love has love's hire, being balanced with good will.
But say, come you to us, or come you rather
To pawn more lands for money to our father?
I know 'tis so; i' God's name spend at large.
What, man? Our marriage day will all discharge.   125
Our father, by his leave, must pardon us.
Age, save of age, of nothing can discuss.
But in our loves the proverb we'll fulfil:
Women and maids must always have their will.
Heigham. [*Coming forward, still to Laurentia.*] Say thou as much,
    and add life to this corpse.   130
Laurentia. Yourself and your good news doth more enforce.
How these have set forth love by all their wit,
I swear in heart, I more than double it.
Sisters be glad, for he hath made it plain,
The means to get our schoolmaster again.   135
But gentlemen, for this time cease our loves;
This open street perhaps suspicion moves.
Fain we would stay, bid you walk in more rather,

---

124. i'] *1830;* a *Qq.*   130. corpse] *this ed.;* Coarse *Qq;* corse *1830.*

---

111. *our three suns*] i.e. the three sisters.
112. *this*] this one (i.e. Marina).
stay] support, strength (physical and psychological).
116. *quick*] imminent, sudden.
117. *Forbids . . . done*] Prevents us from giving you the welcome we would desire.
121. *love's hire . . . will*] love's use; love's (sexual) reward, payment; there may also be a pun on hire/higher (i.e. erection), since the line ends with a good *will* (i.e. penis).
124. *i'*] in.
127. *save of*] except for.
129. *Women . . . will*] proverbial, see Tilley W723 (variations at W626, W715).
138. *Fain we would*] i.e. We would like to.

But that we fear the coming of our father.
Go to th'Exchange, crave gold as you intend;   140
Pisaro scrapes for us, for us you spend.
We say farewell, more sadlier be bold
Than would my greedy father to his gold.
We here, you there, ask gold, and gold you shall;
We'll pay the int'rest and the principal.   *Exeunt sisters.*   145
Walgrave. That's my good girls, and I'll pay you for all.
Harvey. Come to th'Exchange, and when I feel decay,
'Send me such wenches, heavens', I still shall pray.   *Exeunt.*

[1.3]

Enter PISARO, DELION *the Frenchman,* VANDAL *the Dutchman,
and other* MERCHANTS [and STRANGERS], *at several doors.*

Pisaro. Good morrow, Masters Strangers.
Strangers.   Good morrow, sir.
Pisaro. This, loving friends, hath thus emboldened me:
For knowing the affection and the love,
Master Vandal, that you bear my daughter;
Likewise, and that with joy considering too,   5
You, Monsieur Delion, would fain despatch,
I promise you, methinks the time did fit,
And does, by'r Lady too, in mine advice,
This day to clap a full conclusion up.

0.1–2. SD *Enter . . . doors.*] *Qq insert* 'Alvaro the Italian' *after* 'Dutchman'.

---

141. *scrapes*] rakes in, collects.

0.1] Qq have Alvaro enter here, but Pisaro comments on his absence at line 24, and he enters at line 236.

0.2] Qq's speech prefixes seem to require one 'stranger' (merchant?) and one (either English or foreign) 'merchant' (see lines 203–6); the exit direction at line 293 also suggests at least two extras ('*Ex[eun]t* Moore, Browne, Towerson, Strangers, *and* Merchants'). The speeches at 202 and 205 could be spoken by the same person, but I have left Qq's slightly vague prefixes, since they suggest a community of Anglo-foreign merchants; this has required indicating the separate 'strangers' in this scene-opening s.d.

1. *Masters Strangers*] Baugh writes, 'The 1830 editor has a mistaken note, p. 17, suggesting that Pisaro is here "probably addressing 'the other merchants', as he knows Delion and Vandal." He is, of course, addressing the foreigners.' Indeed, Pisaro's next line, which addresses his 'loving friends', suggest that Baugh is correct. The stage direction indicating entry 'at several doors' leaves a number of staging and greeting options open.

8. *by'r Lady*] an oath, 'By Our Lady'.

9. *clap . . . up*] seal the deal, conclude things.

And therefore made I bold to call on you,   10
Meaning – our business done here at the Burse –
That you at mine entreaty should walk home
And take in worth such viands as I have.
And then we would, and so I hope we shall,
Loosely tie up the knot that you desire,   15
But for a day or two; and then church rites
Shall sure conform, confirm, and make all fast.

Vandal. Zeker Meester Pisaro, me do so groterly dank you, dat you
          maak me so sure of de wench, dat ik can niet dank you genough.
Delion. Monsieur Pisaro, mon père, mon vader, O, de grande joy you   20
          give me, écoute, me sal go home to your house, sal eat your bacon,
          sal eat your beef, and sal tack de wench, de fine damoisella.
Pisaro. You shall, and welcome, welcome as my soul.
          But were my third son, sweet Alvaro, here,
          We would not stay at the Exchange today,   25
          But hie us home and there end our affairs.

Enter MOORE *and* TOWERSON.

Moore. Good day, Master Pisaro.
Pisaro.   Master Moore.
          Marry, with all my heart good morrow, sir.
          What news, what news?
Moore. This merchant here, my friend, would speak with you.   30
Towerson. Sir, this jolly south-west wind with gentle blast
          Hath driven home our long-expected ships,
          All laden with the wealth of ample Spain,
          And but a day is passed since they arrived
          Safely at Plymouth, where they yet abide.   35

---

21. écoute] *1830 (ecoute); (econte) Qq.* 27–9.] *Moore.* Good day maister *Pisaro.* /
Pisa. Maister *Moore,* marry with all my heart good morrow sir; What newes? What
newes?' *Qq.*

---

11. *Burse*] the Exchange. See note to 1.1.222.
13. *viands*] meats, offerings (in terms of his dinner and his daughters).
15. *the knot*] the marriage bond.
18. *Zeker*] sure(ly).
groterly] greatly.
20. *mon père, mon vader*] my father (French), mon vader (attempted English).
21. *écoute,*] listen; all Quartos have '*(econte)*', the 'u' apparently turned.
22. *tack*] take, with possible pun on 'to tack' or 'nail' her sexually.
25. *Exchange*] see note to 1.1.222.
26. *hie*] hasten, go quickly.
28. *Marry*] an oath, 'By Mary'.
35. *Plymouth*] seaport in the county of Devon, on the south-west coast of
England.

Pisaro. Thanks is too small a guerdon for such news.
  How like you this news, friends? Master Vandal,
  Here's somewhat towards for my daughter's dowry.
  Here's somewhat more than we did yet expect.
Towerson. But hear you, sir, my business is not done.   40
  From these same ships I did receive these lines,
  And there enclosed this same bill of exchange,
  To pay at sight, if so you please accept it.
Pisaro. Accept it? Why? What, sir, should I accept?
  Have you received letters, and not I?   45
  Where is this lazy villain, this slow post?
  What, brings he every man his letters home
  And makes me nobody? Does he, does he?
  I would not have you bring me counterfeit;
  And if you do, assure you I shall smell it: 50
  I know my factor's writing well enough.
Towerson. You do, sir. Then see your factor's writing.
  I scorn as much as you to counterfeit.
Pisaro. 'Tis well you do, sir.

          Enter HARVEY, WALGRAVE, *and* HEIGHAM.

  What, Master Walgrave and my other friends.   55
  You are grown strangers to Pisaro's house.
  I pray, make bold with me.
Walgrave. [*Aside*]   Ay, with your daughters.
  You may be sworn, we'll be as bold as may be.
Pisaro. Would you have aught with me? I pray now, speak.
Heigham. Sir, I think you understand our suit   60

---

38. daughter's] *1830;* Daughters *Qq.*   43. please] *Q;* please, *Q2, Q3.*

_____

36. *guerdon*] gift.
38. *somewhat towards*] something in advance ('in the bank').
daughter's] I have chosen the singular possessive here for Q's 'daughters' because Pisaro is addressing one daughter at this point and uses the singular 'dowry'.
41. *lines*] i.e. a letter.
42. *bill of exchange*] a notice to pay for goods received (c.o.d.).
43. *pay at sight*] cash on delivery (as opposed to credit).
50. *smell*] perceive, understand (cf. 1.2.83).
51. *factor's*] agent's (a profession comparable with usury to puritanical Elizabethans, since it made money from nothing, from mere speculation). In George Wapull's *The Tide Tarrieth No Man* (1576), a courtier laments the loss of his money to so many factors and middle-men in his dealings: '*Ninubula pluvia imbrem parit,* / A mizeling shower ingendreth great wet, / Which saying *officium proverbia non tarit,* / Many a little maketh a great. / So every of them, by me wrought this feate, / And every of these brybes, being cast to account, / To a good porcion I feele do amounte' (sig. E).

By the repairing we have had to you.
Gentlemen, you know, must want no coin,
Nor are they slaves unto it, when they have.
You may perceive our minds. What say you to't?
Pisaro. Gentlemen all, I love you all,   65
Which more to manifest, this afternoon
Between the hours of two and three repair to me,
And were it half the substance that I have,
Whilst it is mine, 'tis yours to command.
But gentlemen, as I have regard to you,   70
So do I wish you'll have respect to me.
You know that all of us are mortal men,
Subject to change and mutability.
You may, or I may, soon pitch o'er the perch,
Or so, or so, have contrary crosses;   75
Wherefore I deem it but mere equity
That something may betwixt us be to show.
Heigham. Master Pisaro, within this two months
Without fail, we will repay –

Enter BROWNE.

Browne. God save you, gentlemen.
[*All.*]   Good morrow, sir.   80
Pisaro. What, Master Browne, the only man I wished for.
Does your price fall? What, shall I have these cloths?
For I would ship them straight away for Stoade.
I do wish you my money 'fore another.
Browne. Faith, you know my price, sir, if you have them.   85

---

76. it] *1830; not in Qq.*   78–9. months / Without fail, we] *Haz;* months without
faile, / We *Q; single line in Q2, Q3, with 'We' capitalised.*   79. we will repay –] *1830;*
We will repay. *Qq;* we'll repay. *Haz.*   80. SP [*All.*]] *this ed.;* Gentlemen. *Q, Q2;*
Gentel. *Q3.*   82. cloths] *1830;* Cloathes *Qq.*   83. away] *Q; not in Q2, Q3.*

---

66. *manifest*] show, reveal.
67. *repair*] resort, come.
70. *regard*] respect.
74. *pitch o'er the perch*] drop dead.
o'er] over.
75. *contrary crosses*] (1) mishaps (that are contrary to our wishes) (2) disagreements
between us.
76. *mere equity*] complete fairness.
77. *something . . . show*] i.e. some collateral needs to be put down to guarantee the
loan.
82. *Does your price fall?*] Are you charging less?
83. *Stoade*] 'Stade (?) on the Elbe, 22 miles below Hamburg' (Baugh).

Pisaro. You are too dear, in sadness – Master Heigham,
  You were about to say somewhat: pray, proceed.
Heigham. Then this it was: those lands that are not mortgaged –

               Enter POST.

Post. God bless your worship.
Pisaro. [*To Heigham.*] I must crave pardon. [*To Post.*] O, sirrah, are
  you come?   90
            [*The merchants and strangers flock about the* POST,
                        who hands out letters.]
Walgrave. Hoyda, hoyda! What's the matter now?
  Sure, yonder fellow will be torn in pieces.
Harvey. What's he, sweet youths, that so they flock about?
  What, old Pisaro tainted with this madness?
Heigham. Upon my life, 'tis some body brings news.   95
      [*The merchants and strangers separate with their letters.*
                POST *gives* PISARO *letters, apart.*]
  The court breaks up, and we shall know their counsel.
  Look, look, how busily they fall to reading.
Pisaro. I am the last: you should have kept it still.
  Well, we shall see what news you bring with you.
  [*Reads.*] 'Our duty premised, and we have sent unto your worship 100
  sack, Seville oils, pepper, Barbary sugar, and such other commodities as we thought most requisite. We wanted money; therefore we
  are fain to take up £200 of Master Towerson's man, which by a
  bill of exchange sent to him, we would request your worship pay
  accordingly.' You shall command, sir, you shall command, sir. 105
  [*Reads again.*] 'The news here is that the English ships, the *Fortune*,
  your ship, the *Adventure*, and *Good Luck* of London, coasting
  along by Italy towards Turkey, were set upon by two Spanish

---

91. Hoyda, hoyda] *Qq;* Hey day, hey day *1830;* Heyday, heyday *Haz.*   101. Seville]
1830; sivill *Q;* Sivill *Q2, Q3.*   103. £200] *1830;* 200.l. *Q;* 200.li. *Q2;* 230.li. *Q3.*

  86. *in sadness*] seriously, truly (here, with the sense of unfortunately).
  98. *last*] i.e. last to receive a letter.
  101. *Seville oils*] Q's 'sivil' may be a typographical error for 'civit' (i.e. civet), the
musky liquid extraction from anal glands of the civet-cat, used in perfumery, but Q2
and Q3's capitalization to 'Sivil' suggests the proper noun.
  Barbary] north coast of Africa, Algiers.
  105. *You shall command*] Pisaro's scornful response to the letter's 'request' to pay,
emphasizing his own lack of choice in the situation (cf. his use of the term at
1.3.274).
  106. SD] Pisaro could also be looking back at a single letter.

galleys. What became of them we know not, but doubt much by
reason of the weather's calmness.'   110
How is't? Six to one, the weather calm,
Now afore God, who would not doubt their safety?
A plague upon these Spanish-galley pirates!
Roaring Charybdis or devouring Scylla
Were half such terror to the antique world   115
As these same antic villains now of late
Have made the straits 'twixt Spain and Barbary.
Towerson. Now, sir, what doth your factor's letters say?
Pisaro. Marry, he saith these witless, luckless dolts
Have met and are beset with Spanish galleys   120
As they did sail along by Italy.
What a bots made the dolts near Italy!
Could they not keep the coast of Barbary,
Or having passed it, gone for Tripoli,
Being on the other side of Sicily,   125
As near, as where they were, unto the straits?
For by the globe, both Tripoli and it
Lie from the straits some twenty-five degrees,
And each degree makes threescore English miles.
Towerson. Very true, sir,   130

---

111. SP] *not in this ed., 1830; Pisa[.] Qq.*   How is't? Six] *Q2, Q3; How ist six Q.*
calm,] *Q; calme: Q2, Q3; calm? 1830.*   115. Were half] *Q; Were but halfe Q2,*
Q3.   115–6. antique . . . antic] *1830; anticke . . . anticke Qq.*   130–2. Very . . . acco
unt.] *so lineated in this ed.; set in prose in Qq.*

---

109. *galleys*] galleons, large ships.
doubt] fear.
109–10. *by . . . calmness*] since the weather is calm, the loss of the ships must be
due to piracy.
111. *How is't? . . . calm*] 'Six to one' might suggest the relative numbers of enemy
and English ships, but the numbers do not accord with the details in the letter; perhaps
he is saying 'How was the weather calm, when the odds were so much against it?'.
114. *Charybdis . . . Scylla*] Two monsters in Greek mythology who menaced ship-
ping in the straits of Messina between Italy and Sicily. With her six heads on long
necks, Scylla fed on luckless sailors from her Italian shore; meanwhile the male whirl-
pool monster, Charybdis, swallowed and regurgitated sea water and anything in it three
times daily.
115–6. *antique world . . . antic villains*] In the Q texts, 'antique' and 'antic' (i.e. odd,
fantastic) are both spelled 'anticke,' emphasizing the parallel between the two terrors
of ancient and modern worlds.
117. *straits*] narrow sea passage.
119. *dolts*] blockheads, dunces.
122. *bots*] expression of disgust and dismissal (cf. 'pox' = disease, plague).
124. *Tripoli*] east of Tunis, on the north African coast directly south of Sicily.
129. *threescore*] sixty (score = 20).

But it makes nothing to my bill of exchange.
This dealing fits not one of your account.
Pisaro. And what fits yours? A prating, wrangling tongue?
A woman's ceaseless and incessant babbling,
That sees the world turned topsy-turvy with me,   135
Yet hath not so much wit to stay a while
Till I bemoan my late excessive loss?
                    [MOORE *and* TOWERSON *move apart,*
                                        joining the MERCHANTS.]
Walgrave. 'Swounds, 'tis dinner time; I'll stay no longer:
[*To Pisaro.*] Hark you a word, sir –
Pisaro. I tell you, sir, it would have made you whine   140
Worse than if schools of luckless, croaking ravens
Had seized on you to feed their famished paunches,
Had you heard news of such a ravenous rout,
Ready to seize on half the wealth you have –
Walgrave. [*Aside*] 'Sblood, you might have kept at home and be
    hanged!   145
    What a pox care I?

---

142. seized] *Q2, Q3* (seiz'd*); ceasd *Q*.   146. What ... I?] *this line is followed with
the SD 'Enter a Post' in Qq.*

---

132. *fits not*] suits not, is not fitting for.
account] social or professional standing, with pun on the outstanding account that
needs paying.
133. *prating*] (idly) chattering.
wrangling] arguing, quarrelling.
135. *topsy-turvy*] 'an abbreviation of *topside t'other way*' (1830); i.e. upside-down.
Stability of the social order and the increasing social mobility of the middle and lower
ranks, which could make the world seem 'topsy-turvy' to some, were vital issues in the
sixteenth century.
137. *late*] recent, latest, last.
138. *'Swounds*] An oath, 'God's wounds'.
141. *schools*] flocks (used of birds as well as fish in the sixteenth century).
143. *rout*] a word related to 'riot', referring to a group of unruly persons or to their
act of disturbing the peace.
145–6. *'Sblood, you ... I?*] I place this as an aside, since (1) it would seem rather
foolish of Walgrave to dismiss Pisaro's concerns to his face, and (2) Pisaro's speeches
on either side of these lines and those from the Post seem to be two parts of a whole,
and Pisaro does not hear Walgrave or the Post. To argue that this is not an aside, one
might point out that Walgrave *is* 'mad' Ned, after all, and a few lines later Pisaro
laments the lack of concern of one man for another's woe in the present world, exactly
what Walgrave has illustrated.
146. *What a pox*] exclamation of irritation, disgust, dismissal (pox = disease, esp.
one which produces pock marks on the victim).

Post. [*To Pisaro.*] God save your worship, a little money, and so
    forth.
Pisaro. – But men are senseless now of others' woe.
    This stony age is grown so stony hearted
    That none respects their neighbours' miseries.   150
    I wish, as poets do, that Saturn's times,
    The long out-worn world, were in use again,
    That men might sail without impediment.
Post. Ay, marry, sir, that were a merry world indeed. I would hope to
    get more money of your worship in one quarter of a year than I   155
    can do now in a whole twelve-month.

                Enter BALSARO.

Balsaro. Master Pisaro, how I have run about,
    How I have toiled today to find you out!
    At home, abroad, at this man's house, at that.
    Why, I was here an hour ago and more,   160
    Where I was told you were, but could not find you.
Pisaro. Faith, sir, I was here, but was driven home.
    Here's such a common haunt of crack-rope boys,
    That, what, for fear to have m'apparel spoiled,
    Or my ruffs dirted, or eyes struck out,   165
    I dare not walk where people do expect me.
    Well, things, I think, might be better looked unto,

---

165. *dirted*] *1830; durted Qq; dirtied Haz.*

---

147. *and so forth*] possibly a cue for improvisation (cf. 1.2.106–7 and note).

149. *stony hearted*] The irony of the traditionally stony-hearted usurer declaring the
times to be stony hearted would not have been lost on the audience.

151–2. *I wish . . . again*] in *Works and Days* the Greek poet Hesiod (eighth century
BCE) describes five ages of man, declining from the original golden age to the present
iron age; Saturn (Gk *Kronos*) ruled over the golden age, which came to an end when
Saturn's son, Jupiter (Gk *Zeus*), deposed him.

162. *driven*] forced.

163. *common haunt of*] (1) popular gathering place for (2) frequent group of.

crack-rope boys] those that will break a rope with their necks (or their necks with
a rope), hence hanging fodder, rogues. In the usury play *Wily Beguiled* (1596), Will
Cricket calls the spritely Robin Goodfellow, a 'cogging, pettifogging, crackropes, calf-
skin companion' (Haz. vol. 9, p. 238).

165. *ruffs*] pleated fabric collar.

dirted] dirtied, soiled.

167–70. *Well, things . . . uses*] Pisaro seems to be saying that things could be better
taken care of, sorted out (*looked unto*); the 'knaves' are probably the constables of the
watch (see notes to 3.3.15 and 4.1.261), who are paid to keep the peace (or bribed by
Pisaro for special attention?), but who are letting things remain dangerous and unruly
('but do not see things be reformed'); the money, says Pisaro, could be better
employed.

And such coin, too, which is bestowed on knaves –
Which should, but do not, see things be reformed –
Might be employed to many better uses.   170
But what of beardless boys, or such like trash?
The Spanish galleys – O, a vengeance on them!

Post. Mass, this man hath the luck on't! I think I can scarce ever come
to him for money, but this 'a vengeance on' and that 'a vengeance
on' doth so trouble him that I can get no coin. Well, a vengeance   175
on't for my part, for he shall fetch the next letters himself!

Browne. I prithee, when thinkst thou the ships will be
Come about from Plymouth?

Post.   Next week, sir.

Heigham. Came you, sir, from Spain lately?

Post. Ay, sir. Why ask you that?   180

Harvey. Marry, sir, thou seems to have been in the hot countries, thy
face looks so like a piece of rusty bacon. Had thy host at Plymouth
meat enough in the house when thou wert there?

Post. What though he had not, sir? But he had, how then?

Harvey. Marry, thank God for it, for otherwise he would doubtless   185
have cut thee out in rashers to have eaten thee. Thou lookst as
thou wert through broiled already.

Post. You have said, sir, but I am no meat for his mowing, nor yours
neither. If I had you in place where, you should find me tough
enough in digestion, I warrant you.   190

Walgrave. [*Makes to draw a weapon.*] What, will you swagger, sirrah?
Will ye swagger?

Browne. [*To Walgrave.*] I beseech you, sir, hold your hand! [*To Post.*]
Get home, ye patch! Cannot you suffer gentlemen jest with you?

Post. I'd teach him a gentle trick, an I had him of the burse; but I'll   195
watch him a good turn, I warrant him.

Moore. Assure ye, Master Towerson, I cannot blame him.

---

181. seems] *Q; seem'st Q2, Q3.*   188. mowing] *Q2, Q3; moing Q.*

187. *through*] thoroughly.
188. *I . . . mowing*] proverbial, cf. Tilley M832.
mowing] digesting, stomaching; cf. 'Mowing is a corruption of mouthing' (1830).
189. *in place where*] in the right circumstances.
191. *swagger*] bandy, face off.
194. *patch*] fool, clown (derived from the fool's patchwork, 'motley,' clothing; cf.
note to 3.2.79)
195. *gentle*] gentlemanlike.
an . . . burse] i.e. if I could get him away from the Exchange.
196. *watch him a good turn*] ironic, meaning 'return the favour' or 'get him
back'.

I warrant you it is no easy loss.
How think you, Master Stranger? By my faith, sir,
There's twenty merchants will be sorry for it,   200
That shall be partners with him in his loss.
Stranger. Why, sir, what's the matter?
Moore. The Spanish galleys have beset our ships,
That lately were bound out for Syria.
Merchant. What not? I promise you I am sorry for it.   205
Walgrave. What an old ass is this to keep us here –
Master Pisaro, pray, despatch us hence.
Pisaro. [*To Walgrave.*] Master Vandal, I confess I wrong you,
But I'll talk a word or two with him, and straight turn to you.
[*To Balsaro.*] Ah, sir, and how then i'faith?   210
Heigham. Turn to us? Turn to the gallows if you will.
Harvey. 'Tis midsummer-moon with him; let him alone.
He calls Ned Walgrave Master Vandal.
Walgrave. Let it be Shrovetide; I'll not stay an inch.
Master Pisaro –   215
Pisaro. What should you fear? And as I have vowed before,
So now again. My daughters shall be yours,
And therefore I beseech you and your friends
Defer your business till dinner time,
And, what you'd say, keep it for table talk.   220
Harvey. Marry, and shall; a right good motion. –
Sirs, old Pisaro is grown kind of late,
And in pure love hath bid us home to dinner.
Heigham. Good news in truth. – But wherefore art thou sad?
Walgrave. For fear the slave, ere it be dinner time,   225
Remembering what he did, recall his word,
For by his idle speeches you may swear
His heart was not confederate with his tongue.
Harvey. Tut, never doubt. Keep stomachs till anon,

---

205. *SP Merchant.*] *Qq* (March.*)*; STRANG. *1830.* 214–15. Let . . . Pisaro –] *so
lineated in 1830; single line in Qq.* 216. fear? And] *1830* (fear? and*)*; feare: ende *Q*;
feare:end *Q2*; feare:and *Q3.*

---

203. *beset*] set upon, attacked.
207. *despatch*] release, send.
212. *midsummer-moon*] the lunar month in which midsummer day comes; traditionally, a time when lunacy is prevalent.
214. *Shrovetide*] three days leading up to Shrove Tuesday (see note for 1.2.100).
228. *His heart . . . tongue*] cf. *Richard II* 5.3.50–1: Aumerle, 'I do repent me. Read
not my name there. / My heart is not confederate with my hand.' As 'tongue' means
tongue and words, so 'hand' means hand and writing.
229. *stomachs*] (1) stay hungry (2) remain determined, strong.
anon] later, the time appointed.

And then we shall have cates to feed upon.   230
Pisaro. Well sir, since things do fall so crossly out,
   I must dispose myself to patience.
   But for your business, do you assure yourself,
   At my repairing home from the Exchange
   I'll set a helping hand unto the same.   235

Enter ALVARO *the Italian.*

Alvaro. *Buon giorno, Signiore Padre*; why be de malancholy so much,
   and grave in you-a? Wat news make you look so naught?
Pisaro. 'Naught' is too good an epithet by much
   For to distinguish such contrariousness.
   Hath not swift Fame told you our slow-sailed ships   240
   Have been o'ertaken by the swift-sailed galleys,
   And all my cared-for goods within the lurch
   Of that same caterpillar brood of Spain?
Alvaro. Signiore, si, how de Spaniola have almost tack de ship dat go
   for Turkey. My Pader, hark you me one word: I have receive un   245
   lettre from my factor de Venice, dat after un piculo battalion, for
   un half hour de come a wind fra de north, and de sea go tumble
   here, and tumble dare, dat make de galleys run away for fear be
   almost drowned.

---

236. *Buon giorno, Signiore Padre*] *Bon jurno signeour Padre Qq.*   241. swift-
sailed] *Q2, Q3*; swift saile *Q.*   244. si] *Q*; cy *Q2, Q3.*   245. one] *Q2, Q3*; on *Q.*

---

230. *cates*] sweetmeats, delicacies (and punning on a generic name for women,
'Kate').
231. *crossly*] contrary, unfavourably (cf. *Richard II* 2.4.23–4: Salisbury, 'Thy
friends are fled to wait upon thy foes, / And crossly to thy good all fortune goes').
232. *dispose*] set up, fashion.
234. *repairing*] returning.
236. Buon giorno] Good day.
237. *naught*] sad (?).
240. *Fame*] personification of the phenomenon of public report, news; the character
is often depicted blowing a trumpet.
242. *lurch*] reach, possession.
243. *caterpillar brood*] connected pseudo-etymologically with 'piller' (pillager, plun-
derer, etc.), hence rapacious, preying group of beings.
244–5. *how de Spaniola . . . Turkey*] how the Spanish have almost taken the ship
that goes for Turkey.
245. *hark you me one word*] listen to one word of mine.
246. *un piculo battalion*] a little battle (sea-fight).
246–9. *for un half hour . . . drowned*] Alvaro's tale of the Spanish galleys' retreat in
bad weather would have reminded the audience of the miraculous escape of England
and the English navy from the vastly superior Spanish Armada of 1588, which was
grounded on flats in the English Channel and then famously wrecked by 'divine intervention', i.e. bad weather.

Pisaro. How, sir!   250
 Did the wind rise at north, and seas wax rough?
 And were the galleys therefore glad to fly?
Alvaro. Signiore si, and de ship go drite on de Iscola de Candy.
Pisaro. Wert thou not my Alvaro, my beloved,
 One whom I know does dearly count of me,   255
 Much should I doubt me that some scoffing jack
 Had sent thee in the midst of all my griefs
 To tell a feigned tale of happy luck.
Alvaro. Will you no believe me? See dare den, see de lettre.
Pisaro. What is this world, or what this state of man?   260
 How in a moment cursed, in a trice blessed?
 But even now my happy state 'gan fade,
 And now again my state is happy made!
 My goods all safe, my ships all 'scaped away,
 And none to bring me news of such good luck   265
 But whom the heavens have marked to be my son.
 Were I a lord as great as Alexander,
 None should more willingly be made mine heir
 Than thee, thou golden tongue, thou good-news teller.
 Joy stops my mouth!   *The Exchange bell rings.* 270
Balsaro. Master Pisaro, the day is late; the bell doth ring.
 Wilt please you hasten to perform this business?
Pisaro. What business, sir? God's me, I cry you mercy!
 Do it, yes sir, you shall command me more.
Towerson. But sir, what do you mean? Do you intend   275

251–2 Did . . . fly?] *so lineated in 1830; set as prose in Qq.* 253. si] Q; cy Q2, Q3. Candy] Q (*Candy*); Cande Q2; Cande Q3.

---

253. *drite*] i.e. *dritta* starboard (right-hand) side; the ship drifted to the right toward Crete.
 Iscola de Candy] isle of Candy (Crete).
255. *count*] account, hold in esteem.
256. *scoffing jack*] practical joker.
261. *a trice*] an instant.
262. *'gan*] began to.
264. *'scaped*] escaped.
267. *Alexander*] Alexander the Great (356–323 BCE), son of Philip of Macedon; conquered Persia, Syria, and Egypt, and founded the city of Alexandria.
270. *Exchange bell*] bell indicating the end of morning trading at noon. (Balsaro's 'the day is late' at line 271 suggests the end of the day, but at line 289 Pisaro remarks, 'I think 'tis one o'clock'; getting home in time for dinner (i.e. lunch) is mentioned several times; and Heigham notes that during this morning trading session 'Pisaro bade us come to him / 'Twixt two or three o'clock at afternoon' (304–5).)
273. *God's me*] an oath, 'God bless me'.

To pay this bill, or else to palter with me?
Pisaro. Marry, God shield that I should palter with you.
      I do accept it, and come when you please.
      You shall have money; you shall have your money due.
Post. I beseech your worship to consider me.   280
Pisaro. O, you cannot cog. Go to, take that,
      Pray for my life. Pray that I have good luck,
      And thou shalt see, I will not be thy worst master.
Post. Marry, God bless your worship! I came in happy time. What, a
      French crown? Sure he knows not what he does. Well, I'll be gone,   285
      lest he remember himself and take it from me again.
                                                                    Exit.
Pisaro. Come on, my lads: Master Vandal, sweet son Alvaro.
      Come, Don Balsaro, let's be jogging home.
      By'r laken sirs, I think 'tis one o'clock.
                              Ex[eun]t PISARO, BALSARO, ALVARO,
                                          DELION, *and* VANDAL.
Browne. Come, Master Moore, th'Exchange is waxen thin;   290
      I think it best we get us home to dinner.
Moore. I know that I am looked for long ere this.
      Come Master Towerson, let's walk along.
                              Ex[eun]t MOORE, BROWNE, TOWERSON,
                                          STRANGERS, *and* MERCHANT[S].
Heigham. And if you be so hot upon your dinner,
      Your best way is to haste Pisaro on,   295
      For he is cold enough, and slow enough,
      He hath so late digested such cold news.
Walgrave. Marry, and shall. Hear you, Master Pisaro –
Harvey. Many Pisaros here! Why how now, Ned?

293.2. MERCHANTS] *this ed.; Marchant Q; Merchant Q2, Q3.*

---

276. *palter*] talk idly, trick or cheat.
280. *consider me*] take account of (with payment).
281. *cog*] trick, defraud.
285. *French crown*] the *ecu*, valuable French coin; a common play on baldness ('crown' = head) from 'French disease' (venereal disease) does not seem relevant here.
288. *jogging*] making our way.
289. *By'r laken*] an oath, 'By Our Ladykin'.
290. *waxen*] grown.
292. *looked for*] expected.
294. *hot*] intent, eager.
299. *Many Pisaros here!*] The use of 'many' here seems to be an ironic usage, indicating that there are *no* people called Pisaro present. 1830 notes, 'Walgrave, abstracted, does not perceive that Pisaro has gone out, for which Harvey laughs at him, "*Many* Pisaros *here!*" In the same sense, in act v., Laurentia says, "*Many* Balsaros *I.*" '

Where is your Matt, your welcome, and good cheer?   300
Walgrave. 'Swounds, let's follow him. Why stay we here?
Heigham. Nay, prithee, Ned Walgrave, let's bethink ourselves.
    There's no such haste; we may come time enough.
    At first Pisaro bade us come to him
    'Twixt two or three o'clock at afternoon –   305
    Then was he old Pisaro. But since then,
    What, with his grief for loss, and joy for finding,
    He quite forgot himself when he did bid us,
    And afterward forgot that he had bade us.
Walgrave. I care not. I remember't well enough: 310
    He bade us home, and I will go, that's flat,
    To teach him better wit another time.
Harvey. Here'll be a gallant jest when we come there,
    To see how 'mazed the greedy chuff will look
    Upon the nations, sects, and factions   315
    That now have borne him company to dinner.
    But hark you, let's not go to vex the man.
    Prithee sweet Ned, let's tarry, do not go.
Walgrave. Not go? Indeed, you may do what you please.
    I'll go, that's flat – nay, I am gone already.   320
    Stay you two, and consider further of it.
Heigham. Nay, all will go, if one. I prithee, stay.
    Thou'rt such a rash and giddy-headed youth,

---

301. 'Swounds] *Q; Come Q2, Q3.*   308–9. forgot . . . forgot] *this ed.; forgat . . . for-gat Qq.*   309–11. bade . . . bade] *Q;* bad . . . bad *Q2, Q3.*   310. remember't] *Q;* remember it *Q2, Q3.*

Laurentia's case is not quite the same. She is replying to Pisaro's order at 5.1.62–3 to fetch Master Balsaro. Of course, the question inherently requires that Pisaro is aware that Balsaro is not present, differentiating that situation from this one. Laurentia's reply seems to have a similar ironic ring, meaning something like 'I'll have no Balsaros' (or nothing to do with any Balsaros).

    300. *Matt*] short for Mathea.

    302. *Ned Walgrave*] Baugh writes, 'If *Ned* is omitted the line . . . would be a good blank verse line. With *Ned* in it the line will not scan. Perhaps Haughton wrote *Ned* and then, seeing that a two-syllable word was needed, inserted *Walgrave* instead. The printer copied both.' This is a plausible explanation for the hypermetrical line. I have kept the line with its possible fault, since Heigham and Harvey never call Ned by his last name alone.

    311. *flat*] certain, definite, the end of the matter.

    314. *'mazed*] amazed.

    chuff] (1) a greedy clown (2) miser (See Thomas Nashe, *Pierce Penilesse*, where he writes of 'an old, stradling Usurer . . . a fat chuffe it was', McKerrow i, p. 162–3).

Each stone's a thorn. Hoyda, he skips for haste!
Young Harvey did but jest; I know he'll go.   325
Walgrave. Nay, he may choose for me. But if he will,
Why does he not? Why stands he prating still?
If you'll go, come; if not, farewell.
Harvey. Hire a post-horse for him, gentle Frank:
Here's haste, and more haste than a hasty pudding.   330
You mad-man, mad-cap, wild-oats! We are for you!
It boots not stay when you intend to go.
Walgrave. Come away, then!   *Exeunt.*

---

324. Hoyda,] *Qq; Heydey! 1830.*   333. SD *Exeunt*] *Q, Haz; not in Q2, Q3.*

---

324. *Each stone's a thorn*] proverbial, cf. Tilley S894 'Under every stone sleeps a scorpion'.

327. *prating*] talking (excessively).

329. *post-horse*] horse kept at an inn or post-house for riders; a fast way to travel because the rider changes to a fresh horse at each 'post'.

Frank] i.e. Ferdinand (Heigham).

330. *hasty pudding*] a pudding made of flour stirred in boiling milk or water to the consistency of a thick batter (also refers to porridge).

331. *wild-oats*] young, boisterous man, out to sow his 'wild oats'.

332. *boots not*] does not help to, does not advantage (us) to.

ACT 2

[2.1]

Enter PISARO, ALVARO, DELION, *and* VANDAL.

Pisaro. A thousand welcomes, friends. Monsieur Delion,
   Ten thousand ben-venues unto your self.
   Signiore Alvaro, Master Vandal,
   Proud am I that my roof contains such friends.
   Why Mall, Laurentia, Matt! Where be these girls?   5

Enter the three sisters.

   Lively, my girls, and bid these strangers welcome.
   They are my friends, your friends, and our well-willers.
   You cannot tell what good you may have on them.
   God's me, why stir you not? – Hark in your ear:
   These be the men, the choice of many millions,   10
   That I, your careful father, have provided
   To be your husbands; therefore, bid them welcome.
Mathea. Aside Nay, by my troth, 'tis not the guise of maids
   To give a slavering salute to men. –
   If these sweet youths have not the wit to do it,   15
   We have the honesty to let them stand.
Vandal. God's sekerlin, dat's een fraai meiskin, Monsieur Delion, daar
   de grote freister, daar would ik zien, tis een fraaie daughter, daar
   heb ik so long loved, dare heb my desire so long geweest.

---

13. *Aside*] Qq *places '(aside)' at the end of line 14.*

---

  2. *ben-venues*] welcomes.
  5. *Mall*] i.e. Marina.
  6. *Lively*] Quickly.
  13–14. *Nay . . . men.* –] The aside in Q applies to these two lines; the four lines of
the speech could also be played entirely aloud or entirely as an aside.
  13. *guise*] proper action, custom, habit.
  14. *slavering*] slobbering, drooling.
  16. *honesty*] modesty, chastity.
  17–19. *God's sekerlin . . . geweest*] God's sweetness (sweet kin, child), that's a beautiful girl, Mister Delion, there the great lover, there would I be, it is a beautiful daughter,
there (i.e. her) I have loved so long, there my desire so long has been.

Alvaro. Ah, Venice, Roma, Italia, Frauncia, Angliterra, nor all dis orbe   20
can show so much *belliza, veremante de secunda*, Madona de
grande beauty.

Delion. Certes me dincke de mine de petite de little Angloise, de me
Maitresse Pisaro is une nette, un becues, un fra, et un tendre
damoisella.   25

Pisaro. What stocks! What stones! What senseless trunks be these?
When as I bid you speak, you hold your tongue.
When I bid peace, then can you prate and chat
And gossip! But go too, speak and bid welcome,
Or, as I live, you were as good you did.   30

Marina. I cannot tell what language I should speak.
If I speak English – as I can none other –
They cannot understand me, nor my welcome.

Alvaro. Bella madona, dare is no language so *dulce* – '*dulce*': dat is
'sweet' – as de language dat you shall speak, and de velcome dat   35
you sal say sal be well know perfaitemente.

Marina. Pray, sir, what is all this in English?

Alvaro. De usa sal vell teash you vat dat is. And if you sal please, I will
teash you to parler Italiano.

Pisaro. And that, methinks, sir, not without need.   40
And with Italian, to a child's obedience,
With such desire to seek to please their parents,
As others far more virtuous than themselves
Do daily strive to do. But 'tis no matter –

---

21. *belliza, veremante de secunda*] Qq.   35. velcome] *1830;* vell come Q; vel come
Q2, Q3.

21. belliza] i.e. *bellezza* beauty, charm.

veremante de secunda] i.e. *veramente* truly, indeed [Venice, Rome, etc.] are second
to Mathea in beauty. (The verb, *secondare*, means to support or second, and could here
be implied since Alvaro goes on to elaborate on his praise with the phrase, 'Madona
de grande beauty').

23-4. *de petite . . . tendre*] the little (petite) Englishwoman, my Mistress Pisaro is a
beauty, so very [beautiful], that's true, and a tender woman.

24. becues] probably meaning French: *beaucoup* (much, a lot).

fra] probably meaning French: *vrai* (true). It could also be an echo of Vandal's preceding use of the word to mean beautiful; Delion similarly echoes Alvaro's previous
line's 'much' with 'beaucoup' and 'veremante' with 'fra/vrai[ment]'.

26. stocks] trunks of trees without branches, stumps of felled trees.

30. *you were . . . did*] you'll wish you did.

35. *velcome*] welcome.

perfaitemente] perfectly.

39. *De usa*] use of it (language? Alvaro's intentions?).

parler] speak.

I'll shortly pull your haughty stomachs down.   45
I'll teach you urge your father, make you run
When I bid run, and speak when I bid speak.
What greater cross can careful parents have
Than careless children?   *Knock within.*
                    Stir and see who knocks.

          Enter HARVEY, WALGRAVE, *and* HEIGHAM.

Walgrave. Good morrow to my good mistress Mathea.   50
Mathea. As good a morrow to the morrow-giver.
Pisaro. A murren! What make these? What do they here?
Heigham. You see, Master Pisaro, we are bold guests.
    You could have bid no surer men than we.
Pisaro. Hark you, gentlemen. I did expect you   55
    At afternoon, not before two o'clock.
Harvey. Why, sir, if you please, you shall have us here at two o'clock,
    at three o'clock, at four o'clock – nay, till tomorrow this time. Yet
    I assure you, sir, we came not to your house without inviting.
Pisaro. Why, gentlemen, I pray, who bade you now?   60
    Whoever did it sure hath done you wrong,
    For scarcely could you come to worser cheer.
Heigham. It was your own self bade us to this cheer
    When you were busy with Balsaro talking.
    You bade us cease our suits till dinner time,   65
    And then to use it for our table talk.
    And we, I warrant you, are as sure as steel.
Pisaro. [*Aside*] A murren on yourselves, and sureness too!
    How am I crossed! God's me, what shall I do?
    This was that ill news of the Spanish pirates   70
    That so disturbed me. Well, I must dissemble
    And bid them welcome. But for my daughters

---

49. SD *Knock within*] Qq *place this direction after line* 44.   60. bade] Q; bad Q2,
Q3.   63. this] Q2, Q3; your Q.   67. are as sure] Q; as sure Q2, Q3.

45. *haughty stomachs*] pride.
46. *urge*] push (too far).
48. *cross*] burden (But cf. also 1.3.75 and 1.3.231).
49. *Stir*] Move.
52. *A murren*] plague, disease; an exclamation of disbelief or disgust; cf. *Taming of
a Shrew* (Epilogue, 10): Tapster, 'A Lord with a murrain! Come, art thou drunken
still?'.
62. *cheer*] welcome, entertainment.
67. *as sure as steel*] proverbial; this line cited in Tilley S840.
69. *crossed*] (1) contradicted (2) burdened.
71. *dissemble*] hide my true feelings.

I'll send them hence; they shall not stand and prate –
Well, my masters, gentlemen, and friends,
Though unexpected, yet most heartily welcome –　　　　75
[*Aside*] Welcome with a vengeance. – But for your cheer,
That will be small. – [*Aside*] Yet too too much for you. –
Mall, in and get things ready. Laurentia,
Bid Maudlin lay the cloth, take up the meat.
Look how she stirs. You sullen elf, you callet!　　　　80
Is this the haste you make?　　*Exeunt* MARINA *and* LAURENTIA.
Alvaro. Signiore Pisaro, ne soiat so malcontento; de gentlewoman your
filigola did parler but a litella to de gentle homa your grande
amico.
Pisaro. But that 'grande amico' is your grand inimico!　　　　85
One, if they be suffered to 'parlar',
Will poll you, ay, and pill you of your wife.
They love together, and the other two
Loves her two sisters. But 'tis only you
Shall crop the flower that they esteem so much.　　　　90
Alvaro. Do dey so? Vell let me 'lone, sal see me give dem de such grand
mock, sal be shame of dem selves.
Pisaro. Do, sir, I pray you do; set lustily upon them,
And I'll be ready still to second you.

78–9. ready. Laurentia, / Bid] *1830*; readie. / *Laurentia*, bid *Qq*.　83. did] *Q*; dit *Q2*,
Q3.　your] *this ed.*; y our *Q*; our *Q2, Q3*.

79. *Maudlin*] the kitchen woman, often mentioned, but never seen.
80. *sullen*] ill-humoured, gloomy.
elf] small, mischievous child.
callet] lewd woman, strumpet.
82. *ne soiat so malcontento*] do not be distraught.
filigola] (i.e. *figliola*) little daughter.
83. *your*] Q's 'y our' suggests that 'y' was intended to be Alvaro's 'and' in Anglo-
Italian; 'our' also suggests the camaraderie between the strangers and Pisaro. (Poeti-
cally, a slur between 'y' and 'our' might suggest the 'your' of the following line.)
However, this appears to be a compositorial error in Q, since 'your' nicely echoes
Alvaro's 'your filigola' and is echoed itself in Pisaro's play on the word as he responds
with an emphasized '*your* grand inimico'.
83–4. *grande amico*] good (great) friend.
85. *inimico*] enemy.
86. *parlar*] speak.
87. *poll . . . pill*] strip, make bare; pollarding, cutting off of tree-tops (hence, losing
of hair, with suggestion of the likely effects of venereal disease).
90. *crop the flower*] deflower the daughters (take their virginity).
91–2. *grand mock*] big joke, great embarrassment.
93. *lustily*] with vigour.
94. *second you*] support you, back you up.

Walgrave. But Matt, art thou so mad as to turn French?   95
Mathea. Yes, marry, when two Sundays come together.
     Think you I'll learn to speak this gibberish,
     Or the pig's language? Why, if I fall sick
     They'll say the French *et cetera* infected me.
Pisaro. Why, how now, minion! What, is this your service?   100
     Your other sisters busy are employed,
     And you stand idle. Get you in, or –   *Exit* MATHEA.
Walgrave. If you chide her, chide me, Master Pisaro.
     For but for me, she had gone in long since.
Pisaro. I think she had, for we are sprights to scare her.   105
     But ere't be long, I'll drive that humour from her.
Alvaro. [*To Walgrave.*] Signiore, me thinks you soud no mack de
     wenshe so hardee, so disobedient to de padre as ditt Madona
     Matt.
Walgrave. Signiore, me thinkes you should learn to speak before you   110
     should be so foolhardy as to woo such a maiden as that 'Madona
     Matt'.
Delion. Warrant you, Monsieur, he sal parle wen you sal stande out
     the doure.

---

97. I'll] *Q;* I *Q2, Q3.*   gibberish] *1830;* gibberidge *Qq.*   99. *et cetera*] *this ed.;* (*et-cetera*) *Qq.*   105. we] *Qq;* ye *Haz.*   106. ere't] *Q2, Q3;* er't *Q.*   113. Warrant] *1830;* Warrent *Qq.*

---

95. *turn French*] a variation on 'to turn Turk', a common saying in the sixteenth century for betraying one's native attributes (in many cases, Christianity).

97. *I'll*] This Q reading suggests the future tense; Q2 and Q3's 'I' suggests a current action, as if Mathea might already be 'learning French'.

98. *pig's language*] because the French say, 'awee, awee', squealing like a pig; cf. 1.1.172–5.

99. *the French* et cetera *infected me*] the 'French' disease, venereal disease; Mathea may actually say 'et cetera' or the Qq's parentheses around the words may be an implicit stage direction for her to react with improvisation to the bawdy nature of the line.

100. *minion*] See note to 1.1.130.

105. *sprights*] sprites, spirits.

106. *ere't*] i.e. before it.

humour] mood, temper; early modern physiology believed in the body's composition by 'humours', the four substances blood, phlegm, yellow bile, and black bile; the levels of these humours in the body corresponded with temperamental characteristics of the person, respectively sanguine (cheerful), phlegmatic (sluggish, apathetic), choleric (angry), melancholic (sad).

108. *hardee*] i.e. hardy (bold, presumptions).

113. *Warrant you*] Be assured.

113–4. *he sal . . . doure*] he will be inside talking to the woman when you are still outside the front door.

Harvey. Hark you, Monsieur, you would wish yourself half hanged;   115
you were as sure to be let in as he.

Vandal. Maak no doubt de Signiore Alvaro sal do vel enough.

Heigham. Perhaps so, but methinks your best way were to ship yourself
for Stoade, and there to barter yourself for a commodity; for I can
tell you, you are here out of liking.   120

Pisaro. The worst perhaps dislike him, but the best esteem him best.

Harvey. But, by your patience, sir, methinks none should know better
who's lord than the lady.

Alvaro. Den de lady? Vat lady?

Harvey. Marry, sir, the lady Let-her-alone, one that means to let you 125
alone for fear of trouble.

Pisaro. Every man as he may; yet sometimes the blind may catch a
hare.

Heigham. Ay, sir, but he will first eat many a fly.
You know it must be a wonder if a crab catch a fowl.   130

Vandal. Maar hoort eens. If he and ik and Monsieur Delion be de crab,
we sal kash de fowl wel genough, I warrant you.

Walgrave. Ay, and the fool well enough, I warrant you.
And much good may it do ye.

Alvaro. Me dincke such a piculo man as you be sal have no de such   135
grande luck madere.

---

119. barter] Q2, Q3; batter Q.   123. who's lord] Q; who's is lord Q2; who's the
lord Q3; who is lord *1830*.   125. Let-her-alone] *1830*; let her alone Qq.

119. *Stoade*] cf. note to 1.3.83.
barter] bargain.
125. *Let-her-alone*] (1) never mind her, don't worry yourself about her (2) keep
away from her.
127–30. *the blind ... fowl*] ' "The blind eats many a fly" was proverbial, and,
according to Henslowe's *Diary*, formed the title of a play by Tho[ma]s Heywood, under
the date of November 1602' (1830). See Tilley B451. See *Diary* for 23 November 1602,
for a £3 partial payment (p. 220), 30s more on 15 December, and a final instalment
of 30s on 7 January 1603 (p. 221).
131. Maar hoort eens] But listen.
133. *fool*] Walgrave's play on Vandal's 'fowl' above.
135. *piculo*] little. Ned Walgrave is apparently a small man who makes up for his
lack of physical size by his boisterousness and quick temper; his pet name, Ned, often
used to denote close friends in the period, is a diminutive that further suggests his small
size.
136. *madere*] perhaps 'made here'.

Delion. Non; da Monsieur, an he be so grande amorous op de damoisella, he sal have Mawdlyn de witt wenshe in de Kichine by maiter
Pisaro's leave.

Walgrave. By Master Pisaro's leave, Monsieur, I'll mumble you, except   140
you learn to know whom you speak to. I tell thee *François*, I'll
have, maugre thy teeth, her that shall make thee gnash thy teeth
to want.

Pisaro. Yet a man may want of his will, and bate an ace of his wish.
But, gentlemen, every man as his luck serves, and so agree we. I   145
would not have you fall out in my house. Come, come, all this was
in jest. Now let's to't in earnest – I mean with our teeth – and try
who's the best trencher-man.   *Exeunt.*

[2.2]

Enter FRISCO.

Frisco. Ah, sirrah, now I know what manner of thing Paul's is. I did
so mar'l afore what it was out of all count, for my master would
say, 'Would I had Paul's full of gold'. My young mistresses and
Grimkin our tailor would wish they had Paul's full of needles. I
once asked my master half a yard of frieze to make me a coat and   5
he cried whoop holiday, it was big enough to make Paul's a night-

---

2. mar'l] *Haz;* marle *Qq;* marl *1830.*   4–5. I once] *1830;* I, one *Qq.*

---

137. *da*] the.

an] the foreigner here seems to understand the English use of 'and' as 'if', an apparent example of the author's natural English usage inserting itself into the 'foreign'
character's language.

137–8. *grande amorous op de damoisella*] hugely in love with the woman.

138. *witt*] perhaps the term of endearment (pet usage) 'white', here used ironically
(*OED* 'white' a.9).

140. *mumble*] 'maul, handle roughly, maltreat' (*OED* 'mumble' V.5), punning on
the Frenchman's mumbled English pronunciation.

141. François] i.e. Frenchman.

142. *maugre*] in spite of.

142–3. *gnash thy teeth to want*] i.e. respond in a frustrated manner to lacking her
love; there is a touch of hyperbole, as the image recalls lost souls' gnashing of teeth in
hell.

144. *bate an ace*] to abate a jot or a little, to make the slightest abatement (lessening
of something).

148. *trencher-man*] eater; trencher = platter for serving food on, or possibly the
carver of the meat.

1. *Paul's*] See note to 1.2.63.

2. *mar'l*] marvel.

2. *out of all count*] beyond all compare.

5. *frieze*] heavy, napped, woollen cloth.

gown! I have been told that Duke Humphrey dwells here, and that
he keeps open house, and that a brave sort of cammileres dine with
him every day. Now, if I could see any vision in the world towards
dinner, I would set in a foot. But the best is, as the ancient English   10
Roman orator saith, 'So-lame-men, misers, housewives', and so
forth. The best is that I have great store of company that do
nothing but go up and down and go up and down, and make a
grumbling together, that the meat is so long making ready. Well,
if I could meet this scurvy Frenchman, they should stay me, for I   15
would be gone home.

Enter ANTHONY.

Anthony. I beseech you, Monsieur, give me audience.
Frisco. What would you have? What should I give you?
Anthony. Pardon, sir, mine uncivil and presumptuous intrusion, who
endeavour nothing less than to provoke or exasperate you against   20
me.
Frisco. They say a word to the wise is enough. So by this little French
that he speaks, I see he is the very man I seek for. Sir, I pray, what
is your name?
Anthony. I am nominated Monsieur Le Mouche, and rest at your *bon*   25
service.

---

7. *Duke Humphrey*] Stow notes that John Beauchamp, constable of Dover, has a
tomb in St Paul's mistakenly thought by some to be that of Humphrey, Duke of
Gloucester. C. L. Kingsford, in his edition of Stow, notes that 'The aisles, and especially
the neighbourhood of "Duke Humphrey's Tomb," were the recognized haunts of loiter-
ers, needy adventurers, and broken-down gallants'. Such men 'hoped there to earn a
meal by their wits'; ' "to dine with Duke Humphrey" became a proverb for to go din-
nerless' (Stow ii, p. 349) (see also note to 1.2.64).

8. *cammileres*] 'meaning *Cavaliers*' (1830).

10–11. *the ancient . . . '. . . housewives'*] The 1830 editor recognized this as a comically corrupted line from *Dr Faustus*. In response to Dr Faustus's question about why
Lucifer tempts souls, Mephastophilis responds '*Solamen miseris socios habuisse doloris*'
(5.42), misery loves company.

11–12. *and so forth*] possibly said by Frisco, but possibly an implicit stage direction
for him to finish the quotation with improvisation (see notes to 1.2.106–7 and
1.3.147).

15. *stay me*] wait for me, (or possibly) keep me here.

16. *would be*] wish to be.

20. *provoke or exasperate*] Anthony's deliberate misuse of big words to impress the
ignorant Frisco.

22. *a word . . . enough*] proverbial, cf. Tilley W781 'a word to a wise man is enough'
and W799, 'few words show men wise'.

25. *nominated*] affected way of saying 'named'.
Le Mouche] The Fly (*la mouche* can also mean the bull's eye of a target).
bon] good.

Frisco. I understand him partly yea and partly nay. Can you speak
  French? *Content pore vous Monsieur Madamo.*
Anthony. If I could not, sir, I should ill understand you. You speak the
  best French that ever trod upon shoe of leather.   30
Frisco. Nay, I can speak more languages than that. This is Italian, is it
  not: *Nella slurde Curtezana?*
Anthony. Yes, sir, and you speak it like a very natural.
Frisco. I believe you well. Now for Dutch: *Ducky de doe watt heb yee
  gebrought.*   35
Anthony. I pray, stop your mouth, for I never heard such Dutch before
  brocht.
Frisco. Nay, I think you have not met with no peasant. Hear you,
  Master Mouse, – so your name is, I take it – I have considered of
  your learning in these aforesaid languages, and find you reason-   40
  able. So, so, now this is the matter. Can you take the ease to teach
  these tongues to two or three gentlewomen of mine acquaintance,
  and I will see you paid for your labour?
Anthony. Yes, sir, and that most willingly.
Frisco. Why then, Master Mouse, to their use, I entertain ye, which   45
  had not been but for the troubles of the world, that I my self have
  no leisure to show my skill. Well, sir, if you'll please to walk with
  me, I'll bring you to them.   *Exeunt.*

[2.3]

Enter LAURENTIA, MARINA, *and* MATHEA.

Laurentia. Sit till dinner's done? Not I, I swear.
  Shall I stay till he belch into mine ears
  Those rustic phrases, and those Dutch-French terms,
  Stammering half sentences, dogbolt eloquence?
  And when he hath no love, forsooth, why then   5

---

  28. Content . . . Madamo] Happily for you, Mister Madam.
  32. Nella slurde Curtezana] perhaps 'In the filthy courtesan': '*Slurde* may be a
mistake for *lurda* (for *lorda*), foul, impure, lewd' (Baugh).
  34. Ducky de doe] this is apparently gibberish.
  watt heb yee gebrought] what have you brought.
  37. brocht] broached, attempted (?), but perhaps punning on 'gebrought' of the
preceding line, thus Anthony is saying that he is impressed by the Dutch that Frisco
has *brought* with him.
  38. not . . . no] the double negative frequently appears in sixteenth-century texts.

  4. dogbolt] wretched, contemptible.

He tells me cloth is dear at Antwerp, and the men
Of Amsterdam have lately made a law
That none but Dutch as he may traffic there.
Then stands he still and studies what to say,
And after some half hour, because the ass　　　　　　　　10
Hopes – as he thinks – I shall not contradict him,
He tells me that my father brought him to me,
And that I must perform my father's will.
Well, goodman goose-cap, when thou wooest again,
Thou shalt have simple ease for thy love's pain.　　　　15
Mathea. Alas, poor wench. I sorrow for thy hap,
To see how thou art clogged with such a dunce.
Forsooth, my sire hath fitted me far better.
My Frenchman comes upon me with the 'sa, sa, sa.
Sweet madam pardone moy I pra'.　　　　　　　　　　　　20
And then out goes his hand, down goes his head,
Swallows his spittle, frizzles his beard, and then to me:
'Pardone moy mistresse Mathea,
If I be bold, to macke so bold met you,
Think it go' will dat spurs me dus up you.　　　　　　　　25
Dan cast neit off so good and true lover,

---

25. go'] *this ed.;* go *Qq.*

6–8. *He tells . . . there*] cf. Portia's boredom with her suitor, the Neapolitan Prince, who 'doth nothing but talk of his horse, and he makes it a great appropriation to his own good parts that he can shoe him himself' (*Merchant of Venice* 1.2.35–7).

6. *Antwerp*] major trading port for English and European merchants in the sixteenth century, on the Scheldt River in early modern Netherlands, now Belgium.

8. *traffic*] trade and ship goods.

14. *goodman*] vague term for class underneath gentleman.

goose-cap] simpleton, fool.

15. *simple . . . pain*] spoken ironically: Laurentia will flatly rebuff Vandal's advances.

16. *hap*] misfortune.

17. *clogged*] (1) stopped, clogged up (2) encumbered (clog = block of wood hung on an animal to slow it down or stop it escaping) (3) pun on Dutch wooden shoes, or clogs. Line 18's 'sire' seems to extend the animal metaphor.

19–22. *My Frenchman . . . me*] cf. the description of Pilia-Borza in *The Jew of Malta* 4.2.30–4 and 4.3.6–14.

20. *pardone moy*] i.e. *pardonnez moi* = excuse me.

pra'] pray.

22. *frizzles*] twists and springs into tight curls.

24. *met*] with (Dutch; this quoted passage contains words derived from all three foreign languages with which this play is concerned).

25. *go'*] Mathea's imitation French pronunciation of 'good'. Thus the line has Delion claiming that his 'go[od] will' prompts his amorous advances.

dus] thus.

Madama Celestura de la –' I know not what
'– Do oft pray to God dat me would love her'.
And then he reckons a catalogue of names
Of such as love him, and yet cannot get him.   30
Marina. Nay, but your Monsieur's but a mouse in cheese
Compared with my Signiore. He can tell
Of Lady Venus, and her son, blind Cupid;
Of the fair Scilla that was loved of Glaucus,
And yet scorned Glaucus, and yet loved King Minos;   35
Yet Minos hated her, and yet she helped him,
And yet he scorned her, yet she killed her father
To do him good, yet he could not abide her.
Nay, he'll be bawdy, too, in his discourse.
And when he is so, he will take my hand   40
And tickle the palm, wink with his one eye,
Gape with his mouth, and –
Laurentia. And hold thy tongue, I prithee; here's my father!

> *Enter* PISARO, ALVARO, VANDAL, DELION, HARVEY,
> WALGRAVE, *and* HEIGHAM.

Pisaro. Unmannerly, untaught, unnurtured girls!
Do I bring gentlemen, my very friends,   45
To feast with me, to revel at my house,
That their good likings may be set on you,
And you like misbehaved and sullen girls
Turn tail to such as may advance your states?
I shall remember't, when you think I do not.   50
I am sorry, gentlemen, your cheer's no better.
But what did want at board, excuse me for,

---

36. helped] *this ed.;* holp'd *Qq;* holp *Haz.*   38. do him good] *Q2, Q3;* doe her good
Q.

---

27. *Madama Celestura*] French: *céleste* = celestial, heavenly.
31. *a mouse in cheese*] to speak like a 'mouse in a cheese' = to mumble, to speak in
a muffled voice (*OED* 'mouse' I.2); hence, Delion is nothing compared to the garrulous
volubility of Alvaro.
33–4. *Lady Venus . . . Glaucus*] 'This story had become familiar in consequence of
T[homas] Lodge's *Scillaes Metamorphosis*, printed in 1589' (1830). Thomas Lodge's
'The most pithie and pleasant historie of Glaucus and Silla' (1589) tells the first half
of this story in rhymed pentameter. Alvaro has apparently been combining two stories
of Scylla; in one, Glaucus is the sea-god in love with Scylla, and jealous Circe turns
Scylla into the six-headed monster that devours sailors in the Strait of Messina; in
another, Scylla, Daughter of Nisus, king of Megara, betrayed her father to his enemy
Minos, but, when she sought Minos' love, he scorned her.
52. *want at board*] lack at the dinner table.

And you shall have amends be made in bed.
To them, friends, to them! They are none but yours.
For you I bred them, for you brought them up.   55
For you I kept them, and you shall have them.
I hate all others that resort to them.
Then rouse your bloods! Be bold with what's your own.
For I and mine, my friends, be yours, or none.

Enter FRISCO *and* ANTHONY.

Frisco. God-gee god-morrow sir, I have brought you Master Mouse   60
    here to teach my young mistresses. I assure you, forsooth, he is a
    brave Frenchman.
Pisaro. Welcome, friend, welcome. My man, I think,
    Hath at the full resolved thee of my will.
    Monsieur Delion, I pray question him.   65
    I tell you, sir, 'tis only for your sake
    That I mean to entertain this fellow.
Anthony. [*Aside*] A bots of all ill luck! How came these here?
    Now am I 'posed except the wenches help me:
    I have no French to slap them in the mouth.   70
Harvey. [*Aside*] To see the luck of a good fellow: poor Anthony
    Could ne'er have sorted out a worser time.
    Now will the pack of all our sly devices
    Be quite laid ope, as one undoes an oyster.
    Frank Heigham, and mad Ned, fall to your muses   75
    To help poor Anthony now at a pinch,
    Or all our market will be spoiled and marred.
Walgrave. Tut, man, let us alone, I warrant you.
Delion. Monsieur, *Vous êtes très bien venu; de quel pais êtes vous?*

---

55. brought] *Q;* I brought *Q2, Q3.*   69. 'posed] *this ed.;* posde *Q;* pos'd *Q2, Q3.*

58. *rouse your bloods*] (1) be bold (2) get sexually active.
60. *God-gee god-morrow*] God give you good morrow (1830 emends to 'Gi' ye').
62. *brave*] splendid, fine.
64. *resolved thee*] clarified for you, informed you.
67. *entertain*] take in, employ.
68. *bots*] See note to 1.3.122 and 146.
69. *'posed*] exposed ('nonplussed' (Baugh)).
73. *pack*] bundle, set, whole lot; cf. Malvolio in *Twelfth Night*: 'I'll be revenged on the whole pack of you' (5.1.365).
75. *fall to your muses*] rack your brains; in Greek mythology, the muses were the nine daughters of Zeus and Mnemosyne, associated with various arts, and called upon by practitioners for inspiration. (Hazlitt glosses muses as 'inventions').
76. *at a pinch*] quickly, in a desperate situation.
79. vous êtes . . . vous?] You are very welcome; from which country are you?

Anthony. [*To himself.*] 'Vous': that's 'you'. Sure, he says, 'how do men   80
    call you'. [*To Delion.*] Monsieur le Mouche.
Marina. Sister, help, sister! That's honest Anthony,
    And he answers your wooer *cuius contrarium.*
Delion. Monsieur. Vous n'entends pas. Je ne demande puit, votre nom –
Mathea. Monsieur Delion. He that made your shoes made them not in   85
    fashion: they should have been cut square at the toe.
Delion. Madame, my sho met de square toe? Vat be dat?
Pisaro. Why, sauce-box! How now, you unreverent minx!
    Why, in whose stable hast thou been brought up,
    To interrupt a man in midst of speech?   90
    Monsieur Delion, disquiet not yourself,
    But as you have begun, I pray proceed
    To question with this countryman of yours.
Delion. Dat me sal do *très bien,* but de bella Madona de jeune gentle-
    woman do monstre some singe of amour to speak to me, epurce   95
    Monsieur, me sal say but two, tree, four, five word to dis François,
    or sus: *Monsieur Le Mouche, en quelle partie de France êtiez vous*
    né?
Harvey. France!
Heigham.   Ned!
Walgrave.   'Sblood, let me come!
    Master Pisaro, we have occasion of affairs,   100
    Which calls us hence with speed, wherefore I pray
    Defer this business till some fitter time,
    And to perform what at the Exchange we spoke of.
Anthony. [*Aside*] A blessing on that tongue, saith Anthony.
Pisaro. Yes, marry, gentlemen, I will, I will. –   105

---

94. jeune] *1830;* june *Qq.* 95. to me] *this ed.;* lot me *Qq.* 99. 'Sblood] Sbloud *Q;*
What *Q2, Q3.*

---

83. *he . . . contrarium*] he replies contrarily, at odds with (sometimes with the [legal]
sense of argumentation, but here through ignorance).

84. *Vous n'entends . . . nom –*] You don't understand. I didn't ask your name – (the
French could also be punctuated as a question).

88. *unreverent*] irreverent, disrespectful.

minx] pert, flirtatious girl.

94. *très bien*] very well.

jeune] young.

95. *do monstre some singe of amour*] demonstrates something of love (French:
demonstrer).

epurce] and for it (French: *et pour ce*).

97–8. *en quelle . . . né?*] in which part of France were you born?

99. *France!*] i.e. Ferdinand (Heigham); this exclamation might be played as a
comical, echoing panic response to the question, '*en quelle partie de* France êtiez vous
né?'

Alvaro, to your task; fall to your task.
I'll bear away those three, who, being here,
Would set my daughters on a merry pin.
Then cheerly try your lucks; but speak, and speed,
For you alone, say I, shall do the deed.   110
      Exeunt PISARO, HARVEY, WALGRAVE, *and* HEIGHAM.
Frisco. Hear you, Master Mouse. Did you dine today at Paul's with
    the rest of the gentlemen there?
Anthony. No, sir, I am yet undined.
Frisco. Methinks you should have a reasonable good stomach then by
    this time. As for me, I can feel nothing within me from my mouth   115
    to my cod-piece, but all empty, wherefore I think it a piece of
    wisdom to go in and see what Maudlin hath provided for our
    dinner. Master Mouse, will you go in?
Anthony. With as good a stomach and desire as yourself.
Frisco. Let's pass in, then.   *Exeunt* FRISCO *and* ANTHONY.   120
Vandal. Hoe zeg you, dochter, voor wat cause, voor why be de also
    much grooterlie strange, ik zeg you wat, if dat gij speake to me, is
    dat gij love me.
Laurentia. Is't that I care not for you. Is't that your breath stinks. If
    that your breath stinks not, you must learn sweeter English or I   125
    shall never understand your suit.
Delion. Pardonnez moi madame.
Mathea. With all my heart, so you offend no more.
Delion. Is dat an offence to be amorous di one belle gentleawoman?
Mathea. Ay, sir, see your 'belle gentlewoman' cannot be amorous of   130
    you.

---

115. feel] *1830*; sell *Qq.*   116. think it] *Q2, Q3*; thinke *Q.*   121. Hoe] *this ed*;
Han *Qq.*

    108. *merry pin*] merry frame of mind.
    109. *speed*] succeed.
    116. *cod-piece*] padded or pocketed appendage affixed to the front of close-fitting
hose or breeches, and covering the genitals; sometimes used figuratively for genitals, as
in *Measure for Measure* 3.1.358–9: Lucio, 'Why, what a ruthless thing is this in him,
for the rebellion of a codpiece to take away the life of a man!'
    121–3. *Hoe zeg . . . me*] i.e. How say you daughter, for what cause, for why be so
much greatly strange (i.e. why are you being so distant)? I tell you what, if that you
speak to me is that you love me (the final clause may be an interrogative, or it may be
a statement, requiring reading the 'if . . . is' and 'if . . . then').
    124. *Is't that your breath stinks*] These phrases could be punctuated with question
marks. This would depend on an interpretation of the interrogative nature of Vandal's
preceding lines.
    127. Pardonnez moi madame] This could be delivered as a question for the old joke
of the question 'excuse me' as meaning 'what do you mean' being answered with the
reply that takes the question as a statement of apology.
    130. *see*] take note that, understand that.

Marina. Then if I were as that 'belle gentlewoman''s lover, I would
    trouble her no further, nor be amorous any longer.

Alvaro. Madona, yet de belleza of de face beauty, de form of all de
    corpo may be such datt no perriculo, nor all de mal shaunce can   135
    make him leave hir dulce visage.

Laurentia. But Signiore Alvaro, if the 'perriculo' or 'mal shaunce' were
    such that she should love and live with another, then the 'dulce
    visage' must be left in spite of the lover's teeth, whilst he may whine
    at his own ill fortune.   140

Vandal. Dat's waar matress, for it is un true saying: dey wint he taught
    dey verleifd lie scrat zijn gat.

Mathea. And I think, too, y'are like to scratch there, but never to claw
    any of my sister's love away.

Vandal. Dan zal your sistree do 'gainst her vader's will, for your vader   145
    zegt dat ik sal heb haar voor mine wife.

Laurentia. I think not so, sir, for I never heard him say so; But I'll go
    in and ask him if his meaning be so.

Marina. Hark, sister, Signiore Alvaro saith that I am the fairest of all
    us three.   150

Laurentia. Believe him not for he'll tell any lie,
    If so he thinks thou mayst be pleased thereby.
    Come, go with me and ne'er stand prating here;
    I have a jest to tell thee in thine ear
    Shall make you laugh. Come, let your Signiore stand.   155
    I know there's not a wench in all this town
    Scoffs at him more or loves him less than thou.
    Master Vandal, as much I say for you:
    If needs you marry with an English lass,
    Woo her in English, or she'll call you ass.   160

                     [*Exeunt* LAURENTIA *and* MARINA.]

---

143. y'are] *Q2, Q3;* are *Q;* you are *1830.*

---

134. *de belleza*] beauty, charm.

134–5. *de corpo*] the body.

135. *perriculo*] danger, peril.

136. *dulce visage*] sweet face.

139. *in . . . teeth*] regardless of, despite the lover('s appetite, desire); proverbial, cf.
Tilley S764, 'In spite of one's teeth'.

141. *Dat's waar*] That's true.

141–2. *dey wint . . . gat*] a difficult passage, with a dirty joke: it reads something
like 'he (who) wins teaches, he who loves lies scratching his hole (i.e. arse)'.

144. *sister's*] this could be a plural possessive, although Vandal's speech following
suggests the singular.

Mathea. Tut, that's a French cog. Sure I think
   There's ne'er a wench in France not half so fond
   To woo and sue so for your Monsieurship.
Delion. Par may foy, madame, she does tinck dare is no wench so dure
   as you. For de fillee was cree dulce, tendre, and amarous for me   165
   to love hir. Now me tincke dat I, being such a fine man, you should
   love-a me.
Mathea. So think not I, sir.
Delion. But so tincke esh oder damosellas.
Mathea. Nay, I'll lay my love to your command   170
   That my sisters think not so. How say you, sister Mall?
   Why, how now, gentlemen; is this your talk?
   What, beaten in plain field? Where be your maids?
   Nay, then I see their loving humour fades,
   And they resign their int'rest up to me,   175
   And yet I cannot serve for all you three.
   But lest two should be mad, that I love one,
   You should be all alike, and I'll love none.
   The world is scant when so many Jack Daws
   Hover about one corpse with greedy paws.   180
   If needs you'll have me stay till I am dead,
   Carrion for crows, Mathea for her Ned.
   And so, farewell, we sisters do agree
   To have our wills, but ne'er to have you three.   *Ex*[*it*].
Delion. Madama, attendez, madama! Is she allé? Do she mocque de   185
   nous in such sort?

---

179. Jack Daws] *Q, Q2* (Jacke Dawes); Jack-Dawes *Q3*; jackdaws *1830*.   180. corpse]
this ed.; Coarse *Qq;* corse *1830.*   184. SD *Ex*[*it*] *this ed.;* Exeunt *Qq.*   186. nous] *this
ed.;* nows *Q;* uous *(i.e. 'vous' or a turned 'n') Q2, Q3;* vous *1830.*

---

161. *French cog*] French trick.
162. *fond*] foolish.
164. *Par may foy*] By my faith, truly.
so dure] tough, difficult, harsh.
165. *de fillee was cree dulce*] the girl was believed (to be) sweet ('cree' may also
imply 'made' or 'created').
169. *esh oder*] each (i.e. both) of the other women.
173. *in plain field*] in fair fight.
179. *Jack Daws*] (1) jackdaws (black birds) (2) contemptuous epithet for a person:
'daw' = fool; cf. John Day, *Law Tricks* (1608), 'How the daw scours ore his rusty
phrases' 1.39–40 (Malone Society Reprint: Oxford University Press, 1950) (cf. also
Pisaro's 'scoffing jack' 1.3.256, 'Jack Sauce' 4.1.34, 4.1.147, and Mathea's 'Jack Daws'
2.3.179); John Daw is also the name of a gullible character in Jonson's *Epicoene*.
185. attendez] wait.
allé] gone (past tense of French: *aller*).
185–6. *mocque de nous*] mock us (French: *nous*).

Vandal. O, de pestilence! Hoe if dat ik can niet deze Englese spreek
    vel, ik shal haar fader zeg how dit is to pass gekomen?

Enter PISARO.

Alvaro. Ne parlate. See here, Signiores, de fader.
Pisaro. Now, friends, now gentlemen, how speeds your work?   190
    Have you not found them shrewd, unhappy girls?
Vandal. Meester Pisaro, de dochter Matress Laurentia calle me de
    duivel, de ass, for that ik kan niet Englesh spreken.
Alvaro. Ande dat we sal no parler, dat we sal no havar den for de
    wive.   195
Pisaro. Are they so lusty? Dare they be so proud?
    Well, I shall find a time to meet with them.
    In the mean season, pray, frequent my house.

Enter FRISCO, running.

    How now, sirrah, whither are you running?
Frisco. About a little tiny business.   200
Pisaro. What business, ass?
Frisco. Indeed, I was not sent to you. And yet I was sent after the three
    gen'men that dined here, to bid them come to our house at ten
    o'clock at night, when you were a-bed.
Pisaro. Ha! What is this? Can this be true?   205
    What, art thou sure the wenches bade them come?
Frisco. So they said, unless their minds be changed since. For a woman
    is like a weathercock, they say, and I am sure of no more than I
    am certain of. But I'll go in and bid them send you word whether
    they shall come or no.   210

---

187. Hoe] *Q, Q2 (hoe); ho Q3; Ho 1830; O Haz.*   188. gekomen?] *this ed.; gecomen.
Qq, Haz.*   190-1. Now . . . girls?] *so lineated in 1830; single line in Qq.*   203. gen'men]
1830; Gen-men *Qq.*

   187-8. *Hoe . . . gekomen?*] How if I cannot speak this English well, shall I tell her
father how this is come to pass?.

   189. Ne parlate] don't speak, be quiet.

   191. *shrewd*] of children, naught; malicious, mischievous (less harshly, bad); also
shrewish, temperamental.

   192-3. *de duivel*] the devil.

   194. *dat . . . dat*] i.e. if . . . then.

   197. *meet*] give them a talking to, get even.

   198. *mean season*] meantime.

   203. *gen'men*] Frisco's pronunciation of 'gentlemen'.

   207-8. *a woman is like a weathercock*] proverbial, cf. Tilley W653: wavering, variable; *A Woman Is a Weathercock* is the title of a play by Nathaniel Field (Q1, 1612),
included in vol. 2 of *The Old English Drama* (1830).

Pisaro. No, sirrah, stay you here. But one word more:
    Did they appoint them come one by one, or else altogether?
Frisco. Altogether! Lord, that such a young man as you should have
    no more wit! Why, if they should come together, one could not
    make room for them, but coming one by one, they'll stand there   215
    if there were twenty of them.
Pisaro. How this news glads me and revives my soul.
    How say you, sirs? What, will you have a jest
    Worth the telling – nay, worth the acting?
    I have it gentlemen, I have it friends!   220
Alvaro. Signiore Pisaro, I prey de gratia watte maneire sal we have?
    Watt will thee parler? What bon do you know, Signiore Pisaro,
    dicheti noi Signiore Pisaro.
Pisaro. O, that youth so sweet
    So soon should turn to age. Were I as you,   225
    Why this were sport alone for me to do.
    Hark ye, hark ye. Here my man
    Saith that the girls have sent for Master Heigham
    And his two friends. I know they love them dear,
    And therefore wish them late at night be here   230
    To revel with them. Will you have a jest,
    To work my will, and give your longings rest?
    Why then, Master Vandal and you two
    Shall soon at midnight come, as they should do,
    And court the wenches. And to be unknown   235
    And taken for the men, whom they alone
    So much affect, each one shall change his name.
    Master Vandal, you shall take 'Heigham', and you
    'Young Harvey', and Monsieur Delion, 'Ned',
    And under shadows be of substance sped.   240
    How like you this device? How think you of it?

217–20. How . . . friends!] *so lineated in 1830; set as prose in Qq.* 222. thee] *this*
ed.; the *Qq.* 224–6. O, that . . . do] *so lineated in 1830; set as prose in Qq.*

213. *such a young man*] Frisco is being ironic.
221–3. *I prey . . . Pisaro*] 'I pray, if you please, what is your plan for us (what are
we to do)? What do you want to tell us? What 'good' (plan, jest) do you have in mind,
Mr Pisaro? Tell us Mr Pisaro.'
225–6. *So soon . . . you, / Why . . . do*] these lines are prose in Qq, but the rhyme
of 'you/do' confirms the verse.
240. *under shadows*] (1) in disguise (2) shadows of night.
of substance sped] (1) rid of material (bodily) existence (2) succeed substantially.

Delion. O, de brave de galliarde devise. Me sal come by de nite and
contier faire de Anglois gentlehommes dicte nous ainsi Monsieur
Pisaro.

Pisaro. You are in the right, sir.   245

Alvaro. And I sall name me de Signiore Harvey, ende Monsieur Delion
sall be de piculo Signiore Ned, ende when Madona Laurentia sall
say, 'who be dare?' mister Vandal sall say, 'O, my sout laide, hier
be your love mestro Haigham'. Is no dis de bravissime, Master
Vandal?   250

Vandal. [*Sings.*]
  Slaat op de trommel, van ik zal come
  Up to de kamerken van my new Wineken
  Slaat up de trommel, van ik zal come.

Pisaro. Ha, ha, ha, Master Vandal,
  I trow you will be merry soon at night,   255
  When you shall do in deed what now you hope of.

Vandal. I zall u zegger vader, ik sall tesh your daughter such a ting,
  make her laugh too.

Pisaro. Well, my sons all – for so I count you shall –
  What we have here devised, provide me for.   260
  But above all, do not, I pray, forget
  To come but one by one, as they did wish.

Vandal. Maar hoort eens vader, ik weet niet de weg to your huis; hoort
  eens, zal meester Frisco your manneken come to call to me, and
  bring me to u house?   265

Pisaro. Yes, marry, shall he. See that you be ready,

---

256. in deed] *Q*; indeed *Q2, Q3.*   263. weg] *this ed.;* wecke *Q;* wey *Q2, Q3;* way
Haz.

---

242. O, de . . . devise] Oh, what a splendid, valiant (brave, spirited) plan.

242–4. Me . . . Pisaro] another jumbled sentence, whose meaning condenses to: 'So,
I will arrive at night and speak like the English gentlemen, Mister Pisaro'.

243. contier] perhaps *conter* 'to tell, relate,' in the sense of playing the roles of the
Englishmen.

248. sout] sweet (cf. Dutch: 'zoete' and note to 3.4.54).

249. bravissime] most wonderful.

251. Slaat op . . . come] Beat on the drum, because I shall come.

252. *Up to de kamerken . . . Wineken*] Up to the room of my new little thing.

255. trow] think, believe.

257–8. I zall . . . too] 'Let me tel you, father, I shall teach your daughter such a thing
that will make her laugh'; making her laugh with a 'thing' has a sexual suggestion.

260. provide me for] prepare for, get ready (the 'me' is a colloquial addition).

263. Maar hoort . . . huis] i.e. Listen father, I don't know the way to your house;
Q2, Q3 anglicise *Q*'s 'wecke' (i.e. Dutch: *weg*) to 'wey'.

264. manneken] little man.

And at the hour of eleven soon at night. –
[*To Frisco.*] Hie you to Bucklersbury to his chamber,
And so direct him straight unto my house.
My son, Alvaro, and Monsieur Delion,   270
I know, doth know the way exceeding well. –
Well, we'll to the Rose in Barken for an hour.
And, sirrah, Frisco, see you prove no blab.

         Exeunt PISARO, ALVARO, DELION, *and* VANDAL.

Frisco. O, monstrous! Who would think my master had so much wit
    in his old rotten budget. And yet, i'faith, he is not much troubled   275
    with it, neither. Why, what wise man in a kingdom would send
    me for the Dutchman? Does he think I'll not cozen him? O, fine,
    I'll have the bravest sport! O, brave, I'll have the gallantest sport!
    O, come. Now, if I can hold behind while I may laugh a while, I
    care not: Ha, ha, ha!   280

              Enter ANTHONY.

Anthony. Why, how now, Frisco? Why laughest thou so heartily?
Frisco. Laugh, Master Mouse, Laugh! Ha, ha, ha!
Anthony. Laugh? Why should I laugh? Or why art thou so merry?
Frisco. O Master Mouse, Master Mouse, it would make any mouse,
    rat, cat, or dog laugh to think what sport we shall have at our   285
    house soon at night. I'll tell you all. My young mistresses sent me
    after Master Heigham and his friends, to pray them come to our
    house after my old master was abed. Now I went and I went, and
    I ran and I went; and whom should I meet, but my master, Master
    Pisaro, and the strangers. So my master very worshipfully – I must   290
    needs say – examined me whither I went; now, I durst not tell him
    an untruth, for fear of lying, but told him plainly and honestly
    mine errand. Now, who would think my master had such a

---

289. ran] *this ed.;* runne *Qq;* run *1830.*   289–90. master, Master Pisaro] *this ed.;*
Maister and M. *Pisaro Q;* Master, and M. *Pisaro Q2;* Master, and Master *Pisaro Q3;*
master, M. *Pisaro 1830;* master Pisaro *Haz.*   291. went; now] *this ed.;* went now? *Q;*
went? now *Q2;* went: now *Q3;* went. Now, *Haz.*

---

    268. *Bucklersbury*] A street in Cheap Ward: 'This whole streete called Buckles bury
on both the sides throughout is possessed of Grocers and Apothecaries'; 'Buckles berie,
so called of a Mannor . . . This Mannor or great house hath of long time been divided
and letten out into many tenementes' (Stow i, pp. 260, 259) (see Appendix).
    272. *the Rose in Barken*] an inn; 'The Rose tavern in Barking was destroyed in 1649
by an explosion of gunpowder two doors away' (Baugh)
    273. *blab*] tell-tale, chatterbox.
    275. *budget*] head (also pouch, bag: see *The Winter's Tale*'s 'sow-skin budget'
(4.3.20)).
    278–301. *O, brave . . . nothing*] cf. Ithamore in *The Jew of Malta* 3.3.1–28.

monstrous plaguey wit? He was as glad as could be; out of all
scotch and notch glad; out of all count glad. And so, sirrah, he bid   295
the three uplandish-men come in their steads and woo my young
mistresses. Now, it made me so laugh to think how they will be
cozened that I could not follow my master. But I'll follow him; I
know he is gone to the tavern in his merry humour. Now, if you
will keep this as secret as I have done hitherto, we shall have the   300
bravest sport soon as can be. I must be gone. Say nothing.   *Exit.*
Anthony.   Well, it is so.
 And we will have good sport, or it shall go hard;
 This must the wenches know, or all is marred.

     Enter the three sisters.

 Hark you, Miss Moll, Miss Laurentia, Miss Matt,   305
 I have such news, my girls, will make you smile.
Marina.   What be they, Master? How I long to hear it.
Anthony.   A woman right, still longing, and with child,
 For every thing they hear, or light upon.
 Well, if you be mad wenches, hear it now: 310
 Now may your knaveries give the deadliest blow
 To night-walkers, eavesdroppers, or outlandish love,
 That e'er was stricken –
Mathea.   Anthony Mouche,
 Move but the matter; tell us but the jest,

---

307. Master? . . . it.] *this ed.;* Maister, . . . it? *Qq;* master? . . . it! *Haz.*   313. stricken]
Q2, Q3; stristen *Q.*

---

 294. *plaguey*] pernicious, pestilent, vexatious.
 294–5. *out . . . notch*] beyond imagination, excessively.
 296. *uplandish*] outlandish, foreign (cf. 'outlandish' at 2.3.312).
 in their steads] in their places (instead).
 298. *But I'll follow him*] i.e. now that I've stopped laughing so hard.
 303. *it shall go hard*] or else; or there will be trouble; or everything will be
ruined.
 307. *they*] referring to plural 'news' in the previous line.
 308–9. *A woman . . . upon*] i.e. a typical woman, desperately impatient (for 'with
child' we might say 'bursting') for more information on anything they hear about or
find out.
 310. *mad*] eccentric, ready to act (Ned Walgrave is called 'mad Ned' at 2.3.75; cf.
Moll Cutpurse, 'the maddest, fantastical'st girl' in *The Roaring Girl* (2.1.189)).
 312. *night-walkers*] those who walk about by night, especially with criminal
intent.
 eavesdroppers] (sometimes eaves-drippers): those who listen secretively to others'
conversation, traditionally by standing under the 'eaves' of houses where the roof
overhangs the walls, and where the rain water 'drops' or 'drips' on to the ground.
 314. *Move but the matter*] Tell us the plan; get on with it.

And if you find us slack to execute,   315
Never give credence, or believe us more.
Anthony. Then know: the strangers, your outlandish loves,
Appointed by your father, comes this night
Instead of Harvey, Heigham, and young Ned,
Under their shadows to get to your bed.   320
For Frisco simply told him why he went.
I need not to instruct; you can conceive.
You are not stocks, nor stones, but have some store
Of wit, and knavery too.
Mathea.   Anthony, thanks
Is too too small a guerdon for this news.   325
You must be English. Well, Sir Signiore Souse,
I'll teach you tricks for coming to our house.
Laurentia. Are you so crafty? O, that night were come,
That I might hear my Dutchman how he'd swear
In his own mother language that he loves me.   330
Well, if I quit him not, I here pray God
I may lead apes in hell and die a maid,
And that were worser to me than a hanging!

---

317. *outlandish*] foreign (cf. 'uplandish' at 2.3.296).

321. *told him*] revealed (the 'him,' is a colloquial addition; cf. 'me' in line 260).

322. *conceive*] understand (with sexual suggestion).

323. *stocks, nor stones*] dunces, lifeless things (cf. 2.1.26 and note).

325. *guerdon*] gift.

326. *You must be English*] i.e. this plan evidences that you cannot be foreign, despite the disguise, perhaps emphasizing honesty.

Souse] pickled parts of a pig (Mathea is referring to Delion the Frenchman; cf. 1.1.172–5, where Frisco asserts that 'pigs and Frenchmen speak one language').

329. *That I might . . . swear*] The lack of punctuation between 'Dutchman' and 'how' is familiar sixteenth-century grammar.

331. *quit*] requite, pay back.

332. *lead apes in hell*] proverbial, cf. Tilley M37 'old maids lead apes in hell' (apparently, bachelors turn to apes in hell). Shakespeare uses the proverb in *Much Ado* 2.1.39–41 and *Shrew* 2.1.33–4, and it appears in the other extant play in which Haughton had a hand, *Patient Grissill*: when Julia proclaims that she would rather men hate her than love her, Farneze says, 'Then I perceive you mean to lead apes in hell', to which Julia replies, 'That spiteful proverb was proclaim'd against them that are married on earth; for to be married is to live in a kind of hell' (Thomas Dekker, Henry Chettle, William Haughton, *Patient Grissill* (London. Shakespere Society, 1841), pp. 25 6). 1830 cites these instances and continues: 'This does not throw any new light upon the matter, nor explain why old maids are destined in the infernal regions to this duty. If old bachelors were supposed to be transformed there into apes, it would be very intelligible.'

Anthony. Well said, old honest huddles. Here's a heap
   Of merry lasses. Well, for my self,   335
   I'll hie to meet your lovers, bid them mask
   With us at night, and in some corner stay
   Near to our house, where they may make some play
   Upon your rivals, and when they are gone,
   Come to your windows.
Marina.   Do so, good Master.   340
Anthony. Peace, be gone,
   For this our sport somebody soon will mourn.
              Exeunt [the three sisters, manet ANTHONY].

              Enter PISARO.

Pisaro. How favourable heaven and earth is seen,
   To grace the mirthful complot that is laid.
   Night's candles burn obscure, and the pale moon,   345
   Favouring our drift, lies buried in a cloud.
   I can but smile to see the simple girls,
   Hoping to have their sweethearts here tonight,
   Tickled with extreme joy, laugh in my face.
   But when they find the strangers in their steads,   350
   They'll change their note and sing another song.
   Where be these girls here? What! To bed, to bed!
   [*Shouts offstage.*] Maudlin, make fast the doors; rake up the fire!

           Enter the three sisters.

   God's me, 'tis nine o'clock! Hark, Bow-bell rings.   *Knock.*
   Some look down below, and see who knocks.   355

341–2. Peace, . . . mourn] *so lineated in 1830;* Peace, . . . sport, / Some body . . .
mo[o]rne *Qq.* 342.1. SD *Exeunt* [. . . ANTHONY]] *this ed.; Exeunt. Qq.* 353.1. SD
Enter . . . sisters] Q2, Q3; not in Q.

   334. *huddles*] usually applied to usurers and misers (cf. Frisco to Pisaro, 'I go, old
huddle' (4.3.106)); perhaps applied because the daughters are cunningly secretive and
keeping things to themselves.
   342.1. *Exeunt*] it is not entirely satisfactory to have the sisters exit here, since it
causes a lot of stage business in the rest of the scene; withdrawal upstage is an
option.
   manet] remains (on stage).
   344. *complot*] plan made in consort; plot involving several persons.
   345. *Night's candles*] stars.
   346. *drift*] intent, purpose.
   354. *Bow-bell*] bell of St Mary-le-Bow (Bow church), south side of Cheap ward (see
Appendix).

And hark you, girls, settle your hearts at rest,
And full resolve you that tomorrow morn
You must be wed to such as I prefer;
I mean Alvaro and his other friends.
Let me no more be troubled with your nays;   360
You shall do what I'll have, and so resolve.

Enter MOORE.

Welcome, Master Moore, welcome.
What wind, a-God's name, drives you forth so late?
Moore. Faith, sir, I am come to trouble you;
My wife this present night is brought to bed.   365
Pisaro. To bed? And what hath God sent you?
Moore. A jolly girl, sir.
Pisaro. And God bless her. But what's your will, sir?
Moore. Faith, sir, my house being full of friends,
Such as – I thank them – came to see my wife,   370
I would request you, that for this one night
My daughter, Susan, might be lodged here.
Pisaro. Lodge in my house? Welcome, with all my heart.
Matt, hark you, she shall lie with you.
Trust me, she could not come in fitter time,   375
For, hear you, sir, tomorrow in the morning
All my three daughters must be married.
Good Master Moore, let's have your company.
What say you, sir? Welcome, honest friend.

Enter a servant.

Moore. How now, sirrah, what's the news with you?   380
[MOORE *and the servant talk aside.*]
Pisaro. Mouche, hear you. Stir betimes tomorrow,
For then I mean your scholars shall be wed. –
What news, what news, man, that you look so sad?
Moore. He brings me word my wife is new-fall'n sick,
And that my daughter cannot come tonight –   385
Or, if she does, it will be very late.
Pisaro. Believe me, I am then more sorry for it.
But, for your daughter, come she soon or late,

---

370. wife,] Q2, Q3 (Wife,); wife? Q.

365. *brought to bed*] i.e. giving birth.
374. *she shall lie with you*] 'Pisaro seems to forget that this would interfere with his plot concerning the foreigners' (Baugh).
381. *betimes*] early.

Some of us will be up to let her in,
For here be three means not to sleep tonight.   390
Well, you must be gone? Commend me to your wife.
Take heed how you go down; the stairs are bad –
Bring here a light.
Moore.   'Tis well, I thank you, sir.
                              Ex[eunt MOORE *and servant].*
Pisaro. Good night, Master Moore; farewell, honest friend.
[*To the sisters.*] Come, come, to bed, to bed; 'tis nine and past.   395
Do not stand prating here to make me fetch you,
But get you to your chambers.   *Exit.*
Anthony. By'r Lady, here's short work! Hark you girls;
Will you tomorrow marry with the strangers?
Marina. I'faith, sir, no; I'll first leap out at window   400
Before Marina marry with a stranger.
Anthony. Yes, but your father swears you shall have one.
Mathea. Yes, but his daughters swear they shall have none.
These whoreson cannibals, these Philistines,
These tango mongoes shall not rule o'er me!   405
I'll have my will and Ned, or I'll have none.
Anthony. How will you get him? How will you get him?
I know no other way except it be this:
That when your father's in his soundest sleep,
You ope the door and run away with them.   410

---

393. 'Tis well, I] *1830;* 'Tis well I *Qq.*   393.1. SD *Ex[eunt … servant].] this ed.;*
Exit. Qq.   403. swear] *Q3, Haz;* swears *Q, Q2.*

---

389. *Some*] Pisaro could mean (1) someone (i.e. himself, keeping watch), or (2)
several (i.e. the three daughters); the reading will depend on interpretation of the next
line.

390. *three means*] Pisaro probably gestures towards his three daughters here; he
could mean (1) 'here are three reasons for me not to sleep tonight' (because the daughters are cunning and need to be watched), or (2) 'here are three children that themselves
mean to stay awake tonight'.

393. *Bring here a light*] 1) Take a light (said to Moore) ('here' is a colloquial addition) (2) Fetch a light (said to Anthony, Moore's servant, or directed off stage to a
household servant).

396. *prating*] chattering, talking idly.

404. *whoreson*] literally, son of a whore; general term of abuse.

cannibals] possibly meaning 'foreign' and 'alien,' the word 'cannibal' originally
related specifically to anthropophagi, people whose heads grew beneath their shoulders,
and about whom the English learnt from travellers' reports.

Philistines] uncultured, unrefined persons.

405. *tango mongoes*] a puzzling epithet; *tango* is a variation of tanga, the name
given to various coins from Persia, India, and Turkestan (first cited for 1598 in *OED*);
mongoes is an obsolete form of mongoose (earliest *OED* reference = 1698).

All Sisters. So we will, rather than miss of them.
Anthony. 'Tis well resolved, i'faith, and like your selves.
    But hear you: to your chambers presently,
    Lest that your father do descry our drift.   *Exeunt sisters.*
    Mistress Susan should come, but she cannot,   415
    Nor perhaps shall not – yet perhaps she shall.
    Might not a man conceit a pretty jest,
    And make as mad a riddle as this is?
    If all things fadge not, as all things should do,
    We shall be sped; 'faith, Matt shall have her due.   [*Exit.*]   420

413. you:] *this ed.;* you? *Qq;* you. *1830;* you! *Haz.*
420. 'faith, Matt shall have her due] *Haz; Q2, Q3 (without apostrophe);* y'fayth, Matt shall have hue *Q.*

---

    414. *descry*] spy out, detect.
    417. *conceit*] conceive, think up.
    pretty] funny, clever.
    419. *fadge*] See note to 1.2.11.
    420. *sped*] foiled, beaten.

ACT 3

[3.1]

Enter VANDAL *and* FRISCO.

Vandal. Wear be you, Mester Frisco?

Frisco. Here sir, here sir. [*Aside*] Now, if I could cozen him. – Take
  heed, sir, here's a post.

Vandal. Ik be so groterly hot, datt ik swette. O, wen sal we com
  daar?   5

Frisco. Be you so hot, sir? Let me carry your cloak. I assure you, it will
  ease you much.

Vandal. Daar, here, daar; 'tis so dark ey can niet see.

Frisco. Ay, so, so. Now you may travel in your hose and doublet.
  [*Aside, putting on Vandal's cloak.*] Now look I as like the Dutch-   10
  man as if I were spit out of his mouth. I'll straight home and speak
  groote and broode, and toot and gib'rish; and in the dark I'll have
  a fling at the wenches. Well, I say no more. Farewell Master
  Mendall; I must go seek my fortune.   *Exit.*

Vandal. Meester Frisco, Meester Frisco! Wat, sal you no speak? Make   15
  you de fool? Why, Meester Frisco! O, de schelm! He be ga met de
  cloak. Me zal seg his meester han Meester Frisco, waar zeit gei,
  Mester Frisco?   *Exit.*

[3.2]

Enter HARVEY, HEIGHAM, *and* WALGRAVE.

Harvey. Goes the case so well, Signiore Bottle-nose?
  It may be we shall overreach your drift.

---

  3. *a post*] wandering around in the dark, Frisco probably indicates the public theatre's stage-post here.

  4. *groterly*] hugely, greatly (Dutch: *groot* + suffix '-ly').

  9. *hose and doublet*] breeches or stockings attached to close-fitting (sleeved or
sleeveless) jacket.

  11. *as if . . . mouth*] proverbial, cf. Tilley M1246 cites this line (cf. 'spitting
image').

  16. *schelm*] rascal.

  ga] gone.

  17. *han*] how.

  waar zeit gei] where are you (Qq's *sidy* = Dutch: *zijt gij* 'art thee'?).

  1. *Bottle-nose*] the traditionally large nose of the usurer.

This is the time the wenches sent us word
Our bumbast Dutchman and his mates will come.
Well, neat Italian, you must don my shape.   5
Play your part well, or I may 'haps pay you.
What, speechless, Ned? Faith, whereon musest thou?
'Tis on your French co-rival, for my life.
He come *être votre*, and so forth,
Till he hath foisted in a brat or two: 10
How then, how then?
Walgrave.   'Swounds, I'll geld him first,
Ere that infestious losel revel there.
Well, Matt, I think thou knowst what Ned can do.
Shouldst thou change Ned for Noddy, me for him,
Thou didst not know thy loss, i'faith thou didst not.   15
Heigham. Come, leave this idle chat, and let's provide
Which of us shall be scarecrow to these fools
And set them out the way?
Walgrave.   Why, that will I.
Harvey. Then put a sword into a madman's hand.
Thou art so hasty, that but cross thy humour   20
And thou't be ready cross them o'er the pates.
Therefore, for this time, I'll supply the room.
Heigham. And so we shall be sure of chat enough!

---

4. bumbast] *Qq*; bombast *1830*.   9. être votre] *this ed.*; *ete vostre Qq*; *et vostre
1830.*   10. two:] *this ed.*; two? *Qq*; two. *1830.*   11. 'Swounds] *Q*; Nay *Q2, Q3.*
12. infestious] *Q, Q2*; infectious *Q3.*   losel] *Haz*; loszell *Qq*; lozell *1830.*

4. *bumbast*] bombastic; 'bombast' is stuffing, and Qq's spelling of the word plays
on the fat Dutchman's rear end.
5. *neat*] See 'spruce' at 4.1.82.
6. *'haps pay you*] chance to give you what you deserve.
9. être votre] French: to be yours (i.e. [pretending] to be you).
and so forth] this phrase may imply Harvey's improvisation in French (cf. 1.3.147,
etc.).
10. *foisted in a brat*] thrust in, heaved in a child.
11. *geld*] castrate.
12. *infestious*] i.e. infectious, alluding, probably, to 'French' (i.e. venereal) disease.
losel] morally lost person, prodigal, profligate; more generally, a ragamuffin.
14. *Noddy*] fool, simpleton.
16. *provide*] decide.
19. *Then put . . . hand*] proverbial, and Tilley P669 cites this line; ironic version of
'ill putting (put not) a sword into a mad-man's hand'.
20-1. *cross . . . cross*] contradict, disagree . . . hit, deliver a blow.
21. *pates*] heads.
22. *supply the room*] take up the position.

You'll hold them with your flouts and gulls so long
That all the night will scarcely be enough   25
To put in practice what we have devised!
Come, come, I'll be the man shall do the deed.
Harvey. Well, I am content to save your longing.
    But soft, where are we? Ha, here's the house.
    Come, let us take our stands. France, stand you there,   30
    And Ned and I will cross t'other side.
Heigham. Do so – but hush, I hear one passing hither.

                    [HARVEY *and* WALGRAVE *withdraw.*]

                    Enter ALVARO.

Alvaro. O, de favourable aspect of de heaven: 'tis so obscure, so dark,
    so black dat no mortal creature can know de me. I pray a Dio I
    sal have de reight wench. Ah, si, I be recht: here be de huis of   35
    Signiore Pisaro. I sall have de madona Marina, and darvor I sall
    knock to de dore.   *He knocks* [*as* HEIGHAM *gets in his way*].
Heigham. What a pox! Are you mad or drunk?
    What, do you mean to break my glasses?
Alvaro. Wat be dat glass? Wat drunck? wat mad?   40
Heigham. What glasses, sir? Why, my glasses! And if you be so crank,
    I'll call the constable. You will not enter into a man's house, I hope,
    in spite of him?

---

41. What glasses . . . glasses] *Q*; What Glasse . . . Glasse *Q2, Q3*.

24. *flouts*] mockings, insults.
gulls] tricks, deceptions.
28. *save*] relieve, stop.
30. *France*] i.e. Ferdinand (cf. 2.3.99).
31. *t'other side*] the other side (of the street/stage).
34. *a Dio*] to God.
35. *reight . . . recht . . . huis*] right (accented English) . . . right (German) . . . house (Dutch).
36. *darvor*] therefore.
38. *pox*] plague, disease.
39. *do . . . glasses?*] Heigham seems to be pretending to be a glassmaker or seller of drinking glasses who lives at this address; he accuses Alvaro, who has just knocked on his door, of intending to break into his house (line 42) and destroy his wares. This conflict may relate to the high-profile antagonism and competition between English artisans and immigrant craftspersons in late sixteenth-century London and other towns. John Stow records a factory that made drinking glasses on the site of the Crutched Friars priory; it burned down 4 September 1575 and might be alluded to here (Stow i, p. 148). It is also possible to read the 'glasses' as referring to spectacles, since at line 66 he asks Delion 'will you run over me and break my glasses', and the scene is based on the joke of getting lost because of not being able to see (in the dark).
41. *crank*] insistent, bold.

Harvey. [*Aside*] Nor durst you be so bold as to stand there,
    If once the master of the house did know it.   45
Alvaro. Is dit your hous? Be you de Signiore of dis cassa?
Heigham. Signiore me no Signiores, nor cassa me no cassas, but get
    you hence, or you are like to taste of the bastinado.
Harvey. [*Aside*] Do, do, good Ferdinand; pummel the loggerhead!
Alvaro. Is this niet the house of Mester Pisaro?   50
Heigham. Yes, marry, when? Can you tell? How do you? I thank you
    heartily, my finger in your mouth.
Alvaro. Wat be dat?
Heigham. Marry, that you are an ass and a loggerhead to seek Master
    Pisaro's house here.   55
Alvaro. I pray de grazia, wat be dis plashe? Wat do you call dit
    street?
Heigham. What, sir; why, Leadenhall: could you not see the four
    spouts as you came along?
Alvaro. Certenemento Leadenhall. I hit my hed by de way – dare may 60
    be de voer spouts. I pray de grazia, wish be de wey to Crutche
    Friars?
Heigham. How, to Crutched Friars? Marry, you must go along till you
    come to the pump, and then turn on your right hand.
Alvaro. Signiore, *adio*.   *Exit.*

51–7.] *Heigh.* Yes marry when? can you tell: how doe you? / I thanke you heartily,
my finger in your mouth. / *Alva.* Wat be dat? / *Heigh.* Marry that you are an Asse and
a Logerhead, / To seeke maister *Pisaros* house heere. / *Alva.* I prey de gratia, wat be
dis plashe? / Wat doe ye call dit strete? *Qq.*

44. *you*] i.e. Heigham.
46. *cassa*] (i.e. 'casa') house.
48. *bastinado*] a beating with a large stick, cudgel.
49. *pummel*] beat repeatedly.
loggerhead] blockhead.
52. *my finger in your mouth*] 'with one's finger in one's mouth' (1) helplessly inactive (2) with nothing accomplished, looking foolish (*OED* 'finger' verb 3); hence
Heigham is turning a familiar phrase against the addressee, calling Alvaro foolish
instead of himself.
58–9. *the four spouts*] The water-standard at Cornhill and Leadenhall streets,
installed in 1582 by the German ('German or Dutch man borne' (Stow 1598)) Peter
Morris, had four overflow spouts that ran with Thames water at high tide. Stow notes
in the 1603 edition of his *Survey* that it was not working at his time of writing (Stow
i, p. 188); Kingsley notes Stow's response to the non-operative conduit in another
manuscript: 'The Standart at Ledenhall is to be reformed or pulled down; it standeth
as a shadow, or rather a playne mockery yildinge no comodytie to the Citie, suche as
was promised, but contrarywise it comberith the street with the let of cariage' (Stow
ii, p. 243, 302) (see Appendix).
61–2. *Crutche Friars*] See Appendix, and note to 1.2.5.
65. *adio*] goodbye.

Harvey.   Farewell – and be hanged, Signiore!   65
  Now for your fellow, if the ass would come.

Enter DELION.

Delion. By my trot' me do so mush tincke of dit gentlewoman de fine
  wenshe, dat me tincke esh houer ten day, and esh day ten year, till
  I come to her. Here be de huise of sin vader, sal alle and knocke.
                                                    He knocks.
Heigham. What a bots ail you! Are you mad? Will you run over me   70
  and break my glasses?
Delion. Glasses? What glasses? Pray, is Monsieur Pisaro to de
  maison?
Harvey. [*Aside to Walgrave.*] Hark, Ned, there's thy substance!
Walgrave. [*Aside to Harvey.*]   Nay, by the mass,
  The substance's here; the shadow's but an ass.   75
Heigham. What Master Pisaro?
  Loggerhead, here's none of your Pisaros!
Delion. Yes, but dit is the houis of Mester Pisaro.
Walgrave. [*Aside*] Will not this Monsieur Motley take his answer?
  I'll go and knock the ass about the pate.   80
Harvey. [*Holding Walgrave back.*] Nay, by your leave, sir, but I'll
  hold your worship.
  This stir we should have had, had you stood there.
Walgrave. [*Aside to Harvey.*] Why, would it not vex one to hear the
  ass
  Stand prating here of dit and dan, and den and dog?

74–5. Nay, by the mass, / The substance's ... ass.] *this ed.; Qq divides the line at*
'heere, / The shaddow's'.   77. Pisaros!] *this ed.; Pisaros? Qq;* Pisaro's? *1830.*

  be hanged] i.e. go to hell.
  67. *By my trot'*] i.e. By my troth = truly.
  69. *sal alle*] (I) shall go (cf. 2.3.185).
  70. *What a bots ail you*] What the pox is troubling you (i.e. 'what do you think
you're doing?').
  74. *substance*] Harvey comically inverts the sense of the dressed-up character as the
true man's 'shadow' by calling Delion the substantial (i.e. real) man, thus suggesting
Walgrave's secondary, shadowy status. Hiding upstage, Walgrave is, of course, literally
'shadowing' Delion.
  75. *The substance's here*] playing on Harvey's use of the word, Ned calls himself
the substance and his French rival his shadow, i.e. (1) his disguised self and (2) his
empty being.
  79. *Monsieur Motley*] Mister Fool (cf. note to 1.3.194).
  80. *knock ... pate*] hit him on the head; there may be a joke on ass/arse; Walgrave
will knock Delion head over heels, or arse over head.
  82. *stir*] disturbance, fight.

Harvey. One of thy mettle, Ned, would surely do it.   85
    But peace, and hark to the rest.
Delion. Do no de fine gentlewoman matresse Mathea dwell in dit
    plashe?
Heigham. No, sir, here dwells none of your 'fine gentlewoman'. 'Twere
    a good deed, sirrah, to see who you are: you come hither to steal   90
    my glasses, and then counterfeit you are going to your queans.
Delion. I be deceive dis dark neight. Here be no wenshe. I be no in de
    right plashe. I pray, Monsieur, wat be name dis street, and wishe
    be de way to Croshe Friars?
Heigham. Marry, this is Fenchurch Street, and the best way to Crutched   95
    Friars is to follow your nose.
Delion. Vanshe Street? How shaunce me come to Vanshe Street? Vell,
    Monsieur, me must alle to Croshe-friars.   *Exit.*
Walgrave. Farewell, fortipence. Go seek your Signiore.
    I hope you'll find your selves two dolts anon.   100
    Hush, Ferdinand! I hear the last come stamping hither.

Enter FRISCO.

Frisco. Ha, sirrah, I have left my fat Dutchman, and run myself almost
    out of breath, too. Now to my young mistresses go I – somebody
    cast an old shoe after me. But soft, how shall I do to counterfeit
    the Dutchman, because I speak English so like a natural. Tush,   105
    take you no thought for that; let me alone for *squintum squantum.*
    Soft, here's my master's house.

89. gentlewoman] *this ed.;* Gantle-woman *Q;* Gentle-woman *Q2, Q3;* gentle-women
1830. 89–91. No...queans] *so set as prose in 1830;* No...are; / You come...
Glasses. / And then...Queanes. *Qq.* 95–6. Marry...nose] *so set as prose in 1830;*
Marry...*streete,* / And...nose *Qq.* 99. your] *Q, Q3;* you *Q2.*

85. *mettle*] strength, virtue (often compared with, and spelt the same as, 'metal').
87. *fine gentlewoman*] Q's 'Gantle-woman' suggests Delion's amusing pronunciation that Heigham then mocks in the following line.
91. *queans*] i.e. prostitutes.
97. *Vanshe*] Delion's attempt to say 'Fenchurch'.
shaunce] chance(d).
99. *fortipence*] 'a customary amount for a wager' (*OED* 'forty' A.c), hence perhaps
Walgrave referring to their 'bet' against the foreigner(s).
100. *dolts*] blockheads, dunces.
104. *cast...me*] i.e. wish me luck; proverbial, cf. Tilley S372, 'To cast an old shoe
after one for luck' (cf. *Three Ladies* 8.155 and note).
105. *natural*] (1) native of a region (2) deficient in intellect.
106. *let me alone*] count on me.
squintum squantum] the phrase seems to be playing on 'squint': looking askance,
looking into things privily or in an oblique fashion (*OED* 'squint' a.2–4); also, the
sense of joking on speaking and imitating language (cf. 'gibble-gabble').

Heigham. Who's there?

Frisco. Who's there? Why, sir, here is – nay, that's too good English –
    why, here be de growte Dutchman.   110

Heigham. Then there's not only a growte head, but an ass also.

Frisco. What be you? You be an English ox to call a gentle moan
    ass!

Harvey. [*Aside to Walgrave.*] Hark, Ned, yonder's good greeting.

Frisco. But you, an you be Master Mouse that dwell here, tell your 115
    matressa Laurentia dat her sweet heart Master Vandal would
    speak with hord.

Heigham. Master Mendall, get you gone, lest you get a broken pate
    and so mar all. Here's no entrance for Mistress Laurentia's sweet
    heart.   120

Frisco. God's sacaren, wat is the luck now? Shall not I come to my
    friend maister Pisar hoose?

Heigham. Yes, and to Master Pisaro's shoes too, if he or they were
    here.

Frisco. Why, my groute friend, maister Pisaro, doth dwell here.   125

Heigham. Sirrah, you lie! Here dwells nobody but I, that have dwelt
    here this one and forty years, and sold glasses.

Walgrave. [*Whispers loudly to Heigham.*] Lie farther: one and fifty at
    the least.

Frisco. Hoo, hoo, hoo! Do you give the gentleman the lie?

---

119. Laurentia's] *Haz; Laurentios Qq.*

---

110. *growte*] great, large.

111. *not only . . . also*] joking that the fat Dutchman's great head is complemented
by his great ass/arse (cf. Frisco's probable comment on the large size of the Dutchman's
trousers at 3.3.8–9).

112. *gentle moan*] gentleman.

118. *Master Mendall*] Heigham ironically uses Frisco's own mispronunciation of
'Vandal' on him.

121. *God's sacaren*] God's sacraments (an oath).

123. *and . . . too*] Heigham plays on Frisco's faux-Dutch pronunciation of 'house',
which sounds like 'hose', by referring to another item of apparel, Pisaro's 'shoes' (a
word rhyming with Frisco's 'hoose'). Heigham could also be threatening Frisco that if
this *were* Pisaro's house, he would 'come to' 'Master Pisaro's shoes' by getting kicked
out again.

128. *Lie farther*] increase the deception.

129. *Do . . . lie?*] to 'give the lie' in the sixteenth century was to falsely accuse
someone; cf. *As You Like It* 5.4.64–92, where Touchstone relates seven categories of
lie.

[*Heigham.*] Ay, sir, and will give you a lick of my cudgel if ye stay long   130
   and trouble the whole street with your bawling. Hence, dolt, and
   go seek Master Pisaro's house!
Frisco. Go seek Master Pisaro's house? Where shall I go seek it?
Heigham. Why, you shall go seek it where it is.
Frisco. That is here in Crutched Friars.   135
Heigham. How, loggerhead! Is Crutched Friars here?
   I thought you were some such drunken ass,
   That come to seek Crutched Friars in Tower Street.
   But get you along on your left hand, and be hanged!
   You have kept me out of my bed with your bangling   140
   A good while longer than I would have been.
Frisco. Ah, ah, how is this? Is not this Crutched Friars? Tell me, I'll
   hold a crown they gave me so much wine at the tavern that I am
   drunk, and know not on't.
Harvey. [*Aside*] My Dutchman's out his compass and his card.   145
   He's reckoning what wind hath drove him hither.
   I'll swear he thinks never to see Pisaro's.
Frisco. Nay, 'tis so: I am sure drunk. Soft, let me see: what was I about?
   O, now I have it. I must go to my master's house and counterfeit
   the Dutchman, and get my young mistress. Well, and I must turn   150
   on my left hand, for I have forgot the way quite and clean. Fare
   de well good frend; I am a simple Dutchman, I.   *Exit.*
Heigham. Fair weather after you. [HARVEY *and* WALGRAVE *come*
   forward.] And now my lads,
   Have I not played my part as I should do?

---

130. SP [*Heigham.*]] *this ed.; Harv. Qq.*   140. bangling] *Q, Q2;* brangling *Q3.*
154. played] *Q2, Q3;* plide *Q.*

130–2. This speech is assigned to Harvey in Qq, but Harvey and Walgrave remain
hidden until 155. It would be viable to have Harvey and Walgrave come forward at
130 and Harvey deliver this line, but all the men would then be centre stage for the
remainder of the Heigham/Frisco altercation, which seems a less dramatic choice; it
would also break the sequence of Heigham dealing with each foreigner in turn.
   130. *lick*] blow.
   139. *on your left hand*] i.e. on the left hand side, go left (to get to Crutched
Friars).
   140. *bangling*] flapping about (perhaps suggesting talking tongues); in Q3 the word
is brangling, which means disputing or squabbling.
   143. *hold a crown*] bet a crown (crown = a coin worth 5 shillings, a quarter of a
pound).
   144. *on't*] of it, about it.
   145. *out . . . card*] lost his bearings (a mariner's card is variously a sea chart or a
piece of card marked with the points of the compass).
   151. *quite and clean*] completely.

Harvey. 'Twas well, 'twas well. But now let's cast about   155
    To set these woodcocks farther from the house,
    And afterwards return unto our girls.
Walgrave. Content, content. Come, come, make haste.   *Exeunt.*

[3.3]

Enter ALVARO.

Alvaro. I go and turn, and dan I come to dis plashe, I can tell no waer,
    and sall do I can no tell watt, turn by the pump; I pump it fair.

Enter DELION.

Delion. Me alle, end alle, and can no come to Croshe Friars.

Enter FRISCO.

Frisco. O, miserable black-pudding. If I can tell which is the way to
    my master's house, I am a red herring, and no honest gentleman.   5
Alvaro. Who parlato daer?
Delion. Who be der? Who alle der?
Frisco. How's this? For my life, here are the strangers! O, that I had
    the Dutchman's hose, that I might creep into the pockets: they'll
    all three fall upon me and beat me!   10
Alvaro. Who do der ander?
Delion. Amis?

---

155. *cast about*] separate out, set traps.
156. *woodcocks*] traditionally stupid birds.

2. *I pump it*] I exhaust myself (through labour or striving: OED 'pump' v.9, first
reference in 1633); connected to the idea of a pump evacuating something, usually
water, hence pumping energy or perhaps water in the form of sweat.
4. *black-pudding*] large sausage made from pig's blood and fat (term of exasperation); cf. Ulpian Fulwell's *Like Will to Like*, 'But who comes yonder puffing as whot
as a black pudding' (Biv).
5. *I am a red herring*] i.e. I'll be damned; Frisco's sense of deception or cluelessness
may be related to the modern use of red herring as a false clue.
6. *parlato*] speaks.
9. *that I might creep into the pockets*] much comment was made on Continental
fashions, in particular large, baggy trousers, or hose; here, Frisco may simply be referring to Vandal's hose being big because they belong to a fat Dutchman; cf. the tailor
fitting Moll with her fashionable 'great Dutch slop' in Dekker and Middleton's *The
Roaring Girl* 2.2.81–2.
11. *der ander*] the other.
12. *Amis?*] friends?.

Frisco. O, brave, it's nobody but Master Pharo and the Frenchman
    going to our house, on my life. Well, I'll have some sport with
    them, if the watch hinder me not – who goes there?   15

Delion. Who parle der? In wat plashe, in wat street be you?

Frisco. Why, sir, I can tell where I am: I am in Tower Street. Where a
    devil be you?

Delion. Io be here in Lede-hall.

Frisco. In Leadenhall? I trow I shall meet with you anon. [*Aside*] In   20
    Leaden-hall? What a simple ass is this Frenchman. Some more of
    this: where are you, sir?

Alvaro. Moy, I be here in Vanshe Street.

Frisco. [*Aside*] This is excellent in faith, as fit as a fiddle. I in Tower
    Street, you in Leadenhall, and the third in Fenchurch Street; and   25
    yet all three hear one another, and all three speak together. Either
    we must be all three in Leadenhall, or all three in Tower Street, or
    all three in Fenchurch Street – or all three fools!

Alvaro. Monsieur gentle-homme, can you well tesh de wey to
    Croshe-frier?   30

Frisco. How, to Crutched Friars? Ay, ay sir, passing well, if you will
    follow me.

Delion. Ay, dat me sal, Monsieur gentle-homme, and give you tanks.

Frisco. [*Aside*] And, Monsieur Pharo, I shall lead you such a jaunt that
    you shall scarce give me thanks for. – Come, sirs, follow me.   35

---

13. it's] *Q*; tis *Q2, Q3*.

13. *Pharo*] Frisco's mispronunciation of 'Alvaro'.

14. *on my life*] i.e. I swear on my life; to be sure.

15. *the watch*] force comprising a local constable and his men, employed to keep
the peace in an urban district.

16–35.] See the introduction ('Textual Issues: speech assignment') for a discussion
of the speech assignments and language problems of this section.

19. *Io*] Italian for 'I': see the note to lines 16–35.

21–2. *some more of this*] Baugh considers this to be a cue for improvisation in the
vein of 'and so forth' at 1.2.106–7 and 1.3.147; he does not comment on the occur-
rences of the phrase at 2.2.11–12, 3.2.9, and 4.3.101–2. This 'some more' seems quite
different from 'and so forth', however, and would be dramatically effective if read
directly as I have punctuated in the text, and not used as a cue for improvisation.

23. *Moy*] i.e. 'Moi', French for 'me'. See the note to lines 16–35 above.

24. *as fit as a fiddle*] usually refers to physical (good) condition; here applied to the
perfect state of Frisco's comic situation.

29. *tesh*] teach (i.e. tell me).

31. *passing*] exceedingly.

34. *jaunt*] (usually pleasurable) short journey.

[*Aside*] Now for a dirty puddle, the pissing conduit, or a great post,
that might turn these two from asses to oxen by knocking their
horns to their foreheads.

Alvaro. Whaer be de now, Signiore?

Frisco. Even where you will, Signiore, for I know not. Soft, I smell – O,   40
pure nose!

Delion. Wat do you smell?

Frisco. I have the scent of London-stone as full in my nose as Abchurch-
lane of mother Wall's pasties. Sirs, feel about; I smell
London-stone.   45

Alvaro. Wat be dis?

Frisco. Soft, let me see – feel, I should say, for I cannot see. O lads,
pray for my life, for we are almost at Crutched Friars.

Delion. Dat's good. But what be dis post?

Frisco. This post? Why, 'tis the maypole on Ivy-bridge going to   50
Westminster.

Delion. Ho, Wesmistere! How come we to Wesmistere?

---

52. Wesmistere . . . Wesmistere] *Q; Westmistere . . . Westmistere Q2, Q3;* Westminster
. . . Westminster *1830.*

---

36. *pissing conduit, or a great post*] see notes to 3.1.3 (post) and 3.2.58–9
(conduit).

37–8. *turn these . . . foreheads*] Alvaro and Delion, currently asses (recognized by
their long ears) will become oxen (recognizable by the lumps – 'horns' – on their heads
that appear from hitting their heads on spouts and posts in the dark); there is probably
a joke on the cuckold's horns, which the foreigners will get, since their loves will be
taken by the Englishmen. A cuckold was a married person (usually a husband) whose
partner had been unfaithful; the victim of the cuckolding traditionally could be identified by horns that grew on the head.

41. *pure*] perfect, untainted.

43. *London-stone*] 'On the south side of this high streete [Candlewick/Canning/
Cannon Street], near unto the chanell is pitched upright a great stone called London
stone, fixed in the ground verie deepe, fastned with bars of iron, and otherwise so
strongly set, that if Cartes do run against it through negligence, the wheeles be broken,
and the stone it selfe unshaken. The cause why this stone was set there, the time when,
or other memorie hereof, is none, but that the same hath long continued there is manifest, namely since (or rather before) the conquest' (Stow i, p. 224) (see Appendix).

43–4. *as full . . . pasties*] Frisco smells the stone as strongly as Abchurch Lane
savours of the pasties (meat-filled pastries) from a local bakery; 'Mother Wall' may
allude to the pastry 'walls' or sides of a pasty (*OED* cites this meaning for 'wall' 9.b
only from the eighteenth century, on), which would suggest that the name is a generic
one.

50–1. *the maypole . . . Westminster*] Ivy Bridge [Strand] led down to the Thames
west of the City of London in Westminster. 'The May-pole in the Strand stood on the
sight [*sic*] of the present church of St. Mary-le-Strand' (Baugh, after Stow ii, p. 517);

Frisco. Why, on your legs, fools! How should you go? Soft, here's
another. O, now I know indeed where I am: we are at the farthest
end of Shoreditch, for this is the maypole.   55
Delion. Sore diche? O Dio! Dere be some nautie tinge, some spirit do
lead us.
Frisco. [*Aside*] You say true, sir, for I am afeared your French spirit is
up so far already, that you brought me this way, because you
would find a charm for it at the Blue Boar in the Spittle. But soft,   60
who comes here?

Enter a BELLMAN.

Bellman. Maids in your smocks, look well to your locks,
Your fire and your light, and God give you good night.
Delion. Monsieur gentle-homme, I prey parle one, too, tree, fore words
vore us to dis oull man.   65
Frisco. Yes, marry, shall I, sir. I pray, honest fellow, in what street be
we?
Bellman. Ho, Frisco! Whither frisk you at this time of night?
Delion. What, Monsieur Frisco?
Alvaro. Signiore Frisco?   70

---

58. spirit] *Q2, Q3;* spirt *Q.*

rites of the Roman goddess of fertility, Flora, were celebrated in medieval England (28
April to 3 May) with dancing around the maypole, which was decorated with streamers
and flowers. The actors probably indicate a stage post.

55. *Shoreditch*] Ward north of the City of London; the location of Burbage's
Theatre, 1576–98 (see Appendix).

56. *Sore diche*] Delion seems to be comically misunderstanding Frisco to suggest a
sexual danger, which may be male- or female-oriented: a sore dick or a sore 'ditch'
(sore probably from veneral disease).

58–9. *your French spirit is up*] punning on 'spirit' (devil) in the preceding line, Frisco
refers to Delion's sexual spirit (cf. sonnet 129, 'Th'expense of spirit in a waste of shame
/ Is lust in action', where 'spirit' is semen); here, the 'up' has the phallic suggestion of
erection as well as meaning 'brimming' or 'full'.

60. *a charm*] something to calm Delion's 'spirit', which is 'up' (or something to draw
out his spirit, like a snake charmer draws a snake out of its basket).

Blue Boar in the Spittle] presumably an inn and brothel where the *charming* women
will ease Delion's 'spirit'. Stow mentions a 'cookes house called blew Boore' (Stow ii,
p. 2), but it is in south central London, in Queen Hithe ward. The Spital/Spittle, as
well as being a specific place (see Appendix), suggests 'hospital' and thus refers to the
potential need for Delion's cure from sexually transmitted disease.

62. *smocks*] light overgarment to protect clothes while working.

65. *oull*] old.

68. *frisk*] leap, frolic, skip (playing on Frisco's name).

Frisco. The same, the same. Hark ye, honesty, methinks you might do
well to have an 'M' under your girdle, considering how Signiore
Pisaro and this other Monsieur do hold of me.

Bellman. O sir, I cry you mercy! Pardon this fault, and I'll do as much
for you next time.   75

Frisco. Well, passing over superfluical talk, I pray, what street is this?
For it is so dark, I know not where I am.

Bellman. Why, art thou drunk? Dost thou not know Fenchurch
Street?

Frisco. Ay, sir, a good fellow may sometimes be overseen among   80
friends. I was drinking with my master and these gentlemen, and
therefore no marvel though I be none of the wisest at this present.
But I pray thee, goodman Butterick, bring me to my master's
house.

Bellman. Why, I will, I will. Push, that you are so strange nowadays!   85
But it is an old-said saw: honours change manners.

Frisco. Goodman Butterick, will you walk afore?
Come, honest friends, will ye go to our house?

Delion. Oui, Monsieur Frisco.

Alvaro.   *Si*, Signiore *Frisco.*   [*Exeunt.*]

---

77. am.] *1830;* am? *Qq.*   87. afore?] *Haz;* afore: *Qq;* afore *1830.*

71. *honesty*] honest, plain man (said scornfully, because the Belman has just been
too plain and familiar with Frisco).

72. *an 'M'*] Frisco wants to be called by the title 'Master', and not plain 'Frisco'. In
Eastward Ho, Quicksilver asks, 'Must Golding sit upon us?' to which the constable
replies, 'You might carry an M. under your girdle to Master Deputy's worship'
(4.2.208–10).

72–3. *considering how . . . do hold of me*] considering the high regard in which . . .
hold me.

76. *superfluical*] i.e. superfluous, redundant.

80. *overseen*] deceived, deluded, mistaken (sometimes through drinking too
much).

83. *goodman*] cf. note to 2.3.14.

Butterick] an unusual term for an Englishman, perhaps suggesting that the Belman
is fat.

85. *Push*] expression of surprise or exasperation (cf. pish, tush).

86. *honours change manners*] proverbial, Tilley H583 (cites this line).

[3.4]

Enter VANDAL.

Vandal. O, de schelm Frisco! Ik weit niet waar dat ik be. Ik go and hit
my nose op dit post, and ik go and hit my nose op d'andere post –
O, de villain! Well, waar ben ik now? Hoe laat zien; is dit niet
Croche Vrier? Ya, zeker so is't and dit Mester Pisaro's huis. O, de
good shaunce; well, ik zal now have de wenshe Laurentia. – Mestris   5
Laurentia!

Enter LAURENTIA, MARINA, MATHEA, *above.*

Marina. Who's there? Master Harvey?
Mathea. Master Walgrave?
Laurentia. Master Heigham?
Vandal. Ya, my love; here be Meester Heigham, your grote vriend.   10
Marina. How, Master Heigham my 'grote vriend'?
      Out, alas, here's one of the strangers.
Laurentia. Peace, you mammet! Let's see which it is. We may chance
      teach him a strange trick for his learning. Master Heigham: what
      wind drives you to our house so late?   15
Vandal. O, my lief meiske, de love tot u be so groot, dat het bring me
      out my bed voor you.
Mathea. Ha, ha, we know the ass by his ears: it is the Dutchman. What
      shall we do with him?
Laurentia. Peace, let him not know that you are here. Master Heigham,   20
      if you will stay a while that I may see if my father be asleep, and
      I'll make means we may come together.
Vandal. Dat zal ik, my lova. [*Aside*] Is dit no well counterfett? I speak
      so like Meester Heigham as 'tis possible.

---

1. Ik weit niet] *Q;* it we it neit *Q2;* it wee it neit *Q3.*   dat] *Q; not in Q2, Q3.*
2. d'andere] *this ed.;* danden *Qq.*   4. Mester] *this ed.;* Meester *Haz;* M. *Qq.*
16. tot] *this ed.;* tol *Qq.*

---

1. *weit*] know.
2. *d'andere post*] the other post (again suggesting the two posts of the public
stage).
3. *Hoe laat zien*] how late [it] is.
4. *zeker*] surely.
10. *grote vriend*] good/great friend.
13. *mammet*] '= Maumet, literally an idol' (Baugh); puppet, doll, hence general term
of abuse.
14. *for his learning*] (1) for his education (to teach him a lesson) (2) in response to
what he has learned to do (3) in response to his ignorance.
16. *my lief meiske*] my sweet girl.
   tot u] to you.
18. *we know the ass by his ears*] proverbial, cf. Tilley A355 (cites this line).

Laurentia. Well, what shall we do with this lubber? – Lover, I should   25
     say.
Mathea. What shall we do with him? Why, crown him with a –
Marina. Fie, slut! No, we'll use him cleanlier. You know we have never
     a sign at the door: would not the jest prove current to make the
     Dutchman supply that want?   30
Laurentia. Nay, the fool will cry out and so wake my father.
Mathea. Why, then we'll cut the rope and cast him down.
Laurentia. And so jest out a hanging. Let's rather draw him up in the
     basket, and so starve him to death this frosty night.
Marina. In sadness, well advised. Sister, do you hold him in talk, and   35
     we'll provide it the whilst.
Laurentia. Go to, then. Master Heigham; O, sweet Master Heigham.
     Doth my father think that his unkindness can part you and poor
     Laurentia? No, no, I have found a drift to bring you to my chamber,
     if you have but the heart to venture it.   40
Vandal. Ventre, zal ik go to de zee, and bij de zee, and o'er de zee, and
     in de zee voor my sweet love.
Laurentia. Then you dare go into a basket? For I know no other means
     to enjoy your company than so, for my father hath the keys of the
     door.   45

25–7. Well…a –] *so lineated in this ed.; four lines in Qq:* 'Well…Lubber? /
(Lover…say.) / *Math.* What…him? / Why…a –'.   36. the whilst] *Q2, Q3;*
whilst *Q*.   40. venture] *1830;* venter *Qq*.   43. basket?] *Haz;* Basket; *Qq*.

---

25. *lubber*] big, clumsy, stupid person.

27. *crown him with a –*] to 'crown' can mean to beat, but Marina's response suggests something filthy; perhaps Mathea indicates throwing a bedpan and its contents
from the chamber window over Vandal's head ('crown') (cf. Marina's line 4.1.87). She
may also be referring to crowning him with cuckold's horns.

29. *sign*] a sign hanging at the front of the building to indicate the occupant's
trade.
     current] acceptable, appropriate, fashionable.

30. *want*] lack.

33. *jest out a hanging*] (1) the joke will result in killing Vandal by hanging or by
cutting him down and letting him fall to his death (2) the jest will lead the sisters to
the gallows for murder.
     draw] perhaps punning on the punishment of hanging, drawing, and quartering.

34. *starve*] 'starve' was commonly used in the period to mean suffer from cold
temperature, usually in a construction 'starve of cold' or 'starve for cold' ('starve' *OED
v.* entry 2.c.).

35. *sadness*] seriously, truly.

36. *whilst*] in the meantime.

37. *Go to*] Get to it.

41. *Ventre*] Vandal's attempt to say 'venture'.

41–2. *zal ik go … in de zee*] I would go to the sea, and by the sea, and over the
sea, and in the sea.

Vandal. Zal ik climb up tot you? Zal ik fly up tot you? Zal ic? Wat
      zeg dee?
Mathea. [*Aside to Laurentia.*] Bid him do it, sister: we shall see his
      cunning.
Laurentia. O, no, so you may catch a fall!   [*They lower the basket.*]   50
      There, Master Heigham, put yourself into that basket, and I will
         draw you up. But no words, I pray you, for fear my sisters hear
         you.
Vandal. No, no. No word. O, de zoete wenshe, ik come, ik come!
                              [*He climbs into the basket.*]
Laurentia. Are you ready, Master Heigham?   55
Vandal. Ja ic, my zoete lady.
Marina. Merrily, then, my wenches.
                        [*They draw up the basket half-way.*]
Laurentia. How heavy the ass is! Master Heigham, is there any in the
      basket but yourself?
Vandal. Niet, niet, daar be no man.   60
Laurentia. Are you up, sir?
Vandal. Niet, niet.
Marina. Nor never are you like to climb more higher.
      Sisters, the woodcock's caught; the fool is caged!
Vandal. My zoete lady, I be nog niet up: pul me tot u.   65
Mathea. When, can you tell? What, Master Vandal,
      A weather-beaten soldier, an old wencher,
      Thus to be overreached by three young girls!
      Ah, sirrah, now we'll brag with mistress Moore
      To have as fine a parrot as she hath.   70
      Look, sisters, what a pretty fool it is;
      What a green, greasy, shining coat he hath –
      An almond for parrot, a rope for parrot.

---

47. zeg dee] *this ed.;* segdy *Qq, Haz.*   50. you] *Q;* he *Q2, Q3.*   52. sisters] *this ed.;*
Sister *Qq;* sister *1830.*

46–7. *Wat zeg dee?*] What say you?
54, 56, 65. *zoete*] sweet; cf. Alvaro's 'sout' at 2.3.248.
65. *nog niet*] not yet.
68. *overreached*] out-foxed.
70. *parrot*] exotic pets were fashionable among merchant and upper classes in the
early modern period; cf. Jessica's alleged purchase of a monkey in *Merchant of Venice*
3.1.111–12.
73. *An almond for parrot*] the title of a pamphlet by Thomas Nashe (*An Almond
for a Parrot,* 1590)· cf. the modern 'polly wants a cracker', 'Skelton, in his poem, *Speak
Parrot*, has the expression, "Parrot must have an almond". It is met with in Middleton's
Spanish Gypsy, Act ii, Sc. i, in Ben Jonson's *Magnetic Lady*, Act v, Sc. 5, in Dekker's
Fortunatus [*sic*], Act i, Sc. 1, and various other plays' (1830); George Wither (1588–
1667) also has a text entitled *Amygdala Britannica, almonds for parrets* (1647).

Vandal. Do you mocque me zeker zeker? Ik zal zeg your vader.
Laurentia. Do, an you dare, you see here is your fortune.   75
    Disquiet not my father. If you do,
    I'll send you with a vengeance to the ground.
    Well, we must confess we trouble you,
    And over-watching makes a wise man mad,
    Much more a fool. There's a cushion for you.   80
Marina. To bore you through the nose!
Laurentia.   To lay your head on.
    Couch in your kennel, sleep, and fall to rest;
    And so good night, for London maids scorn still
    A Dutchman should be seen to curb their will.   *Exeunt sisters.*
Vandal. Hoort ye daughter, hoort ye? God's seker kin? Will ye no let   85
    me come tot you? Ik bid you let me come tot you. Wat zal ik doen?
    Ik would niet voor un hundred pound Alvaro and Delion should
    see me op dit manier. Well, wat zal ik doen? Ik moet niet cal, voor
    de wenshes wil cut de rope and break my neck! Ik zal here blijven
    til de morning, and dan ik zal cal to Meester Pisaro, and make him   90
    shafe and shite his dochters. O, de schelm Frisco! O, deze cruel
    hores!   [*Manet* VANDAL, *hanging in the basket.*]

74.] *Vand.* Doe you moc que me seger seger, / I sal seg your vader. *Qq.*   Ik] *this ed.;*
I *Q, etc.*   89. blijven] *this ed.;* bleiven *1830;* bleauen *Qq.*

---

74. *zeker zeker*] sure, sure (or, less likely, *seker, seker* = sweet, sweet).
79. *over-watching . . . mad*] proverbial.
81. *To bore . . . nose*] proverbial, cf. Tilley N229 'To bore one's nose' (to trick,
swindle); Hazlitt has the enigmatic note, 'A play on the double meaning of the word
cushion,' and Baugh avoids it. Cf. Middleton and Rowley, *The Old Law*: Gnotho,
' . . . 'tis but a cushion, I warrant thee . . .' / Siren, 'We will not have our noses bored
with a cushion, if it be so' (4.1.164, 167–68); the use of *cushion* may come from an
obsolete from of *cozen* (to trick or cheat), sometimes spelled cussen or cusshen. A sense
of the proverb's absurdity is brought out in the related versions 'to run him through
the nose with a cushion' (Tilley N239) and 'to kill a man with a cushion' (Tilley
M398).
85. *Hoort*] Hear.
God's seker kin?] God's sweet child?.
89. *blijven*] stay, remain.
91. *shafe and shite*] probably 'chafe and chide', deliberately mispronounced for
scatological comic effect (also, *shafe* = obsolete form of sheaf, to bind up(?); *shite* =
obsolete form of *sheet*, to shut up (?)).

ACT 4

[4.1]

Enter PISARO.

Pisaro. I'll put the light out, lest I be espied,
　　For closely I have stolen me forth adoors,
　　That I might know how my three sons have sped.
　　Now, afore God, my heart is passing light,
　　That I have overreached the Englishmen.　　　　　　　　　5
　　Ha, ha, Master Vandal. Many such nights
　　Will 'ssuage your big swollen bulk, and make it lank.
　　When I was young – yet, though my hairs be grey,
　　I have a young man's spirit to the death,
　　And can as nimbly trip it with a girl　　　　　　　　　10
　　As those which fold the spring-tide in their beards.
　　Lord, how the very thought of former times
　　Supples these near-dried limbs with activeness.
　　Well, thoughts are shadows, sooner lost than seen.
　　Now to my daughters and their merry night.　　　　　　　15
　　I hope Alvaro and his company
　　Have read to them moral philosophy,
　　And they are full with it. Here I'll stay,
　　And tarry till my gallant youths come forth.
　　　　　　　　　　　　[*He sits in front of the door.*]

Enter HARVEY, WALGRAVE, *and* HEIGHAM.

---

7. 'ssuage] *this ed.;* swage *Qq;* 'swage *1830;* 'suage *Haz.*

---

2. *closely*] secretly.
adoors] out of doors.
4. *passing*] exceedingly.
7. *'ssuage*] assuage, lessen.
lank] thin.
9. *spirit*] vigour (also sexual ability; cf. note to 3.3.58–9).
death] with sexual pun, since to 'die' could mean to have an orgasm and 'spirit' was
a term for semen.
10. *trip it*] move lightly, caper.
11. *fold the spring-tide*] enclose, wrap in the height of youth, springtime of life.
17. *moral philosophy*] cf. note to 1.1.31.
18. *full*] surfeited, perhaps with bawdy suggestion.

Heigham. You mad-man, wild-oats, mad-cap, where art thou?   20
Walgrave. Here afore.
Harvey. O, ware what love is. Ned hath found the scent,
    And if the cony chance to miss her burrow,
    She's over-borne i'faith; she cannot stand it.
Pisaro. [*Aside*] I know that voice, or I am much deceived.   25
Heigham. Come, why loiter we? This is the door.
    But soft, here's one asleep.
Walgrave.   Come, let me feel:
    O, 'tis some rogue or other: spurn him spurn him!
Harvey. Be not so wilful, prithee, let him lie.
Heigham. Come back, come back, for we are past the house.   30
    Yonder's Mathea's chamber with the light.
Pisaro. [*Aside*] Well fare a head, or I had been descried.
    God's me, what makes the youngsters here so late?
    I am a rogue, and spurn him? Well, Jack Sauce,
    The rogue is waking yet to mar your sport.   35
Walgrave. Matt! Mistress Mathea! Where be these girls?

                Enter MATHEA *alone*[*, above*].

---

34. rogue] *Q2, Q3 (*Rogue*);* Rouge *Q.* him?] him: *Qq.* Jack Sauce] Jacke sauce
Qq; Jack-sauce *1830.* 35. mar] *Q;* spoyle *Q2, Q3.*

   21. *afore*] before, in front.
   22. *O, ware what love is*] i.e. oh beware what love is (or 'ware' and 'what' have
been transposed, the line meaning something like 'what a thing is love').
   Ned hath found the scent] i.e. as if hunting.
   23. *cony*] rabbit, hare.
   chance to miss her burrow] happens to be left out in the open, vulnerable.
   24. *over-borne*] outweighed, borne down (with sexual suggestion of Ned on top of
his cony).
   stand] defend (her 'burrow,' i.e. vagina); she will therefore lie down instead; there
may also be a joke on a 'standing' (i.e. erect) penis.
   28. *spurn him*] reject him, turn him away (usually by kicking; cf. *Comedy of Errors*
2.1.81–2: Dromio E., 'Am I so round with you as you with me, / That like a football
you do spurn me thus?'; and cf. *The Merchant of Venice* 1.3.113–15: Shylock, 'You,
that did void your rheum upon my beard, / And foot me as you spurn a stranger cur
/ Over your threshold'.
   29. *wilful*] forward, violent.
   32. *Well fare a head*] (1) Pisaro compliments himself in thinking 'ahead' (2) Pisaro
congratulates his 'head' on its effective pretence of being asleep (3) Pisaro looks 'ahead'
to good fortune, since luck seems to be with him.
   descried] discovered, found out.
   34. *Jack Sauce*] saucy fellow (Jack = generic name, John); cf. notes to 1.3.256,
2.3.179, 4.1.147; 'jacks' also = young ruffians.

Mathea. Who's there below?
Walgrave. Thy Ned, kind Ned, thine honest, trusty Ned.
Mathea. No, no, it is the Frenchman in his stead,
   That Monsieur motleycoat that can dissemble.   40
   Hear you, Frenchman: pack to your whores in France.
   Though I am Portingale by the father's side,
   And therefore should be lustful, wanton, light,
   Yet, goodman goose-cap, I will let you know
   That I have so much English by the mother   45
   That no base, slavering French shall make me stoop.
   And so, Sir Dan-delion, fare you well.
[*Heigham.*] What, speechless? Not a word? Why, how now Ned?
Harvey. The wench hath ta'en him down; he hangs his head.
Walgrave. You Dan-de-lion, you that talk so well.   50
   Hark you, a word or two, good mistress Matt.
   Did you appoint your friends to meet you here,
   And, being come, tell us of whores in France,
   A Spanish jennet, and an English mare,
   A mongrel, half a dog and half a bitch,   55
   With tran-dido, dil-dido, and I know not what?
   Hear you: if you'll run away with Ned,
   And be content to take me as you find me,
   Why so law, I am yours. If otherwise,

---

47. Dan-delion] *Qq*; Dandelion *Haz*; Dan-de-lion *1830*.   48. SP [*Heigham.*]] *1830*;
Walg. Qq.   49. The . . . head] *so lineated in 1830; two lines in Qq:* 'The . . . downe,
/ He . . . head'.   50. Dan-de-lion] *Q, Q2*; Don-delion *Q3*; Dandelion *Haz.*

40. *Monsieur motleycoat*] see notes to 1.3.194 and 3.2.79.

42–3. *Though I . . . light*] Lustfulness was often attributed to Italians and Africans
in the sixteenth century. However, it could be applied by the English to other Mediterranean and southern European peoples (lustfulness and spritely wit allegedly being
brought on by hot weather, according to early modern geohumoral theory).

44. *goose-cap*] simpleton, fool.

46. *slavering*] dribbling, drooling.

47 (and 50). *Dan-delion (Dan-de-lion)*] Q3 has 'Don-delion' at line 50, giving the
Spanish title, 'Don'; there may also be a suggestion of a dandy lion, one who is showy
and decorous in strength; the flower, dandelion, derives its name from *dent de lion*
(lion's tooth).

48. SP [*Heigham.*]] The 1830 editor assigns this speech to Heigham; Qq have
'Walgrave', which cannot be correct because the line addresses him.

49. *ta'en him down*] beaten him (with words).

54. *jennet*] small, Spanish horse.

56. *tran-dido, dil-dido*] a refrain-type fill for a song; Walgrave seems to be delivering
this part of the speech as a mock lyric.

59. *Why so law*] this seems to have an older sense of 'law' as being something right
or proper in the circumstances (*OED* 'law' *sb*, II.15).

You'll change your Ned to be a Frenchman's trull.   60
Why then, *Madame* Delion, *je vous lassera a Dio, et la bon*
  fortune!
Mathea. That voice assures me that it is my love.
  Say truly: art thou my Ned? Art thou my love?
Walgrave. 'Swounds, who should I be but Ned?
  You make me swear.   65

Enter MARINA, *above.*

Marina. Who spake you to? Mathea, who's below?
Harvey. Marina.
Marina. Young Master Harvey? For that voice saith so.

Enter LAURENTIA, *above.*

Laurentia. Speak, sister Matt; is not my true love there?
Mathea. Ned is.   70
Laurentia. Not Master Heigham?
Heigham.   Laurentia, here.
Laurentia. I'faith, thou'rt welcome.
Heigham.   Better cannot fall.
Mathea. Sweet, so art thou.
Marina. As much to mine.
Laurentia.   Nay, gentles, welcome all.
Pisaro. [*Aside*] Here's cunning harlotries: they feed these off   75
  With welcome and kind words, whilst other lads
  Revel in that delight they should possess.
  Good girls, I promise you I like you well.
Marina. Say, Master Harvey, saw you, as you came,
  That lecher, which my sire appoints my man?   80
  I mean that wanton, base Italian,
  That Spanish-leather spruce companion,

---

60. trull.] *this ed.;* Trull? *Q, Q2;* trull? *Q3;* trull! *Haz.*   65.1. *Enter* MARINA,
above.] this ed.; Enter above Marina Qq.   66. spake] *Q3;* speake *Q, Q2;* speak
Haz.

---

60. *change*] exchange, put aside.
   trull] prostitute.
61. je vous . . . fortune!] I shall leave you to God, and good luck!.
69–74. I have emphasized the apparent (though imperfect) verse lines in this section
to bring out the antiphonal feel of the exchanges; the half-rhymes of 'there/here' and
'fall/all' suggest such a sense of the lines is intended.
72. *fall*] befall, happen.
75. *harlotries*] prostitutes' tricks.
82. *spruce*] trim, neat, dapper (usually with reference to dress).

That antic ape tricked-up in fashion.
Had the ass come, I'd learn him difference been
Betwixt an English gentleman and him.   85
Heigham. How would you use him, sweet, if he should come?
Marina. Nay, nothing, sweet, but only wash his crown.
Why, the ass woos in such an amorous key
That he presumes no wench should say him nay.
He slavers on his fingers, wipes his bill,   90
And swears 'in faith you shall', 'in faith I will',
That I am almost mad to bide his wooing.
Heigham. Look what he said in word, I'll act in doing.
Walgrave. Leave thought of him, for day steals on apace,
And to our loves. Will you perform your words?   95
All things are ready, and the parson stands
To join, as hearts in hearts, our hands in hands.
Night favours us; the thing is quickly done;
Then truss up bag and baggage, and be gone.
And ere the morning, to augment your joys,   100
We'll make you mothers of six goodly boys.
Heigham. Promise them three, good Ned, and say no more.
Walgrave. But I'll get three, an if I get not four!
Pisaro. There's a sound card at maw, a lusty lad;
Your father thought him well when one he had.   105

---

86. How . . . come?] *so lineated in Haz; two lines in Qq*: '(sweet) / If'.   90. on] *Haz; not Qq*.   99. baggage] *Q2, Q3*; Bagages *Q*.

---

83. *antic . . . fashion*] Italian fashion was ridiculed in sixteenth-century England. The English, however, were also known for widely 'aping' other fashions; cf. W[illiam] R[ankins], *The English Ape, the Italian Imitation, the Footsteps of France* (1588), and Portia's commentary on her English suitor, Falconbridge: 'How oddly he is suited! I think he bought his doublet in Italy, his round hose in France, his bonnet in Germany, and his behaviour everywhere' (*The Merchant of Venice* 1.2.61–4).

84. *learn him difference been*] i.e. teach him the difference that has always been.

87. *wash his crown*] cf. 'To wash an ass's head' = to labour in vain; since 'the ass woos in such amorous key', there is no stopping him (*OED* 'wash' I.3.d), but also cf. 'crown' at 3.4.27.

90. *bill*] mouth (and nose).

92. *mad to bide*] i.e. mad from abiding, putting up with.

94. *apace*] quickly.

97. *To join . . . hands*] 1830 and Hazlitt emend 'as' to 'our'; this edition retains the original wording, since there is a clear and uncomplicated comparative of hands being joined in marriage to represent (to be like or *as*) the joining of hearts.

99. *truss up*] tie up, gather.

104. *sound card at maw*] a certain/sure hand; *maw* = card game with 36-card deck.

Heigham. What say you, sweets: will you perform your words?
Mathea. Love to true love, no lesser meed affords.
    We say we love you, and that love's fair breath
    Shall lead us with you round about the earth;
    And that our loves, vows, words may all prove true,   110
    Prepare your arms, for thus we fly to you.   *[Exeunt the sisters.]*
Walgrave. This works like wax. Now ere tomorrow day,
    If you two ply it but as well as I,
    We'll work our lands out of Pisaro's daughters,
    And cancel all our bonds in their great bellies –   115
    When the slave knows it, how the rogue will curse!
        [The sisters appear at the door, peer through the darkness,
                                looking to embrace.]
Mathea. Sweet heart?
Walgrave.   Matt?
Mathea.   Where art thou?
Pisaro.   Here!
Mathea. O Jesus, here's our father!
Walgrave.   The devil he is!
Harvey. Master Pisaro, twenty times good morrow.
Pisaro. Good morrow? Now I tell you, gentlemen,   120
    You wrong and move my patience overmuch.
    What, will you rob me, kill me, cut my throat,
    And set mine own blood here against me, too?
    You huswives! Baggages! Or what is worse,
    Wilful, stubborn, disobedient.   125

---

111. SD [*Exeunt the sisters.*]] *this ed.; they Embrace Q; They embrace Q2, Q3; see line 116 collation.* 116.1. SD *The . . . embrace.*] *this ed.; Qq stage direction placed after line 111.* 119. good] *Q3; God Q, Q2.* 124. You huswives! Baggages!] *this ed.; huswifes? Baggages? Qq; huswives, baggages, Haz.* worse,] *Q; worse. Q2, Q3.*

---

107. *meed*] reward, praise.
    111. [*Exeunt the sisters.*]] Q's '*they Embrace*' is too early here. 1830 notes of the sisters, 'Of course coming down upon the stage first', but there is a further delay, during which the sisters should exit and make their way to the front of the house; the lovers are clearly in the act of approaching each other at lines 117ff (or comically looking for each other in the dark) when Pisaro intervenes.
    112. *works like wax*] i.e. easily (beeswax, sealing wax for receiving impression of a seal on a document); to work something = to manipulate, to craft (create).
    113. *ply*] work, effect.
    115. *cancel all . . . bellies*] i.e. regain the right to our lands by making the daughters pregnant, thus providing heirs to the inheritance.
    116. *slave*] general term of abuse, directed at Pisaro.
    121. *move*] tax, overburden.
    123. *blood*] kin.

Use it not, gentlemen; abuse me not.
Newgate hath room; there's law enough in England.
Heigham. Be not so testy; hear what we can say.
Pisaro. Will you be wived? First learn to keep a wife.
Learn to be thrifty; learn to keep your lands;   130
And learn to pay your debts too, I advise, else.
Walgrave. What else, what lands, what debts? What will you do?
Have you not land in mortgage for your money?
Nay, since 'tis so, we owe you not a penny.
Fret not, fume not; never bend the brow.   135
You take ten in the hundred more than law.
We can complain: extortion, simony –
Newgate hath room; there's law enough in England.
Heigham. Prithee, have done.
Walgrave.   Prithee me no prithees.
                              [*Pulls* MARINA *to him.*]
Here is my wife; 'sblood, touch her, if thou dar'st.   140
Hearst thou: I'll lie with her before thy face,
Against the cross in Cheap, here, anywhere!
What, you old crafty fox, you –
Heigham.   Ned, stop there!
Pisaro. Nay, nay, speak out; bear witness, gentlemen.
Where's Mouche? Charge my musket, bring me my bill!   145

---

127. *Newgate*] a prison (see Appendix) at the principal west gate of the City of London; built in the twelfth century, it burned down in the Great Fire of 1666.
there's law enough] the law is sufficient to deal with you.
128. *testy*] angry, moody.
133–4. *Have you . . . penny*] Pisaro has the Englishmen's lands as pawn for money he has lent them, so Walgrave feels no financial obligation to Pisaro and takes offence at the suggestion he is in debt.
135. *never bend the brow*] do not frown.
136. *You take . . . law*] as a usurer, Pisaro allegedly charges 20 per cent interest on his loans. In 1571 Elizabeth I confirmed the legal rate for usury at 10 per cent. (In fact, Pisaro will admit to an even more 'biting' rate of 22 per cent at 5.1.32–3.)
137. *simony*] buying or selling of ecclesiastical privileges (e.g. pardons, benefices).
141. *lie*] have sex.
142. *the cross in Cheap*] a city landmark and gathering place of great significance, both for patriotism and protest, erected c. 1296 by Edward I, regilded three times in the sixteenth century, defaced in 1581, taken down in 1599, the year after *Englishmen*, restored in 1600, and finally demolished in 1643 (*Hugh Alley's Caveat: The Markets of London in 1598*, ed. Ian Archer, Caroline Barron, Vanessa Harding (London: London Topographical Society, 1988), p. 90) (see Appendix); it gained something of a devotional status, thus Walgrave's threat to commit his act of fornication at a most public and revered site is to the shame of London as well as Pisaro (hence Heigham's worried response).
145. *bill*] billy club, truncheon.

For here are some that mean to rob thy master. –

Enter ANTHONY.

I am a fox with you? Well, Jack Sauce,
Beware, lest for a goose I prey on you.
In, baggages! Mouche, make fast the door.

         Exeunt PISARO *and daughters.*

Walgrave. A vengeance on ill luck!
Anthony.   What? Never storm,   150
  But bridle anger with wise government.
Heigham. Whom? Anthony, our friend? Ah, how our hopes
  Are found too light to balance our ill haps!
Anthony. Tut, ne'er say so, for Anthony
  Is not devoid of means to help his friends.   155
Walgrave. 'Swounds, what a devil made he forth so late?
  I'll lay my life 'twas he that feigned to sleep,
  And we, all unsuspicious, termed a rogue.
  O God, had I but known him; if I had,
  I would have writ such letters with my sword   160
  Upon the bald skin of his parching pate,
  That he should ne'er have lived to cross us more.
Anthony. These menaces are vain, and helpeth naught;
  For I have in the depth of my conceit
  Found out a more material stratagem: 165

---

149. SD *Exeunt . . . daughters*] *placed after line 148 in Qq.*

147–8. *I am . . . you*] cf. the self-characterization of stage Jews as vengeful, based on the assumptions of their enemies: Barabas, 'We Jews can fawn like spaniels when we please, / And when we grin, we bite; yet are our looks / As innocent and harmless as a lamb's' (*The Jew of Malta* 2.3.20–2), and Shylock, 'Thou call'st me dog before thou hadst a cause, / But since I am a dog, beware my fangs' (*The Merchant of Venice* 3.3.6–7).
 149. *baggages*] worthless women.
 150. *storm*] be angry, rave.
 151. *bridle*] rein in, temper.
 153. *haps*] chances, lucks.
 160. *letters*] i.e. marks (cuts) at various angles.
 161. *parching pate*] hot head (because bald and unprotected from the sun by hair).
 162. *cross us*] get in our way, go against us.
 163. *menaces*] threats.
 164. *conceit*] invention, imagination.
 165. *material*] useful, of some matter or import.
stratagem] plan; the words 'policy' and 'stratagem' would have registered with a sixteenth-century audience as Machiavellian terms of intrigue (Machiavelli was a political theorist and statesman from Florence, 1469–1527; the prologue in Marlowe's *The*

Hark, Master Walgrave; yours craves quick despatch:
                              [*He whispers to Walgrave.*]
About it straight; stay not to say farewell.   *Exit* WALGRAVE.
You, Master Heigham: hie you to your chamber
And stir not forth. My shadow, or my self,
Will in the morning early visit you.   170
Build on my promise, sir, and so good night.   *Exit* HEIGHAM.
Last, yet as great in love as to the first:
If you remember, once I told a jest,
How, feigning to be sick, a friend of mine
Possessed the happy issue of his love.   175
That counterfeited humour must you play.
I need not to instruct; you can conceive.
Use Master Browne, your host, as chief in this.
But first, to make the matter seem more true,
Sickly and sadly bid the churl good night;   180
I hear him at the window – there he is.

                    Enter PISARO, *above.*

[*Aside*] Now for a trick to overreach the devil.
[*Aloud to Harvey.*] I tell you, sir, you wrong my master much,
And then, to make amends, you give hard words.
H'ath been a friend to you; nay, more, a father.   185
I promise you, 'tis most ungently done.
Pisaro. [*Aside*] Ay, well said, Mouche, now I see thy love,
And thou shalt see mine one day, if I live.
[*To Harvey.*] None but my daughters, sir, hangs for your tooth:

---

171. so] Q2, Q3; *not in* Q.

Jew of Malta is 'Machevil', and there was a Rose Theatre play by this name playing at
the same time as *The Jew of Malta*).
    166. *yours craves quick despatch*] your role demands swift execution.
    167. *straight*] immediately.
    168. *hie you*] go.
    169. *My shadow*] someone like me (because in disguise).
    171. *Build on*] Pin your hopes on, Trust in.
    175. *issue*] (1) result (2) offspring.
    176. *humour*] character, temperament, physical disposition (sick owing to an imbal-
ance of humours; see note to 2.1.106).
    178. *your host*] It seems that the Englishmen are Browne's house guests for the
present.
    182. *the devil*] i.e. Pisaro; cf. this representation of the usurer conflated with the
Jew-devil in *Merchant of Venice* 1.3.96, 2.2.21–4, 3.1.19–21, 31, and 73–4, 4.1.215
and 285.
    185. *H'ath*] He hath.
    189. *hangs for your tooth*] the sense seems to be 'awaits your tasting' (Tilley T430
cites teeth watering at luscious food).

[*Aside*] I'd rather see them hanged first, ere you get them.   190
Harvey. Master Pisaro, hear a dead man speak,
    Who sings the woeful accents of his end.
    I do confess I love; then let not love
    Prove the sad engine of my life's remove.
    Marina's rich possession was my bliss;   195
    Then in her loss, all joy eclipsed is.
    As every plant takes virtue of the sun,
    So from her eyes this life and being sprung.
    But now, debarred of those clear, shining rays,
    Death for earth gapes, and earth to death obeys.   200
    Each word thou spak'st – O, speak not so again –
    Bore Death's true image on the word ingraven,
    Which – as it flew, mixed with heaven's airy breath –
    Summoned the dreadful sessions of my death.
    I leave thee to thy wish, and may th'event   205
    Prove equal to thy hope and heart's content:
    Marina to that hap that happiest is,
    My body to the grave, my soul to bliss.
    [*Aside to Anthony.*] Have I done well?
Anthony.   Excellent well, in troth.
                                        Exit HARVEY.
Pisaro. Ay, go; ay, go. Your words move me as much   210
    As doth a stone being cast against the air. –
    But soft, what light is that? What folks be those?
    O, 'tis Alvaro and his other friends.
    I'll down and let them in.   *Exit.*

        Enter BELMAN, FRISCO, DELION, *and* ALVARO.

Frisco. Where are we now, gaffer Butterick?   215
Belman. Why, know you not Crutched Friars? Where be your wits?

---

195. bliss;] *1830;* bliss? *Qq;* bliss: *Haz.*   209. *Exit* HARVEY.] *placed after* 'Have I done well?' *in Qq.*   212–14. But soft ... in] *so lineated in 1830; set as prose in Qq.*
214.1. Enter ... ALVARO] *this ed.; Qq include an entry for Vandal here:* 'Frisco, Vandalle, Delion'.

---

194. *engine of*] mechanism for.
remove] ending (death).
204. *sessions*] judgement.
205. *th'event*] the outcome.
207. *hap*] chance, outcome.
210–14. these lines are prose in Qq, but Pisaro usually speaks in verse, and these lines scan into pentameter.
210–11. *as much ... air*] i.e. not at all (air gives little resistance).
215. *gaffer*] old man.

Alvaro. What, be tis Croshe-friers? Vidite padre; dare, tacke you dat;
    me sal troble you no farre.   [*Gives him money.*]
Belman. I thank you, gentlemen; good night. Good night, Frisco.
                                                                Exit.
Frisco. Farewell, Butterick. What a clown it is! Come on, my masters,   220
    merrily. I'll knock at the door.
Anthony. [*Aside*] Who's there? Our three wise wooers; blockhead,
        our man?
    Had he not been, they might have hanged themselves
    For any wenches they had hit upon.
    [*To them.*] Good morrow, or good e'en, I know not whether.   225
Delion. Monsieur de Mouche, wat macke you out de houis so late?

                    Enter PISARO, *below.*

Pisaro. What, what, young men and sluggards? Fie, for shame!
    You trifle time at home about vain toys,
    Whilst others in the mean time steal your brides.
    I tell you, sirs, the English gentlemen   230
    Had wellnigh mated you, and me, and all.
    The doors were open and the girls abroad,
    Their sweethearts ready to receive them, too.
    And gone, forsooth, they had been, had not I –
    I think by revelation – stopped their flight.   235
    But I have cooped them up, and so will keep them.
    But, sirrah, Frisco, where's the man I sent for?
    Whose cloak have you got there? How now, where's Vandal?

219.] *Bell.* I thanke you Gentlemen, good night: / Good night *Frisco. Qq.*   220. it is!
Come on,] it is:/ Come on *Qq.*   225. good e'en] *this ed.;* good den *Qq.*   230. sirs] *this
ed.;* sir *Qq.*   231. mated] *Q, Q2?;* marred *Q3.*   238. Whose . . . Vandal?] *so this
ed.; two lines in Qq:* there? / How now, *and 1830:* How now; / Where's.

---

217. *Vidite padre; dare*] *vedere* = to see, *padre* = father, *dare* = to give; Alvaro seems
to be politely addressing the old Belman as 'father', and giving him some money.

223–4. *Had he . . . upon*] Had Frisco not been with them, they might have gone to
extremes (or got into trouble) to get their women.

225. *good e'en*] good evening.

227. *sluggards*] habitually lazy, inactive persons.

228. *trifle*] waste.

vain toys] unimportant entertainments.

231. *wellnigh*] very nearly.

mated] checkmated, beaten (in the game of chess), with pun on sexually mating with
the women.

232. *abroad*] out of doors.

235. *revelation*] divine intervention.

236. *cooped*] the image is of cooping up chickens.

Frisco. Forsooth, he is not here. Master Mendall you mean, do you
    not?   240
Pisaro. Why, loggerhead, him I sent for: where is he?
    Where hast thou been? How hast thou spent thy time?
    Did I not send thee to my son, Vandal?
Frisco. Ay, Master Mendall; why, forsooth, I was at his chamber, and
    we were coming hitherward, and he was very hot, and bade me   245
    carry his cloak; and I no sooner had it, but he, being very light,
    firks me down on the left hand, and I turned down on the left
    hand, and so lost him.
Pisaro. Why, then you turned together, ass!
Frisco. No, sir, we never saw one another since.   250
Pisaro. Why, turned you not both on the left hand?
Frisco. No, forsooth, we turned both on the left hand.
Pisaro. Hoyda! Why, yet you went both together.
Frisco. Ah, no, we went clean contrary from one another.
Pisaro. Why dolt, why patch, why ass! On which hand turned ye?   255
Frisco. Alas, alas! I cannot tell, forsooth. It was so dark I could not see
    on which hand we turned – but I am sure we turned one way.
Pisaro. Was ever creature plagued with such a dolt?
    My son, Vandal, now hath lost himself,
    And shall all night go straying 'bout the town,   260
    Or meet with some strange watch that knows him not.
    And all by such an arrant ass as this!
Anthony. No, no, you may soon smell the Dutchman's lodging.
    Now for a figure: [*Pointing up at Vandal.*] out, alas! What's
        yonder?
Pisaro. Where?   265

239–40. Forsooth . . . not?] *so 1830; two lines in Qq:* here: / Maister.   255. Why . . .
ye] *so 1830; two lines in Qq:* Asse, / On.   ye?] Q, Q3; ye: Q2.

---

246. *being very light*] playing on the fact that Vandal was lighter, being relieved of
the weight of his cloak, but hardly very light, since he is a fat man.

247. *firks me*] runs off suddenly (the 'me' is a colloquial direct object, implying close
association between speaker and subject of the utterance, but with no modern
equivalent).

253. *Hoyda!*] See note to 1.2.20.

255. *patch*] See note to 1.3.194.

261. *strange watch*] a shift of the night watch who are unfamiliar with the foreigners
(for 'watch' see note to 3.3.15).

arrant] absolute, notorious.

263. *you may . . . lodging*] perhaps another joke on the fat, sweaty Dutchman.

264. *a figure*] (1) (human) shape (2) a working-out, an answer.

Frisco. Hoyda, hoyda, a basket! It turns, ho!

Pisaro. Peace, ye villain, and let's see who's there.
    Go look about the house. Where are our weapons?
    What might this mean?

Frisco. Look, look, look! There's one in it: he peeps out.   270
    Is there ne'er a stone here to hurl at his nose?

Pisaro. What, wouldst thou break my windows with a stone?
    How now, who's there? Who are you, sir?

Frisco. Look, he peeps out again. O, it's Master Mendall, it's Master
    Mendall. How got he up thither?   275

Pisaro. What, my son Vandal! How comes this to pass?

Alvaro. Signiore Vandal; wat, do you go to de wenshe in de basket?

Vandal. O vader, vader, here be sush cruel dochterkens; ik ben also
    wery, also wery, also cold; for be in dit little basket. Ik pray help
    de me.   280

Frisco. He looks like the sign of the Mouth without Bishopsgate:
    gaping, and a great face, and a great head, and no body.

Pisaro. Why, how now, son? What, have your adamants
    Drawn you up so far, and there left you hanging
    'Twixt heaven and earth like Mahomet's sepulchre?   285

Anthony. They did unkindly, whosoe'er they were
    That plagued him here, like Tantalus in hell,

---

266. Hoyda, hoyda,] *Qq;* Hey day! Hey day! *1830.*   basket!] *this ed.;* Basket: *Qq;*
basket? *1830.*   267. there.] *this ed.;* there? *Qq.*   272–3. What . . . sir?] *so lineated
in 1830; single line in Qq.*   277. de basket] *Q;* dit little basket *Q2, Q3.*   280. de
me] *Q2, Q3;* dene *Q.*

277. *in de basket*] Q2 and Q3 read 'in dit little basket,' but this reading is probably
transposed from line 279.

278. *dochterkens*] little daughters.

278–9. *also wery*] so weary.

281–2. *He looks . . . body*] 'A seventeenth-century trade token was issued from a
house with the sign of the Mouth in Bishopsgate Street, and the Mouth appears in the
rhyming list of taverns, which is to be found in Heywood's "Rape of Lucrece" ' (Baugh,
citing P. Norman, *London Signs and Inscriptions* (London, 1893)); the sign of a gaping
mouth might also be connected to an apothecary's shop sign (van Elk).

283. *adamants*] magnets (i.e. attractive women).

285. *Mahomet's sepulchre*] 'It is said that Mahomet's coffin, in the Hadgire of
Medina, is suspended in mid-air without any support . . . the coffin is not suspended at
all' (Baugh, also noting Nashe's reference to the phenomenon in *The Unfortunate
Traveller*, McKerrow ii, p. 249). Tilley also has as proverbial 'to be suspended like
Mahomet's tomb between heaven and earth' (M13, first reference 1649).

287. *Tantalus*] in Greek mythology, Tantalus is punished for giving ambrosia (food
of the gods) to his friends; Zeus's punishment was for Tantalus to stand in a lake,
which dries up when he bends to drink from it; a fruit-laden bough flies up when he
reaches to eat; hence representative of unsatiated desire.

To touch his lips like the desired fruit,
And then to snatch it from his gaping chaps.

Alvaro. A little farder, Signiore Vandal, and dan you may put u hed   290
into de windo and cash de wensh.

Vandal. Ik pray, vader, dat you help de mee, Ik pray, goody vader.

Pisaro. Help you, but how? –

Frisco. Cut the rope.

Anthony.   – Sir, I'll go in and see,
And if I can, I'll let him down to you.   *Exit.*   295

Pisaro. Do, gentle Mouche. Why, but here's a jest.
They say high climbers have the greatest falls.
If you should fall, as how you'll do I know not,
By'r Lady I should doubt me of my son.
Pray to the rope to hold. – Art thou there, Mouche?   300

Enter ANTHONY, *above.*

Anthony. Yes, sir. Now you may choose whether you'll stay till I let
him down, or whether I shall cut him down?

Frisco. Cut him down, Master Mouse, cut him down, and let's see how
he'll tumble.

Pisaro. Why, sauce, who asked your counsel? Let him down.   305
                    [*The basket is lowered.*]
What, with a cushion, too? Why, you provided
To lead your life as did Diogenes,
And for a tub, to creep into a basket.

Vandal. Ik zal zeg u, vader. Ik kwam here to your huis and sprak tot
de dochterken.   310

Frisco. Master Mendall, you are welcome out of the basket. I smell a
rat: it was not for nothing that you lost me.

Vandal. O, schelm! You run away from me.

Pisaro. I though so, sirrah: you gave him the slip!

---

290. you may] Q; 'you' *not in Q2, Q3.* 292. goody] Q2, Q3 *(goodie)*, *1830;*
Goddie Q. 303–4. Cut . . . tumble] *so 1830; two lines in Q:* downe / And, *and Q2,*
Q3: downe, /And. 305. Why . . . down] *so 1830; two lines in Q:* counsaile? / Let,
and Q2, Q3: counsell? / Let. 309. tot] *this ed.;* tol Qq.

---

289. *chaps*] lips.
297. *high climbers . . . falls*] proverbial, cf. Tilley C414 (cites this line).
299. *doubt*] fear.
307–8. *Diogenes, . . . basket*] the cynical philosopher, Diogenes (c. 412–323 BCE)
was traditionally believed to have lived in a tub.
309. *Ik zal zeg u*] I shall tell you.
kwam] came.
311–12. *I smell a rat*] proverbial, cf. Tilley R31.

Frisco. Faw, no forsooth! I'll tell you how it was: when we come from 315
    Bucklersbury into Cornwall, and I had taken the cloak, then you
    should have turned down on your left hand and so have gone right
    forward, and so turned up again, and so have crossed the street;
    and you, like an ass –
Pisaro. Why, how now, rascal! Is your manners such? 320
    You ass, you dolt! Why led you him through Cornhill?
    Your way had been to come through Canning Street.
Frisco. Why, so I did, sir.
Pisaro. Why, thou sayest ye were in Cornhill!
Frisco. Indeed, sir, there was three faults – the night was dark, Master 325
    Mendall drunk, and I sleepy – that we could not tell very well
    which way we went.
Pisaro. Sirrah, I owe for this a cudgelling.
    But, gentlemen, sith things have fall'n out so,
    And for I see Vandal quakes for cold, 330
    This night accept your lodgings in my house,
    And in the morning forward with your marriage.
    Come on, my sons. [*To Frisco.*] Sirrah, fetch up more wood.
                                  Exeunt.

[4.2]

Enter the three sisters.

Laurentia. Nay, never weep, Marina, for the matter.
    Tears are but signs of sorrow, helping not.
Marina. Would it not mad one to be crossed as I,
    Being in the very height of my desire?
    The strangers frustrate all. Our true loves come, 5
    Nay, more, even at the door, and Harvey's arms

---

324. sayest] *1830;* say'st *Q2, Q3;* seest *Q.* 329. fall'n out] *this ed.;* faulne out *Q;* falne out *Q2;* fallen *Q3.*

5. loves] *Haz;* love's *Qq.*

---

315. *Faw*] a variant of 'faugh', a dismissive expression of disgust.
316. *Bucklersbury*] a lane to the east and south of Cheap (see Appendix).
Cornwall] mistake for Cornhill Street, in London (see Appendix); Pisaro corrects Frisco at line 324. (Cornwall is the most south-westerly county in England.)
322. *Canning Street*] i.e. Cannon/Candlewick Street (see, Appendix).
324. *sayest*] This Q2 and Q3 reading fits the exchange better than Q's 'see'st', although the latter is workable.
328. *I owe ... cudgelling*] i.e. I owe you ... beating (with a cudgel, a large stick).
329. *sith*] since.

3. *mad*] enrage.
crossed] thwarted.

Spread as rainbow ready to receive me,
And then my father meet us – O God, O God!
Mathea. Weep who that list for me. I'faith, not I.   10
Though I am youngest, yet my stomach's great.
Nor 'tis not father, friends, nor any one
Shall make me wed the man I cannot love.
I'll have my will, in faith, i'faith I will.
Laurentia. Let us determine, sisters, what to do.
My father means to wed us in the morning,   15
And therefore something must be thought upon.
Marina. We'll to our father and so know his mind,
Ay, and his reason, too; we are no fools,
Or babes neither, to be fed with words.
Laurentia. Agreed, agreed. But who shall speak for all?   20
Mathea. I will.
Marina.   No, I.
Laurentia.   Thou wilt not speak for crying.
Marina. Yes, yes, I warrant you; that humour's left.
Be I but moved a little, I shall speak,
And anger him, I fear, ere I have done.

Enter ANTHONY.

All. Whom, Anthony our friend, our schoolmaster?   25
Now help us, gentle Anthony, or never.
Anthony. What, is your hasty running changed to prayer?
Say, where were you going?

---

7. *rainbow*] referring to (1) the curvature of one's arms held out to embrace another (2) the notion of covenant (God's to Noah; Harvey's vows of love and marriage to Marina).

9. *list*] choose, care (to).

10. *stomach*] inner strength.

16. *thought upon*] planned, worked out.

18–19. *we are . . . words*] the meaning seems to be that the sisters are not so childish as to accept what they are told without question; they will demand logical reason for their father's verbal determination.

21. *I will . . . crying*] I have inset speeches to make one (slightly hypermetrical) pentameter line out of the three lines in Qq; this brings out the rapidity and emotion of the exchange between the sisters.

22. *warrant*] assure, promise.

humour] in this case, melancholy (cf. note to 2.1.106).

left] (1) gone (the crying melancholy that stops her speaking) (2) remains (the speaking choler that she will use to speak).

23. *moved*] prompted, aroused (to anger).

Laurentia.   Even to our father,
   To know what he intends to do with us.
Anthony. 'Tis bootless, trust me, for he is resolved   30
   To marry you to –
Marina.   The strangers?
Anthony.   I'faith, he is.
Mathea. I'faith, he shall not.
   Frenchman, be sure we'll pluck a crow together
   Before you force me give my hand at church.
Marina. Come, to our father. Speech this comfort finds: 35
   That we may scold out grief and ease our minds.
Anthony. Stay, stay, Marina, and advise you better.
   It is not force, but policy must serve.
   The doors are locked; your father keeps the key,
   Wherefore unpossible to 'scape away.   40
   Yet have I plotted, and devised a drift
   To frustrate your intended marriages,
   And give you full possession of your joys.
   Laurentia, ere the morning's light appear,
   You must play Anthony in my disguise.   45
Mathea and Marina. Anthony, what of us? What shall we wear?
Anthony. Soft, soft, you are too forward, girls, I swear.
   For you some other drift devised must be.
   One shadow for a substance: [*Indicating Laurentia.*] this is she.
                    [MATHEA *and* MARINA *weep.*]

---

35. Come, to our father. Speech this comfort finds:] *so pointed in this ed.;* Come to
our Father speach this comfort finds, *Qq (see additional line 35 collation below);* Come
to our father: speech this comfort finds, *1830.*   35. father] *Q;* Fathers *Q2, Q3.*
48. be] *this ed.;* bee? *Qq;* be? *1830;* be: *Haz.*

---

28. *Even*] Straight, Immediately.

30. *bootless*] pointless.

31-2. *To marry . . . not*] As with line 21, I have inset speeches to make one (slightly
hypermetrical) pentameter line for the same reason as before.

33. *we'll pluck a crow together*] set things straight between us, argue out our differences (proverbial, cf. Tilley C855, 'I have a crow to pluck with you') and cf. the
modern 'I have a bone to pick with you'.

34. *hand*] i.e. hand in marriage.

35-6. *Speech . . . minds*] speaking gives this comfort – that we can vent our anger
and sadness to get it out of our systems.

38. *policy*] clever planning (cf. note to 'stratagem' 4.1.165).

41. *drift*] plan.

47. *you . . . swear*] since 'two' is printed 'too' at 3.3.64 (albeit spoken by a foreigner), a similar change here would make the line read, 'you are two forward girls, I
swear,' which retains Qq punctuation; Anthony in such a case would be referring specifically to the forwardness of Mathea and Marina.

forward] bold, immodest.

Nay, weep not, sweets, repose upon my care,   50
For all alike, or good or bad, shall share.
You will have Harvey, you Heigham, and you Ned;
You shall have all your wish, or be I dead.
For sooner may one day the sea lie still
Than once restrain a woman of her will.   55
All. Sweet Anthony, how shall we quit thy hire?
Anthony. Not gifts, but your contentments I desire.
To help my countrymen I cast about,
For strangers' loves blaze fresh, but soon burn out.
Sweet rest dwell here, and frightful fear abjure,   60
These eyes shall wake to make you rest secure.
For ere again dull night the dull eyes charms,
Each one shall fold her husband in her arms;
Which, if it chance, we may avouch it still,
Women and maids will always have their will.   *Exeunt.*   65

[4.3]

Enter PISARO *and* FRISCO.

Pisaro. Are wood and coals brought up to make a fire?
Is the meat spitted, ready to lie down?
For bake meats I'll have none; the world's too hard.
There's geese, too, now I remember me –
Bid Maudlin lay the giblets in paste.   [FRISCO *starts to leave.*]   5
Here's nothing thought upon, but what I do –   [*A bell rings.*]
Stay, Frisco, see who rings. Look to the door,
Let none come in, I charge, were he my father.

---

60. abjure] *Q3*; objure *Q, Q2.*   61. you] *Q2, Q3*; your *Q.*

---

50. *repose*] rest, rely, trust.
51. *or ... or*] whether ... or.
56. *quit thy hire*] requite, pay back your employment, help.
58. *cast about*] try all manner of things.
60. *abjure*] put away, suppress, discard (cf. Prospero in *The Tempest*, 'But this rough magic / I here abjure' (5.1.50–1)).
61. *These eyes*] i.e. Anthony's eyes.

2. *spitted*] roasted on a spit (rod thrust through meat to suspend it and turn it above a fire to cook).
lie down] serve.
3. *bake meats*] pastry, pies.
5. *giblets*] innards (heart, liver, gizzards) of chicken or other fowl.
paste] pastry.
6. *Here's nothing ... do*] familiar master's complaint of servant's lack of initiative.

I'll keep them whilst I have them – Frisco, who is it?
Frisco. She is come, i'faith.
Pisaro.   Who is come?   10
Frisco. Mistress Sushaunce, Mistress Moore's daughter.
Pisaro. Mistress Susan, ass! O, she must come in.
Frisco. [*Aside*] Hang him if he keep out a wench.
          If the wench keep not out him, so it is.

            Enter WALGRAVE *in woman's attire.*

Pisaro. Welcome, Mistress Susan, welcome.   15
          I little thought you would have come tonight,
          But welcome, trust me, are you to my house.
          What, doth your mother mend? Doth she recover?
          I promise you, I am sorry for her sickness.
Walgrave. She's better than she was, I thank God for it.   20
Pisaro. [*Aside*] Now, afore God, she is a sweet, smug girl;
          One might do good on her. The flesh is frail,
          Man hath infirmity, and such a bride
          Were able to change age to hot desire.
          [*To Walgrave.*] Hark you, sweetheart,   25
          Tomorrow are my daughters to be wed;
          I pray you, take the pains to go with them.
Walgrave. If, sir, you'll give me leave, I'll wait on them.
Pisaro. Yes, marry, shall you, and a thousand thanks.
          Such company as you my daughters want;   30
          Maids must grace maids when they are marrièd.
          Is't not a merry life, thinkst thou, to wed,
          For to embrace, and be embraced abed?
Walgrave. I know not what you mean, sir.
          [*Aside*] Here's an old ferret polecat!   35
Pisaro. You may do, if you'll follow mine advice.
          I tell thee, mouse, I knew a wench as nice –

---

    9. *them*] i.e. his daughters.
    13–14. *keep out ... keep not out*] i.e. keep her from entering the house . . . i.e. keep him from entering her sexually.
    21. *smug*] smooth, fair (cf. 1.1.1).
    22. *do good on her*] with sexual suggestion.
    27. *take the pains*] make the effort.
    30. *want*] lack, but with the possible unintentional pun on the modern meaning of 'desire', since one of the daughters *wants* Walgrave.
    35. *ferret polecat*] a ferret is a semi-tame variety of polecat (probably a bawdy joke on the fact that ferrets are used to get into rabbit burrows and animal holes to hunt them out (cf. this sexualized trope at 4.1.22–4).
    37. *mouse*] term of affection.
    nice] (1) warm-hearted, likeable, agreeable (2) simple, innocent (3) dainty.

Well, she's at rest, poor soul, I mean my wife,
That thought, alas, good heart, love was a toy,
Until – well, that time is gone and passed away.   40
But why speak I of this? Hark ye, sweeting,
There's more in wedlock than the name can show;
And now, by'r Lady, you are ripe in years;
And yet, take heed, wench, there lies a pad in straw.
Walgrave. [*Aside*] Old fornicator! Had I my dagger   45
        I'd break his costard.
Pisaro. Young men are slippery, fickle, wavering;
        Constant abiding graceth none but age.
        Then maids should now wax wise, and do so,
        As to choose constant men, let fickle go;   50
        Youth's unregarded, and unhonoured.
        An ancient man doth make a maid a matron,
        And is not that an honour? How say you? How say you?
Walgrave. Yes, forsooth.
        [*Aside*] O, old lust, will you never let me go?   55
Pisaro. You say right well, and do but think thereon,
        How husbands, honoured years, long cared-for wealth,
        Wise stayedness, experient government,
        Doth grace the maid that thus is made a wife,
        And you will wish yourself such, on my life.   60
Walgrave. [*Aside*] I think I must turn womankind altogether
        And scratch out his eyes.
        For as long as he can see me, he'll ne'er let me go.
Pisaro. But go, sweetheart, to bed. I do thee wrong;
        The lateness now makes all our talk seem long.   65

                Enter ANTHONY.

---

55. SD [*Aside*]] *this ed.*; Qq *put line in parentheses, indicating an aside*; [*Aside.*]
1830.

---

38. *my wife*] Stage usurers tend to be widowers, who mention their wives fleetingly,
but affectionately (e.g. *Merchant of Venice* 3.1.100–2).
41. *sweeting*] darling.
43. *ripe*] ready for plucking.
44. *there . . . straw*] there is a hidden danger; proverbial, cf. Tilley P9, 'There is a
pad (toad) in the straw' (toads were thought to be poisonous).
46. *costard*] large apple, thus *head*.
48. *Constant abiding*] Remaining (hence faithfulness).
51. *unregarded*] unrespected.
58. *stayedness*] having the quality of being staid (settled, fixed, sober).
experient] possessing experience (in).
61. *turn womankind*] turn into a woman.

How now, Mouche, be the girls abed?

Anthony. Mathea, an it like you, fain would sleep,

But only tarrieth for her bedfellow.

Pisaro. Ha, you say well. Come, light her to her chamber.

Good rest wish I to thee. Wish so to me, 70

Then Susan and Pisaro shall agree.

Think but what joy is near your bedfellow;

Such may be yours. Take counsel of your pillow.

Tomorrow we'll talk more, and so good night.

Think what is said may be, if all hit right. 75

Walgrave. [*Aside to Anthony.*] What, have I passed the pikes? Knows

he not Ned?

I think I have deserved his daughter's bed!

Anthony. 'Tis well, 'tis well. But this let me request:

You keep unknown, till you be laid to rest – 80

And then a good hand speed you.

Walgrave.   Tut, ne'er fear me:

We two abed shall never disagree.

                              Exeunt ANTHO[NY] *and* WALG[RAVE].

Frisco. I have stood still all this while, and could not speak for laugh-

ing. Lord, what a dialogue hath there been between Age and

Youth! You do good on her? Even as much as my Dutchman will 85

do on my young mistress! Master, follow my counsel: then send

for Master Heigham to help him, for I'll lay my cap to twopence

that he will be asleep tomorrow at night when he should go to bed

to her. Marry, for the Italian, he is of another humour, for there'll

be no dealings with him till midnight; for he must slaver all the 90

wenches in the house at parting, or he is nobody. He hath been

but a little while at our house, yet in that small time he hath licked

more grease from our Maudlin's lips than would have served

---

89. there'll] *Q;* there will *Q2, Q3.*

67. *an it like you*] i.e. if you please.

fain would] would like to.

69. *light her*] lead her with a candle.

75. *may be*] may become reality.

hit] hits home, comes together, makes an impression.

Baugh notes, 'Something seems to have dropped out after this line'. The lines are in fact fine; perhaps Baugh read 'may be' (= could come to pass) as 'maybe,' which would falsely suggest a necessary continuation of the line.

76. *pikes*] long weapon consisting of long stick with pointed blade on one end; hence, line of military defence consisting of pikemen.

84–5. *Age and Youth*] Frisco relates what he has just seen in terms of a Tudor morality play, with antagonists Age and Youth as characters in comic dialogue.

87. *lay*] wager, bet.

89. *humour*] here referring to lechery (for 'humours' see note to 2.1.106).

London kitchen-stuff this twelvemonth. Yet for my money, well
fare the Frenchman. O, he is a forward lad, for he'll no sooner   95
come from the church, but he'll fly to the chamber. Why, he'll read
his lesson so often in the daytime that at night, like an apt scholar,
he'll be ready to sell his old book to buy him a new. O, the generation of languages that our house will bring forth! Why, every bed
will have a proper speech to himself and have the founder's name   100
written upon it in fair capital letters, 'HERE LAY – ', and so
forth.
Pisaro. You'll be a villain still. Look who's at door!   [*Exit.*]
Frisco. Nay, by the mass! You are Master Porter, for I'll be hanged if
you lose that office, having so pretty a morsel under your keeping.   105
I go, old huddle, for the best nose at smelling out a pinfold that I
know. Well, take heed: you may 'haps pick up worms so long that
at length some of them get into your nose, and never out after. But
what an ass am I to think so, considering all the lodgings are taken
up already, and there's not a dog-kennel empty for a strange worm   110
to breed in.   [*Exit.*]

---

101. 'HERE LAY – '] *this ed.; Heere lay, Q; Here lay, Q2, Q3.*

---

94. *kitchen-stuff*] (1) requirements of the city's kitchens (2) kitchen waste (drip-
pings, grease).
95. *forward*] bold, lusty.
97. *lesson*] passage to contemplate.
98. *ready to . . . new*] Frisco seems to be alleging that Delion sexually 'learns' everything about one woman in a day, and by nighttime he is ready to find – 'buy,' suggesting
prostitutes – another.
100. *a proper*] its own.
101–2. *and so forth*] this phrase may indicate an implicit stage direction (see notes
to 1.2.106–7 and 3.3.21–2).
104. *Master Porter*] Frisco might be punning on the 'porter' as the opening to the
stomach (*OED* 'porter' n. 2), since Pisaro has a 'so pretty a morsel' to digest.
105. *morsel*] bit of food (referring to Walgrave, dressed up as Susanna).
106–11.] A difficult passage: relevant allusions may be to the 'greedy worm' as
'avarice or greediness as an itching passion in the heart' (*OED* 'worm' n. 11.c); the
'worm' as a tumor, abscess, or swelling, which the *OED* cites as a problem for a horse's
nose (12.c), and this might relate to the usurer's big nose and the reference to a pinfold.
Frisco may be suggesting that Pisaro is so full of corruption that no more can come to
him.
106. *I go, old huddle*] Frisco is saying he will attend to the door and is referring to
Pisaro as a miserly old person (*OED* 'huddle' 3); cf. note to 2.3.334; Frisco could also
be saying 'Ay, go' to Pisaro, since he then refers to the nose.
smelling out] discovering, intuiting.
pinfold] animal pen.
107. *take heed*] be careful.
'haps] perhaps.

ACT 5

[5.1]

Enter ANTHONY.

Anthony. The day is broke. Mathea and young Ned
    By this time are so surely linked together
    That none in London can forbid the banns.
    Laurentia, she is near provided for,
    So that if Harvey's policy but hold,   5
    Elsewhere the strangers may go seek them wives –
    But here they come.

Enter PISARO *and* BROWNE [*and* FRISCO].

Pisaro. Six o'clock, say you? Trust me, forward days.
    Hark you, Mouche, hie you to church;
    Bid Master Buford be in readiness.   10
    Where go you that way?
Anthony.   For my cloak, sir.
Pisaro. O, 'tis well.   [*Exit* ANTHONY.]
           And Master Browne,
    Trust me, your early stirring makes me muse:
    Is it to me your business?
Browne.   Even to yourself.
    I come, I think, to bring you welcome news.   15
Pisaro. And welcome news more welcome makes the bringer.
    Speak, speak, good Master Browne; I long to hear them.
Browne. Then this it is: young Harvey late last night,
    Full weak and sickly came unto his lodging,
    From whence this sudden malady proceeds.   20
    'Tis all uncertain; the doctors and his friends

---

16. And ... bringer] *so 1830; two lines in Q, Q2:* newes, / More; *second line missing in Q3.*   18. is: young] *this ed.;* is. Young *Qq.*

---

3. *banns*] announcement of marriage before ceremony to provide time for any impediments to be revealed.

4. *near provided for*] almost home and dry.

8. *forward*] (1) as a command, 'onward' (2) early (3) ready, spirited.

10. *Master Buford*] this is the first and last mention of this man, who could be the pastor or sexton, depending on the job Pisaro has in mind for him.

Affirm his health is unrecoverable.
Young Heigham and Ned Walgrave lately left him,
And I came hither to inform you of it.
Pisaro. Young Master Harvey, sick? Now, afore God,   25
The news bites near the bone, for should he die
His living, mortgaged, would be redeemed,
For not these three months doth the bond bear date.
Die now? Marry, God in heaven defend it!
O, my sweet lands; lose thee? Nay, lose my life.   30
And which is worst, I dare not ask mine own,
For I take two and twenty in the hundred,
When the law gives but ten. But should he live,
He careless would have left the debt unpaid.
Then had the lands been mine, Pisaro's own,   35
Mine, mine own land, mine own possession!
Browne. Nay, hear me out.
Pisaro.   You're out too much already,
Unless you give him life, and me his land.
Browne. Whether 'tis love to you, or to your daughter,
I know not certain, but the gentleman   40
Hath made a deed of gift of all his lands
Unto your beauteous daughter, fair Marina.
Pisaro. Ha! Say that word again, say it again:
A good thing cannot be too often spoken.
Marina, say you? Are you sure 'twas she –   45
Or Mary, Margery, or some other maid?
Browne. To none but your daughter, fair Marina.
And for the gift might be more forcible,
Your neighbour, Master Moore, advised us –
Who is a witness of young Harvey's will –   50
Sick as he is, to bring him to your house.
I know they are not far, but do attend,
That they may know what welcome they shall have.

---

23. *lately*] recently.

25-36.] There are several options for delivering sections of this speech directly or as aside.

26-8. *for should . . . date*] because Harvey would die before the due date.

32. *two . . . hundred*] 22 per cent interest on loans; see the discussion of interest rates in the introduction, and cf. note to 4.1.136.

37. *You're out*] (1) You're wide of the mark (2) You're too open, you've said too much.

43-4. *Ha! Say . . . spoken*] cf. Shylock's response to the good news of Antonio's lost ships, 'What, what, what? Ill luck, ill luck?' (*Merchant of Venice* 3.1.84ff).

48. *forcible*] enforceable.

51. *he*] i.e. Harvey.

52. *attend*] wait, stand by.

Pisaro. What welcome, sir? As welcome as new life
    Given to the poor, condemned prisoner.   55
    Return, good Master Browne, assure their welcome.
    Say it – nay, swear it – for they're welcome truly.
                               [Exit BROWNE.]
    For welcome are they to me which bring gold –   *[A knock.]*
    See down who knocks: it may be there they are.
    Frisco, call down my sons, bid the girls rise.   *[Exit* FRISCO.] 60
    Where's Mouche? What, is he gone or no?

        Enter LAURENTIA *in* ANTHONY's *attire.*

    O, hear you, sirrah. Bring along with you
    Master Balsaro, the Spanish merchant.
Laurentia. *[Aside]* Many Balsaros, I! I'll to my love,
    And thanks to Anthony for this escape.   65
Pisaro. Stay, take us with you.
          [He gives her a token. Exit LAURENTIA. *A knock.]*
                Hark, they knock again.
    Come, my soul's comfort, thou good news bringer;
    I must needs hug thee even for pure affection!

    Enter HARVEY *brought in a chair,* MOORE, BROWNE,
        ALVARO, VANDAL, DELION, *and* FRISCO.

Pisaro. Lift softly, good my friends, for hurting him.
    Look cheerly, sir. You're welcome to my house.   70
    [Aside] Hark, Master Vandal, and my other sons,
    Seem to be sad, as grieving for his sickness,
    But inwardly rejoice. *[Aloud.]* Master Vandal,
    Signiore Alvaro, Monsieur Delion,
    Bid my friend welcome; pray, bid him welcome. –   75
    Take a good heart. I doubt not, by God's leave,
    You shall recover and do well enough.
    [Aside] If I should think so, I should hang myself. –
    Frisco, go bid Marina come to me. –   *Exit* FRISCO.
    You are a witness, sir, of this man's will.   80
    What think you, Master Moore? What say you to't?

---

64. *Many Balsaros, I!*] An alternative reading is 'Many Balsaros, ay!' See note to
1.3.299.
   66. *Stay*] Wait.
   67–8. *my soul's . . . thee*] although the 'sick' Harvey – and perhaps Browne as 'news
bringers' of Harvey's condition – is the apparent addressee of this line, Pisaro is referring at base to the 'gold' of line 58. He is like Barabas here, who talks of his 'soul's
sole hope' and 'hugs his bags' in *The Jew of Malta* (2.1.29, 2.1.54 SD).
   70. *cheerly*] cheerful.

Moore. Master Pisaro, follow mine advice.
    You see the gentleman cannot escape:
    Then let him straight be wedded to your daughter.
    So during lifetime she shall hold his land,   85
    When now, being nor kith nor kin to him,
    For all the deed of gift that he hath sealed,
    His younger brother will enjoy the land.
Pisaro. Marry my daughter? No, by'r Lady!
    Hear you, Alvaro, my friend: counsel me,   90
    Seeing young Master Harvey is so sick,
    To marry him incontinent to my daughter,
    Or else the gift he hath bestowed is vain. –
    Marry, an he recover? No, my son,
    I will not lose thy love, for all this land.   95
Alvaro. Hear you, padre, do no lose his lands, his hundred pont per
    anno: 'tis wort to havar. Let him have de matresse Marina in de
    mariage: 'tis but vor me to attendre une day more. If he will no
    die, I sal give him sush a drinck, sush a potion, sal mak him give
    de *bonos noches* to all de world.   100
Pisaro. Alvaro, here's my keys, take all I have:
    My money, plate, wealth, jewels, daughter too!
    Now, God be thanked that I have a daughter
    Worthy to be Alvaro's bedfellow.
    O, how I do admire and praise thy wit: 105
    I'll straight about it. Hear you, Master Moore?

          Enter MARINA *and* FRISCO.

---

83. *cannot escape*] i.e. cannot escape death.
86. *When*] Whereas.
nor . . . nor] neither . . . nor.
88. *younger brother*] English law followed primogeniture, the passing of estates to eldest brothers, the younger getting no portion by automatic right; hence the amused 1830 note, 'There is generally a considerable difference between stage law and statute law'.
92. *incontinent*] (1) immediately (2) in sickness, impotence.
94. *Marry, an he recover?*] i.e. (1) But what if he should recover? (2) Get married, and then recover? (perhaps said after brief, private conference with Alvaro).
96–7. *pont per anno*] pounds per year.
97. *'tis wort to havar*] it's worth having.
98. *attendre*] wait.
99. *potion*] the Italians had a reputation for poisoning in the sixteenth century (cf. Thomas Nashe, *The Unfortunate Traveller*, 'If thou dost but lend half a looke to a *Romans* or *Italians* wife, thy porredge shalbe prepared for thee, and cost thee nothing but thy lyfe' (McKerrow ii, p. 298)).
100. *bonos noches*] good night.

Frisco. Nay, faith, he's sick; therefore, though he be come, yet he can
     do you no good. There's no remedy but even to put yourself into
     the hands of the Italian, that by that time that he hath passed his
     grouth, young Harvey will be in case to come upon it with a sise   110
     of fresh force.   [*Exit.*]
Marina. Is my love come, and sick? [*Aside*] Ay, now thou lov'st me,
     How my heart joys! [*Aloud.*] O, God, get I my will,
     I'll drive away that sickness with a kiss!
     [*Aside*] I need not feign, for I could weep for joy.   115
Pisaro. It shall be so. Come hither, daughter.
     Master Harvey, that you may see my love
     Comes from a single heart unfeignedly,
     See here my daughter: her I make thine own.
     Nay, look not strange; before these gentlemen   120
     I freely yield Marina for thy wife.
Harvey. Stay, stay, good sir, forbear this idle work.
     My soul is labouring for a higher place
     Than this vain, transitory world can yield.
     What, would you wed your daughter to a grave?   125
     For this is but death's model in man's shape.
     [*To Marina.*] You and Alvaro happy live together.
     Happy were I to see you live together.
Pisaro. Come, sir, I trust you shall do well again.
     Here, here, it must be so. God give you joy,   130
     And bless you [*Aside*] not a day to live together.
Vandal. [*To Alvaro.*] Hort ye, broder, will ye let den ander heb your
     wife? Nempt haer, nempt haer yourself!
Alvaro. [*To Vandal.*] No, no. Tush, you be de fool. Here be dat sal
     spoil de marriage of hem. [*Aside*] You have deceve me of de fine   135
     wensh, Signiore Harvey, but I sal deceve you of de mush land.

---

110. grouth] *Qq;* growth *1830.*   126. but] *Q; not in* Q2, Q3.   133. yourself!] *this
ed.;* your selve? *Qq;* yourself? *1830.*

---

110. *grouth*] old spelling of growth (*OED*), suggesting that once Alvaro has gone
as far as he can, Harvey will take over.
     in case] in a situation, in a position.
     sise] (1) sice (a six thrown on a die), hence a high quantity (2) size, i.e. a sizeable
amount (3) assize (?), a trial (of strength).
     131. *And bless ... together*] The breaking-off into a contradictory aside is a tactic
used repeatedly by Marlowe's Barabas.
     132-3. *Hort ye ... wive?*] Hear you, brother, will you let another have your
wife?.
     133. *Nempt haer*] Take her.
     134. *Tush*] dismissive remark (cf. 'Push' at 3.3.85).
     Here be dat] perhaps showing a vial, which purportedly contains poison.

Harvey. Are all things sure, father? Is all despatched?
Pisaro. What interest we have, we yield it you.
    Are you now satisfied, or rests there aught?
Harvey. Nay, father, nothing doth remain, but thanks.   140
    Thanks to yourself first, that, disdaining me,
    Yet loved my lands, and for them gave a wife.
    But next, unto Alvaro let me turn,
    To courteous, gentle, loving, kind Alvaro,
    That rather than to see me die for love,   145
    For very love, would lose his beauteous love.
                      [*He jumps up and embraces* MARINA.]
Vandal. Ha, ha, ha!
Delion. Signiore Alvaro, give him de ting quickly sal make hem dy,
    autrement you sal lose de fine wensh.
Alvaro. Oyime che havesse allhora appressata la mano al mio core,   150
    ô suen curato ate, I che longo sei tu arrivato, ô cieli, ô terra!
Pisaro. Am I awake? Or do deluding dreams
    Make that seem true, which most my soul did fear?
Harvey. Nay, faith, father, it's very certain true:
    I am as well as any man on earth.   155
    Am I sick, sirs? Look here, is Harvey sick?
Pisaro. What shall I do? What shall I say?
    [*To Browne.*] Did not you counsel me to wed my child?
    [*To Alvaro.*] What potion? Where's your help, your remedy?
Harvey. I hope more happy stars will reign today,   160
    And Don Alvaro have more company.

                Enter ANTHONY.

Anthony. [*Aside*] Now, Anthony, this cottons as it should,
    And everything sorts to his wished effect.

---

    138. *interest*] concern, investment.
    139. *rests there aught?*] does anything remain?.
    149. *autrement*] otherwise, or else.
    150–1. Oyime che . . . terra!] Alvaro is crying out in melodramatic pain, lamenting that all his effort has come to nothing; the Italian, which is disjointed and takes on the subjunctive, seems addressed to an unfair heavens, and so we should employ the article 'you' here. This extended Italian without the usual slippage into English perhaps emphasizes Alvaro's sincere distress, or perhaps it simply suggests that Haughton is roughly recalling another Italian text. Alvaro is saying something like 'Alas, that you have now oppressed my heart with your hand – oh, what dream have you wrought, alas, after all this time you come (to me in this way) – O sky, O earth!'
    161. *Don*] a Spanish title, equivalent to 'Lord' in England.
    more company] other female companions.
    162. *cottons*] follows, works (cf. to 'cotton on' to something).
    163. *sorts*] accords, fits in place.

Harvey 'joys Mall; my Dutchman and the French,
Thinking all sure, laughs at Alvaro's hap;   165
But quickly I shall mar that merry vein,
And make your fortunes equal with your friend's.

Pisaro. Sirrah, Mouche, what answer brought you back?
Will Master Balsaro come, as I requested?

Anthony. Master Balsaro? I know not who you mean.   170

Pisaro. Know you not, ass? Did I not send thee for him?
Did not I bid thee bring him, with the parson?
What answer made he: will he come or no?

Anthony. Sent me for him? Why, sir, you sent not me.
I neither went for him, nor for the parson.   175
I am glad to see your worship is so merry.   *Knock.*

Pisaro. Hence, you forgetful dolt! Look down who knocks.

Exit ANTHONY.

Enter FRISCO.

Frisco. O, Master, hang yourself! Nay, never stay for a sessions. Master
Vandal, confess yourself, desire the people to pray for you. For
your bride, she is gone. Laurentia is run away!   180

Vandal. O, de diabolo! De mal-fortune! Is Meestere Laurentia gaan
awech?

Pisaro. First, tell me that I am a lifeless corpse,
Tell me of doomsday, tell me what you will
Before you say Laurentia is gone!   185

Marina. Master Vandal, how do you feel yourself?
What, hang the head? Fie, man, for shame, I say,
Look not so heavy on your marriage day!

Harvey. O, blame him not, his grief is quickly spied,
That is a bridegroom, and yet wants his bride.   190

Enter HEIGHAM, LAURENTIA, BALSARO, *and* ANTHONY.

---

177. Hence . . . knocks] *so 1830; two lines in Qq:* dolt: / Looke . . . knocks?

164. *'joys*] enjoys.
165. *hap*] (mis)fortune.
177. *Hence, you . . . knocks*] this pentameter line is broken into two lines in Qq.
178. *sessions*] trial.
179. *confess*] take confession; admit sins before dying.
181. *de diabolo*] the devil.
mal-fortune] bad luck.
181–2. *gaan awech*] gone away.
189. *spied*] discovered, found out.

Balsaro. Master Pisaro, and gentlemen, good day to all.
    According, sir, as you requested me,
    This morn I made repair unto the Tower,
    Whereas Laurentia now was marrièd.
    And, sir, I did expect your coming thither;   195
    Yet in your absence, we performed the rites.
    Therefore, I pray, sir, bid God give them joy.
Heigham. He tells you true: Laurentia is my wife,
    Who, knowing that her sisters must be wed,
    Presuming also that you'll bid her welcome,   200
    Are come to bear them company to church.
Harvey. You come too late: the marriage rites are done.
    Yet welcome twentyfold unto the feast.
    How say you, sirs, did not I tell you true:
    These wenches would have us, and none of you?   205
Laurentia. I cannot say for these, but on my life
    This loves a cushion better than a wife.
[*Marina.*] And reason, too, that cushion fell out right,
    Else hard had been his lodging all last night.
Balsaro. Master Pisaro, why stand you speechless thus?   210
Pisaro. Anger and extreme grief enforceth me.
    Pray, sir, who bade you meet me at the Tower?
Balsaro. Who, sir? Your man, Mouche – here he is.
Anthony. Who, I, sir? Mean you me? You are a jesting man.
Pisaro. Thou art a villain, a dissembling wretch,   215
    Worser than Anthony, whom I kept last!
    Fetch me an officer: I'll hamper you
    And make you sing at Bridewell for this trick;

---

208. SP [*Marina.*]] *1830; Mall. Qq.*

---

    193. *made repair*] went, resorted.
    Tower] i.e. Tower of London (see Appendix).
    194. *Whereas*] Where.
    now] just now.
    202. *the marriage rites are done*] 'In the Elizabethan Age a betrothal before wit-
nesses and with the consent of the parent(s) or a trothplight sealed by the parties living
together (or its equivalent) was as binding as an actual marriage ceremony and was
often loosely referred to as a marriage' (Baugh).
    207. *This*] i.e. Vandal.
    208. SP [*Marina.*]] Mathea is given this speech in Qq, but she is not on stage at this
time.
    fell out right] worked out nicely, was useful.
    217. *hamper*] stop.
    218. *sing at Bridewell*] i.e. be a 'gaol-bird' at Bridewell prison (see Appendix).

For well he hath deserved it, that would swear
He went not forth adoors at my appointment.   220
Anthony. So swear I still: I went not forth today.
Balsaro. Why, arrant liar! Wert thou not with me?
Pisaro. How say you, Master Browne, went he not forth?
Browne. He, or his likeness, did; I know not whether.
Pisaro. What likeness can there be, besides himself?   225
Laurentia. Myself, forsooth, that took his shape upon me.
    I was that Mouche that you sent from home,
    And that same Mouche that deceived you,
    Effected to possess this gentleman,
    Which to attain, I thus beguiled you all.   230
Frisco. This is excellent. This is as fine as a fiddle! You, Master
    Heigham, got the wench in Mouche's apparel; now let Mouche
    put on her apparel and be married to the Dutchman. How think
    you? Is it not a good 'vice?
Moore. Master Pisaro, shake off melancholy: 235
    When things are helpless, patience must be used.
Pisaro. Talk of patience? I'll not bear these wrongs.
    Go call down Matt and mistress Susan Moore.
    'Tis well that, of all three, we have one sure.
Moore. Mistress Susan Moore? Who do you mean, sir?   240
Pisaro. Whom should I mean, sir, but your daughter?
Moore. You're very pleasant, sir. But tell me this:
    When did you see her, that you speak of her?
Pisaro. I? Late yesternight, when she came here to bed.
Moore. You are deceived: my daughter lay not here,   245
    But watched with her sick mother all last night.
Pisaro. I am glad you are so pleasant, Master Moore;
    You're loth that Susan should be held a sluggard.

---

234. 'vice?] *this ed.;* vize *Qq;* vise? *1830;* vice? *Haz.*   244. I?] *Haz;* I, *Qq.*

220. *appointment*] command, instruction.
222. *arrant*] absolute, notorious.
224. *whether*] which (one).
229. *Effected*] So disguised, Made thus in order.
231. *fine as a fiddle!*] cf. note to 'as fit as a fiddle' (3.3.24).
234. *'vice*] device, idea (?), trope.
236–7. *patience . . . patience*] another familiar plea to usurers: cf. *Hog* 5.3.20, and the Jews of Malta imploring Barabas to have patience: *The Jew of Malta* 1.2.170ff.
242. *pleasant*] merry, joking.
244. *I?*] this could read 'Ay,' but more likely responding to the '*When* did *you*' of Moore's question, thus '*I? Late yesternight*'.
248. *loth*] averse (to the idea).
sluggard] habitually lazy person.

What, man, 'twas late before she went to bed,
And therefore time enough to rise again.   250
Moore. Master Pisaro, do you flout your friends?
    I well perceive, if I had troubled you
    I should have had it in my dish ere now.
    Susan lie here? I'm sure when I came forth
    I left her fast asleep in bed at home.   255
    'Tis more than neighbourhood to use me thus.
Pisaro. Abed at your house? Tell me I am mad!
    Did not I let her in adoors myself?
    Spoke to her, talked with her, and canvassed with her?
    And yet she lay not here? What say you, sirrah?   260
Anthony. She did, she did. I brought her to her chamber.
Moore. I say he lies, that saith so, in his throat.
Anthony. Mass, now I remember me, I lie indeed!
Pisaro. O, how this frets me! Frisco, what say you?
Frisco. What say I? Marry, I say if she lay not here, there was a familiar   265
    in her likeness. For I am sure my master and she were so familiar
    together that he had almost shot the gout out of his toes' ends to
    make the wench believe he had one trick of youth in him. Yet now
    I remember me, she did not lie here; and the reason is because she
    doth lie here, and is now abed with Mistress Mathea: witness   270

---

249. 'twas] *1830.;* t'was *Q;* t was *Q2;* twas *Q3.*   254. I'm] *1830;* 'am *Q, Q2;* I am
Q3.

---

251. *flout*] scorn, disdain.

253. *in my dish*] proverbial, cf. Tilley T155 'to lay (cast) a Thing in one's dish'; '=
to reproach or taunt him with it'.

256. *neighbourhood*] neighbourly behaviour.
    use] treat.

259. *canvassed*] petitioned, put my case forward. Baugh notes, 'So Q1. The reading
is not quite free from suspicion of corruption, though the NED gives as meanings of
canvass (4d and 5) "to debate; to discuss" and "? To bargain or deal with; to sound
or try as to their expectations". The last sense would especially suit the passage in
the text. The word may, however, be an error for "conuerst" to which Q3 changes it'
(pp. 230–1); *conversed* is possible, since it goes with 'spoke' and 'talk' as a line of
repetitions.

262. *in his throat*] a lie constituting a challenge and requiring substantiation by the
accuser, or retaliation form the accused (cf. note to 3.2.129).

264. *frets*] worries, disturbs.

265. *familiar*] demonic likeness, spirit, double.

267. *gout*] disease producing painful inflammation of joints, usually in the feet and
legs; traditionally a usurer's disease.

268. *trick*] spark.

whereof, I have set to my hand and seal, and mean presently to
fetch her.   *Exit.*
Pisaro. Do so, Frisco. Gentlemen and friends,
   Now shall you see how I am wronged by him.
   Lay she not here? I think the world's grown wise: 275
   Plain folks, as I, shall not know how to live.

                     Enter FRISCO.

Frisco. She comes, she comes; a hall, a hall!

        Enter MATHEA, *and* WALGRAVE *in woman's attire.*

Walgrave. Nay, blush not, wench; fear not, look cheerfully.
   Good morrow, father; good morrow, gentlemen.
   Nay, stare not; look you here, no monster, I,   280
   But even plain Ned. And here stands Matt, my wife.
   Know you her, Frenchman? But she knows me better.
   Father, pray father, let me have your blessing,
   For I have blessed you with a goodly son.
   'Tis breeding here, i'faith, a jolly boy.   285
Pisaro. I am undone! A reprobate, a slave,
   A scorn, a laughter, and a jesting stock!
   Give me my child; give me my daughter from you!
Moore. Master Pisaro, 'tis in vain to fret
   And fume and storm: it little now avails.   290
   These gentlemen have, with your daughters' help,
   Outstripped you in your subtle enterprises.
   And, therefore, seeing they are well descended,
   Turn hate to love, and let them have their loves.
Pisaro. Is it even so? Why, then, I see that still,   295
   Do what we can, women will have their will.
   Gentlemen, you have outreached me now,
   Which ne'er, before you, any yet could do.
   You that I thought should be my sons indeed

---

296. we] *Q, Q2;* you *Q3.*

---

271. *hand and seal*] mock legality of Frisco's statement: he has applied his own
signature and seal to affirm his words.
   274. *him*] i.e. Moore.
   275. *grown wise*] said ironically (i.e. the world has gone mad).
   277. *a hall!*] a cry to clear a room for an event.
   282. *Know . . . knows me*] Recognize . . . knows me sexually.
   285. *here*] i.e. in Mathea's womb.
   286. *undone*] foiled, ruined.
   reprobate] (usually morally) wicked, depraved person.
   293. *well descended*] of good birth, high social class.
   297. *outreached*] cf. 'overreached' at 3.4.68 and note.

Must be content, since there's no hope to speed.   300
Others have got what you did think to gain,
And yet, believe me, they have took some pain.
Well, take them, there; and with them, God give joy.
And, gentlemen, I do entreat tomorrow
That you will feast with me, for all this sorrow.   305
Though you are wedded, yet the feast's not made:
Come, let us in, for all the storms are passed,
And heaps of joy will follow on as fast.   [*Exeunt.*]

FINIS.

307. passed] *this ed.*; past *Qq.*

300. *speed*] be successful.
307. *passed*] Qq's 'past' is possible; since 'tomorrow' in line 304 implies the future, talking of things as being 'in the past' seems to maintain a pleasing lexical balance.

THE HOG HATH LOST HIS PEARL

THE ACTORS' NAMES

OLD LORD WEALTHY.
YOUNG LORD [WEALTHY], *his son.*
MARIA, *his daughter.*
CARRACUS,
ALBERT, } *two gentlemen, near friends.* 5
LIGHTFOOT, *a country gentleman.*
HADDIT, *a youthful gallant.*
HOG, *a usurer.*
REBECCA, *his daughter.*
PETER SERVITUDE, *his man.* 10
ATLAS, *a porter.*
PRIEST.
PLAYER.
SERVINGMAN.
NURSE. 15
[ECHO.]
[Servants.]
[Satyrs.]

THE ACTORS' NAMES] *Placed after Prologue in* Q. CARRACUS...] Carracus *and* Albert, *two Gentlemen, nere friends* Q.

---

4. *CARRACUS*] A carrack is a large warship or galleon, perhaps indicating the character's steadfastness among the play's storms of adversity. Caracas, as the capital of Venezuela, may be relevant; named by the Spanish in 1567, it seems to be used (spelled 'Corrucus') in early modern drama to denote a distant location of loss, the unknown, or the impossible (it might be better applied to the reclusive Albert): see, for example, George Chapman's *The Blind Beggar of Alexandria* (1598), where 'Corrucus' is used in this way multiple times (2.106; 4.146; 5.89).

7. *HADDIT*] The name suggests the past tense of possession – Haddit the prodigal had it all, but now it's gone.

8. *HOG*] Usurers were proverbially compared with pigs because they are greedy, slothful, and useful as meat only after death; see the introduction to the play for references to this trope.

PROLOGUE

Our long-time-rumoured Hog – so often crossed
By unexpected accidents, and tossed
From one house to another, still deceiving
Many men's expectations, and bequeathing
To some lost labour – is at length got loose,   5
Leaving his servile yoke-stick to the goose,
Hath a knight's licence, and may range at pleasure,
Spite of all those that envy our Hog's treasure.
And thus much let me tell you, that our swine
Is not, as diverse critics did define,   10
Grunting at State affairs, or invecting
Much at our city vices; no, nor detecting
The pride or fraud in it; but, were it now
He had his first birth, wit should teach him how
To tax these times' abuses, and tell some   15
How ill they did in running oft from home,
For to prevent – O men more hard than flint! –
A matter that shall laugh at them in print.

---

10. define] *Q;* devine *Dod MS.*

1. *long-time-rumoured*] anticipated, talked about (perhaps with direct reference to Mayor Swinnerton – see the introduction to the play).
crossed] thwarted, opposed.
3. *house*] i.e. playhouse.
6. *yoke-stick to the goose*] stick or sticks attached to animals neck as a yoke or harness to work machinery; a goose is a proverbial fool (*OED* 'goose' 1.e, f).
7. *knight's licence*] i.e. patronage; permission to play. Presumably Sir George Buck, whose name appears in the Stationers' Register and at the end of the 1614 play-text.
11–12. *Grunting ... vices*] Discussing (and possibly slandering) personages in national and local politics. Discussion of matters of State or Church on stage were banned by an Act of 1559; see the introduction to the play for a discussion of *Hog's* commentary on 'city vices'.
11. *invecting*] inveighing, uttering invectives (denunciatory, railing language); this line is cited in *OED*.
13–18. *were it now ... in print*] these lines may allude to George Withers, *Abuses Stript and Whipt* (1613), which spends the bulk of its time listing the moral and political abuses of the city's traders, merchants, and authorities.

Once, to proceed in this play we were mindless,
Thinking we lived 'mongst Jews, that loved no swine's flesh: 20
But now that trouble's passed. If it deserve a hiss,
As questionless it will through our amiss,
Let it be favoured by your gentle sufferance:
Wise men are still indued with patience:
We are not half so skilled as strolling players,   25
Who could not please here, as at country fairs:
We may be pelted off, for aught we know,
With apples, eggs, or stones, from thence below;
In which we'll crave your friendship, if we may,
And you shall have a dance worth all the play;   30
And if it prove so happy as to please,
We'll say 'tis fortunate, like Pericles.

---

19. Once, to] *this ed.;* Once to *Q, etc.*   21. passed] *this ed.;* past *Q, Dod, etc.*   32. Pericles] *Q prints the prologue in italic and this word in roman font. Dod, Reed, Coll all italic; Scott, Haz all roman.*

---

19. *were mindless*] did not think of it; were careless.

20. *Thinking . . . swine's flesh*] i.e. thinking that there would not be many Hog-lovers to complain about our representation; usury was proverbially the trade of Jews.

25. *strolling*] travelling, journeymen.

28. *from thence below*] from that part of the audience standing or sitting down in front (or lower than, hence below) the stage.

30. *a dance*] a jig commonly followed play performances.

32. *Pericles*] Prince of Tyre, subject of a Shakespearean romance play. The word may refer to the title of the play, noting its commercial success. Steevens, writing a note for Reed's edition, writes, 'Perhaps a sneer was designed. To say that a dramatic piece was *fortunate*, is not to say it was *deserving*: and why of all the pieces supposed to be written by our great Author was this particularized?' (Reed, p. 379). The simple answer is perhaps that the fortunate character, not the play, is being ostensibly referred to by the Prologue. Collier responded to Steevens's note with his own: 'There is good reason to dispute this interpretation of the word fortunate, but Mr. Steevens seems to have discovered many sneers at Shakespeare that were never intended' (Collier p. 331).

ACT I

Act 1, Scene 1

Enter LIGHTFOOT, *a country gentleman, passing over the stage,
and knocks at the other door.*

Lightfoot. Ho, who's within here?

Enter ATLAS, *a porter.*

Atlas. Ha' ye any money to pay, you knock with such authority, sir?

Lightfoot. What if I have not? May not a man knock without money,
    sir?

Atlas. Seldom. Women and sergeants, they will not put it up so, sir.   5

Lightfoot. How say you by that, sir? But, I prithee, is not this one Atlas
    his house, a porter?

Atlas. I am the rent-payer thereof.

Lightfoot. In good time, sir.

Atlas. Not in good time neither, sir, for I am behind with my landlord   10
    a year and three-quarters at least.

Lightfoot. Now, if a man would give but observance to this fellow's
    prating, 'a would weary his ears sooner than a barber. D'ye hear,
    sir? Lies there not one Haddit, a gentleman, at this house?

Atlas. Here lies such a gentleman, sir, whose clothes – were they not   15
    greasy – would bespeak him so.

Act 1, Scene 1] *Q has* 'Actus primi Scena prima' *under the title, which is ranged as
follows:* 'THE / HOGGE HATH / lost his Pearle'.   5. sergeants] *this ed.;* Seriaunts
Q; servants *Dod, etc.*

  0.2. the other door] This stage direction assumes two doors in the *frons scenae.*

  2. *money*] for lodging, or for generous tips.

  5. *sergeants*] Dodsley et al. emend to 'servants', suggesting a domestic – and perhaps
sexual – connection between the groups mentioned here; 'sergeants', however, seems
to refer credibly to the city watch not putting up with noise in the street by the poor.

  put it up so] (1) put up with it (2) put in a receptacle for safe keeping (continuing
the possible sexual suggestion).

  9–10. *In good time . . . neither*] i.e. (1) Finally, an answer (2) Never mind about
that; tell me about it later (3) You answered the door very slowly . . . This is not a
happy period in my life because I'm in financial trouble.

  13. *prating*] chattering.

  weary . . . a barber] Barbers were proverbially garrulous, since they heard and
imparted all the town's gossip.

  16. *bespeak him so*] i.e. show him to be a gentleman.

[*Lightfoot.*] Then I pray, sir, when your leisure shall permit, that you
  would vouchsafe to help me to the speech of him.

Atlas. We must first crave your oath, sir, that you come not with intent
  to molest, perturb, or endanger him; for he is a gentleman, whom   20
  it hath pleased Fortune to make her tennis ball of, and therefore
  subject to be struck by every fool into hazard.

Lightfoot. In that I commend thy care of him, for which friendship
  here's a slight reward [*Gives Atlas money.*]; tell him a countryman
  of his, one Lightfoot, is here, and he will not any way despair of   25
  his safety.

Atlas. With all respect, sir; pray, command my house.   *Exit.*

Lightfoot. So, now I shall have a sight of my cousin gallant: he that
  hath consumed eight hundred pound a year in as few years as he
  hath ears on his head; he that was wont never to be found without   30
  three or four pair of red breeches running before his horse or
  coach; he that at a meal hath had more several kinds than I think
  the ark contained; he that was admired by niters for his robes of
  gallantry, and was indeed all that an elder brother might be –
  prodigal; yet he, whose unthriftiness kept many a house, is now   35
  glad to keep house in a house that keeps him the poor tenant of a
  porter. And see his appearance! I'll seem strange to him.

Enter HADDIT in poor array.

---

17. SP [*Lightfoot.*]] *Dod, etc.; not in* Q.   25. he] *Dod, etc.; not in* Q, *Coll;* [he]
Haz.   34–5. be – prodigal; yet he,] *Haz;* be, prodigall, yet he, *Q;* be, prodigal; yet
he, *Dod, Reed, Coll.*   36. tenant] *Dod, etc.;* tente Q.

---

  18. *vouchsafe*] grant.
  to the speech of him] i.e. to his presence, to converse with him.
  21–2. *tennis-ball . . . hazard*] the hazards in the game of 'real' tennis, an indoor
pastime, are openings in the wall into which balls are hit to score points; Haddit is
being battered around by others for their own gain.
  27. *command my house*] make yourself at home, ask for whatever you will.
  31. *red breeches*] i.e. servants with livery (uniform).
  33. *niters*] 'If this be not a corrupted, it must be an affected, word, coined from the
Latin word *niteo*, to shine, or be splendid. He was admir'd by those who *shone* most
in the article of dress' (Reed p. 382). Reed cites Marston's *Satires*, printed with *Pyg-
malion* in 1598, 'O dapper, rare, compleat, sweet nittie youth!' Collier adds to Reed,
'Niters however may be a corruption of *niflers*. Chaucer uses *nifles* for *trifles*. See
Sompnour's Tale . . . "He served him with *nifles* and with fables"' (Collier p. 334). I
don't find convincing connections of the word to clothing, as Reed suggests; 'nitre's'
connection to saltpeter or something volatile might be relevant (*OED* 'nitre' I.1.a).
  35–6. *kept . . . keep . . . keeps*] managed, was in charge of . . . reside, fend for himself
domestically . . . maintains, imprisons.
  37. *strange*] unknown, a stranger.
  37.1. *poor array*] meagre apparel.

Haddit. Cousin Lightfoot, how dost? Welcome to the city.

Lightfoot. Who calls me cousin? Where's my cousin Haddit? He's
surely putting on some rich apparel for me to see him in. I ha' been   40
thinking all the way I came up, how much his company will credit
me.

Haddit. My name is Haddit, sir, and your kinsman, if parents may be
trusted; and therefore you may please to know me better when you
see me next.   45

Lightfoot. I prithee, fellow, stay: is it possible thou shouldst be he?
Why, he was the generous spark of men's admiration.

Haddit. I am that spark, sir, though now raked up in ashes;
Yet when it pleaseth Fortune's chops to blow
Some gentler gale upon me, I may then   50
From forth of embers rise and shine again.

Lightfoot. O, by your versifying I know you now, sir. How dost? I
knew thee not at first; thou'rt very much altered.

Haddit. Faith, and so I am, exceeding much since you saw me last:
about eight hundred pound a year; but let it pass, for passage   55
carried away the most part of it – a plague of Fortune!

Lightfoot. Thou'st more need to pray to Fortune than curse her; she
may be kind to thee when thou art penitent, but that, I fear, will
be never.

Haddit. O, no, if she be a woman, she'll ever love those that hate her.   60
But, cousin, thou art thy father's firstborn; help me but to some
means, and I'll redeem my mortgaged lands, with a wench to
boot.

Lightfoot. As how, I pray thee?

Haddit. Marry thus: Hog the usurer hath one only daughter.   65

Lightfoot. Is his name Hog? It fits him exceeding well, for as a hog in
his lifetime is always devouring, and never commodious in aught
till his death, even so is he, whose goods at that time may be put
to many good uses.

---

49. chops] *Q, Dod, etc.;* chaps *Haz.* 53. thou'rt] thart *Q.* 57. Thou'st] *Dod,
etc.;* That'st *Q.* Fortune] *Haz;* fortune *Q, Dod, etc.*

41. *credit*] benefit me (in my business in the city).
49. *chops*] lips, mouth.
55. *let it pass*] never mind about that.
   passage] the word suggests legitimate trade, but passage is also a game at dice (*OED*
IV.15): 'Passage is a game at dice to be play'd at but by two, and it is performed with
three dice. The caster throws continually till he hath thrown dubblets under ten, and
then he is out and loseth; or dubblets above ten, and then he *passeth* and wins' (*Compleat Gamester* 1680, p. 119).
62. *means*] benefit, (way to get) money.
62-3. *to boot*] in addition.

Haddit. And so I hope they shall before his death. This daughter of his   70
    did, and I think doth love me; but I, then thinking myself worthy
    of an empress, gave but slight respect unto her favour, for that her
    parentage seemed not to equal my high thoughts, puffed up –
Lightfoot. With tobacco, surely.
Haddit. No, but with as bad a weed: vainglory.   75
Lightfoot. And you could now be content to put your lofty spirits into
    the lowest pit of her favour. Why, what means will serve, man?
    'Sfoot, if all I have will repair thy fortunes, it shall fly at thy
    command.
Haddit. Thanks, good coz; the means shall not be great, only that I   80
    may first be clad in a generous outside, for that is the chief attrac-
    tion that draws female affection. Good parts, without any habili-
    ments of gallantry, are no more set by in these times than a good
    leg in a woollen stocking. No, 'tis a glistering presence and audac-
    ity brings women into fools' felicity.   85
Lightfoot. Y'ave a good confidence, coz; but what d'ye intend your
    brave outside shall effect?
Haddit. That being had, we'll to the usurer, where you shall offer some
    slight piece of land to mortgage, and if you do it to bring ourselves

---

71. I, then] *Haz;* I then *Q, Dod, etc.*   82–3. habiliments] *Dod, etc.;* abilements
Q.   84. stocking] *Dod, etc.;* stocken *Q.*   85. fools'] *this ed.;* fooles *Q;* fool's *Dod,*
etc.   86. d'ye intend] *this ed.;* deendien *Q;* do ye think *Dod, etc.*

---

71. *then*] at that time.
    74. *tobacco*] Smoking (or 'drinking' tobacco, as the saying went) was very fashion-
able among gallants in early seventeenth-century England.
    76–7. *lofty . . . favour*] bawdiness: 'spirit' was slang for semen, 'pit' and 'favour'
could both suggest vagina; cf. *Englishmen* 'your French spirit is up so far already'
(3.3.58–9), and *Hamlet*: 'Then you live about her waist, or in the middle of her favour?
/ Faith, her privates we' (2.2.27–9), and *King Lear*: 'Down from the waist . . . / There's
the sulphurous pit' (4.6.121, 125).
    78. *'Sfoot*] God's foot (a mild oath).
    80. *coz*] i.e. cousin (used in the period for unrelated friends as well as blood
relatives).
    81. *outside*] i.e. clothing.
    82–3. *habiliments*] clothing, outfitting.
    84. *woollen*] wool was the familiar, cheap, English cloth of the masses.
    86. *d'ye intend*] Q's 'deendien' is clearly corrupt, and Dodsley's 'do ye think' is his
personal replacement. This edition's 'd'ye intend' captures something of the sound of
the corrupt set of letters that remain, and it is a favoured term of Tailor's: exactly the
same phrase is used at 1.4.82, the comparable 'To what intent d'ye' appears at 2.4.31,
there are multiple related incidences of questions and statements with 'intend' or
'intent', and five instances of 'd'ye'.

into cash, it shall be ne'er the further from you, for here's a project   90
will not be frustrate of this purpose.

Lightfoot. That shall be shortly tried. I'll instantly go seek for a habit
for thee, and that of the richest too; that which shall not be subject
to the scoff of any gallant, though to the accomplishing thereof all
my means goes. Alas, what's a man unless he wear good clothes?   95
Exit.

Haddit. Good speed attend my suit. Here's a never-seen nephew, kind
in distress; this gives me more cause of admiration than the loss of
thirty-five settings together at passage. Ay, when 'tis performed –
but words and deeds are now more different than Puritans and
players.   100

Enter ATLAS.

Atlas. Here's the player would speak with you.

Haddit. About the jig I promised him – my pen and ink! I prithee, let
him in, there may be some cash rhymed out of him.

Enter PLAYER.

Player. The Muses assist you, sir: what, at your study so early?

Haddit. O, chiefly now, sir; for *Aurora Musis amica.*   105

Player. Indeed, I understand not Latin, sir.

Haddit. You must then pardon me, good Master Change-coat; for I
protest unto ye, it is so much my often converse that, if there be
none but women in my company, yet cannot I forbear it.

---

108. unto ye] *this ed.;* untee *Q;* unto you *Dod, etc.*

90–1. *it shall . . . purpose*] [the land] can hardly be considered out of your hands
because this is a foolproof plan.

91. *frustrate*] thwarted.

92. *a habit*] set of clothes.

94. *scoff*] derision.

though] even if.

96. *suit*] (1) plan (2) suit of clothes.

98. *thirty-five settings*] i.e. thirty-five sittings, losing thirty-five times in a row.

99–100. *Puritans and players*] the ultimate comparative of difference; there were
many Puritan anti-theatrical tracts published in early modern England.

105. Aurora Musis amica] Latin: Dawn is friend of the Muses.

107. *Master Change-coat*] i.e. because the addressee is a player, who changes
apparel frequently.

108. *often converse*] usual mode of conversation.

109. *women*] i.e. those who would not understand.

yet cannot I forbear it] still I cannot resist (or help myself) using it (i.e. Latin).

Player. That shows your more learning, sir; but, I pray you, is that   110
     small matter done I entreated for?
Haddit. A small matter! You'll find it worth *Meg of Westminster*,
     although it be but a bare jig.
Player. O Lord, sir, I would it had but half the taste of garlic.
Haddit. Garlic stinks to this: prove that you have not more whores to   115
     see this than e'er garlic had, say I am a boaster of mine own works,
     disgrace me on the open stage, and bob me off with ne'er a
     penny.
Player. O Lord, sir, far be it from us to debar any worthy writer of his
     merit; but I pray you, sir, what is the title you bestow upon it?   120
Haddit. Marry, that which is full as forcible as garlic. The name of it
     is, 'Who buys my four ropes of hard onions?' by which four ropes
     is meant four several kind of livers; by the onions, hangers-on, as
     at some convenient time I will more particularly inform you in so
     rare a hidden and obscure mystery.   125
Player. I pray, let me see the beginning of it. I hope you have made no
     dark sentence in't; for I'll assure you our audience commonly are
     very simple, idle-headed people, and if they should hear what they
     understand not, they would quite forsake our house.
Haddit. O, ne'er fear it, for what I have writ is both witty to the wise   130
     and pleasing to the ignorant, for you shall have those laugh at it
     far more heartily that understand it not than those that do.

---

115. prove] *Q;* if it prove *Dod, etc.*   125. mystery] *Dod, etc.;* a mystery *Q.*   127–8.
assure you our audience commonly are very simple] *Qc; Qu* omits 'you' and
'are'.   131–2. those . . . those] *Qc;* these . . . those *Qu.*

---

112. *worth Meg of Westminster*] i.e. excellent, highly popular (as evidenced by
Henslowe's *Diary*). Collier notes that in Field's *Amends for Ladies*, the name denotes
a 'conspicuous damsel'; he adds, 'Perhaps this was the title [of] general approbation'.
Indeed, this play's penchant for reference to other drama suggests it may well refer to
'Moll' of *The Roaring Girl* herself. Meg of Westminster is also a character in one of
Thomas Deloney's (1543?–1600) stories in his prose fiction collection *The Gentle Craft;*
there is also the later short extant book entitled *The Life of Long Meg of Westminster,*
containing the mad merry pranks she played in her lifetime . . . (1635).
     113. *bare*] simple, unadorned.
     114. *taste of garlic*] spice, verve.
     115. *to this*] compared with this.
     115–16. *whores . . . garlic*] garlic was used to disguise bad breath; there seems to
be a play on the name of a jig in Tailor's possible allusion to his namesake John
Taylor, the water poet, who refers to 'the Jig of Garlic, or the Punk's Delight' (*OED*
'garlic' n. (2).
     117. *bob me off*] get rid of me, send me away.
     123. *livers*] persons, examples of social group.
     125. *mystery*] art, cunning.
     127. *dark sentence*] mysterious, difficult sayings, allusions.
     129. *house*] i.e. playhouse.

Player. Methinks the end of this staff is a foot too long.

Haddit. O, no, sing it but in tune, and I dare warrant you.

Player. Why, hear ye: 135

    He sings.

    And you that delight in trulls and minions

    Come buy my four ropes of hard St Thomas onions.

    Look you there: 'St Thomas' might very well have been left out;

    besides, 'hard' should have come next the 'onions'.

Haddit. Fie, no! The dismembering of a rhyme to bring in reason shows   140
    the more efficacy in the writer.

Player. Well, as you please; I pray you, sir, what will the gratuity be?
    I would content you as near hand as I could.

Haddit. (*Aside*) So I believe. [*To him again.*] Why, Master Change-
    coat, I do not suppose we shall differ many pounds; pray, make   145
    your offer: if you give me too much, I will, most doctor-of-physic-
    like, restore.

Player. You say well; look you, sir, there's a brace of angels, besides
    much drink of free cost, if it be liked.

Haddit. How, Master Change-coat! A brace of angels, besides much   150
    drink of free cost, if it be liked? I fear you have learned it by heart;
    if you have powdered up my plot in your sconce, you may home,
    sir, and instruct your poet over a pot of ale the whole method on't.
    But if you do so juggle, look to't. Shrove Tuesday is at hand, and
    I have some acquaintance with bricklayers and plasterers.   155

---

133. Methinks] *Dod, etc.;* Me thinke *Q.*   staff] *Q;* stave *Dod, etc.*   137. St Thomas]
this ed., after Q (S. Thomas); sir Thomas's *Dod, Reed;* Sir Thomas's *Scott;* S. Thomas's
Coll; St Thomas's *Haz.*   146. doctor-of-physic-like] *Haz, after Dod (as Hazlitt, but
unhyphenated) and Qc* (Doctor of Phisicke like); Doctor of Phicke like *Qu.*

    133. *staff*] i.e. stave, a line of music.

    foot] metrical measure (in scanning poetry); the player's line here is hypermetrical,
and, if intended to be poetry, a foot too long.

    137. *St Thomas*] a variety of onion; *OED* cites Barnabe Rich, *His farewell to mili-
tary profession* (1581), 'They are sometimes rounde like to Saincte Thomas onions'
(1846, p. 218).

    146–7. *doctor-of-physic-like*] like a doctor of medicine.

    148. *a brace of angels*] a pair of angels (gold coins each worth 10 shillings – half a
pound – stamped with the image of the arch angel Michael killing Satan as a dragon).

    152. *powdered up*] preserved, stored up (hence, remembered).

    sconce] head.

    154. *juggle*] cheat.

    Shrove Tuesday] The holiday preceding the beginning of Lent with carnival, holiday,
and opportunity for riotous behaviour by apprentices; Dekker's play *The Shoemaker's
Holiday* is based around such festivity.

    155. *bricklayers and plasterers*] apprentices who will apparently gather up in
support of him; there is probably a class-biased suggestion that these are two of the
professions most likely to yield combative men.

Player. Nay, I pray, sir, be not angry, for as I am a true stage-trotter,
   I mean honestly; and look ye, more for your love than otherwise,
   I give you a brace more.

Haddit. Well, good words do much. I cannot now be angry with you,
   but see henceforward you do like him that would please a new-   160
   married wife: show your most at first, lest some other come between
   you and your desires, for I protest, had you not suddenly shown
   your good nature, another should have had it, though't had been
   for nothing.

Player. Troth, I am sorry I gave you such cause of impatiency; but you   165
   shall see hereafter, if your invention take, I will not stand off for
   a brace more or less, desiring I may see your works before
   another.

Haddit. Nay, before all others; and shortly expect a notable piece of
   matter, such a jig whose tune with the natural whistle of a carman,   170
   shall be more ravishing to the ears of shopkeepers than a whole
   consort of barbers at midnight.

Player. I am your man for't; I pray you, command all the kindness
   belongs to my function, as a box for your friend at a new play,
   although I procure the hate of all my company.   175

Haddit. No, I'll pay for it rather; that may breed a mutiny in your
   whole house.

Player. I care not. I ha' played a king's part any time these ten years;
   if I cannot command such a matter, 'twere poor, i'faith.

Haddit. Well, Master Change-coat, you shall now leave me, for I'll to   180
   my study; the morning hours are precious, and my Muse meditates
   most upon an empty stomach.

Player. I pray, sir, when this new invention is produced, let not me be
   forgotten.

Haddit. I'll sooner forget to be a jig-maker.   *Exit* PLAYER.   185

---

163. though 't had] *this ed.;* though t'ad *Q;* tho' it had *Dod;* though it had *Reed,*
etc. 169. shortly] *Dod, etc.;* shotly *Q.* 179. if] *Q;* and if *Dod, etc.* 185–6.
I'll ... So] *Haz; line break* (I'll ... / So) *in Dod, etc.*

---

157. *I mean honestly*] My intentions are honourable.

166. *if your invention take*] if your muse takes hold, if your wit is fruitful.

170. *carman*] one who drives a car, or cart, of goods around the city.

171–2. *shopkeepers ... midnight*] the tune will be so fabulous that a simple carman
delivering goods to the shopkeepers would charm them with singing it more than would
a group of barbers, proverbially good harmony singers; the time of 'midnight' suggests
that there may be a play on 'shopkeepers' as keepers of brothels looking forward to
'ravishing' visits from barbers.

174. *as*] such as.

a box] suggesting an indoor, private theatre.

175. *procure the hate ... company*] i.e. because depriving them of the income they
would receive from the box that the player is providing *gratis.*

So, here's four angels I little dreamt of. Nay, an there be money
to be gotten by foolery, I hope Fortune will not see me want. Atlas,
Atlas!

Enter ATLAS.

What, was my country coz here since?
Atlas. Why, did he promise to come again, seeing how the case stood   190
wi' ye?
Haddit. Yea, and to advance my downfallen fortunes, Atlas.
Atlas. But ye are not sure 'a meant it ye, when he spake it.
Haddit. No, nor is it in man to conjecture rightly the thought by the
tongue.   195
Atlas. Why, then I'll believe it when I see it. If you had been in prosper-
ity when he had promised you this kindness –
Haddit. I had not needed it.
Atlas. But being now you do, I fear you must go without it.
Haddit. If I do, Atlas, be it so; I'll e'en go write this rhyme over my   200
bed's head:
Undone by folly, Fortune lend me more.
Canst thou, and wilt not? Pox on such a whore!
And so I'll set up my rest. But see, Atlas, here's a little of that that
damns lawyers; take it in part of a further recompense.   205
Atlas. No, pray keep it; I am conceited of your better fortunes, and
therefore will stay out that expectation.
Haddit. Why, if you will, you may, but the surmounting of my fortunes
is as much to be doubted as he whose estate lies in the lottery:
desperate.   210
Atlas. But ne'er despair. 'Sfoot, why should not you live as well as a
thousand others that wear change of taffeta, whose means were
never anything?
Haddit. Yes, cheating, theft, and panderizing, or, maybe, flattery – I
have maintained some of them myself. But come, hast aught to   215
breakfast?

191. wi' ye] *Haz;* wye *Q;* w'ye *Dod, etc.*   192. Yea] *Dod, etc.;* Ye *Q.*   197. kindness
–] *Dod, etc.;* kindenesse, *Q.*   205. damns] *Dod, etc.;* dambs *Q.*   212. taffeta] *this
ed.;* taffety *Q, Dod, etc.;* taffata *Haz.*

188. *want*] lack, go without.
202–3. *Fortune,. . . a whore!*] Fortune's a whore because she visits many men –
seemingly randomly and unfairly – with 'favours'.
204. *set up my rest*] risk, venture, hazard all on something (*OED* 'rest' n.² (7)).
204–5. *that that damns lawyers*] i.e. money (used for lawyers' bribes).
206. *am conceited*] have an opinion, am favourably minded.
207. *stay out that expectation*] wait it out, take the risk on my hunch.
212. *taffeta*] referring to various fabrics over time, but usually with the sense of a
high-quality material, either a fine linen or a silk cloth.
214. *panderizing*] being a male bawd, pimping.
215. *maintained*] practised.

Atlas. Yes, there's the fag-end of a leg of mutton.
Haddit. There cannot be a sweeter dish; it has cost money the
    dressing.
Atlas. At the barber's, you mean.   *Exeunt [ambo].*   220

[1.2]

                    Enter ALBERT, *solus.*

Albert. This is the green, and this the chamber window,
    And see, th'appointed light stands in the casement,
    The ladder of ropes set orderly; yet he
    That should ascend, slow in his haste, is not
    As yet come hither.   5
    Were't any friend that lives but Carracus,
    I'd try the bliss which this fine time presents.
    Appoint to carry hence so rare an heir,
    And be so slack? 'Sfoot, 'a doth move my patience!
    Would any man that is not void of sense   10
    Not have watched night by night for such a prize?
    Her beauty's so attractive that, by heav'n,
    My heart half grants to do my friend a wrong.
    Forgo these thoughts, for, Albert, be not slave
    To thy affection; do not falsify   15
    Thy faith to him whose only friendship's worth
    A world of women. He is such a one,
    Thou canst not live without his good:
    'A is and was ever as thine own heart's blood.
                            MARIA *beckons him in the window.*
    'Sfoot, see, she beckons me for Carracus!   20
    Shall my base purity cause me neglect

1–5. This . . . hither] *so lineated in Reed, etc.; set in prose in Q, Dod.*   2. th'appointed]
this ed.; appointed Q; the appointed Dod, etc.   9. 'a] *Q; it Dod.*   11. prize] *Dod,
etc.; prise Q.*   12. beauty's] *Dod, etc.; beauties Q.*   15. affection] *Dod, etc.; effec-
tion Q.*   19. SD MARIA . . . window] *Q places this to the right of lines 20–1.*

    217. *fag-end*] remnant, after use by another.
    219. *the dressing*] to prepare, to season.
    220. *the barber's*] i.e. hairdressing, playing on 'dressing' of the previous line and
probably also on the sense of 'mutton' as slang for 'meat' or prostitute.

    0.1. solus] alone.
    9. *move my patience*] provoke me, anger me.
    13. *grants*] allows me, consents.
    19. *'A*] He.
    20. *for*] instead of, thinking me to be.

This present happiness? I will obtain it,
Spite of my timorous conscience. I am in person,
Habit, and all so like to Carracus,
It may be acted, and ne'er called in question.   25
Maria. [*Calling.*] Hist! Carracus, ascend:
  All is as clear as in our hearts we wished.
Albert. Nay, if I go not now, I might be gelded, i'faith!

> ALBERT *ascends, and, being on the top of the ladder,*
> *puts out the candle.*

Maria. O love, why do you so?
Albert. I heard the steps of some coming this way.   30
  Did you not hear Albert pass by as yet?
Maria. Nor any creature pass this way this hour.
Albert. Then he intends, just at the break of day,
  To lend his trusty help to our departure.
  'Tis yet two hours' time thither, till when, let's rest,   35
  For that our speedy flight will not yield any.
Maria. But I fear,
  We, possessing of each other's presence,
  Shall overslip the time. Will your friend call?
Albert. Just at the instant: fear not of his care.   40
Maria. Come then, dear Carracus; thou now shalt rest
  Upon that bed, where fancy oft hath thought thee,
  Which kindness until now I ne'er did grant thee,
  Nor would I now, but that thy loyal faith
  I have so often tried; even now,   45
  Seeing thee come to that most honoured end,
  Through all the dangers which black night presents,
  For to convey me hence and marry me.
Albert. If I do not do so, then hate me ever.
Maria. I do believe thee, and will hate thee never.   *Exeunt.*   50

---

26. *Maria* [*Calling.*]] *this ed.; Ma.* Cals Q.   29. why do you so] *Qc;* why do so
Qu.   37–9. But … call] *so lineated in Reed, etc.; set in prose in Q, Dod.*

---

23. *Spite*] In spite.
timorous] fearful.
28. *gelded*] castrated.
36. *For that*] Because.
39. *overslip*] forget about, let pass, let slip by.
40. *at the instant*] exactly on time.

[1.3]

Enter CARRACUS.

Carracus. How pleasing are the steps we lovers make,
    When in the paths of our content we pace
    To meet our longings. What happiness it is
    For man to love. But O, what greater bliss
    To love and be beloved! O, what one virtue   5
    E'er reigned in me, that I should be enriched
    With all earth's good at once? I have a friend,
    Selected by the heavens as a gift
    To make me happy whilst I live on earth,
    A man so rare of goodness, firm of faith,   10
    That earth's content must vanish in his death.
    Then for my love, and mistress of my soul,
    A maid of rich endowments, beautified
    With all the virtues nature could bestow
    Upon mortality, who this happy night   15
    Will make me gainer of her heav'nly self –
    And see how suddenly I have attained
    To the abode of my desired wishes.
    This is the green; how dark the night appears.
    I cannot hear the tread of my true friend.   20
    Albert, hist, Albert! He's not come as yet,
    Nor is th'appointed light set in the window.
    What if I call Maria? It may be
    She feared to set a light, and only hark'neth
    To hear my steps; and yet I dare not call,   25
    Lest I betray myself, and that my voice,
    Thinking to enter in the ears of her,
    Be of some other heard. No, I will stay
    Until the coming of my dear friend, Albert.
    But now think, Carracus, what the end will be   30
    Of this thou dost determine: thou art come
    Hither to rob a father of that wealth
    That solely lengthens his now drooping years,
    His virtuous daughter, and all of that sex left,
    To make him happy in his agèd days.   35
    The loss of her may cause him to despair,
    Transport his near-decaying sense to frenzy,

---

4. For] *Dod, etc.; not in* Q.   9. on] *Dod, etc.;* one Q.   21. Albert, hist, Albert!]
this ed.; Albert, hist *Albert,* Q; Albert! Hist, Albert! – *Dod, etc.*

2, 11. *content*] contentment.

Or to some such abhorred inconvenience,
Whereto frail age is subject. I do too ill in this,
And must not think but that a father's plaint   40
Will move the heavens to pour forth misery
Upon the head of disobediency.
Yet reason tells us parents are o'erseen
When with too strict a rein they do hold in
Their child's affections, and control that love   45
Which the high pow'rs divine inspires them with,
When in their shallowest judgements they may know,
Affection crossed brings misery and woe.
But whilst I run contemplating on this,
I softly pace to my desired bliss.   50
I'll go into the next field, where my friend
Told me the horses were in readiness.   *Exit.*

[1.4]

ALBERT *descending from Maria.*

Maria. But do not stay? What if you find not Albert?
Albert. I'll then return alone to fetch you hence.
Maria. If you should now deceive me, having gained
          What you men seek for –
Albert. Sooner I'll deceive my soul. [*Aside*] And so, I fear, I have.   5
Maria. At your first call, I will descend.
Albert. Till when, this touch of lips be the true pledge
          Of Carracus' constant true devoted love.
Maria. Be sure you stay not long. Farewell,
          I cannot lend an ear to hear you part.   *Exit.*   10
Albert. But you did lend a hand unto my entrance.   *He descends.*
          How have I wronged my friend, my faithful friend!
          Robbed him of what's more precious than his blood,
          His earthly heaven, th'unspotted honour
          Of his soul-joying mistress, the fruition of whose bed   15
          I yet am warm of, whilst dear Carracus
          Wanders this cold night through th'unshelt'ring field,
          Seeking me, treacherous man! Yet no man neither,
          Though in an outward show of such appearance,
          But am a devil indeed; for so this deed   20

1. stay?] *this ed.;* stay, *Q;* stay. *Dod, etc.* 4. for –] *Dod, etc.;* for. *Q.* 8. Carracus'] *Dod, etc.;* Carracus *Q.* 9. long. Farewell] *this ed.;* long, farewell, *Q;* long;
farewell, *Dod;* long; farewell; *Reed, etc.* 18. man! Yet] *this ed.;* man, yet *Q;* man;
yet *Dod, etc.*

1. *But do not stay?*] Are you not going to wait?

Of wronged love and friendship rightly makes me.
I may compare my friend to one that's sick,
Who, lying on his deathbed, calls to him,
His dearest-thought friend, and bids him go
To some rare-gifted man that can restore   25
His former health. This his friend sadly hears,
And vows with protestations to fulfil
His wished desires with his best performance;
But then, no sooner seeing that the death
Of his sick friend would add to him some gain,   30
Goes not to seek a remedy to save,
But, like a wretch, hies him to dig his grave;
As I have done for virtuous Carracus.
Yet, Albert, be not reasonless, to endanger
What thou mayst yet secure; who can detect   35
The crime of thy licentious appetite?
I hear one's pace! 'Tis surely Carracus.   [*Withdraws.*]

Enter CARRACUS.

Carracus. Not find my friend? Sure, some malignant planet
Rules o'er this night, and, envying the content
Which I in thought possess, debars me thus   40
From what is more than happy, the loved presence
Of a dear friend and love.
Albert. 'Tis wronged Carracus by Albert's baseness:
I have no power now to reveal myself.
Carracus. The horses stand at the appointed place,   45
And night's dark coverture makes firm our safety.
My friend is surely fall'n into a slumber
On some bank hereabouts; I will call him.
Friend Albert, Albert!
Albert. [*Coming forward.*] Whate'er you are that call, you know my
    name.   50
Carracus. Ay, and thy heart, dear friend.
Albert. O Carracus, you are a slow-paced lover!
Your credit had been touched, had I not been.

---

32. hies] *Haz;* hides Q, Dod, Coll.   37. hear] *Dod, etc.;* here Q.   41–2. From . . .
love] *so lineated in Reed, etc.; single line in* Q, Dod.

---

    32. *hies*] hurries; Q's 'hides' can be made sense of, but Hazlitt's emendation to 'hies'
is convincing.
    46. *coverture*] covering.
    53. *Your credit . . . been*] The overt meaning is 'your reputation would have been
marred, if I had not been there to defend you'; the underlying meaning is something
like 'how good you are (sexually) would have been tested (to "touch" is to test a metal),
if I had not been there in your place'.

Carracus. As how, I prithee, Albert?

Albert. Why, I excused you to the fair Maria,   55
 Who would have thought you else a slack performer;
 For coming first under her chamber window,
 She heard me tread, and called upon your name;
 To which I answered with a tongue like yours,
 And told her I would go to seek for Albert,   60
 And straight return.

Carracus. Whom I have found, thanks to thy faith and heav'n,
 But had not she a light when you came first?

Albert. Yes, but hearing of some company,
 She at my warning was forced to put it out.   65
 (*Aside*) And had I been so too, you and I too
 Had still been happy.

Carracus. See, we are now come to the chamber window.

Albert. Then you must call, for so I said I would.

Carracus. Maria.   70

Maria. My Carracus, are you so soon returned?
 I see you'll keep your promise.

Carracus. Who would not do so, having passed it thee,
 Cannot be framed of aught but treachery.
 Fairest, descend, that by our hence departing   75
 We may make firm the bliss of our content.

Maria. Is your friend Albert with you?

Albert. Yes, and your servant, honoured lady.

Maria. Hold me from falling, Carracus.   *She descends.*

Carracus. I will do now so, but not at other times.   80

Maria. You are merry, sir,
 But what d'ye intend with this your scaling-ladder,
 To leave it thus, or put it forth of sight?

Carracus. Faith, 'tis no great matter which,
 Yet we will take it hence, that it may breed   85
 Many confused opinions in the house

---

66. SD *(Aside)*] *placed after line 67 in Q.* 66–7. And . . . happy] *so lineated in Reed, etc.; single line in Q, Dod.* 84. Faith, 'tis no] *Dod, etc.; Faithts Q.*

 56. *slack performer*] continuing the sexual suggestion in line 53, this phrase suggest a limp lover.

 61. *straight*] immediately.

 66. *had I been so too*] i.e. 'put out' of the house by Maria, instead of let in for a sexual liaison.

 73. *passed it thee*] uttered it to you.

 74. *framed of aught*] made of anything.

 79–80. *falling . . . other times*] playing on the notion of 'falling' as a woman lying down for sex.

Of your escape here. Albert, you shall bear it;
It may be you may chance to practise that way,
Which when you do, may your attempts so prove
As mine have done – most fortunate in love.   90
Albert. May you continue ever so.
   But it's time now to make some haste to horse:
Night soon will vanish. (*Aside*) O, that it had power
For ever to exclude day from our eyes,
For my looks then will show my villainy!   95
Carracus. Come, fair Maria, the troubles of this night
Are as forerunners to ensuing pleasures.
And, noble friend, although now Carracus
Seems, in the gaining of this beauteous prize,
To keep from you so much of his loved treasure,   100
Which ought not be mixed, yet his heart
Shall so far strive in your wished happiness,
That if the loss and ruin of itself
Can but avail your good –
Albert. O friend, no more! Come, you are slow in haste.   105
Friendship ought never be discussed in words,
Till all her deeds be finished. Who, looking in a book,
And reads but some part only, cannot judge
What praise the whole deserves, because his knowledge
Is grounded but on part. (*Aside*) As thine, friend, is,   110
Ignorant of that black mischief I have done thee.
Maria. Carracus, I am weary; are the horses far?
Carracus. No, fairest, we are now even at them.
   Come, do you follow, Albert?
Albert. Yes, I do follow. [*Aside*] Would I had done so ever,   115
And ne'er had gone before.   *Exeunt.*

---

87. *escape here. Albert*] *this ed.;* escape here: *Albert Q;* escape. Here, Albert *Dod,
etc.*   93. SD (*Aside*)] *placed after line 95 in Q.*   103–4 That . . . good –] *so lineated
in Reed, etc.; single line in Q, Dod.*   104. *good*–] *Dod, etc.;* good *Q.*   106. *discussed*]
Dod, etc. (discuss'd); distrust *Q.*   110. SD (*Aside*)] *placed after line 110 in Q.*

87–8. *bear it; . . . that way*] carry it (i.e. the ladder); one day you might have to do
the same thing again for your own love.
   107. *Who, looking*] i.e. A person who looks.
   110. *thine*] i.e. your knowledge.
   116. *gone before*] i.e. sexually been with Maria before Carracus.

ACT 2

Act 2[, Scene 1]

Enter HOG *the usurer, with* PETER SERVITUDE,
trussing his points.

Hog. What, hath not my young Lord Wealthy been here this
morning?
Peter Servitude. No, in very deed, sir; 'a is a towardly young gentleman;
shall 'a have my young mistress, your daughter, I pray you, sir?
Hog. Ay, that 'a shall, Peter; she cannot be matched to greater honour   5
and riches in all this country. Yet the peevish girl makes coy of it;
she had rather affect a prodigal, as there was Haddit, one that by
this time cannot be otherwise than hanged, or in some worse estate;
yet she would have had him. But I praise my stars she went without
him, though I did not without's lands. 'Twas a rare mortgage,   10
Peter.
Peter Servitude. As e'er came in parchment; but see, here comes my
young lord.

Enter YOUNG LORD WEALTHY.

Young L. Wealthy. Morrow, father Hog. I come to tell you strange
news: my sister is stolen away tonight, 'tis thought by necromancy   15

Act 2[, Scene 1]] *this ed.;* Actus Secundus. Q.   3. 'a is] *this ed.;* is Q; he is *Dod,*
etc.   10. lands. 'Twas] *Coll, Haz;* lands 'twas Q; lands; 'twas *Dod, etc.*   15–16. necromancy . . . necromancy] *Haz;* Nigromancy . . . Nigromancy Q, *Dod, etc.*

0.2. trussing his points] fastening the laces that attach the hose (trousers) to the
doublet (close-fitting body garment).
7. *affect*] favour, show affection for.
as there was] in other words.
8. *estate*] situation (ironic, since this supposition is a state worse than hanging); the
term usually refers in this period to social standing (specifically related to financial
health).
10. *rare*] precious, fine.
15. *necromancy*] the art of communicating with the dead to predict future events;
more generally, magic, the 'black' arts.

– what necromancy is, I leave to the readers of *The Seven Cham-*
pions of Christendom.

Hog. But is it possible your sister should be stolen? Sure some of the
household servants were confederates in't.

Young L. Wealthy. Faith, I think they would have confessed, then, for   20
I am sure my lord and father hath put them all to the bastinado
twice this morning already – not a waiting-woman, but has been
stowed, i'faith.

Peter Servitude. Trust me, 'a says well for the most part.

Hog. Then, my lord, your father is far impatient.   25

Young L. Wealthy. Impatient! I ha' seen the picture of Hector in a
haberdasher's shop not look half so furious; he appears more terrible than wildfire at a play. But father Hog, when is the time your
daughter and I shall to this wedlock druggery?

Hog. Troth, my lord, when you please; she's at your disposure, and I   30
rest much thankful that your lordship will so highly honour me.
She shall have a good portion, my lord, though nothing in respect
of your large revenues. Call her in, Peter; tell her my most respected
Lord Wealthy's here, to whose presence I will now commit her

16–17. *Seven . . . Christendom*] *this ed.; not italicized or capitalized in Q, Dod; capi-*
talized in Reed, Scott, Coll; capitalized and in quotation marks in Haz.   29. *druggery*]
Q; drudgery Dod, etc.

16–17. The Seven Champions of Christendom] a prose romance by Richard Johnson
published in two parts (1596 and 1597), involving many episodes of magic and
enchantment, and the tales of the named necromancers Ormondine (Part 1, ch. 10) and
Osmond (Part 1, ch. 19).

21. *bastinado*] method of punishment involving hitting the victim on the soles of
the feet with a large stick; here probably simply means a 'dry beating', beating with a
blunt instrument, usually a cudgel.

23. *stowed*] locked up.

26. *Hector*] hero of the Trojans, killed by Achilles; the haberdasher's shop may be
a quip about Hector's epithet as the one 'of the flashing helmet'.

27–8. *more terrible . . . play*] an apparent allusion to the fire that burned down the
Globe playhouse on 29 June 1613 during a performance of *Henry VIII.*

29. *druggery*] this word is emended to 'drudgery' by Dodsley and all editors after
him; the *OED* notes 'druggery' as an obsolete form of 'drudgery' (the double 'gg' pronounced as soft letters), and we find a similar phrase in Marlowe's *Dido Queen of
Carthage* where Aeneas declares 'I may not dure this female drudgery' (4.3.55) as he
prepares to abandon Dido; the emendation, then, is sound, but the Q form of the word
allows for the suggestion of the addictive and/or narcotic nature of the wedding (related
as it is to a financial agreement).

30. *disposure*] disposal (i.e. to do with as you wish).

32. *portion*] Money, goods, or estate brought by an unmarried woman to her
husband; cf. a 'dowry', which was brought by a widow to her remarriage. The two
terms were often used synonymously in early modern texts.

[*Exit* PETER.]; and I pray you, my lord, prosecute the gain of her   35
affectation with the best affecting words you may, and so I bid
good morrow to your lordship.   *Exit.*
Young L. Wealthy. Morrow, father Hog. 'To prosecute the gain of her
affectation with the best affecting words' – as I am a lord, a most
rare phrase! Well, I perceive age is not altogether ignorant, though   40
many an old justice is so.

          Enter PETER [SERVITUDE].

How now, Peter, is thy young mistress up yet?
Peter Servitude. Yes, indeed, she's an early stirrer, and I doubt not
hereafter but that your lordship may say she's abroad before you
can rise.   45
Young L. Wealthy. Faith, and so she may, for 'tis long ere I can get
up, when I go foxed to bed. But, Peter, has she no other suitors
besides myself?
Peter Servitude. No, an it like your lordship; nor is it fit she should.
Young L. Wealthy. Not fit she should? I tell thee, Peter, I would give   50
away as much as some knights are worth – and that's not much –
only to wipe the noses of some dozen or two of gallants, and to
see how pitifully those parcels of man's flesh would look when I
had caught the bird which they had beaten the bush for.

---

35. SD [*Exit* PETER.]] *Reed, etc.; not in Q, Dod.*   36. affectation] *Q;* affection *Dod,
etc.*   38. Morrow] *Dod, etc.;* Moreover *Q.*   39. affectation] *Q;* affection *Dod,
etc.*   49. nor is it fit] *Dod, etc.;* nor is fit *Q.*   53. man's] *this ed.;* mans *Q;* mens
Dod; men's *Reed, Haz.*

35–6. *prosecute . . . affecting words*] pursue, draw out the winning of her affection,
of her 'affecting' you with your most affecting/effective words (of love); Young Lord
Wealthy is suitably ironically impressed by this bombastic utterance from Hog.
43. *early stirrer*] (1) gets up early in the morning (2) quickly excites, stirs up the
blood.
44–5. *abroad before you can rise*] (1) gets up too early for you (2) gets bored waiting
for you to 'rise' (have an erection) and goes 'abroad' to seek sex elsewhere.
46–7. *'tis . . . bed*] (1) I sleep in a long time when I go to bed drunk (2) It takes a
long time for me to have an erection when I go to bed drunk.
51. *that's not much*] an allusion to the perceived cheapening of the title of knight
after the accession of James I and the 'inflation of honours', whereby knighthoods were
given out more freely and titles could be purchased.
52. *to wipe the noses*] to cheat (*OED* 'nose' 10.b).
gallants] fashionable, showy gentleman.
54. *the bird . . . for*] referring to the method of catching birds by beating the bush
they rest in and catching them in a net as they attempt to fly away – known as 'bat
fowling'.

Peter Servitude. Indeed, your lordship's conquest would have seemed 55
the greater.
Young L. Wealthy. Foot! As I am a lord, it angers me to the guts that
nobody hath been about her.
Peter Servitude. For anything I know, your lordship may go without
her. 60
Young L. Wealthy. An I could have enjoined her to some pale-faced
lover's distraction, or been envied for my happiness, it had been
somewhat.

Enter REBECCA, Hog's *daughter.*

But see where she comes. I knew she had not power enough to stay
another sending for. (*Aside*) O lords! What are we? Our very 65
names enforce beauty to fly, being sent for. – Morrow, pretty Beck,
how dost?
Rebecca. I rather should enquire your lordship's health, seeing you up
at such an early hour. Was it the toothache, or else fleas disturbed
you? 70
Young L. Wealthy. Do ye think I am subject to such common infirmities? Nay, were I diseased, I'd scorn but to be diseased like a lord,
i'faith. But I can tell you news: your fellow virgin-hole player, my
sister, is stolen away tonight.
Rebecca. In truth, I am glad on't; she's now free from the jealous eye 75
of a father. Do not ye suspect, my lord, who it should be that hath
carried her away?
Young L. Wealthy. No, nor care not: as she brews, so let her bake – so
said the ancient proverb. But lady mine that shall be, your father
hath wished me to appoint the day with you. 80
Rebecca. What day, my lord?

---

61. enjoined] Q (injoin'd); enjoy'd Dod, etc.

---

57. *Foot!*] God's foot! (a mild oath).
58. *about her*] wooing her, pestering her.
61. *An*] If.
63. *somewhat*] something (of substance).
64. *stay*] wait out.
71-2. *common infirmities*] Young Lord Wealthy is offended by the suggestion that
he might take accommodations where there are fleas.
73. *virgin-hole*] a crass sexual pun on the lady's instrument, the virginals, a key-
board instrument in a box that sits on a table.
78. *as . . . bake*] as she sows, so let her reap.
80. *wished me to*] desired that I, asked that I.

Young L. Wealthy. Why, of marriage; or as the learned historiographer
writes, Hymen's holidays, or nuptial ceremonious rites.

Rebecca. Why, when would you appoint that, my lord?

Young L. Wealthy. Why, let me see. I think the tailor may despatch all   85
our vestures in a week; therefore, it shall be directly this day
se'ennight.

Peter Servitude. God give you joy!

Rebecca. Of what, I pray you, impudence! [*Aside*] This fellow will go
near to take his oath that he hath seen us plighted faiths together;   90
my father keeps him for no other cause than to outswear the truth.
– My lord, not to hold you any longer in a fool's paradise, nor to
blind you with the hopes I never intend to accomplish, know I
neither do, can, or will love you.

Young L. Wealthy. How! Not love a lord? O indiscreet young woman!   95
Indeed, your father told me how unripe I should find you. But all's
one; unripe fruit will ask more shaking before they fall than those
that are, and my conquest will seem the greater still.

Peter Servitude. [*Aside*] Afore God, he is a most unanswerable lord,
and holds her to't, i'faith.   100

Young L. Wealthy. Nay, ye could not a' pleased me better than seeing
you so invincible, and such a difficult attaining to. I would not give
a pin for the society of a female that should seem willing; but give
me a wench that hath disdainful looks,
For 'tis denial whets on appetite,   105
When proffered service doth allay delight.

Rebecca. [*Aside*] The fool's well read in vice. – My lord, I hope you
hereafter will no further insinuate in the course of your affections;
and, for the better withdrawing from them, you may please to
know I have irrevocably decreed never to marry.   110

---

89. Of . . . impudence!] *this ed.;* Of what I pray you impudence, *Q;* Of what, I pray,
you impudence? *Dod, etc.* 90. plighted] *Q;* plight *Dod, etc.* 99. he] *Dod, etc.;*
not in Q. 105. whets on] *Q;* whet's an *Dod;* whets an *Reed, etc.*

---

82. *learned historiographer*] 'This was probably Samuel Daniel, who was an histo-
rian as well as a poet. The work above alluded to is probably *Hymen's Triumph*; a
Pastoral Tragi-comedy, acted at the Queen's Court in the Strand, at the nuptials of
Lord Roxborough' (Reed, p. 400).

83. *Hymen's holidays*] Fleay notes that this alludes to William Rowley's *Hymen's
Holiday*, and 'shows that [it] was written for a marriage, probably that of the Earl of
Dunbar's daughter with Lord Waldon, interrupted by the Earl's death 29th Jan. 1612.
It was acted at Court 24th Feb.' (ii, p. 257); Hymen: Greek god of marriage.

86. *vestures*] clothing.

87. *se'ennight*] seven nights, a week.

90. *plighted faiths*] promised (exchanged) vows.

105. *whets on*] urges, incites.

106. *proffered*] offered.

Young L. Wealthy. Never to marry! Peter, I pray bear witness of her
words, that when I have attained her, it may add to my fame and
conquest.

Peter Servitude. Yes, indeed, an't like your lordship.

Young L. Wealthy. Nay, ye must think, Beck, I know how to woo; ye   115
shall find no bashful university man of me.

Rebecca. Indeed, I think y'ad ne'er that bringing up. Did you ever
study, my lord?

Young L. Wealthy. Yes, faith, that I have, and the last week too, three
days and a night together.   120

Rebecca. About what, I pray?

Young L. Wealthy. Only to find out why a woman, going on the right
side of her husband the daytime, should lie on his left side at night;
and, as I am a lord, I never knew the meaning on't till yesterday.
Malapert, my father's butler, being a witty jackanapes, told me   125
why it was.

Rebecca. By'r Lady, my lord, 'twas a shrewd study, and I fear hath
altered the property of your good parts, for I'll assure you, I loved
you a fortnight ago far better.

Young L. Wealthy. Nay, 'tis all one whether you do or no; 'tis but a   130
little more trouble to bring ye about again; and no question, but
a man may do't, I am he. 'Tis true, as your father said, the black
ox hath not trod upon that foot of yours.

Rebecca. No, but the white calf hath, and so I leave your lordship.

Exit.

Young L. Wealthy. Well, go thy ways; th'art as witty a marmalade-   135
eater as ever I conversed with. Now, as I am a lord, I love her
better and better. I'll home and poetize upon her good parts presently. Peter, here's a preparative to my further applications [*Gives*

---

135. marmalade] *Dod, etc.;* marmaled *Q.*

---

112. *that*] so that.

116. *bashful university man*] shy, studious type.

125. *Malapert*] the name means 'presumptuous', 'saucy'.

witty jackanapes] cheeky monkey, naughty fellow.

127. *By'r Lady*] A mild oath on the Virgin Mary.

131. *but*] if.

132-3. *black . . . foot*] misfortune, adversity (*OED* 'ox' 4.b) has not affected you.

134. *white calf*] i.e. the leather of her shoes, on which she proceeds to walk away.

135-6. *marmalade-eater*] *OED* speculates that this phrase means 'one daintily
brought up' ('marmalade' 3.a).

137. *poetize*] write or extemporize poetry.

138. *a . . . applications*] a preparation for my future rendezvous (i.e. money, a
bribe); specifically in a medieval sense, something to prepare the body for a course of
treatment.

money.]; and, Peter, be circumspect in giving me diligent notice
    what suitors seem to be peeping.   140
Peter Servitude. I'll warrant you, my lord, she's your own; for I'll give
    out to all that come near her that she's betrothed to you, and if
    the worst come to the worst, I'll swear it.
Young L. Wealthy. Why, godamercy, and if ever I do gain my
    request,   145
    Thou shalt in braver clothes be shortly dressed.   *Exeunt.*

[2.2]

Enter OLD L[ORD] WEALTHY, *solus.*

Old L. Wealthy. Have the fates then conspired, and quite bereft
    My drooping years of all the blessed content
    That age partakes of, by the sweet aspect
    Of their well-nurtured issue, whose obedience,
    Discreet and duteous 'haviour, only lengthens   5
    The thread of age, when on the contrary,
    By rude demeanour and their headstrong wills,
    That thread's soon ravelled out? O, why, Maria,
    Couldst thou abandon me now at this time,
    When my grey head's declining to the grave?   10
    Could any masculine flatterer on earth
    So far bewitch thee to forget thyself,
    As now to leave me? Did nature solely give thee me,
    As my chief, inestimable treasure,
    Whereby my age might pass in quiet to rest,   15
    And art thou proved to be the only curse
    Which heav'n could throw upon mortality?
    Yet I'll not curse thee, though I fear the fates
    Will on thy head inflict some punishment,
    Which I will daily pray they may withhold.   20
    Although thy disobediency deserves
    Extremest rigour, yet I wish to thee
    Content in love, full of tranquillity.

Enter YOUNG [LORD] WEALTHY.

---

140. peeping] *Dod, etc.;* pee-ping Q.

0.1. SD [*Enter . . . solus.*]] *this ed.; not in Q, Dod, etc.*   13. solely] *Dod, etc.;* soly Q.
23.1. SD *Enter . . .* WEALTHY.] *placed at the end of line 23 in Q: Enter young Wealthy.*

---

  139. *be circumspect*] be wary, keep your eyes open.
  140. *peeping*] looking in, coming to see Rebecca.
  146. *braver*] finer.

   5. *'haviour*] behaviour.

But see where stands my shame, whose indiscretion
Doth seem to bury all the living honours   25
Of all our ancestors; but 'tis the fates' decree,
That men might know their weak mortality.
Young L. Wealthy. Sir, I cannot find my sister.
Old L. Wealthy. I know thou canst not: 'twere too rare to see
Wisdom found out by ignorance.   30
Young L. Wealthy. How, father? Is it not possible that wisdom should
be found out by ignorance? I pray, then, how do many magnificoes
come by it?
Old L. Wealthy. Not buy it, son, as you had need to do.
Yet wealth without that may live more content   35
Than wit's enjoyers can, debarred of wealth.
All pray for wealth, but I never heard yet
Of any but one that e'er prayed for wit.
He's counted wise enough in these vain times
That hath but means enough to wear gay clothes   40
And be an outside of humanity. What matters it a pin
How indiscreet soe'er a natural be,
So that his wealth be great? That's it doth cause
Wisdom in these days to give fools applause.
And when gay folly speaks, how vain soe'er,   45
Wisdom must silent sit, and speech forbear.
Young L. Wealthy. Then wisdom must sit as mute as learning among
many courtiers. But, father, I partly suspect that Carracus hath got
my sister –
Old L. Wealthy. With child, I fear, ere this.   50
Young L. Wealthy. By'r Lady, and that may be true. But, whether 'a
has or no, it's all one; if you please, I'll take her from under his
nose, in spite on's teeth, and ask him no leave.
Old L. Wealthy. That were too headstrong, son;
We'll rather leave them to the will of heaven,   55
To fall or prosper; and though young Carracus
Be but a gentleman of small revenues,

---

29. SP *Old L. Wealthy.*] *Reed, Haz (O. Lord W.); Fa. Q, and throughout scene; Father.*
Dod. 54–5. That . . . heaven] *so lineated in Reed, etc.; single line in Q, Dod.*

30. *Wisdom . . . ignorance*] referring to his son as a morality play character, personifying ignorance.
32. *magnificoes*] grand, exalted persons of the city.
34. *Not buy it*] Old Lord Wealthy seems to be playing on Young Lord Wealthy's phrase 'come by/buy it' in the preceding line.
42. *natural*] fool ('natural' was also used of an illegitimate child in the period).
43. *So*] Provided.
53. *in spite on's teeth*] in spite of him, in defiance of him.

Yet he deserves my daughter for his virtues,
And, had I thought she could not be withdrawn
From th' affecting of him, I had ere this   60
Made them both happy by my free consent,
Which now I wish I had granted, and still pray,
If any have her, it may be Carracus.
Young L. Wealthy. Troth, and I wish so too; for, in my mind, he's a
gentleman of a good house, and speaks true Latin.   65
Old L. Wealthy. Tomorrow, son, you shall ride to his house,
And there enquire of your sister's being.
But as you tender me and your own good,
Use no rough language savouring of distaste,
Or any uncivil terms.   70
Young L. Wealthy. Why, do ye take me for a midwife?
Old L. Wealthy. But tell young Carracus these words from me,
That if he hath, with safeguard of her honour,
Espoused my daughter, that I then forgive
His rash offence, and will accept of him   75
In all the fatherly love I owe a child.
Young L. Wealthy. I am sure my sister will be glad to hear it, and I
cannot blame her, for she'll then enjoy that with quietness which
many a wench in these days does scratch for.
Old L. Wealthy. Come, son, I'll write   80
To Carracus, that my old hand may witness
How much I stand affected to his worth.   *Exeunt.*

[2.3]

Enter HADDIT, *in his gay apparel, making him ready,*
and with him LIGHTFOOT.

Haddit. By this light, coz, this suit does rarely! The tailor that made it
may hap to be saved, an't be but for his good works; I think I shall
be proud of 'em, and so I was never yet of any clothes.

---

59. thought] *Dod, etc.;* though *Q.*   80. write] *Dod, etc.;* wright *Q.*   80–2. Come
. . . worth] *Coll., Haz.; set in prose in Q, Dod, Reed, Scott.*

0.1. SD HADDIT] *Dod, etc.;* Haddid *Q.*

---

71. *midwife*] Midwives were proverbially loose with their unsavoury language.

79. *scratch for*] scrape for, try desperately to get; also with sexual suggestion of (1)
'enjoying' in safe and clean circumstances the sex that causes other women to 'scratch'
themselves when they get diseased, and (2) other women 'scratch' themselves because
they cannot find a husband to do it for them.

2. *hap*] happen, chance.
good works] the Catholic doctrine of good works – where good deeds on earth are
tallied and speak well for the actor in heaven – was not one for the Reformed theolo-
gian, to whom everyone was predestined to salvation or damnation.

Lightfoot. How, not of your clothes? Why, then you were never proud
of anything, for therein chiefly consisteth pride, for you never saw   5
pride pictured but in gay attire.

Haddit. True, but in my opinion, pride might as well be portrayed in
any other shape, as to seem to be an affecter of gallantry, being
the causes thereof are so several and diverse. As some are proud
of their strength, although that pride cost them the loss of a limb   10
or two by over-daring; likewise, some are proud of their humour,
although in that humour they be often knocked for being so; some
are proud of their drink, although that liquid operation cause them
to wear a nightcap three weeks after; some are proud of their good
parts, although they never put them to better uses than the enjoying   15
of a common strumpet's company, and are only made proud by
the favour of a waiting-woman; others are proud –

Lightfoot. Nay, I prithee, coz, enough of pride; but when do you intend
to go yonder to Covetousness the usurer, that we may see how
near your plot will take for the releasing of your mortgaged   20
lands

Haddit. Why, now presently; and if I do not accomplish my projects
to a wished end, I wish my fortunes may be like some scraping
tradesman, that never embraceth true pleasure till he be threescore
and ten.   25

Lightfoot. But say Hog's daughter, on whom all your hopes depend,
by this be betrothed to some other.

---

19. usurer]   *Dod, etc.;* Usurer Q.

5–6. *pride . . . attire*] The pride of clothing was considered particularly heinous by
extreme moralists of the day; see the introduction to the play.

8. *being*] since.

11. *humour*] character, behaviour.

12. *knocked*] struck for being at odds; cf. *Henry V*, where Nim says to Pistol 'I have
an humour to knock you indifferently well' (2.1.48–9).

14. *nightcap*] (1) because sleepy or ill from drink (2) to hide their cuckold's horns
because a sober man has got his wife.

14–15. *their good parts*] (1) good features (2) genitals.

19. *Covetousness the usurer*] The allusion is to a morality-type character of the
medieval drama and Tudor interlude.

19–20. *how . . . take*] how soon your plan will succeed, how successful your plan
will be.

24–5. *threescore and ten*] seventy, the proverbial age for the end of life; hence, true
pleasure only comes to the poor ('scraping tradesman') in death.

Haddit. Why, say she were; nay more, married to another, I would be
    ne'er the further of the effecting of my intents. No, coz, I partly
    know her inward disposition; and, did I but only know her to be   30
    womankind, I think it were sufficient.
Lightfoot. Sufficient for what?
Haddit. Why, to obtain a grant of the best thing she had: chastity, man.
    'Tis not here as 'tis with you in the country, not to be had without
    father's and mother's goodwill; no, the city is a place of more   35
    traffic, where each one learns by example of their elders to make
    the most of their own, either for profit or pleasure.
Lightfoot. 'Tis but your misbelieving thoughts makes you surmise so:
    if women were so kind, how haps you had not by their favours
    kept yourself out of the claws of poverty?   40
Haddit. O, but coz, can a ship sail without water? Had I had but such
    a suit as this to set myself afloat, I would not have feared sinking.
    But come, no more of need; now to the usurer, and though
    All hopes do fail, a man can want no living,
    So long as sweet desire reigns in women.   45
Lightfoot. But then yourself must able be in giving.   *Exeunt.*

[2.4]

                    Enter ALBERT, *solus.*

Albert. Conscience, thou horror unto wicked men,
    When wilt thou cease thy all-afflicted wrath,
    And set my soul free from the labyrinth
    Of thy tormenting terror? O, but it fits not!
    Should I desire redress, or wish for comfort,   5
    That have committed an act so inhumane,
    Able to fill shame's spacious chronicle?
    Who but a damned one could have done like me?

29. ne'er ... intents] *this ed.;* neare the further of them effecting of my intents *Q*;
ne'er the farther from effecting of my intents. *Dod, etc.;* ne'er the farther from effecting
my intents *Coll, Haz.* 33–4. had: chastity, man. 'Tis] *this ed.;* had, Chastity, Man
tis *Q*; had, chastity. Man, 'tis *Dod, etc.* 35. city] *Dod, etc.;* City *Q*. 43–6. though
/ All ... giving] *Coll (tho'), Haz; set in prose in Q;* usurer: / And, tho' ... living, /
So ... giving. *Dod, Reed, Scott.*

2. all-afflicted] *this ed.;* all afflicted *Q*; all-afflicting *Dod, etc.*

29. *ne'er ... intents*] no whit further from achieving my ends.
36. *traffic*] (1) goings on, exchange (2) sex.
39. *kind*] (1) financially helpful (2) sexually promiscuous.
haps] happens, chances.

4. *it fits not*] it is not fitting, appropriate (for me to ask for such easing of my
suffering).

Robbed my dear friend, in a short moment's time,
Of his love's high-prized gem of chastity,   10
That which so many years himself hath stayed for.
How often hath he, as he lay in bed,
Sweetly discoursed to me of his Maria?
And with what pleasing passions 'a did suffer
Love's gentle war-siege. Then he would relate   15
How he first came unto her fair eyes' view,
How long it was ere she could brook affection,
And then how constant she did still abide.
I, then, at this would joy, as if my breast
Had sympathized in equal happiness   20
With my true friend. But now, when joy should be –
Who but a damned one would have done like me?
He hath been married now at least a month,
In all which time I have not once beheld him:
This is his house.   25
I'll call to know his health, but will not see him;
My looks would then betray me, for, should he ask
My cause of seeming sadness, or the like,
I could not but reveal, and so poured on,
Worse unto ill, which breeds confusion.   *He knocks.*   30

                    Enter SERVINGMAN.

Servingman. To what intent d'ye knock, sir?
Albert. Because I would be heard, sir; is the master of this house
    within?
Servingman. Yes, marry, is 'a, sir; would you speak with him?
Albert. My business is not so troublesome.   35
    Is 'a in health, with his late espoused wife?
Servingman. Both are exceeding well, sir.
Albert. I'm truly glad on't; farewell, good friend.
Servingman. I pray you, let's crave your name, sir; I may else have
    anger.   40
Albert. You may say one Albert, riding by this way, only enquired their
    health.
Servingman. I will acquaint so much.   *Exit.*

---

15. gentle] *Dod, etc.;* genle Q.   24–5. In . . . house] *so lineated in Reed, etc.; single
line in Q, with* 'This' *capitalized; single line in Dod:* 'him. This'.

---

11. *himself hath stayed*] he has waited.
17. *ere*] before, until.
    brook] stand, bear.

Albert. How like a poisonous doctor have I come,
    To inquire their welfare, knowing that myself   45
    Have given the potion of their ne'er recovery;
    For which I will afflict myself with torture ever.
    And since the earth yields not a remedy
    Able to salve the sores my lust hath made,
    I'll now take farewell of society   50
    And th'abode of men, to entertain a life
    Fitting my fellowship, in desert woods,
    Where beasts like me consort; there may I live
    Far off from wronging virtuous Carracus.
    There's no Maria that shall satisfy   55
    My hateful lust; the trees shall shelter
    This wretched trunk of mine, upon whose bark
    I will engrave the story of my sin.
    And there this short breath of mortality
    I'll finish up in that repentant state,   60
    Where not th'allurements of earth's vanities
    Can e'er o'ertake me; there's no baits for lust,
    No friend to ruin; I shall then be free
    From practising the art of treachery;
    Thither then, steps, where such content abides,   65
    Where penitency, not disturbed, may grieve,
    Where on each tree and springing plant I'll carve
    This heavy motto of my misery:
    'Who but a damned one could have done like me?'
    Carracus, farewell; if e'er thou see'st me more,   70
    Shalt find me curing of a soul-sick sore.   *Exit.*

---

46. potion . . . recovery] *Dod, etc*; portion of their nere recovery *Q.*   57. bark] *this ed.*; backe *Q*; barks *Dod, etc.*   71. soul-sick] *Dod, etc.*; sole-sicke *Q.*

---

44. *poisonous doctor*] There was a proverbial confluence of the idea of medicine and poison in the period.

46. *potion of their ne'er recovery*] poison from which they can never be remedied.

55. *There's*] i.e. in the woods.

71. *Shalt find . . . sore*] Carracus shall find me recovering from my wounded conscience (as with the medicine/poison binary, though 'cure' also has the sense of 'taking care of', 'maintaining', thus Albert simultaneously promises to get better from the sore of conscience and to keep his pain alive).

ACT 3

Act 3[, Scene 1]

Enter CARRACUS, *driving his* [SERVINGMAN] *before him.*

Carracus. Why, thou base villain! Was my dearest friend here, and
    couldst not make him stay?
Servingman. 'Sfoot, sir, I could not force him against his will. An he
    had been a woman –
Carracus. Hence, thou untutored slave!   *Exit* SER[VINGMAN].   5
    But couldst thou, Albert, come so near my door,
    And not vouchsafe the comfort of thy presence?
    Hath my good fortune caused thee to repine,
    And, seeing my state so full replete with good,
    Canst thou withdraw thy love to lessen it?   10
    What could so move thee? Was't because I married?
    Didst thou imagine I infringed my faith
    For that a woman did participate
    In equal share with thee? Cannot my friendship
    Be firm to thee because 'tis dear to her?   15
    Yet no more dear to her than firm to thee.
    Believe me, Albert, thou dost little think
    How much thy absence gives cause of discontent.
    But I'll impute it only to neglect;
    It is neglect indeed when friends neglect   20
    The sight of friends, and say 'tis troublesome,
    Only ask how they do, and so farewell,
    Showing an outward kind of seeming duty,
    Which in the rules of manhood is observed,

Act 3[, Scene 1]] *this ed; Actus Tertius Q.*   0.1. SD [SERVINGMAN]] *this ed.; Man Q;*
Dod, etc.   1–4. Why . . . woman –] *so lineated in Q, Dod, etc.; four lines in Haz:*
dearest / friend . . . will: / An'.   3–4. will. An he had . . . woman –] *this ed.;* wil, an
a had been a woman. *Q;* will: an' he had been a woman – *Coll;* will, an he had been
a woman. *Dod, Reed, Scott;* will: An' he had been a woman – *Haz.*   6–7. But . . . pres-
ence] *so lineated in Reed, Haz.; single line in Q, Dod.*

3–4. *An . . . woman*] i.e. if he had been a woman (I *could* have forced her against
her will).
  5. *untutored slave!*] ignorant fool!
  7. *vouchsafe*] grant, bestow, confer.
  8. *repine*] feel discomfort, complain.

And think full well they have performed their task,   25
When of their friend's health they do only ask,
Not caring how they are, or how distressed:
It is enough they have their loves expressed
In bare enquiry. And in these times, too,
Friendship's so cold that few so much will do.   30
And am not I beholden then to Albert?
He, after knowledge of our being well,
Said he was truly glad on't. O rare friend!
If he be unkind, how many more may mend?
But whither am I carried by unkindness?   35
Why should not I as well set light by friendship,
Since I have seen a man whom I late thought
Had been composed of nothing but of faith
Prove so regardless of his friend's content?

Enter MARIA.

Maria. Come, Carracus, I have sought you all about.   40
Your servant told me you were much disquieted;
Prithee, love, be not so. Come, walk in,
I'll charm thee with my lute from forth disturbance.
Carracus. I am not angry, sweet; though, if I were,
Thy bright aspect would soon allay my rage.   45
But, my Maria, it doth something move me
That our friend Albert so forgets himself.
Maria. It may be 'tis nothing else; and there's no doubt
He'll soon remember his accustomed friendship.
He thinks as yet, peradventure, that his presence   50
Will but offend, for that our marriage rites
Are but so newly passed.
Carracus. I will surmise so too, and only think
Some serious business hinders Albert's presence.
But what ring's that, Maria, on your finger?   55
Maria. 'Tis one you lost, love, when I did bestow
A jewel of far greater worth on you.

---

31. beholden] *Dod, etc.*; beholding Q.   48. be 'tis] *this ed.*; be 'ts Q; be, 'tis *Dod,
etc.*

---

43. *from forth disturbance*] out of your troubled state.
46. *move*] anger.
47. *forgets himself*] behaves himself improperly.
48. *'tis nothing else*] i.e. that he merely forgets himself and there's no *substantial*
reason for his behaviour.
50. *peradventure*] perhaps, maybe.
52. *but*] only, just.
57. *jewel*] i.e. her virginity.

Carracus. At what time, fairest?
Maria. As if you knew not! Why d'ye make't so strange?
Carracus. Y'are disposed to riddle; pray, let's see't.   60
    I partly know it; where was't you found it?
Maria. Why, in my chamber, that most gladsome night,
    When you enriched your love by my escape.
Carracus. How, in your chamber?
Maria. Sure, Carracus, I will be angry with you   65
    If you seem so forgetful. I took it up
    Then, when you left my lodge, and went away,
    Glad of your conquest, for to seek your friend.
    Why stand you so amazed, sir? I hope that kindness,
    Which then you reaped, doth not prevail   70
    So in your thoughts, as that you think me light.
Carracus. O, think thyself, Maria, what thou art!
    This is the ring of Albert, treacherous man,
    He that enjoyed thy virgin chastity!
    I never did ascend into thy chamber,   75
    But all that cold night through the frozen field
    Went seeking of that wretch, who ne'er sought me,
    But found what his lust sought for, dearest thee!
Maria. I have heard enough, my Carracus,
    To bereave me of this little breath –   *She swoons.*   80
Carracus. All breath be first extinguished! Within there, ho!

        Enter NURSE *and servants.*

    O nurse, see here, Maria says she'll die.
Nurse. Marry, God forbid! O mistress, mistress, mistress!
    She has breath yet; she's but in a trance: good sir,
    Take comfort, she'll recover by and by.   85
Carracus. No, no, she'll die, nurse, for she said she would;
    An she had not said so, 't had been another matter;
    But you know, nurse, she ne'er told a lie:
    I will believe her, for she speaks all truth.

---

60. Y'are] *this ed.;* Yare *Q;* You are *Dod, etc.* 69. amazed, sir? I] *Dod, etc.;*
*(*amaz'd, sir? I*) Haz;* amaz'd, sir I *Q.* 79–80. I . . . breath] *so lineated in this ed.;*
single line in Q, Dod, etc.; bereave / Me *Haz.* 80. SD *She swoons.*] *Dod, etc;* she
sounds. *Q.* 83–5. Marry . . . by] *so lineated in this ed.;* set in prose in *Q. Dod,*
etc. 86–9. No . . . truth] *so lineated in this ed.;* set in prose in *Q, Dod, Reed, Scott,*
Coll; 87–9. *set in prose in Haz, line* 89 *single line of verse.* 87. 't had] *Dod, etc.*
('thad*);* tad *Q.*

59. *Why . . . strange?*] Why are you acting as if you don't know what I'm talking
about?
81. *All . . . extinguished*] i.e. 'Let *all* breathing stop before Maria should die'.

Nurse. His memory begins to fail him. Come, let's bear   90
    This heavy spectacle from forth his presence;
    The heavens will lend a hand, I hope, of comfort.
                      Exeunt; CA[RRACUS] *manet.*
Carracus. See how they steal away my fair Maria.
    But I will follow after her as far
    As Orpheus did to gain his soul's delight,   95
    And Pluto's self shall know, although I am not
    Skilful in music, yet I can be mad,
    And force my love's enjoyment, in despite
    Of hell's black fury. But stay, stay, Carracus.
    Where is thy knowledge and that rational sense   100
    Which heaven's great architect endued thee with?
    All sunk beneath the weight of lumpish nature?
    Are our diviner parts no noblier free
    Than to be tortured by the weak assailments
    Of earth-sprung griefs? Why is man then accounted   105
    The head commander of this universe,
    Next the Creator, when a little storm
    Of nature's fury straight o'erwhelms his judgement?
    But mine's no little storm: 'tis a tempest
    So full of raging, self-consuming woe,   110
    That nought but ruin follows expectation.
    O my Maria! What unheard-of sin
    Have any of thine ancestors enacted,
    That all their shame should be poured thus on thee?
    Or what incestuous spirit, cruel Albert,   115
    Left hell's vast womb for to enter thee,
    And do a mischief of such treachery?

             Enter NURSE, *weeping.*

    O nurse, how is it with Maria?
    If e'er thy tongue did utter pleasing words,
    Let it now do so, or hereafter e'er be dumb in sorrow.   120

---

   90. *His memory . . . him*] possibly an aside, the nurse makes fun of Carracus'
idealism.
   92.1. *manet*] remains (on stage).
   95. *Orpheus*] Orpheus followed his stolen love, Eurydice, to the underworld to try
to win her back; he enchanted Pluto with his music and was allowed to lead Eurydice
back to earth provided he did not look back at her during the journey; he could not
resist looking back to her, and he lost her for ever.
   96. *Pluto's*] God of the Underworld.
   99. *stay*] wait.
   105. *accounted*] considered, nominated.
   107. *Next*] Next to.

Nurse. Good sir, take comfort: I am forced to speak
    What will not please: your chaste wife, sir, is dead.
Carracus. 'Tis dead, indeed! How did you know 'twas so, nurse?
Nurse. What, sir?
Carracus. That my heart was dead. Sure, thou hast served   125
    Dame Nature's self, and knowst the inward secrets
    Of all our hidden powers. I'll love thee for't,
    And if thou wilt teach me that unknown skill,
    Shalt see what wonder Carracus will do.
    I'll dive into the breast of hateful Albert,   130
    And see how his black soul is round encompassed
    By fearful fiends! O, I would do strange things,
    And know to whose cause lawyers will incline
    When they had fees on both sides; view the thoughts
    Of forlorn widows, when their knights have left them;   135
    Search through the guts of greatness, and behold
    What several sin best pleased them; thence I'd descend
    Into the bowels of some pocky sir,
    And tell to lechers all the pains he felt,
    That they thereby might warned be from lust.   140
    Troth, 'twill be rare! I'll study it presently.
Nurse. [*Aside*] Alas, he is distracted! What a sin
    Am I partaker of, by telling him
    So cursed an untruth? But 'twas my mistress' will,
    Who is recovered, though her griefs never   145
    Can be recovered. She hath vowed with tears
    Her own perpetual banishment; therefore to him
    Death were not more displeasing than if I
    Had told her lasting absence.
Carracus. I find my brains too shallow far for study.   150
    What need I care for being a 'rithmetician?
    Let citizens' sons stand, an they will, for ciphers;
    Why should I teach them, and go beat my brains
    To instruct unapt and unconceiving dolts?
    And, when all's done, my art, that should be famed,   155
    Will by gross imitation be but shamed.
    Your judgement, madam?

---

150. brains] *Q (*braines*); brain's *Haz.*

---

129. *Shalt*] i.e. Thou shalt (impersonal).
137. *thence*] then, after that.
138. *pocky*] affected with the pox (usually syphilis), pock-marked.
142. *distracted*] mad.
151. *'rithmetician*] pedantic schoolmaster.
152. *citizens' sons*] average students, beneath Carracus' sense of his new-found intellectual greatness/madness.
    ciphers] zeros, worthless persons.

Nurse. Good sir, walk in; we'll send for learned men
   That may allay your frenzy.
Carracus. But can Maria so forget herself   160
   As to debar us thus of her attendance?
Nurse. She is within, sir; pray you, will you walk to her?
Carracus. O, is she so? Come, then, let's softly steal
   Into her chamber. If she be asleep,
   I'll laugh, shalt see, enough, and thou shalt weep.   165
   Softly, good long-coat, softly.   *Exeunt.*

[3.2]

                    Enter MARIA *in page's apparel.*

Maria. Cease now thy steps, Maria, and look back
   Upon that place where distressed Carracus
   Hath his sad being, from whose virtuous bosom
   Shame hath constrained me fly, ne'er to return.
   I will go seek some unfrequented path,   5
   Either in desert woods or wilderness,
   There to bewail my innocent mishaps,
   Which heaven hath justly poured down on me,
   In punishing my disobediency.

                 Enter YOUNG LO[RD] WEALTHY.

   O, see, my brother.   *Exit.*   10
Young L. Wealthy. Ho, you, three-foot-and-a-half! Why, page, I say!
   'Sfoot, 'a is vanished as suddenly as a dumb show. If a lord had
   lost his way now, so 'a had been served. But let me see; as I take
   it, this is the house of Carracus. A very fair building, but it looks
   as if 'twere dead; I can see no breath come out of the chimneys.   15
   But I shall know the state on't by and by, by the looks of some
   servingman. What ho, within here!   *Beats at the door.*

                    Enter SER[VINGMAN].

158–9. Good . . . frenzy] *so lineated in Haz, Reed; single line of prose in Q,*
Dod.   159. may] *Q; can Dod, etc.*   164. chamber. If] *this ed.; chamber, if Q, Dod,*
etc.; chamber; if Haz.

12. 'a] *this ed.; not in Q, Dod; he Haz.*   17. SD [Beats at the door.]] *Haz.; not in*
Q, Dod, etc.

---

   166. *long-coat*] one who wears a long coat, here the nurse.

   11. *three-foot-and-a-half*] i.e. little man, youth, young page.
   13. *so 'a had been served*] this is how he would have been treated/helped.
   15. *breath*] i.e. smoke.
   16. *state on't*] state of it, situation in the house.

Servingman. Good sir, you have your arms at liberty. Will't please you
   to withdraw your action of battery?
Young L. Wealthy. Yes, indeed, now you have made your appearance.   20
   Is the living-giver within, sir?
Servingman. You mean my master, sir?
Young L. Wealthy. You have hit it, sir, praised be your understanding.
   I am to have conference with him; would you admit my
   presence?   25
Servingman. Indeed, sir, he is at this time not in health, and may not
   be disturbed.
Young L. Wealthy. Sir, an 'a were in the pangs of childbed, I'd speak
   with him.

Enter CARRACUS.

Carracus. Upon what cause, gay man?   30
Young L. Wealthy. [*Aside*] 'Sfoot, I think 'a be disturbed indeed; 'a
   speaks more commanding than a constable at midnight. – Sir, my
   lord and father, by me, a lord, hath sent these lines enclosed, which
   show his whole intent.
Carracus. Let me peruse them; if they do portend   35
   To the state's good, your answer shall be sudden,
   Your entertainment friendly; but if otherwise,
   Our meanest subject shall divide thy greatness.
   You'd best look to't, ambassador.
Young L. Wealthy. Is your master a statesman, friend?   ·   40
Servingman. Alas, no, sir; 'a understands not what 'a speaks.
Young L. Wealthy. Ay, but when my father dies, I am to be called in
   for one myself, and I hope to bear the place as gravely as my suc-
   cessors have done before me.
Carracus. Ambassador, I find your master's will   45

---

40. your master] *Dod, etc.;* yous Mr. Q.

---

   18. *You ... liberty*] (1) You are brandishing your weapons (2) You are free with
your knocking.
   19. *action of battery*] (1) assault on person or defences (2) hard knocking.
   23. *hit it*] got it.
   30. *gay*] brash, careless, assertive.
   31. *disturbed*] (1) annoyed, unsettled (2) mad.
   32. *more commanding ... midnight*] i.e. because the officer would need to take
control of a situation so late at night.
   38. *Our meanest ... greatness*] (1) We shall measure your worth at a low rate (2)
Our lowliest citizen shall cut you up.
   39. *look to't*] be careful.
   ambassador] Carracus's mad identification of the message-carrying Young Lord
Wealthy.

Treats to the good of somewhat, what it is –
You have your answer, and may now depart.
Young L. Wealthy. I will relate as much, sir; fare ye well.
Carracus. But stay, I had forgotten quite our chiefest affairs:
    Your master father writes, some three lines lower,   50
    Of one Maria that is wife to me,
    That she and I should travel now with you
    Unto his presence.
Young L. Wealthy. Why, now I understand you, sir; that Maria is my
    sister, by whose conjunction you are created brother to me, a   55
    lord.
Carracus. But, brother lord, we cannot go this journey.
Young L. Wealthy. Alas, no, sir, we mean to ride it. My sister shall
    ride upon my nag.
Carracus. Come, then, we'll in and strive to woo your sister.   60
    I have not seen her, sir, at least these three days.
    They keep her in a chamber, and tell me
    She's fast asleep still; you and I'll go see.
Young L. Wealthy. Content, sir.
Servingman. [*Aside*]   Madmen and fools agree.   *Exeunt.*

[3.3]

Enter HADDIT and REBECCA.

Rebecca. When you have got this prize, you mean to lose me.
Haddit. Nay, prithee, do not think so. If I do not marry thee this instant
    night, may I never enjoy breath a minute after. By heaven, I respect
    not his pelf thus much, but only that I may have wherewith to
    maintain thee.   5
Rebecca. O, but to rob my father, though 'a be bad, the world will
    think ill of me.
Haddit. Think ill of thee? Can the world pity him that ne'er pitied any
    besides? Since there is no end of his goods nor beginning of his
    goodness, had not we as good share his dross in his lifetime, as let   10
    controversy and lawyers devour it at's death?

55–6. brother to me, a lord] *Dod;* brother, to me a lord *Q;* brother to me a lord
Haz.

8–9. any besides? Since] *this ed.;* any, besides since *Q;* any? besides, since *Dod, etc.*

57–9. *But, brother lord . . . my nag*] These lines could be pointed with Carracus's
line 57 and Young Lord Wealthy's reply 'Alas, no, sir' as either questions or
statements.

4. *pelf*] money.
    thus much] i.e. not at all, probably with a dismissive gesture.

Rebecca. You have prevailed. At what hour is't you intend to have
    entrance into his chamber?
Haddit. Why, just at midnight, for then our apparition will seem most
    fearful. You'll make a way that we may ascend up like spirits?   15
Rebecca. I will, but how many have you made instruments herein?
Haddit. Faith, none but my cousin Lightfoot and a player.
Rebecca. But may you trust the player?
Haddit. O, exceeding well. We'll give him a speech 'a understands not.
    But now I think on't, what's to be done with your father's man,   20
    Peter?
Rebecca. Why, the least quantity of drink will lay him dead asleep – but
    hark, I hear my father coming; soon in the evening I'll convey you
    in.
Haddit. Till when, let this outward ceremony be the true pledge of our   25
    inward affections. [*He kisses her.*]   *Exit* REB[ECCA].
    So, this goes better forward than the plantation in Virginia – but
    see, here comes half the West Indies, whose rich mines this night
    I mean to be ransacking.   [*Withdraws.*]

    Enter HOG, LIGHTFOOT, *and* PETER [SERVITUDE].

Hog. Then you'll seal for this small lordship, you say? Tomorrow your   30
    money shall be rightly told up for you to a penny.
Lightfoot. I pray, let it, and that your man may set contents upon every
    bag.

---

27. plantation in Virginia ... West Indies] *Dod, etc.* (west Indies); *Plantation in Virginia ... west Indies* Q.

---

    16. *instruments*] partakers.
    23–4. *convey you in*] provide access to you.
    27. *plantation in Virginia*] After Raleigh's failed Roanoke Island colony of 1584, English colonists settled Jamestown as the first permanent New World settlement in 1607.
    28. *half the West Indies*] Haddit directs this comment at Hog; he will steal Hog's treasure, which includes his daughter. The comparison of the female beloved to New World treasure became a poetic commonplace; it is a trope employed with both irony and directness by Donne, who finds 'both the Indias of spice and mine' (i.e. east and west) in his lover ('The Sun Rising') and apostrophizes 'O my America, my new found land' in 'Elegy 8: To His Mistress Going to Bed'. The conceit is parodied in a mock-blazonic dialogue in *The Comedy of Errors*, where Antipholus and Dromio of Syracuse are describing Nell ('Luce' in the Folio) the kitchen wench as having 'America, the Indies' 'upon her nose': 'all o'er embellished with rubies, carbuncles, sapphires' (3.2.131–3).
    rich mines] treasures, material and sexual.
    30. *seal*] contract, seal a bond.
    31. *told*] counted.
    32–3. *set contents ... bag*] mark every bag with the amount of money it holds.

Haddit. [*Aside*] Indeed, by that we may know what we steal without
 labour for the telling on't o'er. [*Coming forward.*] How now,   35
 gentlemen, are ye agreed upon the price of this earth and clay?
Hog. Yes, faith, Master Haddit, the gentleman your friend here makes
 me pay sweetly for't. But let it go; I hope to inherit heaven, an't
 be but for doing gentlemen pleasure. – [*Aside*] Peter!
Peter Servitude. [*Aside*] Anon, sir.   40
Hog. [*Aside*] I wonder how Haddit came by that gay suit of clothes;
 all his means was consumed long since.
Peter Servitude. [*Aside*] Why, sir, being undone himself, 'a lives by the
 undoing – or, by Lady, it may be by the doing – of others; or peradventure both. A decayed gallant may live by anything, if 'a keep   45
 one thing safe.
Hog. Gentlemen, I'll to the scrivener's, to cause these writings to be
 drawn.
Lightfoot. Pray do, sir; we'll now leave you till the morning.
Hog. Nay, you shall stay dinner; I'll return presently. Peter, some beer   50
 here for these worshipful gentlemen. – Come, Peter.
                                       Ex[*eunt*] HOG [*and* PETER].
Haddit. We shall be bold, no doubt, and that, old penny-father, you'll
 confess by tomorrow morning.
Lightfoot. Then his daughter is certainly thine, and condescends to all
 thy wishes?   55
Haddit. And yet you would not once believe it, as if a female's favour
 could not be obtained by any but he that wears the cap of
 maintenance,

---

39. Peter!] *this ed.; new line with* SP 'Hog. Peter.' Q; 'Hog. Peter!' *Dod, etc.*   51. Come,
Peter.] *Q, placed after the SD to exit; phrase omitted by Dod, etc.*   51.1. Ex[*eunt*]
HOG [*and* PETER]] *this ed.; Exit Hogge, Q; Exit Hog and Peter Dod, etc.*

---

   39. *but*] only.
   43–4. *undone . . . undoing . . . doing*] ruined (financially) . . . ruining . . . having sex
with.
   46. *one thing safe*] i.e. his genitals from disease.
   47. *scrivener's*] scribe's, associated directly with money-lenders in plays, where they
act as the middle man to find borrowers and to broker the loan through its bond
date.
   50. *stay dinner*] stay for dinner (literally, make dinner wait upon you).
   51. *– Come, Peter & SD*] This phrase, followed in Q only by an exit for Hog, suggests a bit of stage business such as Hog leaving and then shouting back for Peter to
follow him. Dodsley and all editors following him omit this phrase.
   54. *condescends*] agrees.
   57–8. *the cap of maintenance*] headgear denoting great civic standing; here perhaps
meaning one who is well-off and trustworthy financially (see *OED* 'cap' n[1] 4.g and
'maintenance' (6)), since Haddit seems to be promoting attitude and youthful
forwardness.

When 'tis nothing but acquaintance and a bold spirit,
That may the chiefest prize 'mongst all of them inherit.   60
Lightfoot. Well, thou hast got one deserves the bringing home with
trumpets, and falls to thee as miraculously as the one thousand
pound did to the tailor, thank your good fortune. But must Hog's
man be made drunk?
Haddit. By all means, and thus it shall be effected: when 'a comes   65
in with beer, do you upon some slight occasion fall out with
him, and if you do give him a cuff or two, it will give him cause
to know y'are the more angry; then will I slip in and take up the
matter, and, striving to make you two friends, we'll make him
drunk.   70
Lightfoot. It's done in conceit already – see where he comes.

Enter PETER.

Peter Servitude. Will't please you to taste a cup of September beer,
gentlemen?
Lightfoot. Pray, begin; we'll pledge you, sir.
Peter Servitude. It's out, sir.
Lightfoot. Then my hand in, sir! *Lightfoot cuffs him.* Why, goodman   75
Hobby-horse, if we out of our gentility offered you to begin, must
you out of your rascality needs take it?
Haddit. Why, how now, sirs, what's the matter?
Peter Servitude. The gentleman here falls out with me upon nothing in   80
the world but mere courtesy.
Haddit. By this light, but 'a shall not; why, cousin Lightfoot!
Peter Servitude. Is his name Lightfoot? A plague on him: he has a heavy
hand.

Enter YOUNG LORD WEALTHY.

---

74. Pray ... sir.] *Qc; not in Qu.*   75–6. It's ... *cuffs him.*] *single line in Q.*

---

62. *trumpets*] i.e. with fanfare.
falls to thee] (1) comes into your possession (2) sexually 'falls' for you.
62–3. *one ... tailor*] another topical reference: 'The lottery for the benefit of the
Virginian Colonies, drawn 29th July 1612, in which Thomas Sharpliffe, a tailor, gained
the £1000 prize (*Stow*, p. 1002)' (Fleay ii, p. 257).
67. *cuff*] blow, punch.
71. *conceit*] imagination.
72. *September beer*] beer brewed in autumn; cf. 'March beer', 'a strong beer with
good keeping qualities, brewed in the spring' (*OED* 'March' II.2.b), and Francis Beaumont, *Knight of the Burning Pestle*, in which the Wife promises Rafe 'a cold capon
a-field, and a bottle of March beer' for his performance (5.161–2).
75. *It's out*] Here's my drink offered for pledge.
76. *my hand in*] here's my hand to punch you.
77. *goodman Hobby-horse*] Master buffoon.

Young L. Wealthy. Peace be here, for I came late enough from a　85
　madman.

Haddit. My young lord, God save you.

Young L. Wealthy. And you also – I could speak it in Latin, but the
　phrase is common.

Haddit. True, my lord, and what's common ought not much to be dealt　90
　withal; but I must desire your help, my lord, to end a controversy
　here between this gentleman my friend and honest Peter – [*Aside*]
　who, I dare be sworn, is as ignorant as your lordship.

Young L. Wealthy. That I will; but, my masters, thus much I'll say
　unt'ye: if so be this quarrel may be taken up peaceably without the　95
　endangering of my own person, well and good; otherwise I will
　not meddle therewith, for I have been vexed late enough already.

Haddit. Why then, my lord, if it please you, let me, being your inferior,
　decree the cause between them.

Young L. Wealthy. I do give leave, or permit.　100

Haddit. Then thus I will propound a reasonable motion: how many
　cuffs, Peter, did this gentleman out of his fury make thee partaker
　of?

Peter Servitude. Three at the least, sir.

Haddit. All which were bestowed upon you for beginning first,　105
　Peter?

Peter Servitude. Yes indeed, sir.

Haddit. Why then, hear the sentence of your suffering. You shall both
　down into Master Hog's cellar, Peter; and whereas you began first
　to him, so shall he there to you; and as he gave you three cuffs, so　110
　shall you retort off, in defiance of him, three black-jacks, which,
　if he deny to pledge, then the glory is thine, and he accounted by
　the wise discretion of my lord here a flincher.

Omnes. A very reasonable motion.

---

90. my lord] *Dod, etc.;* my Lords Q.　95. unt'ye] *this ed.;* untee Q; unto you *Dod,
etc.*

87. *God save you*] Greetings.

88–9. *Latin . . . common*] Young Lord Wealthy dismisses the 'common' again, as in
2.1.71–2. Reed notes that Young Lord Wealthy is 'Alluding to the use of it in Cooke's
City Gallant, commonly called Green's *Tu quoque*' (Reed, p. 240), 'then on the stage
at the Bull', adds Fleay (ii, p. 257).

95. *if so be*] if it might be that.

111. *retort*] reply, pay back (by drinking).

black-jacks] large, leather beer jugs.

112. *glory*] victory.

113. *flincher*] one who passes the bottle, refuses to drink; one who backs down from
a danger.

114. SP Omnes] All.

Young L. Wealthy. Why so; this is better than being among madmen 115
    yet.
Haddit. Were you so lately with any, my lord?
Young L. Wealthy. Yes, faith; I'll tell you all in the cellar how I was
    taken for an ambassador, and being no sooner in the house, but
    the madman carries me up into the garret for a spy, and very 120
    roundly bad me untruss; and had not a courteous servingman
    conveyed me away whilst he went to fetch whips, I think in my
    conscience, not respecting my honour, 'a would a' breeched me!
Haddit. By Lady, and 'twas to be feared! But come, my lord, we'll hear
    the rest in the cellar. 125
    And honest Peter, thou that hast been grieved,
    My lord and I will see thee well relieved. *Exeunt.*

---

122. fetch]   *Dod, etc.;* feteh *Q.*

---

   120. *garret*] uppermost room of a house, turret in a tower.
   121. *roundly bad me untruss*] curtly, bluntly told me to undress.
   123. *breeched me*] whipped me on the buttocks.
   127. *relieved*] recompensed, but also perhaps 'relieved' of duty by being made
drunk.

ACT 4

Act 4[, Scene 1]

Enter ALBERT *in the woods.*

Albert. How full of sweet content had this life been
　If it had been embracèd but before
　My burdenous conscience was so fraught with sin!
　But now my griefs o'ersway that happiness.
　O, that some lecher or accursed betrayer   5
　Of sacred friendship might but here arrive,
　And read the lines repentant on each tree
　That I have carved t'express my misery!
　My admonitions now would sure convert
　The sinful'st creature; I could tell them now,   10
　How idly vain those humans spend their lives
　That daily grieve, not for offences past,
　But to enjoy some wanton's company,
　Which when obtained, what is it but a blot,
　Which their whole life's repentance scarce can clear?   15
　I could now tell to friend-betraying man,
　How black a sin is hateful treachery,
　How heavy on their wretched souls 'twill sit
　When fearful death doth plant his siege but near them,
　How heavy and affrightful will their end   20
　Seem to appeach them, as if then they knew
　The full beginning of their endless woe
　Were then appointed; which astonishment,
　O, blest repentance, keep me, Albert, from!
　And suffer not despair to overwhelm,   25
　And make a shipwreck of my heavy soul!

Enter MARIA, *like a page.*

Act 4[, Scene 1]] *this ed.*; Actus Quartus *Q.* 10. tell] *Qc; not in Qu.* 15. life's]
Dod, etc.; lives *Q.* 17. a] *Dod, etc.; not in Q.* 21. appeach] *Q*; approach *Dod,
etc.* knew] *Dod, etc.*; knew, *Q.* 23. astonishment,] *Dod, etc.*; astonishment
Q. 24. repentance,] *Dod, etc.*; repentance *Q.*

---

21. *appeach*] Q's reading here suggests judgment upon the dying; Dodsley's emendation to 'approach' works well with the metaphor of death's military siege.

Who's here? A page. What black, disastrous fate
Can be so cruel to his pleasing youth?
Maria. So now, Maria, here thou must forgo
What nature lent thee to repay to death.   30
Famine, I thank thee, I have found thee kindest;
Thou sett'st a period to my misery.
Albert. It is Maria, that fair innocent,
Whom my abhorred lust hath brought to this:
I'll go for sustenance, and, O you powers,   35
If ever true repentance won acceptance,
O, show it Albert now, and let him save
His wronged beauty from untimely grave!   *Exit.*
Maria. Sure, something spake, or else my feebled sense
Hath lost the use of its due property –   40
Which is more likely, than that in this place
The voice of human creature should be heard.
This is far distant from the paths of men;
Nothing breathes here but wild and ravening beasts,
With airy monsters, whose shadowing wings do seem   45
To cast a veil of death on wicked livers,
Which I live dreadless of, and every hour
Strive to meet death, who, still unkind, avoids me,
But that now gentle famine doth begin
For to give end to my calamities.   50
See, here is carved upon this tree's smooth bark
Lines knit in verse – a chance far unexpected!
Assist me, breath, a little to unfold
What they include.

The Writing.
I that have writ these lines am one whose sin   55
Is more than grievous, for know that I have been
A breaker of my faith with one whose breast
Was all composed of truth; but I digressed,
And fled th'embrace of his dear friendship's love,

38. His] *Q, Dod;* This *Reed, etc.*   46. cast a veil of death on] *Haz.;* taste a veil of
death in *Q;* cast a vail of death in *Dod, Coll.*   53–4. Assist ... include] *so lineated
in Reed, etc.; single line in Q, Dod.*   54.1. *The Writing*] *Q, ranged right at lines 55–6.*
59. th'embrace] *Dod, etc.;* them brats *Q.*

35. *go for sustenance*] fetch food and drink.
46. *cast ... on*] Hazlitt's convincing emendation here builds on Dodsley's 'cast a
vail of death in'. Q's 'taste a veil of death in' can be made to work, if we read it to
mean 'experience the proximity of death', but the easy confusion of a small secretary
hand 't' with 'c' might explain the taste/caste misreading.
52. *knit*] couched, entwined, apparelled.

Clasping to falsehood, did a villain prove,   60
As thus shall be expressed. My worthy friend
Loved a fair beauty, who did condescend
In dearest affection to his virtuous will;
He then a night appointed to fulfil
Hymen's blessed rites, and to convey away   65
His love's fair person, to which peerless prey
I was acquainted made, and when the hour
Of her escape drew on, then lust did pour
Enraged appetite through all my veins,
And base desires in me let loose the reins   70
To my licentious will; and that black night,
When my friend should have had his chaste delight,
I feigned his presence, and, by her thought him,
Robbed that fair virgin of her honour's gem;
For which most heinous crime upon each tree   75
I write this story, that men's eyes may see
None but a damned one would have done like me.

Is Albert then become so penitent,
As in these deserts to deplore his facts,
Which his unfeigned repentance seems to clear?   80
How good man is when he laments his ill.
Who would not pardon now that man's misdeeds,
Whose griefs bewail them thus? Could I now live,
I would remit thy fault with Carracus.
But death no longer will afford reprieve   85
Of my abundant woes. Wronged Carracus, farewell;
Live, and forgive thy wrongs, for the repentance
Of him that caused them so deserves from thee;
And since my eyes do witness Albert's grief,
I pardon Albert, in my wrongs the chief.   [*She faints.*] 90

Enter ALBERT, *like a hermit.*

Albert. How? Pardon me? O sound angelical!
But see, she faints! O heavens, now show your power,
That these distilled waters, made in grief,
May add some comfort to affliction.
Look up, fair youth, and see a remedy.   95
Maria. O, who disturbs me? I was hand in hand,
Walking with death unto the house of rest.

68. pour] *Dod, etc.;* power *Q.* 84. I would] *Dod, etc.;* I'de *Q.*

80. *unfeigned*] true, genuine.
93. *distilled waters*] tears.

Albert. Let death walk by himself; if 'a want company,
    There's many thousands, boy, whose agèd years
    Have ta'en a surfeit of earth's vanities;   100
    They will go with him when he please to call.
    Do drink, my boy; thy pleasing, tender youth
    Cannot deserve to die; no, it is for us,
    Whose years are laden by our often sins,
    Singing the last part of our blessèd repentance,   105
    Are fit for death; and none but such as we
    Death ought to claim, for when 'a snatcheth youth,
    It shows him but a tyrant, but when age,
    Then is 'a just, and not composed of rage.
    How fares my lad?   110
Maria. Like one embracing death with all his parts,
    Reaching at life but with one little finger;
    His mind so firmly knit unto the first,
    That unto him the latter seems to be
    What may be pointed at, but not possessed.   115
Albert. O, but thou shalt possess it!
    If thou didst fear thy death but as I do,
    Thou wouldst take pity – though not of thyself,
    Yet of my agèd years. Trust me, my boy,
    Thou'st struck such deep compassion in my breast   120
    That all the moisture which prolongs my life
    Will from my eyes gush forth, if now thou leav'st me.
Maria. But can we live here in this desert wood?
    If not, I'll die, for other places seem
    Like tortures to my griefs. May I live here?   125
Albert. Ay, thou shalt live with me, and I will tell thee
    Such strange occurrents of my fore-passed life,
    That all thy young-sprung griefs shall seem but sparks
    To the great fire of my calamities.
[Maria.] Then I'll live only with you for to hear   130
    If any human woes can be like mine.
    Yet since my being in this darksome desert,
    I have read on trees most lamentable stories.

---

102. Do] *Dod, etc.;* To Q.   111. with all] *Dod;* withall Q.   130. SP *[Maria.]*]
Dod, etc.; not in Q.

---

98. *want*] lack.
100. *surfeit*] excess, superfluity.
107. *'a*] he.
113. *knit*] tied, connected.
113–14. *first . . . latter*] i.e. death . . . life.
127. *occurrents*] happenings, events.
128. *young-sprung griefs*] troubles of youth.
129. *To*] Compared with.

Albert. 'Tis true indeed: there's one within these woods
    Whose name is Albert, a man so full of sorrow,   135
    That on each tree he passeth by he carves
    Such doleful lines for his rash follies past,
    That whoso reads them and not drowned in tears,
    Must have a heart framed forth of adamant.
Maria. And can you help me to the sight of him?   140
Albert. Ay, when thou wilt; he'll often come to me
    And at my cave sit a whole winter's night,
    Recounting of his stories. I tell thee, boy,
    Had he offended more than did that man
    Who stole the fire from heaven, his contrition   145
    Would appease all the gods, and quite revert
    Their wrath to mercy. But come, my pretty boy,
    We'll to my cave, and after some repose
    Relate the sequel of each other's woes.   *Exeunt.*

[4.2]

Enter CARRACUS.

Carracus. What a way have I come, yet I know not whither.
    The air's so cold this winter season,
    I'm sure a fool: would any but an ass
    Leave a warm, matted chamber and a bed
    To run thus in the cold? And, which is more,   5
    To seek a woman – a slight thing called woman;
    Creatures, with curious nature framed, as I suppose,

---

136. on] *Dod, etc.;* one *Q.*   140. me] *Dod, etc.; not in Q.*

1–2. What … whither, / The … season] *Q, Dod., Scott, Reed;* What … not / Whither … season, *Coll, Haz.*   7. with] *Q;* which *Dod, etc.* framed,] *Dod, etc.* *(*fram'd,*);* framed *Q.*

---

138. *whoso*] whoever.
  not] is not.
139. *adamant*] hard rock, associated in the seventeenth century with diamond.
142. *winter's night*] i.e. long night, proverbially a time for long tales of romance, courage, or magic.
144–5. *that man … heaven*] Prometheus stole fire from heaven to keep his human creations warm on earth. His continued disdain for the gods and his avoidance of their intended punishments led to his temporary punishment having his liver repeatedly eaten while bound to Mount Caucasus.

7. *with curious Nature framed*] designed/made by complicated/cunning/mysterious Nature. Dodsley's emendation from 'with' to 'which' makes an easier grammatical statement, but 'with' is clear too.
7–8. *framed, … treasury*] designed (with seductive form) to ensure receipt of men's 'rent' (semen) to reproduce humanity.

For rent-receivers to her treasury.
And why I think so now, I'll give you instance:
Most men do know that nature's self hath made them   10
Most profitable members; then if so,
By often trading in the commonwealth
They needs must be enriched; why, very good.
To whom ought beauty then repay this gain,
Which she by nature's gift hath profited,   15
But unto nature? Why, all this I grant.
Why then, they shall no more be called women,
For I will style them thus, scorning their leave:
Those that for nature do much rent receive.
This is a wood, sure; and, as I have read,   20
In woods are echoes which will answer men
To every question which they do propound. Echo!
Echo.   Echo.
Carracus. O, are you there? Have at ye then, i'faith.
Echo, canst tell me whether men or women
Are for the most part damned?
Echo.   Most part damned.   25
Carracus. Of both indeed; how true this echo speaks.
Echo, now tell me if 'mongst a thousand women
There be one chaste or none?
Echo.   None.
Carracus. Why, so I think; better and better still.
Now further, Echo: in a world of men,   30
Is there one faithful to his friend, or no?
Echo.   No.
Carracus. Thou speakst most true, for I have found it so.
Who said thou wast a woman, Echo, lies;
Thou couldst not then answer so much of truth.
Once more, good Echo: 35

---

22. Echo! / *Echo.* Echo.] *this ed.*; *Echo, Echo, Echo.* Q; *Echo. / Echo.* Echo. *Dod, etc.* 22–43.] *Q places Echo's replies to the right of each prompting line.* 30. further] Q; farther *Dod, etc.*

21. *In woods are echoes*] Echo was a wood nymph who fell in love with Narcissus. He supposed she was mocking him as she repeated just the tail-end of his phrases. Her unrequited love caused her physically to pine away, leaving just her voice. Echoes in drama tend to provide answers or warnings to those in quandary or peril; the trope foregrounds artificiality and is often found in romance and seventeenth-century entertainments.
23. *Have at ye*] Come on then.

Was my Maria false by her own desire,
    Or was't against her will?
Echo.   Against her will.
Carracus. Troth, it may be so; but canst thou tell,
    Whether she be dead or not?
Echo.   Not.
Carracus. Not dead?
Echo.   Not dead.   40
Carracus. Then without question she doth surely live.
    But I do trouble thee too much; therefore,
    Good speak-truth, farewell.
Echo.   Farewell.
Carracus. How quick it answers. O, that councillors
    Would thus resolve men's doubts without a fee!   45
    How many country clients then might rest
    Free from undoing; no plodding pleader then
    Would purchase great possessions with his tongue.
    Were I some demigod, or had that power,
    I would straight make this echo here a judge: 50
    He'd spend his judgement in the open court,
    As now to me, without being once solicited
    In's private chamber; 'tis not bribes could win
    Him to o'ersway men's right, nor could he be
    Led to damnation for a little pelf;   55
    He would not harbour malice in his heart,
    Or envious hatred, base despite, or grudge,
    But be an upright, just, and equal judge.
    But now imagine that I should confront
    Treacherous Albert, who hath raised my front!   60
    But I fear this idle prate hath
    Made me quite forget my *cinquepace.*   *He danceth.*

                    Enter ALBERT.

Albert. I heard the echo answer unto one,
    That by his speech cannot be far remote

---

38. Troth, it] *Haz; Troth't Q;* Troth it *Dod, Coll.*   50. I would] *Haz.;* I'de *Q;* I
wou'd *Dod, Coll.*   55. Led] *Dod, etc.;* Lead *Q.*   61–2. But . . . hath / Made] *so
lineated in Q, Dod, Reed, Scott;* But . . . me / Quite *Coll, Haz.*   62. cinquepace] *this
ed.;* cinque pace *Q, Dod, etc.*

---

60. *raised my front*] (1) faced up to me in defiance, offended me (2) provoked me
to anger, defiance.
    61. *prate*] chatter.
    62. cinquepace] lively dance.

From off this ground – and see, I have descried him.   65
O heavens! It's Carracus, whose reason's seat
Is now usurped by madness and distraction,
Which I, the author of confusion,
Have planted here by my accursèd deeds.
Carracus. O, are you come, sir? I was sending   70
The tavern-boy for you; I have been practising
Here, and can do none of my lofty tricks.
Albert. Good sir, if any spark do yet remain
Of your consumed reason, let me strive –
Carracus. To blow it out, troth, I most kindly thank you,   75
Here's friendship to the life. But Father Whey-beard,
Why should you think me void of reason's fire,
My youthful days being in the height of knowledge?
I must confess your old years gain experience,
But that's so much o'erruled by dotage,   80
That what you think experience shall effect,
Short memory destroys. What say you now, sir?
Am I mad now, that can answer thus
To all interrogatories?
Albert. But though your words do savour, sir, of judgement,   85
Yet when they derogate from the due observance
Of fitting times, they ought not be respected,
No more than if a man should tell a tale
Of feigned mirth in midst of extreme sorrows.
Carracus. How did you know my sorrows, sir?   90
What, though I have lost a wife,
Must I be therefore grieved? Am I not happy
To be so freed of a continual trouble?
Had many a man such fortune as I,
In what a heaven would they think themselves,   95
Being released of all those threat'ning clouds,
Which in the angry skies – called women's brows –

---

65. off] *Dod, etc.;* of *Q.*   70–2. O . . . tricks] *so lineated in Haz; set in prose in Q,*
Dod, Reed, Scott, Coll.   87. not] *Q;* to *Dod, etc.*   95. themselves,] *Reed, etc.;*
themselves? *Q, Dod.*

65. *From off*] This emendation from Q's 'From of' reflects common usage of the
period.
66. *reason's seat*] i.e. brain.
72. *lofty*] showy, clever.
76. *Whey-beard*] white-beard, old man (whey is the serum or watery part of milk
after the separation of the curd, usually for the manufacture of cheese).
80. *dotage*] feebleness (usually associated with old age), foolish affection.
86. *derogate*] detract, withdraw.

                    Sit, ever menacing tempestuous storms?
                    But yet I needs must tell you, old December,
                    My wife was clear of this; within her brow   100
                    Sh'had not a wrinkle nor a storming frown,
                    But, like a smooth, well-polished ivory,
                    It seemed so pleasant to the looker-on.
                    She was so kind, of nature so gentle,
                    That if sh'had done a fault, she'd straight go die for't –   105
                    Was not she then a rare one?
                    What, weepst thou, agèd Nestor?
                    Take comfort, man, Troy was ordained by fate
                    To yield to us, which we will ruinate.
Albert.   Good sir, walk with me but where you see   110
                    The shadowing elms, within whose circling round
                    There is a holy spring about encompassed
                    By dandling sycamores and violets,
                    Whose waters cure all human maladies.
                    Few drops thereof, being sprinkled on your temples,   115
                    Revives your fading memory, and restores
                    Your senses lost unto their perfect being.
Carracus.   Is it clear water, sir, and very fresh?
                    For I am thirsty; gives it a better relish
                    Than a cup of dead wine with flies in't?   120
Albert.   Most pleasant to the taste; pray, will you go?
Carracus.   Faster than you, I believe, sir.
                              Exeunt[, CARRACUS running ahead].

[4.3]

                              Enter *Maria.*

Maria.   I am walked forth from my preserver's cave
                    To search about these woods, only to see
                    The penitent Albert, whose repentant mind

---

101. Sh'had] *this ed.;* sh'ad *Q;* She had *Dod, etc.*   105. sh'had] *this ed.;* sh'ad *Q;*
she'd *Dod, etc.*   110. you see] *Q, Dod, etc.;* you [may] see *Haz.*   119–20. thirsty;
gives it . . . in't?] *Q, Dod.;* thirsty? gives *Reed, etc.;* thirsty, [which] gives it . . . in't?
Haz.

---

   99. *old December*] old man (assignation of months to characters to represent age
was a familiar pastoral and lyric poetic trope of the period).
   102. *ivory*] i.e. ivory carved object.
   107. *Nestor*] Wise old man of the Greek army in Homer's *Iliad.*
   113. *dandling*] The *OED* cites this line as 'dandle' mistaken for 'dangle' ('dandle'
(5)). However, 'dandle' is a term usually applied to caressing or rocking a baby, and
this nicely suggests personification as the elms move up and down (*OED* 'dandle' 1.b)
(in the breeze?) and lean protectively over the 'holy spring'.

Each tree expresseth. O, that some power divine
Would hither send my virtuous Carracus –   5
Not for my own content, but that he might
See how his distressed friend repents the wrong
Which his rash folly, most unfortunate,
Acted against him and me, which I forgive
A hundred times a day, for that more often   10
My eyes are witness to his sad complaints.
How the good hermit seems to share his moans,
Which in the daytime he deplores 'mongst trees,
And in the night his cave is filled with sighs;
No other bed doth his weak limbs support   15
Than the cold earth; no other harmony
To rock his cares asleep but blustering winds,
Or some swift current, headlong rushing down
From a high mountain's top, pouring his force
Into the ocean's gulf, where, being swallowed,   20
Seems to bewail his fall with hideous words;
No other sustentation to suffice
What nature claims, but raw, unsavoury roots
With troubled waters, where untamèd beasts
Do bathe themselves.

> *Enter Satyrs, dance, and exeunt.*

                    Ay me! What things are these?   25
What pretty harmless things they seem to be,
As if delight had nowhere made abode,
But in their nimble sport.

> *Enter* ALBERT [*and* CARRACUS].

Yonder's the courteous hermit, and with him
Albert, it seems. O, see, 'tis Carracus!   30
Joy, do not now confound me!   [*Withdraws.*]
Carracus. Thanks unto heavens and thee, thou holy man,
I have attained what doth adorn man's being,
That precious gem of reason, by which solely
We are discerned from rude and brutish beasts,   35

---

11. sad] *Dod, etc.;* said *Q.*   26. be,] *this ed.;* be? *Q, Dod;* be! *Reed, etc.*   34. solely]
Dod, etc.; soly *Q.*

---

10. *for that*] because.
13. *deplores*] laments, moans.
22. *sustentation*] sustenance, provision.
35. *discerned from rude*] differentiated from simple.

No other difference being 'twixt us and them.
How to repay this more than earthly kindness
Lies not within my power, but in his
That hath indued thee with celestial gifts,
To whom I'll pray he may bestow on thee   40
What thou deserv'st, blessed immortality.
Albert. Which unto you befall, thereof most worthy.
But virtuous sir, what I will now request
From your true generous nature is that you would
Be pleased to pardon that repentant wight,   45
Whose sinful story upon yon trees' bark
Yourself did read, for that you say to you
Those wrongs were done.
Carracus. Indeed they were, and to a dear wife lost;
Yet I forgive him, as I wish the heavens   50
May pardon me.
Maria.   So doth Maria too.   *She discovers herself.*
Carracus. Lives my Maria, then? What gracious planet
Gave thee safe conduct to these desert woods?
Maria. My late mishap – repented now by all,
And therefore pardoned – compelled me to fly,   55
Where I had perishèd for want of food,
Had not this courteous man awaked my sense,
In which death's self had partly interest.
Carracus. Alas, Maria! I am so far indebted
To him already for the late recovery of   60
My own weakness, that 'tis impossible
For us to attribute sufficient thanks
For such abundant good.
Albert. I rather ought to thank the heaven's creator
That he vouchsafed me such especial grace   65
In doing so small a good, which could I hourly
Bestow on all, yet could I not assuage
The swelling rancour of my fore-passed crimes.
Carracus. O sir, despair not, for your course of life –
Were your sins far more odious than they be –   70
Doth move compassion and pure clemency
In the all-ruling judge, whose powerful mercy

46. story] *Dod, etc,;* stories *Q.*   46. yon trees'] *this ed.;* yon trees *Q;* yon tree's *Dod, etc.*   64. creator] *Dod;* Creator *Q, Coll, Haz.*   72. judge] *Dod, etc.;* Judge *Q.*

45. *wight*] person.
54. *late*] recent.
65. *vouchsafed*] granted, conferred on.
67–8. *assuage ... rancour*] ease, mitigate the growing rancidity, smell.

O'ersways his justice, and extends itself
To all repentant minds. He's happier far
That sins, and can repent him of his sin,   75
Than the self-justifier, who doth surmise
By his own works to gain salvation,
Seeming to reach at heaven and clasp damnation.
You then are happy, and our penitent friend,
To whose wished presence please you now to bring us,   80
That in our gladsome arms we may enfold
His much-esteemed person, and forgive
The injuries of his rash follies passed.
Albert. Then see false Albert prostrate at your feet,
Desiring justice for his heinous ill.   *He discovers himself.* 85
Carracus. Is it you, Albert's self, that hath preserved us?
O blessed bewailer of thy misery!
Maria. And wofullest liver in calamity!
Carracus. From which, right worthy friend, it's now high time
You be released; come then, you shall with us.   90
Our first and chiefest welcome, my Maria,
We shall receive at your good father's house,
Who, as I do remember, in my frenzy
Sent a kind letter which desired our presence.
Albert. So please you, virtuous pair, Albert will stay   95
And spend the remnant of this wearisome life
In these dark woods.
Carracus. Then you neglect the comforts heaven doth send
To your abode on earth. If you stay here,
Your life may end in torture by the cruelty   100
Of some wild ravenous beasts, but if 'mongst men
When you depart, the faithful prayers of many
Will much avail to crown your soul with bliss.
Albert. Loved Carracus, I have found in thy converse
Comfort so blessed, that nothing now but death   105
Shall cause a separation in our being.
Maria. Which heaven confirm!
Carracus. Thus by the breach of faith our friendship's knit
In stronger bonds of love.
Albert.   Heaven so continue it!   *Exeunt.*

---

78. and clasp] *Q*; he clasps *Dod, etc.*   81. may] *Dod, etc.; not in Q*.   85. SD *He discovers himself.*] *placed after line 84 in Q, Dod, etc.*

74–8. *He's happier . . . damnation*] It is a more effective easing of the conscience to acknowledge one's sin and to repent than to rely on the mistaken doctrine of good works to 'buy' oneself into heaven.
90. *with*] i.e. come with.

ACT 5

Act 5[, Scene 1]

Enter HOG *in his chamber, with* REBECCA *laying down his bed,*
and, seeming to put the keys under his bolster,
conveyeth them into her pocket.

Hog. So, have you laid the keys of the outward doors under my
    bolster?
Rebecca. Yes, forsooth.
Hog. Go your way to bed then.   *Exit* RE[BECCA].
    I wonder who did at the first invent   5
    These beds, the breeders of disease and sloth.
    'A was no soldier, sure, nor no scholar,
    And yet 'a might be very well a courtier,
    For no good husband would have been so idle,
    No usurer neither – yet here the bed affords   10
    Store of sweet golden slumbers unto him.   *Discovers his gold.*
    Here sleeps command in war; Caesar by this
    Obtained his triumphs; this will fight man's cause
    When fathers, brethren, and the nearest of friends
    Leaves to assist him; all content to this   15
    Is merely vain; the lovers whose affections
    Do sympathize together in full pleasure,
    Debarred of this, their summer sudden ends;
    And care, the winter to their former joys,
    Breathes such a cold blast on their turtles' bills,   20

Act 5[, Scene 1]] *this ed.;* Actus Quintus *Q.* 8. very *Dod, etc.;* vety *Q.* 11. SD
Discovers his gold.] placed after line 10 in Q, Dod, etc. 15. Leaves] *Q;* Leave *Dod,*
etc.

    0.1. laying down] turning down.
    0.2. bolster] pillow, generally long and rounded.
    9–10. *idle . . . No usurer neither*] not even a usurer would have been that idle;
usurers do no work for their financial gain, and are therefore proverbially idle.
    11. Discovers] uncovers, reveals.
    12. *Caesar*] Julius Caesar (100-44 BCE), Emperor of Rome.
    15. *Leaves to assist*] Abandons.
content] contentment, comfort.
    18. *Debarred of*] Denied.
    20. *turtles*] turtle doves, love-birds.

Having not this to shroud them from his storms,
They straight are forced to make a separation,
And so live under those that rule o'er this.
The gallant, whose illustrious outside draws
The eyes of wantons to behold with wonder   25
His rare-shaped parts, for so he thinks they be,
Decked in the robes of glistering gallantry,
Having not this attendant on his person,
Walks with a cloudy brow, and seems to all
A great condemner of society,   30
Not for the hate he bears to company,
But for the want of this ability.
O silver! Thou that art the basest captive
Kept in this prison; how many pale offenders
For thee have suffered ruin? But, O my gold!   35
Thy sight's more pleasing than the seemly locks
Of yellow-haired Apollo, and thy touch
More smooth and dainty than the down-soft white
Of ladies' tempting breast; thy bright aspect
Dims the greatest lustre of heaven's wagoner.   40
But why go I about to extol thy worth,
Knowing that poets cannot compass it?
But now give place, my gold, for here's a power
Of greater glory and supremacy

---

21. them from] *this ed.;* him forth *Q;* him from *Dod;* them forth *Haz.*   26. His]
Haz. Hir *Q, Dod, etc.*   39. ladies'] *this ed.;* Ladies *Q;* lady's *Dod, etc.*

---

21. *to . . . storms*] to protect them from care's afflictions; Q's 'shroud him forth his
storms' could mean something like 'to cover up and put away (as in shrouding the
dead) the things that afflict him', but the singular 'him' is grammatically incorrect and
to 'shroud something forth' is not a familiar phrase.

23. *this*] i.e. gold.

24. *outside*] outer appearance (clothing).

26. *rare-shaped parts*] i.e. fabulous body.

28. *this*] i.e. gold (placed in the extended metaphor of peace of mind, sleep).

30. *condemner of society*] the phrase suggests a misanthrope, a hater of people; but
the following line shifts the meaning to envy for those in possession of the satisfaction
of possession of gold.

32. *want*] lack.

37. *Apollo*] God of the sun, and therefore golden-haired.

39. *aspect*] appearance.

40. *heaven's wagoner*] i.e. Apollo, who drives his sunny wagon around the world.

41. *go I about*] do I attempt.

extol] praise.

42. *compass*] encompass.

43. *give place*] move aside.

Obscures thy being; here sits enthronised   45
The sparkling diamond, whose bright reflection
Casts such a splendour on these other gems,
'Mongst which he so majestical appears,
As if – now my good angels guard me!

A flash of fire, and LIGHTFOOT *ascends like a spirit*
[through a trap door in the floor].

Lightfoot. Melior vigilantia somno.   50
Stand not amazed, good man, for what appears
Shall add to thy content. Be void of fears;
I am the shadow of rich kingly Croesus,
Sent by his greatness from the lower world
To make thee mighty, and to sway on earth   55
By thy abundant store, as he himself doth
In Elysium; how he reigneth there,
His shadow will unfold: give thou then ear.
In under-air, where fair Elysium stands,
Beyond the river stylèd Acheron,   60
He hath a castle built of adamant,
Not framed by vain enchantment, but there fixed
By the all-burning hands of warlike spirits,
Whose windows are composed of purest crystal,
And decked within with oriental pearls.   65
There the great spirit of Croesus' royal self
Keeps his abode in joyous happiness;

49.1–2. *A . . . floor*]] *this ed.; Q ranges SD to the right of lines 48–50.*

49. *my good angels*] an appeal to heavenly protection in a moment of fear; punning on protection by his gold ('angels' are gold coins worth 10 shillings each).

50. Melior vigilantia somno] Latin: Better wakefulness than sleep.

53. *Croesus*] Wealthy king of Lydia c. 560-547 BCE.

57. *Elysium*] fields of rest (often for military heroes) in the afterlife.

58. *shadow*] ghost (returned spirits from the underworld were known as 'shades' or 'shadows').

give thou then ear] listen.

59. *under-air*] the underworld.

60. *stylèd*] named, called.

Acheron] 'river of woe', one of the rivers of the underworld across which Charon ferries souls of the dead.

61. *adamant*] See note to 4.1.139.

62. *framed by vain enchantment*] made, invented by mere magic.

fixed] placed.

63. *all-burning*] because in hell.

65. *oriental*] eastern, valuable.

He is not tortured there, as poets feign,
With molten gold and sulphury flames of fire,
Or any such molesting perturbation,   70
But there reputed as a demigod,
Feasting with Pluto and his Proserpine
Night after night with all delicious cates,
With greater glory than seven kingdoms' states.
Now further know the cause of my appearance: 75
The kingly Croesus, having by fame's trump
Heard that thy loved desires stand affected
To the obtaining of abundant wealth,
Sends me, his shade, thus much to signify,
That if thou wilt become famous on earth,   80
He'll give to thee even more than infinite,
And after death with him thou shalt partake
The rare delights beyond the Stygian lake.
Hog. Great Croesus' shadow may dispose of me
To what he pleaseth.
Lightfoot.   So speaks obediency.   85
For which I'll raise thy lowly thoughts as high
As Croesus' were in his mortality.
Stand then undaunted whilst I raise those spirits
By whose laborious task and industry
Thy treasure shall abound and multiply.   90
      Ascend, Ascarion, thou that art
      A powerful spirit, and dost convert

---

75. *further*] Q; *farther Dod, etc.*   84–5. *Great . . . me / To . . . pleaseth*] *so lineated in Reed, etc.; single line in Q, Dod.*   91–5. *Ascend . . . will*] *so lineated in Reed, etc.; set in prose and italic font in Q, Dod.*

68. *as poets feign*] as poets pretend, invent in their poetic stories.
70. *perturbation*] disturbance, disquieting.
72. *Pluto and his Proserpine*] God of the underworld and his wife (Persephone in Greek), whom he stole from the world of the living; Pluto complied with Mercury's demand to free her, but first he gave her six pomegranate seeds to eat, which kept her with him six months of the year and allowed her to live on earth the other six months.
73. *cates*] edible delicacies.
74. *seven kingdoms' states*] probably referring to the heptarchy of the Anglo-Saxon kingdoms: East Anglia, Essex, Mercia, Northumbria, Kent, Sussex, and Wessex.
76. *fame's trump*] the trumpet of fame; the character Fame is usually depicted in images as having a trumpet to announce the glories of great persons.
79. *signify*] relate, impart.
83. *Stygian lake*] 'pertaining to the River Styx, or, in wider sense to the infernal regions of classical mythology' (*OED* 'Stygian').
91. *Ascarion*] Unclear who this is supposed to be; it may be a corruption of (Judas) Iscariot, as one who lusted after gold at the expense of Christ.

Silver to gold; I say ascend
And on me, Croesus' shade, attend,
To work the pleasure of his will.   95

The PLAYER [*as Ascarion*] *appears* [*through the trap door*].

Player. What, would then Croesus list to fill
     Some mortal's coffers up with gold,
     Changing the silver it doth hold?
     By that pure metal, if't be so,
     By the infernal gates I swear,   100
     Where Rhadamanth doth domineer,
     By Croesus' name and by his castle,
     Where winter nights he keepeth wassail,
     By Demogorgon and the fates,
     And by all these low-country states;   105
     That after knowledge of thy mind,
     Ascarion, like the swift-paced wind,
     Will fly to finish thy command.
Lightfoot. Take, then, this silver out of hand,
     And bear it to the river Tagus,   110
     Beyond th'abode of Archi-Magus,
     Whose golden sands upon it cast,
     Transform it into gold at last,
     Which, being effected, straight return,
     And sudden too, or I will spurn   115
     This trunk of thine into the pit,
     Where all the hellish furies sit,
     Scratching their eyes out. Quick, be gone!

---

94. on] *Dod, etc.;* one *Q.*   118. out. Quick, be gone!] *this ed., after Haz.* (out.
Quick, begone!)*;* out quicke begon. *Q;* out. Quick! begone! *Dod, etc.*

---

96. *list*] want, desire.
101. *Rhadamanth*] Rhadamanthus, judge of the underworld. In Thomas Kyd's *The
Spanish Tragedy* (1587), Andrea tells how Rhadamanthus sits with Minos and Aeacus,
and all three discuss Andrea's proper region of residence there before sending him to
Pluto for determination (1.1.32–54).
103. *wassail*] salutation, health-drinking.
104. *Demogorgon*] ancient creative pagan deity, sometimes conflated in the early
modern period with Ovid's Demiurge, who created the universe.
fates] three goddesses that determine the length of human life.
105. *low-country states*] i.e. underworld regions.
109. *out of hand*] at once, immediately.
110. *river Tagus*] largest river in the Iberian peninsula, passing through Aranjuez,
Toledo, and Alcántara in Spain, and Lisbon in Portugal.
111. *Archi-Magus*] Arch magician; cf. Archimago in Spenser's *Faerie Queene.*
115. *spurn*] cast aside.
117. *furies*] avenging goddesses sent from the underworld.

Player. Swifter in course than doth the sun.   *Exit.*
Lightfoot. How farest thou, mortal? Be not terrified   120
  At these infernal motions; know that shortly
  Great Croesus' ghost shall, in the love he bears thee,
  Give thee sufficient power by thy own worth
  To raise such spirits.
Hog. Croesus is much too liberal in his favour   125
  To one so far desertless as poor Hog.
Lightfoot. Poor Hog? O, speak not that word 'poor' again,
  Lest the whole apple tree of Croesus' bounty,
  Cracked into shivers, overthrow thy fortunes!
  For he abhors the name of poverty,   130
  And will grow sick to hear it spoke by those
  Whom he intends to raise. But see, the twilight
  Posteth before the chariot of the sun,
  Brings word of his approach:
  We must be sudden, and with speed raise up   135
  The spirit Bazan, that can straight transform
  Gold into pearl; be still and circumspect.
    Bazan, ascend up from the treasure
    Of Pluto, where thou didst at pleasure
    Metamorphize all his gold   140
    Into pearl, which 'bove a thousand-fold
    Exceeds the value; quickly rise
    To Croesus' shade, who hath a prize
    To be performèd by thy strength.

    [HADDIT *as*] *Bazan ascends* [*through the trap door*].

Haddit. I am no fencer, yet at length,   145
  From Pluto's presence and the hall
  Where Proserpine keeps festival,

---

120. farest] *this ed.;* fair'st Q; far'st Dod, *etc.* 128. Lest] *Dod, etc.;* Least Q. 133. Posteth] *Q;* Posting Dod, etc. 138–44. Bazan . . . strength] *so lineated in* Reed, *etc.;* *set in prose and italic font in* Q, Dod. 138, 144.1. Bazan . . . Bazan] *Dod, etc.;* Bazon . . . Bazon Q, 145. SP Haddit.] *so* Reed, etc.; Bazon Q, Dod.

133. *Posteth . . . sun*] Hurries before the sunrise.
136. *Bazan*] I cannot find this spirit; it may be a corruption of the verb 'baze', meaning 'to stupefy, frighten, alarm' (*OED* cites a 1603 instance), which is certainly what these spirits are designed to do.
145. *fencer*] swordsman (he is responding to Lightfoot's 'prize' at line 143, which he takes to mean a fencing contest).
147. *festival*] an odd usage, since Prosperpine was not happy to be in the underworld; it might be taken with irony, or be read simply as meaning she observes the required annual sojourn in the underworld.

I'm hither come; and now I see
To what intent I'm raised by thee:
It is to make that mortal rich,   150
That at his fame men's ears may itch
When they do hear but of his store.
He hath one daughter and no more,
Which all the lower powers decree,
She to one Wealthy wedded be,   155
By which conjunction there shall spring
Young heirs to Hog, whereon to fling
His mass of treasure when 'a dies –
Thus Bazan truly prophesies.
But come, my task: I long to rear   160
His fame above the hemisphere.
Lightfoot. Take then the gold which here doth lie,
And quick return it by and by,
All in choice pearl; whither to go
I need not tell you, for you know.   165
Haddit. Indeed I do, and Hog shall find it so.   *Exit.*
Lightfoot. Now, mortal, there is nothing doth remain
'Twixt thee and thine abundance, only this:
Turn thy eyes westward, for from thence appeareth
Ascarion with thy gold, which, having brought   170
And at thy foot surrendered, make obeisance;
Then turn about, and fix thy tapers eastward,
From whence great Bazan brings thy orient pearl;
Who'll lay it at thy feet much like the former.
Hog. Then I must make to him obeisance thus.   175
Lightfoot. Why, so; in meantime, Croesus' shade will rest
Upon thy bed; but above all, take heed
You suffer not your eyes to stray aside
From the direct point I have set thee at,

---

149. I'm raised] *this ed.;* 'Ime rai'sd *Q;* I'm rais'd *Dod, etc.*   166. Indeed . . . so]
Dod. makes this an aside; not in Haz.   169. westward] *Q;* eastward *Dod,*
etc.   172. eastward] *this ed.;* westward *Q, Dod etc.*

---

151. *itch*] i.e. because irritated with envious response, and because touched by
Fame's words; cf. Milton, *Lycidas*, 'But not the praise, / Phoebus replied, and touched
my trembling ears' (lines 76–7).

169–72. *westward . . . eastward*] i.e. westward to see gold arriving from the New
World . . . eastward to see the approaching of your Oriental pearl. Dodsley etc. strangely
alter the first 'westward' to 'eastward'; Q has 'westward' at both lines, and the Malone
reprint rightly tells us to read 'eastward' at line 172.

172. *tapers*] candles.

For though the spirit do delay the time,   180
And not return your treasure speedily –
Hog. Let the loss light on me if I neglect
Or overslip what Croesus' shade commands.
Lightfoot. [*Aside*] So, now practise standing, though it be nothing
    agreeable to your Hog's age. Let me see, among these writings is   185
    my nephew Haddit's mortgage; but in taking that it may breed
    suspect on us, wherefore this box of jewels will stand far better,
    and let that alone. It is now break of day, and near by this the
    marriage is confirmed betwixt my cousin and great Croesus'
    friend's daughter here, whom I would now leave to his most   190
    weighty cogitations. –
So, gentle sir, adieu; time not permits
To hear those passions and those frantic fits
You're subject to, when you shall find how true
Great Croesus' shade hath made an ass of you.   [*Exit.*]   195
Hog. Let me now ruminate to myself why Croesus should be so great
    a favourer to me – and yet to what end should I desire to know?
    I think it is sufficient it is so. And I would 'a had been so sooner,
    for he and his spirits would have saved me much labour in the
    purchasing of wealth; but then indeed it would have been the   200
    confusion of two or three scriveners which, by my means, have
    been properly raised. But now imagine this only a trick, whereby
    I may be gulled! But how can that be? Are not my doors locked?
    Have I not seen with my own eyes the ascending of the spirits?
    Have I not heard with my own ears the invocations wherewith they   205
    were raised? Could any but spirits appear through so firm a floor
    as this is? 'Tis impossible. But hark! I hear the spirit Ascarion
    coming with my gold. O bountiful Croesus! I'll build a temple to
    thy mightiness!

    Enter YOUNG LO[RD] WEALTHY *and* PETER [SERVITUDE].

183. Or] *Dod, etc.;* I *Q.* shade] *Dod, etc.;* suit *Q.* 190. would] *Q;* will *Dod,*
etc. 205. invocations] *Q, Dod, etc.* invocation *Haz.*

183. *shade*] Q's 'suit', or command, works in the context, but Dodsley's emendation
is a good one considering the phrase 'Croesus' shade' appears as a kind of mantra
throughout the scene (lines 94, 143, 176, and 195).
    187. *stand far better*] do better, be much more appropriate.
    188. *near by this*] just about this time.
    191. *cogitations*] thoughts.
    204. *the ascending . . . spirits*] i.e. entering up through the trapdoor, not exiting up
into the stage heavens.

Young L. Wealthy. O Peter, how long have we slept upon the   210
    hogshead?

Peter Servitude. I think a dozen hours, my lord; and 'tis nothing: I'll
    undertake to sleep sixteen upon the receipt of two cups of
    muscadine.

Young L. Wealthy. I marvel what's become of Haddit and Lightfoot.   215

Peter Servitude. Hang 'em, flinchers! They slunk away as soon as they
    had drunk as much as they were able to carry, which no generous
    spirit would a' done, indeed.

Young L. Wealthy. Yet I believe Haddit had his part, for, to my think-
    ing, the cellar went round with him when 'a left us. But are we   220
    come to a bed yet? I must needs sleep.

Peter Servitude. Come softly by any means, for we are now upon the
    threshold of my master's chamber, through which I'll bring you to
    Mistress Rebecca's lodging. Give me your hand, and come very
    nicely.   *Peter falls into the hole.*   225

Young L. Wealthy. Where art, Peter?

Peter Servitude. O, O, O!

Young L. Wealthy. Where's this noise, Peter? Canst tell?

Hog. I hear the voice of my adopted son-in-law.

Young L. Wealthy. Why, Peter, wilt not answer me?   230

Peter Servitude. O my Lord above, stand still. I am fallen down at least
    thirty fathom deep. If you stand not still till I recover, and have
    lighten a candle, y'are but a dead man.

Hog. I am robbed, I am undone, I am deluded! Who's in my
    chamber?   235

Young L. Wealthy. 'Tis I, the lord, your son that shall be; upon my
    honour, I came not to rob you!

---

215. Lightfoot.] *this ed.; Lighfoote? Q*; Lightfoot! *Dod, etc.*   216. Hang'em, flinchers! They] *this ed.;* Hang 'em flinchers they *Q*; Hang 'em, flinchers; they *Dod, etc.*
227. O, O, O!] *this ed.;* O oh o. *Q*; O ho! *Dod, etc.;* O, O! *Haz.*

---

211. *hogshead*] barrel.

214. *muscadine*] i.e. muscatel, a wine made from the muscat variety of grape.

217. *carry*] tolerate, bear.

218. *spirit*] (1) gentleman, man of good character (2) alcoholic drink (3) ghost.

219. *had his part*] had his share of drink, drank enough.

220. *went round with him*] spun around for him (because he was drunk).

224–5. *come very nicely*] proceed very cautiously, gingerly (*OED* 'nicely' 4.d).

232. *thirty fathom*] a measure of depth (also of length), measured variously in the
period as the distance from forefinger to forefinger with arms outstretched and from
head to toe (earlier, the cubit (length of the forearm)).

232–3. *If you stand . . . dead man*] If you move without a candle to see by in this
pitch darkness before I get out, you'll fall down in this pit and die.

Hog. I shall run mad! I shall run mad!
Young L. Wealthy. Why, then, 'tis my fortune to be terrified with
madmen.   240

Enter PETER [SERVITUDE,] *with a candle.*

Peter Servitude. Where are you, my lord?
Hog. Here, by'r lady! Where are you, rogue, when thieves break into
my house?
Peter Servitude. Breaking my neck in your service – a plague on't!
Young L. Wealthy. But are you robbed, indeed, father Hog? Of how   245
much, I pray?
Hog. Of all, of all! See here, they have left me nothing but two or three
rolls of parchment; here they came up like spirits and took my
silver, gold, and jewels. Where's my daughter?
Peter Servitude. She's not in the house, sir. The street doors are wide 250
open.
Young L. Wealthy. Nay, 'tis no matter where she is now. She'll scarce
be worth a thousand pound, and that's but a tailor's prize.
Hog. Then you'll not have her, sir?
Young L. Wealthy. No, as I hope to live in peace.   255
Hog. Why, be't so, be't so; confusion cannot come in a more fitter time
on all of us. O bountiful Croesus, how fine thy shadow hath
devoured my substance!
Peter Servitude. Good my lord, promise him to marry his daughter, or
'a will be mad presently, though you never intend to have her.   260
Young L. Wealthy. Well, father Hog, though you are undone, your
daughter shall not be, so long as a lord can stand her in any stead.
Come, you shall with me to my lord and father, whose warrants

242. by'r Lady] *this ed.;* my Lady? *Q;* my lady *Dod, etc.* 253. prize] *Dod, etc.;*
prise *Q.* 256. more fitter] *Q;* deleted in *Dod MS, not in Dod, etc.* 262. a lord]
Dod, etc.; a Lords *Q.*

239. *fortune*] destiny; Young Lord Wealthy is thinking back to his encounter with
Carracus in 3.2.
242. *by'r Lady*] so Q; Dodsley and Hazlitt think Hog should say 'my Lady' as a
play on Peter Servitude's 'my Lord'.
253. *a thousand . . . prize*] a victory (a wife) for a – proverbially poor – tailor (also
see note to 3.3.62–3).
256. *confusion*] overthrow, ruin, destruction.
257. *fine*] (1) completely, with finality (2) cleverly, cunningly.
261. *undone*] ruined; followed by possible sexual play on Rebecca's status as *done*
or *undone* (i.e. sexually 'known' or a virgin) because Young Lord Wealthy will marry
her and have sex with her.
262. *stand her in any stead*] hold her in any regard, place her in any position (of
quality).

we will have for the apprehending of all suspicious livers, and,
though the labour be infinite, you must consider your loss is so.   265
Hog. Come, I'll do anything to gain my gold.
Peter Servitude. Till which be had, my fare will be but cold. *Exeunt.*

[5.2]

        Enter HADDIT, REB[ECCA,] LIGHTFOOT, *and* PRIEST.

Haddit. Now, Master Parson, we will no further trouble you; and, for
the tying of our true love- knot, here's a small amends.
                                              [*Gives money.*]
Priest. 'Tis more than due, Sir, yet I'll take it all.
  Should kindness be despised? Goodwill would fall
  Unto a lower ebb, should we detest   5
  The grateful giver's gift, *verissimo est.*
Haddit. It's true, indeed; good morrow, honest parson.
Priest. Yet, if you please, Sir John will back surrender
  The overplus of what you now did tender.
Haddit. O, by no means; I prithee, friend, good morrow.   10
Lightfoot. Why, if you please, Sir John, to me restore
  The overplus, I'll give it to the poor.
Priest. O, pardon, sir, for, by your worship's leave,
  We ought to give from whence we do receive.
Haddit. Why, then, to me, Sir John.   15
Priest. To all a kind good morrow.   *Exit.*
Haddit. A most fine vicar: there was no other means to be rid of him.
  But why are you so sad, Rebecca?
Rebecca. To think in what estate my father is
  When he beholds that he is merely gulled.   20

3, 8, 13, 16. SP *Priest*] *Dod, etc.*; Prie., Pe., Pe., Pri. *Q.*   4. despised? Goodwill] *this
ed.*; dispis'd, good will *Q*; despis'd, good-will *Dod, etc.*

267. *my . . . cold*] my food will be cold; my reward will be unsatisfying.

4–6. *Should kindness . . .* verissimo est] These lines seem corrupt; it appears that two
partial versions of this passage have been printed together without one being struck.
One would be 'Should kindness be despised, good-will would fall / Unto a lower
ebb . . .' and the other 'Good-will would fall / Unto a lower ebb, should we detest /
The grateful giver's gift . . .'. I have repunctuated line 3 with a question mark to make
sense of the lines as they stand in Q.
6. verissimo est] Latin: it is most true.
8. *back surrender*] return.
9. *overplus*] overpayment.
19. *estate*] state, situation.
20. *merely gulled*] utterly fooled, cheated.

Haddit. Nay, be not grieved for that which should rather give you
cause of content, for 'twill be a means to make him abandon his
avarice and save a soul almost incurable. But now to our own
affairs: this marriage of ours must not yet be known, lest it breed
suspicion. We will bring you, Rebecca, unto Atlas his house, whilst   25
we two go unto the old Lord Wealthy's, having some acquaintance
with his son-in-law Carracus, who I understand is there, where no
question but we shall find your father proclaiming his loss. Thither
you shall come somewhat after us, as it were to seek him, where
I doubt not but so to order the matter, that I will receive you as   30
my wife from his own hands.
Rebecca. May it so happy prove.
Lightfoot. Amen, say I; for, should our last trick be known, great
Croesus' shade would have a conjured time on't.
Haddit. 'Tis true; his castle of adamant would scarce hold him. But   35
come, this will be good cause for laughter hereafter.
Then we'll relate how this great bird was pulled
Of his rich feathers, and most finely gulled.   *Exeunt.*

[5.3]

Enter OLD LO[RD] WEALTHY, *with* CAR[RACUS,]
MA[RIA,] *and* ALBERT.

Old L. Wealthy. More welcome, Carracus, than friendly truce
To a besiegèd city all distressed.
How early this glad morning are you come
To make me happy; for pardon of your offence
I've given a blessing, which may heaven confirm   5
In treble manner on your virtuous lives.
[*Carracus.*] And may our lives and duty daily strive
To be found worthy of that loving favour,
Which from your reverend age we now receive
Without desert or merit.   10

---

25. Atlas his] *Q; Atlas's Dod, etc.*   36. hereafter] *Dod, etc.; heteafter Q.*

1. SP Old L. Wealthy] *so Reed, etc.; Lo. throughout Q.*   7. SP [*Carracus.*]] *Dod, etc.; not in Q.*

24. *lest*] in case.
34. *conjured time*] difficult time, dangerous comeuppance, with pun on the conjuring trick they have played.
35. *scarce*] hardly.
37. *Then . . . pulled*] Then we'll tell the story of how this important personage was plucked (made bare), cheated.
38. *finely gulled*] wonderfully, cunningly cheated.

Enter YOUNG [LORD] WEAL[THY,] HOG, *and* PETER.

Young L. Wealthy. Room for a desirer of justice! What, my sister
    Maria! Who thought to have met you here?

Maria. You may see, brother, unlooked-for guests prove often
    troublesome.

Young L. Wealthy. Well, but is your husband there any quieter than   15
    'a was?

Carracus. Sir, I must desire you to forget all injuries, if, in not being
    myself, I offered you any.

Albert. I'll see that peace concluded.

Young L. Wealthy. Which I agree to, for patience is a virtue, father   20
    Hog.

Old L. Wealthy. Was it you, son, that cried so loud for justice?

Young L. Wealthy. Yes, marry was it, and this the party to whom it
    appertains.

Hog. O my most honoured lord! I am undone, robbed this black night   25
    of all the wealth and treasure which these many years I have hourly
    laboured for!

Old L. Wealthy. And who are those have done this outrage to you?

Hog. O, knew I that, I then, my lord, were happy.

Old L. Wealthy. Come you for justice then, not knowing 'gainst
    whom   30
    The course of justice should extend itself?
    Nor yet suspect you none?

Hog.   None but the devil.

Young L. Wealthy. I thought 'a was a cheater, e'er since I heard two
    or three Templars swear at dice the last Christmas that the devil
    had got all.   35

Enter HADDIT *and* LIGHTFOOT.

Haddit. My kind acquaintance; joy to thy good success.

Carracus. Noble and freeborn Haddit, welcome.

Lightfoot. Master Hog, good day –

Hog. For I have had a bad night on't!

Lightfoot. Sickness is incident to age. What, be the writings ready to   40
    be sealed we entreated last day?

---

13. prove] *Dod, etc.;* proofe *Q.*   30–2. Come ... devil.] *this ed.; set in prose in Q,
Dod, etc.*   39. For ... on't] *Q, Dod, Reed, Scott, Coll;* [Good day,] for ... on't
Haz.

---

   34. *Templars*] barristers or other members of the law courts (Inner or Middle
Temple).

   39. *For I have ... on't*] Hazlitt adds 'Good day' in square brackets at the beginning
of this line, but Hog seems to be using Lightfoot's 'good day' as the beginning of his
own line; repeating the phrase also makes the joke rather heavy-handed.

Hog. Yes, I think they are – would the scrivener were paid for the
  making them.
Lightfoot. 'A shall be so, though I do't myself. Is the money put up,
  as I appointed?   45
Hog. Yes, 'tis put up – confusion seize the receivers!
Lightfoot. Heaven bless us all! What mean you, sir?
Hog. O sir, I was robbed this night of all I had;
  My daughter, too, is lost, and I undone!
Lightfoot. Marry, God forbid! After what manner, I pray?   50
Hog. O, to recount, sir, will breed more ruth
  Than did the tale of that high Trojan duke
  To the sad-fated Carthaginian queen!
Haddit. What exclamation's that?
Lightfoot. What you will grieve at, coz: 55
  Your worshipful friend, Master Hog, is robbed.
Haddit. Robbed! By whom, or how?
Lightfoot. O, there's the grief: 'a knows not whom to suspect.
Haddit. The fear of hell o'ertake them, whatsoe'er they be! But where's
  your daughter? I hope she is safe.   60

                    Enter RE[BECCA].

Hog. Thank heaven, I see she's now so. Where hast thou been, my
  girl?
Rebecca. Alas, sir, carried by amazement I know not where! Pursued
  by the robbers, forced to fly, amazed, affrighted, through all the
  city streets, to seek redress, but that lay fast asleep in all men's   65
  houses, nor would lend an ear to the distressed.
Haddit. O, heavy accident! But see, you grieve too much,
  Being your daughter's found. For th'other loss,
  Since 'tis the will of heaven to give and take,

---

46. seize] *Dod, etc.*; cease *Q.* 61. Thank] *Dod, etc.*; Thankes *Q.* 64. amazed,
affrighted,] *Dod (amaz'd), etc.*; as mad affright, *Q.* 65. city] *Dod, etc.*; City *Q.*

44–6. *put up . . . put up*] got ready, made available . . . set upon, stolen.

46. *receivers*] thieves (punning on the multiple meaning of the word as one who
receives or holds goods or money for someone and as one who receives stolen
goods).

51. *ruth*] sadness.

52. *Trojan duke*] Aeneas.

53. *Carthaginian queen*] Dido, to whom Aeneas told his tale of the fall of Troy; she
was sad-fated, because she killed herself when Aeneas abandoned her to found his new
Troy.

54. *What exclamation's that?*] What is this about? (Haddit's interrogative perhaps
suggests he and Carracus have been talking aside and out of earshot up to this point
until interrupted by Hog's exclamation).

55. *What*] One that.

Value it as nothing; you have yet sufficient   70
To live in blessed content, had you no more
But my small mortgage for your daughter here,
Whom I have ever loved in dearest affection.
If so you please so much to favour me
I will accept her, spite of poverty,   75
And make her jointure of some store of land,
Which, by the loss of a good agèd friend,
Late fell to me: what, is't a match or no?
Hog. It is.
[*Haddit.*] Then I'll have witness on't. My lord and gentlemen,   80
Please you draw near to be here witnesses
To a wished contract 'twixt this maid and I.
Omnes. We all are willing.
Hog. Then in the presence of you all, I give my daughter freely to this
gentleman as wife; and to show how much I stand affected to him,   85
for dowry with her I do back restore his mortgaged lands; and, for
their loves, I vow ever hereafter to detest, renounce, loathe, and
abhor all slavish avarice,
Which doth ascend from hell, sent by the devil
To be 'mongst men the actor of all evil.   90
Omnes. A blessed conversion!
Old L. Wealthy. A good far unexpected. And now, gentlemen,
I do invite you all to feast with me
This happy day, that we may all together
Applaud his good success, and let this day be spent   95
In sports and shows, with gladsome merriment.
Come, blessed, converted man, we'll lead the way,
As unto heaven I hope we shall.
Hog.   Heaven grant we may!
Carracus. Come, my Maria and repentant friend,
We three have tasted worst of misery,   100
Which now adds joy to our felicity.

---

80. SP [*Haddit.*]] *Dod, etc.; not in Q, since line 80 appears to immediately follow
line 78; line 79 is printed to the right of line 78.* 99. repentant] *Q, 'a' uninked or
missing in all Q copies.* 101. adds] *Dod, etc.; adde Q.*

---

75. *spite*] in spite.
76. *jointure*] a joint holder, a piece of land in joint ownership.
77. *loss*] death.
78. *fell to me*] came into my possession.
101. *adds*] Dodsley's emendation here seems correct; Q's 'adde' could be made to
work by considering the word 'add' a command, ordering the experience of misery
now to add joy to their felicity.

Haddit. We three are happy we have gained much wealth,
    And though we have done it by a trick of stealth,
    Yet all, I trust, are pleased, and will our ill acquit,
    Since it hath saved a soul was hell's by right.   105
Young L. Wealthy. To follow after, then, our lot doth fall –
    Now rhyme it, Peter.
Peter Servitude.   A good night to all.   *Exeunt omnes.*

FINIS.

EPILOGUE

Now expectation hath at full received
What we late promised; if in aught we've pleased,
'Tis all we sought to accomplish, and much more
Than our weak merit dares to attribute
Unto itself, till you vouchsafe to deign,   5
In your kind censure, so to gratify
Our trivial labours. –
If it hath pleased the judicial ear,
We have our author's wish, and, void of fear,
Dare ignorant men to show their worst of hate.   10
It not detracts, but adds unto that state
Where desert flourisheth.
We'll rest applauded in their derogation,
Though with a hiss they crown that confirmation.
For this our author saith: if't prove distasteful,   15
He only grieves you spent two hours so wasteful,
But if it like, and you affect his pen,
You may command it, when you please, again.

---

2. we've] *Dod, etc.*; we have *Q.*   14. a] *Haz.*; an *Q, Dod, etc.*   17. if it like] *Q, Coll*; if it likes *Dod, etc.*

---

5. *deign*] condescend, think it worthy.
8. *judicial*] judging, discerning.
13. *derogation*] lessening, weakening, detraction of honour.
17. *if it like*] if it pleases you.
affect his pen] are drawn to, appreciate his writing.
18. *command*] order, ask for.

APPENDIX
MAP OF THE CITY OF LONDON
SHOWING PLACES MENTIONED IN
ENGLISHMEN FOR MY MONEY

1 Bridewell
2 Newgate (prison)
3 St Paul's Cathedral
4 Cheap Cross
5 St Mary-le-Bow Church
6 Bucklersbury
7 London Stone, on Candlewick (Cannon) Street
8 Abchurch Lane
9 Fenchurch Street
10 Barking
11 Tower Hill
12 Crutched Friars
13 Aldgate
14 Aldgate Street
15 Cornhill Street
16 Leadenhall
17 Water standard (the four spouts)
18 Royal Exchange
19 Bishopsgate
20 St Mary Spital (Spital field)
21 *to* Shoreditch *and* The Theatre
22 The Rose Theatre
23 The Globe Theatre (from 1599)

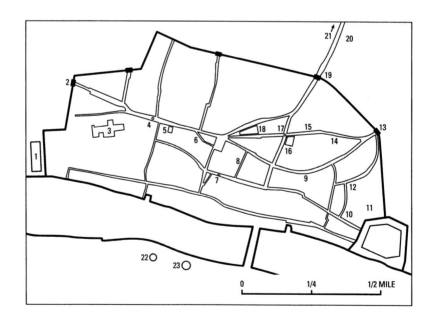

These indexes provide a list of proper names and selected terms related to usury in the introduction, followed by play indexes listing all words and phrases from the annotations to all three plays; an asterisk before a word in an annotations index indicates that it alters or adds to an *OED* entry.

INTRODUCTION

THE THREE LADIES OF LONDON

ENGLISHMEN FOR MY MONEY

de fillee was cree dulce 2.3.165
de petite . . . tendre 2.1.23-4
De usa 2.1.39
death 4.1.9
delight 1.1.101
der ander 3.3.11
descried 4.1.32
descry 2.3.414
despatch 1.3.207
devil, the 4.1.182
dey wint . . . gat 2.3.141-2
Diogenes, . . . basket 4.1.307-8
dirted 1.3.165
dispose 1.3.232
dissemble 2.1.71
distinct 1.1.86
do . . . glasses? 3.2.39
Do . . . lie? 3.2.129
do any good on them 1.2.103-4
do good on her 4.3.22
do monstre some singe of
    amour 2.3.95
dochterkens 4.1.278
Does you price fall? 1.3.82
dog 1.1.174
dogbolt 2.3.4
dolts 1.3.119, 3.2.100
Don 5.1.161
doubt 1.3.109, 4.1.299
dowries 1.1.80
draw 3.4.33
drift 1.2.68, 2.3.346, 4.2.41
drite 1.3.253
driven 1.3.162
drop and curdle . . . fire 1.1.159-
    60
Ducky de doe 2.2.34
Duke Humphrey 2.2.7
dulce visage 2.3.136
dus 2.3.25

Each several 1.1.23
Each stone's a thorn 1.3.324
eavesdroppers 2.3.312
écoute 1.3.21
Effected 5.2.229

effectual 1.2.43
elf 2.1.80
en quelle . . . né? 2.3.97-8
engine of 4.1.194
enquire about 1.1.162
entertain 2.3.67
epurce 2.3.95
ere 1.1.100
ere't 2.1.106
esh oder 2.3.169
être votre 3.2.9
Even 4.2.28
Exchange 1.1.222, 1.3.25
Exchange bell 1.3.270
Exchange time full 1.1.222
Exeunt 2.3.342.1
[*Exeunt the sisters.*] 4.1.111
experient 4.3.58

factor's 1.3.51
fadge 1.2.11, 2.3.419
Fain we would 1.2.138
fain would 4.3.67
fall 4.1.72
fall to your muses 2.3.75
Fame 1.3.240
familiar 5.1.265
father 1.1.79
Faw 4.1.315
fell out right 5.1.208
ferret polecat 4.3.35
Fie 1.1.63
figure, a 4.1.264
filigola 2.1.82
fine as a fiddle! 5.2.231
fine gentlewoman 3.2.87
firks me 4.1.247
fit 1.1.203
fits not 1.3.132
flat 1.3.311
*flaunte taunte 1.1.168-9
flout 5.1.251
flouts 3.2.24
flurjill 1.1.130
foisted in a brat 3.2.10
fold the spring-tide 4.1.11

THE HOG HATH LOST HIS PEARL

Shrove Tuesday 1.1.154
signify 5.1.79
slack performer 1.4.56
so 'a had been served 3.2.13
So 2.2.43
solus 1.2.0.1
somewhat 2.1.63
SP *Omnes* 3.3.114
spirit 5.1.218
spite 5.3.75
Spite 1.2.23
spurn 5.1.115
St Thomas 1.1.137
staff 1.1.133
stand far better 5.1.187
stand her in any stead 5.1.262
state on't 3.2.16
stay 2.1.64, 3.1.99
stay dinner 3.3.50
stay out that expectation 1.1.207
stowed 2.1.23
straight 1.4.61
strange 1.1.37
strolling Pro. 25
Stygian lake 5.1.83
stylèd 5.1.60
suit 1.1.96
surfeit 4.1.100
sustentation 4.3.22

taffeta 1.1.212
tapers 5.1.172
taste of garlic 1.1.114
Templars 5.3.34
tennis-ball . . . hazard 1.1.21–2
that 2.1.112
that man . . . heaven 4.1.144–5
that that damns lawyers 1.1.204–5
that's not much 2.1.51
their good parts 2.3.14–15
then 1.1.71
Then . . . pulled 5.2.37
thence 3.1.137
There's 2.4.55
thine 1.4.110
Thinking . . . swine's flesh Pro. 20

thirty fathom 5.1.232
thirty-five settings 1.1.98
this 5.1.23, 5.1.28
though 1.1.94
thousand . . . prize, a 5.1.253
three-foot-and-a-half 3.2.11
threescore and ten 2.3.24–5
thus much 3.3.4
timorous 1.2.23
'tis . . . bed 2.1.46–7
'tis nothing else 3.1.48
To 4.1.129
to . . . storms 5.1.21
to boot 1.1.62–3
to the speech of him 1.1.18
to this 1.1.115
to wipe the noses 2.1.52
tobacco 1.1.74
told 3.3.31
traffic 2.3.36
Trojan duke 5.3.52
trumpets 3.3.62
trussing his points 2.1.0.2
turtles 5.1.20

under-air 5.1.59
undone 5.1.261
undone . . . undoing . . . doing 3.3.43–4
unfeigned 4.1.80
untutored slave! 3.1.5

verissimo est 5.2.6
vestures 2.1.86
virgin-hole 2.1.73
vouchsafe 1.1.18, 3.1.7
vouchsafed 4.3.65

want 1.1.188, 4.1.98, 5.1.32
wassail 5.1.103
weary . . . a barber 1.1.13
went round with him 5.1.220
were it now . . . in print Pro. 13–18
were mindless Pro. 19
westward . . . eastward 5.1.169–72

Lightning Source UK Ltd.
Milton Keynes UK
UKOW03f1149090414

229651UK00001B/4/P